Realism for the Masses

Realism for the Masses

Aesthetics, Popular Front Pluralism, and U.S. Culture, 1935–1947

Chris Vials

University Press of Mississippi / *Jackson*

www.upress.state.ms.us

The University Press of Mississippi is a member
of the Association of American University Presses.

Copyright © 2009 by University Press of Mississippi
All rights reserved
Manufactured in the United States of America

First printing 2009

∞

Library of Congress Cataloging-in-Publication Data

Vials, Chris.
Realism for the masses : aesthetics, popular front pluralism, and U.S. culture, 1935–1947 / Chris Vials.
    p. cm.
Includes bibliographical references and index.
ISBN 978-1-60473-123-1 (cloth : alk. paper) 1. Popular culture—United States—History—20th century. 2. United States—Civilization—1918–1945. 3. United States—Intellectual life—20th century. 4. Liberalism—United States—History—20th century. 5. Cultural pluralism—United States—History—20th century. 6. Cultural industries—United States—History—20th century. 7. Aesthetics, American—History—20th century. 8. Realism—Social aspects—United States—History—20th century. 9. American literature—20th century—History and criticism. I. Title.
E169.V623 2009
973.91—dc22   2008034577

British Library Cataloging-in-Publication Data available

For Cathy

Contents

ix   Acknowledgments

xi   INTRODUCTION. **The People's Form Finds Its Audience**
        Popular Front Realism and the Culture Industries

3   CHAPTER ONE. **Taking Down the Great White Hope**
        The Popular Front Boxing Narrative

37   CHAPTER TWO. **Radio Soaps, Broadway Lights**
        Lillian Hellman, Shirley Graham, and the Interpellation of Female Audiences

80   CHAPTER THREE. **Realism with a Little Sex in It**
        Erskine Caldwell's Challenge to *Gone with the Wind*

110   CHAPTER FOUR. **Asian Yeoman and Ugly Americans**
        Carlos Bulosan, H. T. Tsiang, and the U.S. Literary Market

149   CHAPTER FIVE. **The Popular Front in the American Century**
        Life Magazine, Margaret Bourke-White, and Partisan Objectivity

191   Notes

213   Works Cited

225   Index

Acknowledgments

I owe a singular debt of gratitude to Seetha Srinivasan, Walter Biggins, and the readers at University Press of Mississippi, not only for their insightful feedback but for the faith they showed in my work from its very early stages. The support they have given me from the very beginning has been truly invaluable. This book began as a dissertation, and I would like to thank everyone who helped shape its foundations: Randall Knoper, whose kind, patient guidance and insights on American realism were indispensable; Jim Smethurst, whose encouragement, feedback, and knowledge of the Popular Front was essential to this project; Jules Chametzky, who not only gave me the privilege of being his last student, but who provided essential scholarly and experiential knowledge of the 1930s and 1940s. I also owe a debt of gratitude to Kathy Peiss for her guidance on chapter 5; her historian's perspective challenged me to push my thinking, writing, and research harder. The day-to-day guidance of other mentors at the University of Massachusetts–Amherst was essential, particularly that of Joe Skerrett and Jenny Spencer. Judith Smith and Rachel Rubin of the American Studies Department at the University of Massachusetts–Boston have also been very supportive of my work. I also want to thank Cannon Schmitt at *Criticism* for publishing an earlier version of chapter 3 in January 2006; Mary Grover and Chris Hopkins for publishing an early draft of the same piece for the University of Dundee's "Working Papers on the Web" years ago; and to Steven Fink and Jared Gardner of *American Periodicals* for publishing an earlier version of chapter 5. Their feedback, as well as that of audiences and fellow panelists at the conferences of the American Studies Association, MELUS, the Asian American Studies Association, and the American Literature Association helped push this project in new directions.

The librarians at the Schlesinger Library at the Radcliffe Institute for Advanced Study were of great help in guiding me through the Shirley Graham

Du Bois papers. I want to express my deepest appreciation to my friends at current colleagues at Buffalo State College (SUNY) for giving me the space and the support to complete this book, particularly Ralph Wahlstrom, Ann Colley, Irving Massey, Barish Ali, and Peter Ramos. Additionally, the institutional support of Susan Tracy, Norm Holland, Laurie Nisonoff, and L. Brown Kennedy at Hampshire College was of immense value. I would also like to thank Eric Schocket, and not only for supporting my scholarship and my teaching: his life and work was an inspiration.

This project owes much to a number of older friends and colleagues as well. Conversations with Ben Balthaser, Daniel Mahoney, Anita Mannur, Seongho Yoon, Asha Nadkarni, Carrie Ruzicka, and Jesse Barba not only helped push my thinking on aesthetics, history, and cultural politics but, more fundamentally, kept me going. I must also thank James Lampidis, who introduced me to the literature of the 1930s in the first place. I would also like to express my appreciation to the Graduate Employee Organization at UMass–Amherst (U.A.W. Local 2322). My work in this organization informed my scholarship on many levels—chiefly, on the relationship between theory and practice and the impossibility of engaging in political action from a pure space.

I would also like to thank my parents Judy and Pete Vials and my sister Jan Sheehy for their love, support, and encouragement throughout the years. The lives of James C. Fennel and Benjamin Fennel Jr. ("Bubba") are examples that continue to guide me; they, along with Paul Jones III ("Bunky"), have instilled in me, more than any theory, the idea that history is a living thing. And finally, I owe infinite gratitude to my wife Cathy Schlund-Vials. Her edits and patient rereadings have been essential in shaping this project, her brilliant insights have shaped my thinking in countless ways, and her love and encouragement kept me writing.

INTRODUCTION

The People's Form Finds Its Audience
Popular Front Realism and the Culture Industries

Released in January 1942, Preston Sturges's film *Sullivan's Travels* embodies a number of assumptions about American realism and the mid-century left that have guided many scholars and critics through the Cold War and beyond. The film is about a socially committed, Hollywood director named John L. Sullivan who has become tired of making light comedies and wants to do a "serious" social protest picture called *O Brother Where Art Thou*. The opening scene of *Sullivan's Travels* is a film within a film—we see two men grapple atop a speeding train, lose their balance, then fall to their deaths in the water below, forming the tragic end to a political drama. The lights come on to reveal a screening room, where Sullivan has been showing this picture to two studio executives, Mr. Hadrian and Mr. LeBrand, to whom he then pitches his next film project:

> SULLIVAN: You see the symbolism of it? Capital and labor destroy each other. It teaches a lesson, a moral lesson, it has social significance.
> MR. HADRIAN: Who wants to see that kind of stuff? It gives me the creeps.
> SULLIVAN: Tell him how long it played over at the Music Hall.
> MR. LEBRAND: It was held over for a fifth week.
> MR. HADRIAN: Who goes to the Music Hall? Communists!
> SULLIVAN: Communists? This picture is an answer to communism. It shows we're awake and not ducking our heads in the sand like a bunch of ostriches. I want this picture to be a commentary on modern conditions. Stark realism. The problems that confront the average man.
> MR. LEBRAND: But with a little sex in it.

SULLIVAN (*impatiently*): A little sex in it, but I don't want to stress it. I want this picture to be a document. I want to hold a mirror up to life. I want this to be a picture of dignity, a true canvas of the suffering of humanity.

Sullivan's butler later adds to the skepticism of the executives but in a more plebeian vein, telling the idealistic director "... The subject [of poverty] is not an interesting one. The poor know all about poverty, and only the morbid rich would find the topic glamorous." After a series of plot twists, Sullivan is sentenced to six years of hard labor due to a case of mistaken identity. When the guards at his prison camp decide to treat the inmates to a movie at a local African American church, the erstwhile serious director, who has lost everything and has finally experienced hardship, finds himself laughing hysterically at the chosen fare: a Disney cartoon featuring Pluto the dog. In the end, Sullivan decides not to make *O Brother Where Art Thou*, as his experience in the school of hard knocks has taught him that people in difficult circumstances want to laugh, and not to see realist representations of poverty and hardship.

Sullivan's Travels thus confirms the original skepticism of both the butler and the studio heads, affirming the social value of light, apolitical comedy—Sturges's chosen genre—over Sullivan's initial inclinations. While scholars of Sturges have tended to use the label *tragedy* to describe the object of his satire, I find what his character called "stark realism" to be the more precise target of the film. When Sullivan conceptually links "a commentary on modern conditions," "the problems that confront the average man," "a document," and the verisimilitude of "holding a mirror up to life," his author places him within the tradition of American realism. Contemporary reviewers noted this as well. Bosley Crowther of the *New York Times* wrote, for instance, that the film was "a stinging slap at those fellows who howl for realism on the screen" (25). Those who "howled" for realism on the screen in 1941 tended to be motivated by their social consciousness, and Sturges wanted his "slap" to show them that realism had no power to reach the broad audience required for political efficacy. Realism, in other words, had no appeal to the masses. Rather, he presumes it to be an elite aesthetic mode appealing only to "the morbid rich" and to educated communists who attend repertoire theaters like "the Music Hall" (in the opening scene, Mr. Hadrian also argued that the realist film touted by Sullivan "died in Pittsburgh," presumably before a mass audience).

It is no coincidence that Sturges connected realism and political didacticism. When he wrote the script in 1941, realism was the aesthetic of choice of a tremendous social and cultural movement—the Popular Front—that had diffused its message throughout American culture. The Popular Front was an international social and cultural movement initially set in motion by the Soviet-dominated Communist International in order to combat the rising influence of fascism, and it assumed a life of its own in each national arena. American communists forged alliances with other left and liberal organizations to create a common, pro-labor, antiracist, and antifascist culture that drew on national icons such as George Washington and Abraham Lincoln for coherence. This movement had so relentlessly diffused its message through the country that a *Fortune* poll in 1942 found that 25 percent of Americans "favored socialism" while another 35 percent "had an open mind about it" (Denning 4).

As a socially committed director, Sullivan was Sturges's surrogate for the many individuals affiliated with the Popular Front social movement who had become well established in the culture industries by 1942. He is arguably an amalgam of two rather different Popular Front figures in Hollywood: Frank Capra and John Garfield. Like the fictional Sullivan, Capra had turned to social-commentary films after years of making screwball comedies, and he is explicitly referenced in the opening scene. When Mr. Hadrian quips that Sullivan's idea sounds "like Capra," the latter responds, "What's the matter with Capra?" Also like Sullivan, the politicized actor John Garfield had a stint riding the rails in his youth, which was used to sell his image by Hollywood's publicity apparatus. Sturges reportedly conceived the idea for *Sullivan's Travels* after he heard Garfield recount his early hobo adventures (Swindell 46). In its final scene, the film also reveals that *O Brother Where Art Thou*, the novel that Sullivan initially wanted to adapt to the screen, was authored by "Sinclair Beckstein," a fusion of the socialistically inclined, realist authors John Steinbeck, Sinclair Lewis, and Upton Sinclair. (The names of these authors are also reconfigured to sound Jewish, reflecting the contemporary association of the movement with Jews.) All in all, *Sullivan's Travels* remains one of the most sophisticated jabs at both the representational practices of the Popular Front social movement and the tradition of American realism.

I begin with this film because it underscores widespread assumptions and silences regarding the aesthetics of the mid-century left, the politics of the 1930s and 1940s, and the relationship between realism and U.S. popular culture. This book challenges the premise that realism and commercial viability have been mutually exclusive in the twentieth century; it also affirms a historical feature of realism that has since been forgotten: its centrality to the mid-century left. Warren Susman perhaps took Sturges's message at face value when he wrote that the Disney film spoke to the fears and anxieties of the average American better than any other text of the age, and that cultural critics would come to see the

1930s as "the age of Mickey Mouse" (196–97). Yet as a writer and director of comedies who steered clear of political activism, Sturges felt compelled to respond to realism because, when he wrote the script in 1941, this aesthetic (as well as the social movement that carried it) was seemingly everywhere. Indeed, none of his films approached the commercial success of John Ford's *Grapes of Wrath* or Capra's *Meet John Doe* and *Mr. Smith Goes to Washington*.[1]

Such a widespread diffusion of the genre this late in the twentieth century might seem strange to literary scholars in particular, as the twentieth century is not generally seen as its heyday. American realism is usually associated with the late nineteenth century within literary studies, but as this book will illustrate, realism as an aesthetic language had more thoroughly saturated U.S. popular culture in the 1930s and 1940s. It could be found atop the best-seller lists with John Steinbeck's *Grapes of Wrath*, Richard Wright's *Native Son* and *Black Boy*, Margaret Mitchell's *Gone With the Wind* (the novel, I will argue in chapter 3, should be seen in the tradition of American realism), Pearl Buck's *Dragon Seed* and *The Good Earth*, Ann Petry's *The Street*, with Erskine Caldwell's novels of the South, countless detective pulp fictions available at newsstands, and more. While the realist works of Zola, Tolstoy, Twain, and Flaubert were among bestsellers in the late nineteenth century United States, what marks the 1930s and 1940s is the more common appearance of American realists on the bestseller lists, and more importantly the unprecedented diffusion of realism beyond the printed page into other arenas of U.S. popular culture. On the screen, a kind of plebeian realism that was combined with melodrama, fitted for mass consumption, and reclaimed from the bourgeois realism of early American cinema could be found in gangster pictures, detective thrillers, boxing dramas, and celluloid narratives of young street "toughs." On Broadway the success of productions authored or inspired by Lillian Hellman, Sidney Kingsley, Elmer Rice, Richard Wright, Claire Booth Luce, and Erskine Caldwell attests to the appeal of the genre, while the Federal Theater Project brought realist theater to an even broader audience who could not afford the tickets prices of the commercial stage. On the new medium of radio, earlier realist work by Theodore Dreiser, Mark Twain, Leo Tolstoy, Heinrich Ibsen, Henry James, Stephen Crane, Edith Wharton, and Ambrose Bierce, as well as newer work by Maxwell Anderson, Donald Ogden Stewart, Claire Booth Luce, Sinclair Lewis, Sidney Kingsley, John Steinbeck, Arthur Miller, and Lillian Hellman, were blended with melodrama and could be heard on such national "prestige drama" programs such as *The Lux Radio Theatre* (one of the most popular shows on the air), *The Columbia Workshop, Favorite Story, The NBC Theater of the Air,* and *The Ford Theater*.[2] In addition to the evening broadcasts of new and old realist work, the new daytime serial genre of the soap opera drew upon innovations from the realist stage.

In 1946 James T. Farrell noted that "the works of writers designated as realists and naturalists—including mine—are being made available to a larger public in reprint editions," and he felt compelled to try to redefine the term *realism* in light of both its constant use by critics and its popular appeal (Foreword). The "reprint editions" to which Farrell referred were part of the paperback revolution of the early 1940s; in the field of literature, this paperback revolution helped enable the diffusion of realism. With the success of Pocket Books, established in 1939, as well as its followers in the paperback market, most notably Penguin (1939), Avon (1941), Dell (1943), and Bantam (1946), book prices were brought down from the often inaccessible Depression-era range of two to three dollars to a mere twenty-five to forty cents. With the U.S. entrance into the war, the restriction of leisure activities for soldiers and on gas and travel for civilians also led to an increased market for books (Schick 79–81). But while increased demand, new print technologies, and fresh marketing practices help explain an enlarged market for books, they do not explain why readers chose realism over other items on the book rack. Rather, the culture created by the Popular Front cultivated a predilection for realist-inspired literature, drama, film, and radio. Indeed, the ubiquity of realism in American culture by 1941 can be seen as a marker of the success of the Popular Front social movement. Popular Front writers and artists who strongly drew from the tradition of American realism and who self-identified as realists injected their work into U.S. mass culture in the 1930s and 1940s like never before, and this book will follow the creation of what I call their "mass-mediated realisms." In tracing the complex and widespread fusions of realist and mass-culture forms, it aims to show a significant and heretofore unexplored aesthetic means by which Popular Front subjects were created.

The revival of realism in the mid-twentieth century, despite its inheritance, was not simply a repetition of earlier conventions established by the likes of William Dean Howells, Mark Twain, Edward Sheldon, or Jacob Riis, or even of socialistically minded naturalists Jack London, Upton Sinclair, or Lewis Hine. Nor were Popular Front writers and artists the first realists with an intimate relationship to mass culture. As Amy Kaplan has argued, American realism of the late nineteenth century was largely intended as a competing mode of representation with an emergent mass culture upon which it depended (12–13). The realist-inspired work of the 1930s and 40s, however, was produced by individuals who had grown up in a world where there was increasingly no space left untouched by the culture industries. In addition to late-nineteenth-century amusements such as vaudeville, Tin Pan Alley, dime novels, story papers, and penny arcades, the explosion of narrative cinema, radio, records, and paperbacks by the mid-twentieth century had left few cultural forms independent of mass culture.

Realism was no exception. The realism of the 1930s and 1940s was in actuality a hybrid genre permeated by mass-culture forms and tropes to a much greater extent than its nineteenth-century incarnation—and in ways not always conscious to its own creators. It was, to borrow from Sturges, realism "with a little sex in it." This was perhaps the most astute line in *Sullivan's Travels*, as it acknowledged how the culture industries were not passively carrying realism, but transforming it. In 1942 literary scholar Alfred Kazin also noted the changes to realism wrought by mass culture. Labeling the dominant style of the 1930s "left-wing naturalism," he wrote that writers in this naturalist mode were "technicians of sensation, opportunists who learned from every native source ... Hollywood, radio, the slick new journalism, the trickery of smooth, paper fiction ..." (388). In reframing this hybrid form less pejoratively as mass-mediated realism, I retain the label *realism* not only because its creators often proclaimed themselves to be realists (not naturalists), but also because their work bears a number of underlying and important formal similarities to their nineteenth- and turn-of-the-century forebears. In other words, by using the term I refer neither to a static form nor to a general, artistic desire for verisimilitude but to a historically specific and evolving aesthetic mode that emerged in France in the 1830s and took shape on the U.S. scene in the late nineteenth century, one which retained underlying characteristics traceable to this origin through its twentieth-century permutations in literary, visual, and aural cultures. The underlying characteristics of realism, as I define it, are a focus on "ordinary" individuals and their vernacular culture; a placement of these individuals in specific contemporary (or near contemporary), sociohistorical contexts, ones that are not mere backdrops but influence the characters in some way; the use of a transparent, accessible form that does not call attention to signification; an impulse toward social intervention and "social significance"; a rejection of sentimentality; and individualized, complex characters.

Tracing the diffusion of realism within mass culture is not merely a stylistic exploration, however. The sometimes unconscious fusions of realism and mass culture are important to understanding the redefinition of the American people at mid-century, as the tradition of American realism carried with it certain epistemologies that delineated who and what should be visible, and the mass culture of the era diffused that realist-based epistemology to an unprecedented degree, converting it, albeit temporarily, into "common sense." The Popular Front, mass-mediated realisms I investigate in this book built upon an earlier aesthetic to intertwine class, race, and ethnicity into complex subjectivities that contemporary scholars do not generally associate with American culture before postmodernity. At the same time, discourses surrounding realism constrained a thoroughgoing interrogation of gender, impeding a genuinely pluralistic idea of the body politic. This book thus seeks to intervene in the literary scholarship on American realism by investigating what happens to the relationship between realism and mass culture—a relationship that has been thoroughly explored for the nineteenth century and the turn of the century—when one extends one's frame well into the twentieth. This particular intervention also underscores my contribution to the study of 1930s and 1940s cultural production. This book is not the first to posit a relationship between the mid-century left and popular culture. The most influential and ambitious treatment of this relationship is Michael Denning's seminal work *The Cultural Front*, which asserted that Popular Front cultural productions created a "laboring" of U.S. culture, wherein American mass culture became much more vernacular and much closer to the values and aesthetic forms of the American working class (xx).[3] In other words, the Popular Front achieved a kind of hegemony in U.S. culture well into the postwar period, in no small part because of the presence of its artists and writers in the cultural industries.

But this book is the first to posit realism—and more specifically the hybrid form that I call "mass-mediated realism"—as a significant site of left-wing intervention into popular culture at mid-century, and to highlight the importance of realism as a vehicle for disseminating the left's oppositional notions of "the people." The 1930s and 1940s can be seen as a time when a political sense of American selfhood, based on the primacy of the ordinary individual, found its fullest expression in an aesthetic that took the lives of common people as its ontological ground. Cultural producers used realism to merge an aesthetic about the masses with a politics for the masses, and at mid-century their efforts created the widest audience for the genre in its history. If there is one thing that has united the more recent scholarship on left cultural production of the 1930s and 1940s, it is the need to break with Cold War paradigms for understanding the various "cultural fronts" of mid-century radicalism. However, a closer examination of realism is needed to complete this break. One of these Cold War paradigms—exhibited, for example, by *The Partisan Review* in its anti-Stalinist rebirth—is that communists and their fellow travelers exalted a hackneyed realism while rejecting a richer and more innovative modernism. In doing so, according to anticommunist critics such as Alfred Kazin and Lionel Trilling, the communist left revealed its intellectual crudeness. But as James Murphy, Jim Smethurst, Alan Wald, and Barbara Foley have all shown, this is an untenable position since writers and critics around journals such as *The New Masses* rejected neither modernism nor formal experimentation (Smethurst 6; Foley 54–63; Murphy 138–47; Wald 33–34, 309–11). While I am in full agreement that the left was not opposed to modernism, I also feel it is important not to elide the topic of realism merely because its association with the Popular Front smacks of the clichés and oversimplifications of anticommunist critics. We should take seriously the words of so many left-wing artists who, like their satirical foil Sullivan, explicitly proclaimed themselves to be "realists," and we should not take lightly the very tangible presence of turn-of-the-century realist formal structures in their work. With the notable exception of Barbara Foley, none of the in-depth studies on left-wing cultural production in the 1930s and 1940s has looked at realism in detail. Even Denning's seminal work on the Popular Front mentions it only in passing. In short, it is high time to "return" to realism in evaluating oppositional cultural production of the 1930s and 1940s. Given that the exaltation of modernist ambiguity by the New Critics was also one of the aesthetic pillars of the Cold War hegemonic order in the United States—and arguably the reason for the continued privileging of modernism within noncultural studies and literary scholarship of the first half of the twentieth century—we continue to allow Cold War paradigms to obscure our evaluation of the period by ignoring aesthetics that do not easily merit the modernist label. The persistent difficulty in literary studies of seeing realism as a significant, mid-twentieth-century aesthetic is arguably a residual Cold War barrier to understanding the "Old Left" that has yet to be removed. (Film studies, by contrast, has not had nearly as much difficult in seeing realism beyond the turn of the century.)[4] This barrier needs to be lifted, because when one shifts the focus to mass-mediated realism one gets a different story of the relationship between the Popular Front, popular culture, and the politics of inclusion. As I will show, one also sees a set of genres and cultural forms that do not retain their politics across the second half of the twentieth century.

A Tale of Two Pluralisms
"We're the People" and "The People's Century"

If the satire of Popular Front aesthetics by *Sullivan's Travels* exposes scholarly tasks that remain to be done, its lampoon of Popular Front pluralism highlights more popular misconceptions about the era's politics that linger to this day. In placing Frank Capra and John Steinbeck at the center of its explicit critique, the film makes only one side of Popular Front pluralism—its most remembered side—stand in for the whole.[5] Capra and Steinbeck put forth an implicitly white, exceptionalist variety of Popular Front pluralism, one that often drew on the iconography of the republican, yeoman farmer. Echoed in various ways within Roy Stryker's editing and presentations of photography for the Farm Security Administration, in the documentaries of Pare Lorentz, in James Agee and Walker Evans's *Let Us Now Praise Famous Men*, and in the Federal Theater Project drama *Native Ground* (to name a few examples), this brand of pluralism is embodied by the phrase "We're the people," which was uttered not only by Ma Joad in *Grapes of Wrath*, but also by the character John Doe/Long John Willoughby in Frank Capra's 1941 film *Meet John Doe*. Ma Joad's assertion "We're the people" has stood as one of the most memorable phrases in John Steinbeck's masterwork, and more broadly, has served as emblematic expression of the politics and culture of the Depression decade. Within the novel it is a rallying cry at a moment of desperation for the Joad family. Ma tells Tom: "Why Tom—us people will go on livin' when all them people is gone. Why, Tom, we're the people that live. They ain't gonna wipe us out. Why, we're the people—we go on ... Rich fellas come up an' they die, an' their kids ain't no good, an' they die out. But Tom, we keep a-comin'. Don' you fret none, Tom. A different time's a comin'" (280). John Ford highlighted these words quite dramatically in his 1940 film adaptation by using them as the very last lines of dialogue in the script. In the movie, Ma Joad repeats these words almost verbatim as she, Pa Joad, and their son Al pull out of a migrant camp and into the landscape. Thus Ford uses her words to fit Hollywood's preference for an optimistic ending while retaining the Popular Front spirit of the novel—a common dynamic, as I will show, in the industry's adaptations of oppositional writers.

"We're the people" evoked the language of the Constitution within a contemporary narrative of dislocation and class conflict, and made one group within a social struggle in California—the poor, white, dispossessed migrants and not the affluent "best families"—the true bearers of the American revolutionary tradition. The Joads, a white, rural farm family, were easily recognizable as the face of the nation, since the yeoman farmer had long been the symbol of national virtue within the discourses of both republicanism and Jeffersonian agrarianism. In showing their merciless exploitation at the hands of large California landowners and their repressive institutions, the novel attempted to illustrate that modern class structures were out of step with America's noble traditions. In simultaneously evoking national traditions *and* questioning the nation's class structures, *The Grapes of Wrath* is decidedly a product of the Popular Front, as the movement prompted coalition members to draw from the national icons of their respective countries. But it is no ordinary artifact of the period. Not only is Steinbeck's narrative of the Dust Bowl and Okie exodus the most resonant, single aesthetic expression of the Popular Front, it also stands as perhaps the most frequently accessed text of the Depression decade.[6]

However, despite the social extension inherent in Steinbeck's notion of the people, more recent scholars have rightly questioned the politics of using the Joads and the Migrant Mother as the face of the nation, as well as the historical accuracy of viewing them as truly reflective of the diversity within the ranks of the Popular Front social movements (Denning 259, Lye 143).[7] Steinbeck's synecdochal use of a white, Protestant, rural, middle-American farm family is especially problematic considering that even within the California fields he investigates, an estimated 75 percent of the migrant worker disputes upon which he based the strikes in *Grapes of Wrath* and *In Dubious Battle* were driven by Mexican workers (Gregory 58–62). His erasure of nonwhites exposes the limitations of republican notions of the people, which, as Ronald Takaki and Matthew Frye Jacobson have observed, are only those "fit for self-government," only those with innate powers of reason granting them the ability to grasp the responsibilities of democracy.[8] By one estimate, moreover, only 6 percent of migrants to California in the 1930s were from the Dust Bowl; many may well have been blue-collar wage workers rather than farmers (Gregory 15–17). And by looking at the field of literature alone, it almost goes without saying that the Joads do not capture the diversity of oppositional cultural production during the 1930s and 1940s. Ultimately, Steinbeck's "We're the people," while it made visible the suffering of a heretofore ignored group of white migrants, also enters and perpetuates a long history of American nationalism that homogenizes (and silences) the heterogeneous populations within U.S. borders. It is no coincidence that in the film *Meet John Doe*, when Capra's character Doe/Willoughby lifts "We're the people" from *Grapes of Wrath* and uses in his pivotal speech, he generates uproarious applause in his audience and spawns a plebeian but almost exclusively white social movement centered around "John Doe Clubs."

After 1941, it was increasingly clear that this brand of exceptionalist pluralism had reached beyond its Anglo-Saxon core to bring Southern and Eastern Europeans into the fold. A slightly expanded version of "We're the people" could be seen in wartime films such as *Bataan* (1943) and Frank Capra's *Why We Fight* series, which stressed the practical need for people of different ethnic backgrounds to come together for the purposes of wartime. It could also be seen in the short film starring Frank Sinatra called "The House I Live In" (1945), which David Roediger has recently discussed as emblematic of all Popular Front pluralisms (*Working Toward Whiteness* 235–44). Given the racialization of the Japanese in these texts, the limited scope of their inclusions, or their elision of deep, structural racial divisions, this expanded version of "We're the people" merely admitted several new groups to the club of whiteness without questioning the Otherness upon which it was predicated.

The spirit of the movement, however, could be much more inclusive, and its inclusiveness could be found just as often in the war years as in the Depression. Carlos Bulosan's essay "Freedom From Want," published in the *Saturday Evening Post* in March 1943, stands as a relatively overlooked yet highly significant Popular Front articulation of the people, one elided by Sturges and lost to popular memory. Bulosan's piece was one of a series of essays published by the *Post* to articulate Franklin Delano Roosevelt's "Four Freedoms," which had become a shorthand version of "Why We Fight" during World War II. The three freedoms Bulosan did not write on—Freedom of Speech and Expression, Freedom of Worship, and Freedom from Fear—were standard tropes within the history of Western liberalism. But Roosevelt's "Freedom from Want" expanded the dominant notion of freedom, adding a form of economic equality to a notion of liberty originally envisioned in the U.S. Constitution in terms of private property and public expression (it added an "equality of means" to the "equality of rights," to use the terms of French historian George Lefebvre [178]). Bulosan was well positioned to write on this freedom: as an author now known for his writing on the brutality experienced by migrant Filipinos along the west coast of the U.S., as well as several fictional works dealing with the cultures of anti-imperial resistance in the Philippines, it had been his specialty. Bulosan defined Roosevelt's fourth freedom quite clearly, writing: "It is only when we have plenty to eat—plenty of everything—that we begin to understand what freedom means." Not surprisingly, his essay is based on the premise that "freedom from want" had not been achieved even within the United States, let alone the rest of the world.

Like Steinbeck, Bulosan aimed to make visible a real people, but he goes farther. His people are not only Okies but also "factory hands, field hands, mill hands," and with his line "waiting for work," they are also unemployed. While Bulosan does not specify the race of the people suffering from want, he alludes to a multiracial workforce. For instance, he writes that "We are multitudes . . . in Alaskan canneries," an industry which, as he reveals in his 1946 *America Is in the Heart*, was largely composed of Filipino workers. He also writes that "we" are "Under the lynch tree amidst hysterical mobs," and asserts "all men, whatever their color, race, religion, or estate, should be given equal opportunity" (color and race, it should be noted, come first in this call for inclusion). In common with many other Popular Front pluralisms, he subverts conventional patriotism by staking the country's future on its most marginalized subjects, who in turn become the new national emblems. "We are the mirror of what America *is*," he writes. "If America wants us to be living and free, then we must be living and free. If we fail, then America fails." Also in common with this movement, Bulosan affiliates himself not with the extant nation but with an unfulfilled idea of "America" that leftist social movements were to realize by building upon its best traditions. Despite their contributions, for instance, and the fact that they hold it an "honor to walk upon the American earth," he asserts in his *Post* essay that workers have not been made to feel a constituent part of the land, because brutality and "want" have made them experience as outsiders the nation that they have created. And in a rhetorical move used by early-twentieth-century African American intellectuals, he urges readers to identify with the nation on the basis of the collective contributions that all of its people have invested in it (Dawahare 84). As such, Bulosan's "Freedom From Want" is not merely a powerful call for a more just and inclusive United States; it also illustrates how politicized articulations of race in 1940s did not always adhere to a black/white frame.

The rather different representations of the people offered by Bulosan and Steinbeck both drew from a tradition of realist aesthetics. Steinbeck placed "We're the people" within a narrative that attempted to represent the totality of the Joads' social environment: their every encounter is recorded in minute detail, and the existence of a part/whole relationship between the Joads and American social structures is underscored through almost biblical narrative interludes about the Okies and the growers as groups, told by an omniscient narrator. Further, Steinbeck follows William Deal Howells's famous call to represent "the phrase and carriage of everyday life," to render the exact language of the people as dutifully as one can, and to cultivate a national environment of sympathy and understanding in the process. One should note in this context that "We're the people," unlike the formal "We the People" of the constitution, is a vernacular expression. By rendering the old constitutional phrase in the accent of the common man and woman, the national tradition could be claimed by them. In short, Steinbeck used realism to give the Joads a place in the national imagination, and it was on the basis of realism that they entered American popular culture. Likewise, when Bulosan challenges middle-class readers of the *Post* with the line, "You usually see us working or waiting for work, and you think you know us, but our outward guise is more deceptive than our history," he is asserting that the people are not only workers, but workers who have not been seen in deep social context, a context which would make them recognizable as the basis of the nation. "Freedom From Want," and Bulosan's prose as a whole, becomes a realist project in part because it attempts to document that deep context. His well-received 1946 autobiography *America Is in the Heart* derived its authority from its claims to realism, expressed in the clear, brutal details he used to render the movement of his narrator through his shifting social environment.

The realism of the Joads—and to a lesser extent, that of the racialized workers in "Freedom From Want"—also stemmed from the fact that they entered seamlessly into a popular iconography already prepared for them by the widely-diffused, documentary images of the Farm Security Administration (FSA).[9] The visual counterpart to Bulosan's piece in *The Saturday Evening Post* was a realism of a different sort—Norman Rockwell's naturalistically rendered painting of white, middle-class family feasting on a turkey. Perhaps intended to illustrate the opposite of "want," this image nonetheless made it much more difficult to "see" the workers rendered by Bulosan. Dorothea Lange had amply documented the presence of Filipino farm workers in California both in her independent work and in her widely circulated photographs taken for the FSA in the 1930s and beyond. But it was another Lange photo—"Migrant Mother"—that became the most famous single image of both the Farm Security Administration and the Depression era, emerging as the iconic visual counterpart to Ma Joad. As with other FSA images, its authority to speak for the authenticity of its subjects derived not only from the "indexical" quality of the photograph—the sense that what lies within the photographic frame really existed on some level—but also from a tradition of realist aesthetics that positioned common people in everyday situations as quintessentially "real."[10] As the number one best-seller in 1939, and with its audience multiplied as a critically and commercially successful film in 1940, Steinbeck's realist narrative built upon these documentary images to become mass culture in the truest sense. His marriage of older republican discourses to the demands of modern workers within the sphere of popular culture greatly served the social movements of the 1930s and 1940s. Indeed, the mass-produced story of *Grapes of Wrath* single-handedly made the plight of migrant workers in California into a national political issue. Soon after the publication of this novel, politicians and journalists began commenting on the Joads as if they were actual people (Lye 143).

If Bulosan's workers represent one "face" of Popular Front pluralism, Steinbeck's Okies represent another. Bulosan's renderings of a real people did not saturate U.S. mass culture to the sustained degree of those of Steinbeck, and they were generally more difficult to "see." But this does not mean that more racially inclusive representations of the body politic at mid-century were insignificant or even uncommon. Indeed, the more racially conscious, realist articulations of the people circulating in mass culture are the focus of this book, which will follow them through not only the Asian/Asian American antifascism of Carlos Bulosan but the southern best-sellers of Erskine Caldwell, the photography of Margaret Bourke-White for *Life* magazine, the domestic dramas of Lillian Hellman, and through Popular Front boxing narratives by the likes of

Nelson Algren, Richard Wright, and Clifford Odets in fiction, drama, reportage, and film. Popular culture, then as now, was a battleground, and these mass-mediated realisms intervened in an overwhelmingly racist culture industry to contest its representations and to link class consciousness to that contestation. Not surprisingly, however, access to most media professions was highly restricted. Although the degree of exclusion varied in recording, radio, film, and publishing, the color line afforded relatively few spaces for people of color to work in the culture industries, particularly as writers or directors. So while mass mediated-realism did question racial hierarchies at mid-century, it was oftentimes—but not always—white or liminally white realists who were allowed to pose the questions before the largest of audiences, and this fact would affect the nature and the depth of its antiracism. Thus this book will also look at what might have been in the form of a number of works that could not circulate on a mass basis in the 1930s and 1940s, including the realist work of Shirley Graham for radio and popular stage, and the powerful novel *And China Has Hands* (1937) by H. T. Tsiang. These works are instructive for illustrating what media executives were and were not ready to accept, thereby underscoring the preconditions for the visibility of race.

It is not my intention to evoke Bulosan's "Freedom From Want" as a replacement for Ma Joad's "We're the people" as the true master narrative of the Popular Front years. Rather, I see the "people" as imagined by Steinbeck and Bulosan as forming two streams within the Popular Front, each with its popular and official adherents. Both of these pluralisms, moreover, contended with "the American Century," media baron Henry Luce's imperial, consumerist vision of the nation that was furthered by films such as *Sullivan's Travels*. My evocation of Bulosan and Steinbeck is intended to underscore the complexity of the political subject arising from the Popular Front years, and to suggest a palpable link between the cultural production of this subject and official rhetoric. Like those who spoke of the Joads as if they were actual people (one of whom was F.D.R.), Vice-President Henry Wallace also referred to Erskine Caldwell's best-selling proletarian novel *Tobacco Road* as if it were an actual place. In a 1944 article in the *New York Times*, Wallace wrote that fascism "may be encountered in Wall Street, Main Street, or Tobacco Road," a sign that the more racially conscious, mass-mediated realisms of the era had created a common set of metaphors even in the highest offices in the country (Wallace also called the naturalist classic *The Jungle* by Upton Sinclair "the most powerful novel of the century") (134, 163).

Wallace attempted to express the antiracist pluralisms of Bulosan and Caldwell with the labels "The Century of the Common Man" and "The People's Century." Positioning himself against "the American Century," Henry Luce's imperial manifesto of 1941, Wallace wrote in 1942: "Some have spoken of the 'American Century.' I say that the century on which we are entering—the century which will come out of this war—can and must be the century of the common man" (193). Wallace's work significantly influenced the rhetoric of the president himself, and as such, can be seen as having far more weight than even Steinbeck's influential novel (Singh 480). Wallace defined the political specificity of the People's Century as follows in a 1942 speech which was repeated almost verbatim in Carlos Bulosan's "Freedom from Want:" "... when the farmers have an opportunity to buy land at reasonable prices and to sell the produce of their land through their own organizations, when workers have the opportunity to form unions and bargain through them collectively, and when the children of all the people have an opportunity to attend schools which teach them truths of the real world in which they live—when these opportunities are open to everyone, then the world moves straight ahead" (191–92). Like Steinbeck, Wallace was rooted in older, republican notions of the body politic, which included a belief that education was a precondition for national self-consciousness, an opposition between a "slave world" and a "free world," and a reliance on the notion of "self-government" (190–91). On closer inspection, however, we find that the People's Century is much more inclusive and broadly imagined than the image offered by the Joads. In short, Wallace, like Bulosan, not only saw "the people" as a more racially diverse category, but also one that did not stop at national borders. Wallace broke with the tradition of republicanism in subscribing to the views of anthropologist Franz Boas, who held that culture, and not innate racial characteristics, was the basis of difference across human societies. Though Wallace lauded Boas before the U.S. entrance into the war, his Boasian idea of cultural difference guided his denunciations of fascism during the conflict itself.[11] In the same 1942 speech quoted above, Wallace broke with the racialized notion of "fitness for self-government" by stating "there are no backward peoples which are lacking in mechanical sense. Russians, Chinese, and the Indians both of India and the Americas all learn to read and write and operate machines just as well as your children and my children" (191). On this basis, he continued: "Those who write the peace must think of the whole world. There can be no privileged peoples. We ourselves in the United States are no more of a master race than the Nazis" (194). Thus he envisioned the people's century, in part, as a "third kind of democracy" wedged between the political democracy of the U.S. and the economic democracy of the U.S.S.R.; he called this third democracy an "ethnic democracy" (198). Simply put, he understood ethnic democracy to mean that "the different races and minority groups must be given the same equality of economic opportunity" (198).

While African American intellectuals such as Angelo Herndon and Ralph Ellison rightly questioned the sincerity of the administration's call for the ethnic democracy of the People's Century, the rhetorical positions of Wallace and F.D.R. vis-à-vis the People's Century marked a profound shift in official U.S. notions of race (Singh 474). As Nikhil Pal Singh has argued, a package of legislation came with this shift that can be regarded as the real inauguration of "the Second Reconstruction." This included Executive Order 8802, which required a certain level of African American employment in the defense industries, and the creation of the Fair Employment Practices Commission (480). But much like the New Deal itself, the "People's Century" was not simply the autonomous creation of government officials, but rather was animated by much larger left and African American social movements. The early legislation of the Second Reconstruction was a response to A. Philip Randolph's March on Washington movement, which threatened to bring 100,000 African Americans to Washington, D.C., in 1941 to protest discrimination in the defense industries; the effectiveness of the black press; the work of the 1.2 million-strong National Negro Congress and El Congreso del Pueblo de Habla Española (the Spanish-Speaking Congress), both of which were Popular Front organizations; Popular Front anti-fascism, and daily acts of resistance by African American and Mexican American workers in particular, all of which threatened the national unity necessary for the impending war.[12] While it is important not to overstate the extent to which this policy shift was felt in the everyday lives of most people of color in the United States in the 1940s, it can be regarded as setting the stage for the civil rights movement of the 1950s and 1960s. The mass-mediated realisms in the chapters that follow were enabled by and participated in this widespread activism. In part, this book is intended to illuminate the origins of Wallace's complex notions of citizenship by looking at significant and underscrutinized narratives circulating within popular culture, showing how the "cultural fronts" of U.S. civil society participated in the rise of "the Second Reconstruction." In other words, it seeks the origins of the People's Century in the culture wars from the decade preceding Wallace's 1942 speech.

Defining the Popular Front Subject(s)

The term *Popular Front* requires a more precise definition. Michael Denning succinctly defines it as "a radical historical bloc uniting industrial unionists, Communists, independent socialists, community activists, and émigré anti-fascists around laborist social democracy, anti-fascism, and anti-lynching" (4). In the most basic sense, the term—put in motion by the Moscow-based Communist International in 1935—denotes a phase in international communist strategy spanning from 1935 to 1939. In the attempt to halt the rise of fascism, the Party jettisoned the policy of the "Third Period" (1928–1935), which was marked by calls for proletarian revolution, class war, and communist vanguardism, in favor of a less sectarian policy of coalition-building with other left and liberal organizations. The rallying cry of this new phase of policy was not "the worker" but "the people." Earl Browder, the chair of the Communist Party of the United States (CPUSA) during the Popular Front period, made it clear in his essay "Who Are the Americans?" that "working" made one eligible to be included in the category of "the people," but he was very careful not to define the nature of that work, nor to attach a specific race, ethnicity, gender, or even income level to its performance. Combating the idea that Anglo-Saxons were the only legitimate heirs to the national tradition, he wrote "We are a mongrel breed, and we glory in it" (14). The rhetorician Kenneth Burke lauded the linguistic shift to "the people" in 1935, rightly noting that it opened up a political space for those who did not identify with the term "worker" and also helped Americans associate the socialist movement with a positive, constitutional symbolism with which they were familiar. To Burke, the rhetorical change from "the worker" to "the people" marked a change from a "propaganda by exclusion" to a "propaganda by inclusion" ("Revolutionary Symbolism" 93).

The positions of party leaders like Browder were highly influential, but they were not followed to the letter. Denning and other recent scholars of the period have rejected the traditional core/periphery model of the Popular Front, which saw the CPUSA leading a broad-based coalition of left-leaning "fellow travelers" by the nose in matters of both aesthetics and politics; I reject this model as well.[13] It is more accurate to view the Popular Front as something that moved far beyond its Comintern origins to assume a life of its own within American culture. Writers on the left in the late 1930s and 1940s rarely maintained a strict adherence to the "party line," nor was there any institution in the U.S. context which could have forcefully compelled them to do so. To return to the beginning of this introduction, the fact that Sullivan's film could be associated with communism and yet be hailed by its leftist creator as "an answer to communism" illustrates how even some critics of the Popular Front recognized its cultural wing as neither controlled by nor fully disconnected from the global communism of its era. Because of the partial independence of the Popular Front from the Communist Party, I have also chosen not to end this book at 1939, when the Hitler-Stalin Pact officially ended the Popular Front period. While Party membership rolls dropped precipitously due to what many regarded as both "a deal with the devil" and a moral and ideological betrayal, the markers of the "people's culture" engendered by the Popular Front continued well into the war years and slightly beyond. This book thus retains the label *Popular Front* up until 1947 to reflect this continuity. The last Popular Front text I consider in detail is the film *Body and Soul,* released in 1947, but I am not suggesting that Popular Front culture ended abruptly in that year.

While Denning has decentered the institutional structure of the Old Left, other scholars have decentered its subject. Like so many others in the 1930s and 1940s, cultural producers often tried to find a language to articulate race, class, and ethnicity (and sometimes gender) without privileging one category over the other, and this book joins a wave of scholarship that, each in its own unique way, attempts to illuminate this complex negotiation of subjectivity. Contrary to a standard view arising from both Cold Warriors and the New Left, much of the secondary work on the 1930s and 1940s has implicitly shown that those turbulent decades were not nearly as class-centered as previously assumed. Whether scholars focus on the Popular Front, the Communist Party, labor unions, or nascent civil rights movements, it is clear that, at the time, a worldview was on the rise that held as a central political goal the crossing of national, racial, and ethnic boundaries in the name of a transnational class consciousness (my terminology is defined at the end of this chapter).[14]

While the nationalist component of Popular Front rhetoric was strategically valuable in building left social movements on a number of levels, a question remains as to whether it fostered a problematic form of subjectivity that foreclosed wider global allegiances. Was this rhetoric exceptionalist? Did it create hard boundaries that prevented cultural producers from imagining affiliations and identities that reached beyond the borders of nation-states? Activists and cultural producers in the Popular Front labored to cultivate a concrete, tangible sense of "the people" within an ideology that paradoxically sought to exalt national traditions and, at the same time, cross national borders in the effort to raise class consciousness. This project was fraught with complications. Communist Party theoreticians worldwide had tried to define the agents of history—hence its subjects and allies—through a number of shifting positions on the issue of nationalism. When the Comintern switched to the Popular Front line in 1935, the novelty of the new position lay not in its embrace of nationalism per se, but in the type of nationalism it now advocated. Throughout its "Third Period" (1928–1934), the Party argued that nationalism was to be encouraged within oppressed nations subjected to imperial capitalism.[15] People living in imperialist countries were to eschew the patriotism of their homelands and promote solidarity with those whom their leaders subjected abroad. But in its effort to co-opt fascist movements in imperial countries, the party deemphasized anti-imperial nationalism. Now, the national traditions within each imperial country were to be positively evoked within a new aesthetic envisioning Marxism as the realization of the nation's cultural heritage. Browder, who was also known for the phrase "Communism is twentieth century Americanism," did not repeat the older line that nationalism should be jettisoned on the road to internationalism. Rather, like Wallace he implied that the American nation was always already international (albeit in a more Eurocentric vein than the vice president).[16] In "Who Are the Americans?" Browder argued that American traditions had been constituted by people and ideas outside of its borders, from the founding fathers who read European Enlightenment philosophy, to immigrants building their communities in its cities, and finally to Marxist ideas entering the country from Europe. The CPUSA did not officially renounce its position on anti-imperial nationalism during the Popular Front period (indeed, Browder mentions the black belt thesis briefly in *What is Communism?*), but it was no longer a point of emphasis.

Gauged in this light, Browder did not exactly "harden" national boundaries, as he argued that the United States must continue to incorporate ideas and peoples from outside of its borders in order to reach its full development. And, to be sure, the real "center" of Browder's national identity is difficult to locate, as the "nation" he imagined was a strategic articulation of a class identity. On a more subtle level, however, Browder and much of U.S. Popular Front culture did harden boundaries by encouraging people to see "America" as the central locus of multiplicity. Moreover, Browder's position (unlike the Third Period line) did not encourage writers to look to foundations other than 1776, nor to imagine multiple, national identities that did not lead back to the Soviet Union. Nonetheless, this did not prevent individual writers from doing so, as I will highlight in my chapter on Carlos Bulosan and H. T. Tsiang.

Realism and Mass Culture
A Brief History

Realism, to reiterate, was a primary vehicle for disseminating Popular Front subjectivity, a means of uniting the politics of the people with an aesthetic for the people. However, the privileging of modernism within literary studies of the first half of the twentieth century has made this cultural process difficult to see. The overvaluation of modernism in twentieth-century studies has had an impact on pedagogy as well, and can be viewed in the accepted order of genre-based

American literature courses: realism in the late nineteenth century, then modernism in the 1920s, then postmodernism after World War II. One simply follows the next, with no looking back. But while it would be an oversimplification to collectively label all cultural work emerging from the 1930s and 1940s as *realist*, there was a definite resurgence of "matter of fact," accessible documentary modes pioneered in the U.S. by Mark Twain and Jacob Riis after the explosion of modernism in the world of arts and letters. By the 1930s realism was an aesthetic strategy widely employed by socially committed authors in the United States and Europe.[17] In literature, John Steinbeck, Myra Page, Richard Wright, Jack Conroy, Agnes Smedley, Carlos Bulosan, and countless others resurrected realism in order to expose social contradictions, while in photography, Dorothea Lange, Walker Evans, Margaret Bourke-White, Russell Lee, and many more employed by the Farm Security Administration reversed the 1920s tendency toward abstract modernism with a new emphasis on social documentary. On the commercial stage realism was increasingly acceptable to audiences in the 1910s and 1920s, and became entrenched as the primary mode of serious dramatic fare in the Depression years. By the 1930s realism had even been adopted as the official artistic genre of the Soviet Union; long after the war, artists would be praised or denounced within communistic circles to the degree that their work conformed to shifting definitions of realism. Some of the primary calling cards of modernism—the emphasis on the defamiliarization of form and the positioning of the artist as a vanguard figure—were certainly present in the arts and letters of the 1930s and 1940s. But these are not motifs that pervade the cultural productions of the Depression and war years, a time often assumed to be dominated by modernist aesthetics. And the search for a universal, quasi-religious aesthetic that marked much of 1920s "high modernism" was in disrepute as that decade faded from view.

More significantly, realism had made a profound leap outside of the arts and into the realm of mass culture by the 1930s. Even in advertising, copywriters rejected the highly aestheticized modernism of the 1920s in favor of a more hard-boiled, "ugly," and to-the-point aesthetic (Marchand 300–306). As my chapter on *Life* will show, the new practice of photojournalism had also become thoroughly infused with realist aesthetics by mid-century. And with the introduction of the paperback format by the publishing industry in the early 1940s, realist-inflected novels by American authors such as Erskine Caldwell, Ann Petry, Richard Wright, and Nelson Algren joined those of James T. Farrell to truly become "mass" culture. Film was perhaps most significant given the size and frequency of its audience. From its very beginnings in the studios of Thomas Edison and the Lumiere brothers, the desire of filmmakers to use the new medium to provide a transparent rendering of reality was present. In its first two decades, however, the formal structures of American cinema were dominated by modes drawn from the urban, working-class culture of its audience: either melodrama or nonlinear, "presentational" modes such as vaudeville, magic lantern shows in the home, street entertainers, circuses, and fairground acts. In the effort to attract more affluent viewers, studios began employing narrative styles drawn from realist theater—individualized characters, linear, continuous narration and editing, realistic, nongestural acting—which had achieved respectability among more affluent, turn-of-the-century theater audiences. This shift was traceable in films as early as Edwin S. Porter's *The Great Train Robbery* (1903), but it achieved a more complete expression with the work of D. W. Griffith (Burch 93–94, Hallam 18–23, Pearson 50). By the onset of the "Classic Period" of American cinema in 1930, mainstream U.S. film was already developing into an amalgam of melodrama and realism (Bodnar xxvi). Popular Front filmmakers of this period would reclaim the realist aspects of the medium from their bourgeois origins, as would the left with realism in general. As chapter 2 will show, the relationship between stage and screen continued to develop in the 1930s and 1940s, when left-wing playwrights brought further innovations from realist theater to Hollywood.

But the presence of realism in mass culture did not begin in the twentieth century, and the Depression cohort were not the first realists to engage with the culture industries. Nineteenth-century American realism arose with the mass publishing market, the first artistic genre to enter an America in which the written word had become a commodity (Borus 24). The relationship between nineteenth-century realism and mass culture was a tense one, however. As Amy Kaplan reminds us, the work of the late-nineteenth-century American realists constituted a "debate" with mass culture, conceived by the likes of Wharton, Dreiser, and Howells as an alternate mode of representation to literary realism (12–13). Realism was imagined by many of its advocates as a form opposed to both an earlier elite, genteel culture and mass culture, with Howells making a sharp distinction between the function of realism and the function of mass culture: the former was to produce social knowledge, while the latter produced mere entertainment (21). Despite this opposition, mass-culture forms were sometimes incorporated into turn-of-the-century realism, sometimes unconsciously: for example, Dreiser's *Sister Carrie* bore the marks of sentimental fiction, and Stephen Crane unconsciously replicated the pop cultural forms of the minstrel show and the freak show in his story "The Monster" (Brown 213–20; Kaplan 140–60). And despite the profound ambivalence of realists toward the culture industries, they nonetheless wanted a viable place for their "serious" writing within the emergent and largely entertainment-driven market (Borus 24, 64).

Both the turn-of-the-century realists and the Depression-era cohort were historically situated at moments when it would have been difficult not to notice massive transformations in everyday life wrought by consumerism. Both produced their work having freshly experienced moments of explosive consumer culture expansion (the 1890s or the 1920s, respectively). The transformations of the 1920s did not go unnoticed by those working in the Popular Front over the two decades that followed; what often did go unnoticed, however, was the degree to which mass-culture forms infused their realisms.

But two main factors separated Popular Front-era realists from their turn-of-the-century forebears in regard to their relationship to the mass market. First, there was much less "outside" of mass culture in the post-1920s world they inhabited. For Howells and Wharton, the culture industries existed alongside a world of older, face-to-face modes of communication—a world Mike Gold represented through his father, the teller of "traditional" Romanian parables and aficionado of the *doina*, a genre of Romanian shepherd song (*Jews without Money* 118). The degree to which mass media permeated everyday life by the 1930s, however, would have been truly astounding to the earlier William Dean Howells. The Depression cohort had grown up in a world where a commercial culture of nickelodeons and movie houses, dance halls and saloons, Tin Pan Alley and radio, dime novels and tabloids was inescapable. As Joseph Freeman wrote of his tenement childhood, "we were molded not only by home, school and companions, but by newspapers and magazines. Happy Hooligan and Buster Brown marched across our imaginations with Jean Valjean and d'Artagnan" (57). And while this world had made incursions into the work of turn-of-the century-realism, its incursions into 1930s and 1940s realism was profound. To put it another way, while fusions of mass-culture forms and realism had been present at the turn of the century, by the mid-twentieth century this fusion had moved to center stage, becoming pervasive and ubiquitous. As I will show in subsequent chapters, an often contradictory blend of realism and melodrama, the latter of which was a dominant aesthetic and epistemological mode in popular working-class theater in the nineteenth century, emerged as a common and powerful outcome of this fusion in popular literature, film, radio, theater, and even photojournalism in the 1930s and 1940s.

A second difference between turn-of-the-century and Depression-era writers is not so much the subject position of the authors, but the subject positions of realist audiences. Using realism as a way of seeing meant something very different by the 1930s—its founding manifestoes had been written long ago, and while it had not become the only mode of representation in the U.S., it was no longer the genteel literary form it was in the heyday of *Atlantic Monthly*.

Though realist literature appeared in the nation's leading publications in the 1880s and 1890s, it never achieved dominance among writers, readers, or critics at that time (Borus 16). The late-nineteenth-century bastion of realism, the *Atlantic Monthly*, reached a small, highly educated audience; even later "popular" magazines in which realist stories were published—*Century, The Cosmopolitan, McClure's*—were consumed primarily by the professional managerial class and never exceeded a circulation of 1 percent of the U.S. population at their peak in the mid-1890s (Ohmann 119).[18] The relative diffusion of the genre during the Depression, appearing in film, radio, best-selling fiction and even advertising, greatly expanded its audience, further blurring the line between realism and popular culture. Espousing a hard-boiled realism, as did many of the editors of the *New Masses*, was less an exploration into fresh ways of seeing as it was a way of getting a much larger audience to accept the underlying principles of an aesthetic which had long since made its mark in the world of arts and letters.

The question remains as to how realist form affected the politics of representing the people by the writers and photographers covered in the chapters that follow. In short, the traditions of realism and naturalism that the culture workers of the 1930s and 40s inherited—and diffused into mass culture—both impeded and positively facilitated a more genuinely pluralistic image of the people. But what were the relevant traits and features of realist epistemology emerging from the nineteenth century? First, Raymond Williams writes that one common feature shared by all realisms is the element of "social extension," or, a narrative focus on characters of nonelite ranks (the other two unifying features of realism, in his reading, are a contemporary or near-contemporary setting and the emphasis on secular rather than metaphysical action) (61–74). The presence of nonelite or even poor, working-class characters in a novel is not inherently democratic, as Nancy Glazener has documented in her study of the *Atlantic Monthly* and similar magazines in the nineteenth century. Produced by established writers and consumed by bourgeois readers, characters of humble origins such as Huck Finn or Silas Lapham could become vehicles for class stratification, legitimizing bourgeois authority by creating a sense of shared interest between plebeian characters and their social betters (22–23, 40–41). Yet the element of social extension paved the way for a representation of "the people" to emerge in the twentieth century that was more inclusive and genuinely democratic in scope, creating the preconditions for a genuine pluralism.

Second, and intimately related to social extension, is the focus on everyday life in realist narratives. In direct contrast to the subject of much Victorian and "genteel" art in the late nineteenth century, and the prior history of American letters in which the lives of "common" or "low" characters were often employed for comic relief or ridicule, this facet of realist representation made the daily, often mundane struggles of nonelite ranks an important subject meriting the "serious" consideration of art.

Several other aesthetic qualities inherited from the nineteenth century speak to the genre's ability to interpellate a wide audience and hence to its marketability—its usability within mass culture, as it were. A third inheritance from the previous century was realism's move toward accessibility. While its advocates in the *Atlantic Monthly* vacillated between populist exhortation and a discourse of connoisseurship, it is significant that the former was the more remembered quality of the genre by writers and critics in the twentieth century.[19] The democratic inclinations of early realism were contradictory at best, yet it exhibited at least the beginnings of a desire for accessible representation. Indeed, Howells had written that the capacity to appreciate art lay within everyone's power and wanted what has been "observed and known" by "the mass of common men" to form the basis of a new literary criticism (12). Central to the realist drive for accessibility was the use of common speech within realist narrative, rather than the use of a separate, elevated language found only in art and rhetoric (Borus 22). While many poststructuralist critics have seen the attempt to achieve narrative transparency as the main flaw of the genre, a concealment of the fact of its authorship and hence the often repressive authority behind it, it is important to remember that the drive for representational transparency was, especially in the twentieth century, part of a drive for accessibility. It came out of a desire to spread a serious and socially committed art to those unschooled (as both readers and writers) in the history of aesthetic tradition—schooling necessary to interpret much of the work promoted by poststructuralism.[20]

Fourth, as Michael Davitt Bell has shown, there was a deep ambivalence toward literary culture within Howellsian realism—the theories of which proved decidedly influential for the Popular Front—and I would add that this ambivalence was transferred to much of 1930s and 1940s realism as well (48). This discomfort was bound to a notion of political commitment, for in Howells's paradigmatic plot, the protagonist moved from irresponsible, aesthetic detachment to a morally and politically responsible realism, with the implication that political, moral commitment is tied to a rejection of the aesthetic realm (54). One sees this image of the detached literary world quite clearly echoed in Mike Gold's manifesto "Proletarian Realism." In his denunciation of Proust, the "master-masturbator of the bourgeois literature," he renounces the literary as a separate sphere of production, proclaiming that "Proletarian realism deals with the *real conflicts* of men and women who work for a living. It has nothing to do with the sickly mental states of the idle Bohemians" (206). While Bell has remarked on the negative implications of this aspect of Howellsian realism for the gender politics of the genre (more on this momentarily), it also had the effect of abolishing the notion of the artist as a heroic, exalted, or vanguard figure, a common marker of both romanticism and modernism. Interestingly, the protagonists of 1930s and 1940s literature are almost never artists, which arguably makes their lives and struggles more germane to the majority of readers.

Finally, one inherited feature of nineteenth-century realism that would put constraints on the aesthetics of Popular Front pluralism was the nature of its break with sentimental codes, which had lent discourses on realism a masculinist tone they never overcame. All nineteenth-century American realisms shared a desire to break with the romantic codes of narrative that were popular before and immediately after the Civil War (Borus 19). The largely female-authored genre of sentimental fiction, to be sure, was one of these codes. As "sentiment" was generally understood as feminine, this break carried with it an implicit rejection of women and what was understood to be women's subjectivity. Howells's seminal story "Editha," which places a destructive sentimentality squarely in its central and highly active female character, stands as a case in point. Bell has linked Howells's rejection of the literary world to his embarrassment with his chosen profession as a fiction writer, which was not regarded as a properly masculine profession in the mid-nineteenth century. Howells's advocacy of the new genre of "realism" was thus inseparable from his desire to re-create the world of the artist as a masculine one, and such masculine overtones became even more pronounced with naturalism (24–25). As I will show in chapter 2, female authors have successfully used realism to call attention to the struggles of women and to critique patriarchy. Indeed, as Paula Rabinowitz has noted, the publication of Agnes Smedley's *Daughter of Earth* in 1929 marked "the beginnings of proletarian realism as a literary movement in the United States" and was acknowledged as such by contemporary critics (*Labor* 10). But since discourses surrounding the genre have tended to code realism as male and melodrama as female, it was often the case that women encountered substantial obstacles in being recognized as realists and faced more hurdles in their attempts to gain access to mass audiences in this role. All in all, it is not a coincidence that the Popular Front valued this male-coded genre so highly. While it laudably united a critique of American class and racial formations as never before, patriarchy too often remained a blind spot within its pluralist imaginings.

As for race and ethnicity, I have found nothing inherent within the form of realism that either facilitates or inhibits a critique of the color line. In nineteenth-

and early-twentieth-century practice, realism was used both to solidify racial hierarchies (London, Norris, Harte) as well as to question them (Twain, Chesnutt, Hopkins, Sin Far, Cahan), a dynamic that continued into the 1930s. It must be noted, however, that although cultural production in the 1930s and 1940s often remained essentialist, the attempt to articulate race, class, and ethnicity in equivalent, oppositional ways is generally much more sophisticated in Depression-era works than those of most class-conscious, turn-of-the-century realists (with the notable exception of Abraham Cahan). London, Dreiser, Norris, Howells, and Sinclair turned out novels, in some instances explicitly socialist in their politics, that were highly critical of the abuses of American capitalism. But the racial and ethnic politics of these authors fell short in a number of ways. By and large, London and Norris did not even attempt to link their exposés of the economic system to a critique of the racial hierarchies of the dominant order. In this sense their writing corresponded to the racial politics of much of the turn-of-the-century labor and socialist movements. Eugene V. Debs, it must be remembered, once stated, "We have nothing special to offer the Negro," while A.F.L. President Samuel Gompers co-authored a pamphlet in 1902, the very title of which underscores its nativism: "Meat vs. Rice: American Manhood against Asiatic Coolieism. Which Shall Survive?" Another strand of class-conscious turn-of-the-century authors—namely, Sinclair and Dreiser—constructed more nuanced linkages between ethnicity and class, but ultimately fell back on class as the ultimate affiliation. Twain and Chesnutt, conversely, were much more critical of U.S. racial formation, but they did not ally themselves with any particular social class.[23] And while Howells endorsed the N.A.A.C.P., his use of dialect often racialized his nonwhite characters (Nettles 87–104). Artistic forms need not always generate a consistent set of political effects, and it is not my intention to suggest as much with the history of realism I have provided here. Suffice to say here that the openness of the form in regard to racial formation allowed for its later and productive use within Popular Front definitions of the people.

In the nineteenth century, realism was not yoked to a single political project. It was touted by some advocates as a language of social critique and by others as an establishment form; among elite Boston philanthropists it could be both at the same time (Glazener 28-33). Marx and Engels left a significant precedent for receiving realism as an oppositional mode by hailing it as the best artistic genre for revealing the totality of capitalist social relations, and their enthusiasm for its class politics would carry to the other side of the Atlantic. Howells valued the genre precisely for its "communistic taste," and he later took the highly unpopular stance of defending the Haymarket anarchists (8). Yet even when it sought to oppose the interests of the establishment, nineteenth-century realism in practice was hamstrung as a democratic project. Despite his call for accessibility and his ambivalence toward the figure of the artist, Howells's narrative voice in his fiction—as was the case with many nineteenth-century realists—retained a Victorian density that dramatically separated it from the vernacular expressions of the characters it described. Indeed, realism's highly educated advocates often represented it within the *Atlantic*-group magazines as a form about the people but not *for* the people, as something "too good" for the average reader (Glazener 48). Granville Hicks, a key literary critic of the communist left in the 1930s, faulted Bret Harte, William Dean Howells, Mark Twain, Stephen Crane, and even Jack London as insufficiently realist because the politics of their work lacked a fundamental connection to the popular social movements of their day (44–45, 93, 193). Following Antonio Gramsci, nineteenth-century realism was not generally a "national-popular" literature, because the "feelings of the people [were] not lived by the writers as their own" (365).

And despite its embrace by Marx, the nineteenth century left did not wholeheartedly embrace the creation of new realist work accessible to the masses. Nineteenth-century socialists by and large stressed a mastery of the classics, not a new proletarian culture (Denning, *Three Worlds* 56). In January 1896, for example, the major socialist newspaper *Appeal to Reason* listed almost no fiction in the column "Books Workers Should Read," and featured advertisements for "Penny Classics" as late as 1909.[21] The impulse to create a realist, proletarian culture gained ground after the Bolshevik Revolution, when creating a new society was much more tangible to those on the left. By the late 1920s, the communist journal the *New Masses* hosted its own cultural critics to evaluate the flood of original, aesthetic production from oppositional writers and artists. The self-proclaimed realists of the 1930s lessened the distance between author and audience, coming much closer to the accessibility Howells sometimes championed, and to the unity of popular and intellectual cultures which Gramsci referred to as "the national popular." The realist rejection of the cultural producer as a "special" figure, as well a more consistent use of simpler prose after the late nineteenth century, would help lessen the gulf between artists and audiences, facilitating the rise of realism as a true "people's" form.[22]

Resurrecting the Body and Soul of the People's Century

If *Sullivan's Travels* stands as a clear lampoon of "We're the people," its implicit silencing of "The People's Century" is emblematic of the place of the more racially inclusive Popular Front pluralism in the historical memory of the U.S.

dominant culture. On the most basic level, Sturges severs antiracism from the 1930s left by withholding any discernable racial politics from his character Sullivan. But as I have noted, Sullivan is also drawn from another Hollywood leftist—John Garfield—who is not explicitly referenced anywhere in the film. Garfield was an avid participant in the People's Century. As I will discuss in chapter 2, he went on to produce the film *Body and Soul* in 1947, a boxing story that wedded a moral rejection of acquisitive individualism to a critique of whiteness.

Sullivan's Travels, by contrast, participates in the very racialization fought by those, like Garfield, who tried to make the People's Century a reality. It uses its one reappearing African American character—billed as "Colored Chef"—for minstrel humor, and the climactic scene, where a largely white band of prisoners file into a church while the black parishioners sing "Go Down, Moses," ultimately trivializes the history of African American vernacular culture. As the people in the church sing the old spiritual, two main shots depict the prisoners entering—the first shows their stooped silhouettes plodding toward the church from the swamp outside, and the second is a close-up of their chained feet slowly shuffling down the center aisle. Both shots convey resignation and, acoustically paired with the spiritual, make "Go Down Moses" the soundtrack of defeat and a defeated people. Their sense of defeat is soon reversed by the Disney film to which they are treated by the minister; this allows the multiracial audience to laugh hysterically and the prisoners to hold their heads up high. Thus *Sullivan's Travels* situates the mass-produced Hollywood comedy as the best, most effective remedy for a history of suffering, the form most capable of instilling the sense of agency that African American vernacular culture could never provide. Considering that the scene appeared when the Communist Party was turning to black folk culture as a culture of resistance, and African American writers and poets affiliated with the left were drawing on black folk songs and stories as a usable past for their own insurgent voices (Paul Robeson even sang "Go Down Moses" at communist events), the church scene can be seen as a rebuke to the lesser-known Popular Front pluralism as well.[24] In sum, the People's Century is an absent presence in *Sullivan's Travels*. Such representations have enabled Americans to forget that there was an active fight against racism in the 1930s and 1940s, not to mention a movement that linked class and racial formations. It also helped many scholars to forget an important strand of antiracism within the history of American realism. For examples one needs to look no further than the postwar critics of Sturges, who missed the contemporaneous racial politics of the church scene in their praise of its proto-postmodern self-referentiality.[25]

The various chapters of this book resurrect instances of antiracist Popular Front realism with particular emphasis on those that were commercially successful. Chapter 1 examines a completely overlooked yet major popular genre of the movement—the Popular Front boxing narrative—and traces it through fiction, drama, music, and film, devoting special attention to the work of Nelson Algren, Clifford Odets, Richard Wright, and John Garfield. Neonaturalist in form, Popular Front boxing narratives authored by Jewish American writers often served as a way to make the struggles of working-class, white "ethnics" visible within mass culture. At the same time, these writers explored the barriers to genuine pluralism by critiquing the competitive masculinity and the psychology of whiteness exhibited by their prizefighter antiheroes. At the same time, a number of boxing narratives were created by African American writers and musicians, most of which exalted Joe Louis as a racial hero. The "Brown Bomber" became a media icon whose meaning was contested by various groups, and African Americans affiliated with the Popular Front, most notably Richard Wright, entered the terrain of mass culture to make him a usable icon of racial pride while also questioning his mythic status. But while a partial critique of American masculinity appears in Popular Front boxing narratives, their representations of women reveal the limitations of the genre in dealing with the gender politics of both realist discourse and popular culture.

While chapter 2 illustrates one of several attempts by the left to use "male" popular genres to reach audiences, chapter 3 explores several Popular Front attempts to interpellate women through mass culture. The 1930s saw the corporate consolidation of radio, and women formed the primary audience for this new medium. Born of the Depression, the new serial genre of the "soap opera" in particular was a means for advertisers to directly address the concerns of female listeners (it was also, as I will show, not untouched by innovations from the realist stage). This chapter will examine the attempts of playwrights Lillian Hellman and Shirley Graham to challenge the politics of "soaps" through their particular brands of mass-mediated realism adapted to stage, screen, and radio. The soap opera foregrounded the agency and the struggles of women in ways that male-authored Popular Front productions often did not, but projected a thoroughly white, middle-class world amenable to consumption. Hellman and Graham represented alternative domestic spaces for their audiences; they showed the home as playing a vital role in producing the class and racial hierarchies legible as "political" in the public debates of the 1930s and 1940s. Yet the work of these two women met with very different outcomes: Hellman became one of the best-paid screenwriters in Hollywood and her drama was broadcast on one of the most popular programs on the dial, while Graham's realist work for radio and stage, despite its intricate tailoring for the mass market, remained obscure and sometimes unaired.

Chapter 3 looks at the ways in which the best-selling novels of Erskine Caldwell and Margaret Mitchell vied with one another to create a narrative of the South in the national imagination. While *Gone with the Wind* remains as a "classic" worldwide, a little-known fact is that Caldwell's story of poor Georgia farmers, *God's Little Acre*, outsold Mitchell's famous work until the 1960s, and it was the third-best selling work of fiction in the United States for the first seventy years of the twentieth century. Building on traditions of local-color realism, both authors jettisoned the agrarian figure of the yeoman in order to propose problematic, yet diametrically opposed, relationships between class, race, and gender. Ironically, despite Mitchell's avowed hostility to the Popular Front, she stayed much closer than Caldwell to the proscriptions for realist writing advocated by cultural theorists on the left. In so doing, she also illustrates the malleability of realism as a mode of representing the people. Mitchell anticipated the racialized rejection of the very idea of plurality that would vex liberal Cold Warriors in the decades after the war, and Caldwell, while providing a stunning and largely unexplored instance of how a "proletarian" novel could achieve commercial success, also revealed how some of the most famous Popular Front cultural productions failed to interrogate gender. This chapter will also explore notions of realism commonly held by literary critics on the left in both the United States and Europe in the 1930s and 1940s, and ask whether it was necessary for Caldwell to depart from these notions in order to achieve financial success.

Chapter 4 shows how Carlos Bulosan and H. T. Tsiang, part of an Asian/Asian American Popular Front, diverged from other Popular Front figures I investigate by exploring the ways in which the U.S. nation-state was an inadequate construct for imagining "the people." Bulosan was able to make Asian diaspora visible within an Orientalist literary market, I argue, because he drew upon agrarian notions of the "folk" that were in wide circulation in Depression-era popular culture, as well as a relationship between Asia and modernity assumed by many U.S. readers. Tsiang, on the other hand, fundamentally questioned the ability of U.S. cultural institutions, especially its culture industries, to facilitate a tolerance for racial diversity, and his work was thus highly marginalized. This chapter will also briefly explore how the best-selling realist novels of Pearl Buck, the reportage of Edgar Snow, and the film *Back to Bataan* by Edward Dmytryk established American images of a "real" Asia that framed U.S. readings of Bulosan and Tsiang. The obstacles faced by Shirley Graham, as well as those confronting Tsiang and Bulosan, illustrate the ways in which people of color had a tremendously difficult time entering mass culture and New Deal agencies as realists. For instance, while the musical theater of Graham was produced and met with tremendous success, the realist plays of African American women playwrights were consistently rejected by the Federal Theater Project and never made it to Broadway in the 1930s and 1940s.

Chapter 5 looks at the impact of Margaret Bourke-White, a Popular Front figure grounded in an oppositional history of realism, on the layout of the explicitly conservative *Life* magazine. As such, it is an exploration of how the aesthetics and the pluralism of the Popular Front could be co-opted by Henry Luce's "The American Century," the influential worldview that imagined a world unified by American consumer goods. By exploring the impact of Bourke-White on *Life*'s signature photo-essay format, I also show how "The American Century" paradoxically relied upon Popular Front aesthetics for coherence.

I should note here that my use of "mass culture" is not synonymous with my use of "popular culture." I use the term *mass culture* to refer to a set of experiences produced for a profit by a small number of specialists working within culture industries that reaches a mass or larger-than-local audience. The element of simultaneity vital to some definitions of mass culture is not essential to mine; that is to say, a given text need not be encountered by millions of people at the same time to be part of mass culture—records and books mass-produced by companies with a national scope constitute mass culture just as much as newspapers and radio. I use *popular culture* to denote forms consumed by "the people" that do not require an advanced level of formal education or cultural capital to access. This broad category encompasses mass culture but also includes oral, vernacular culture, unrecorded music, and the productions of state apparatuses and nonprofit institutions. A pop cultural text can be encountered by millions, or simply hundreds. Thus an accessible short story published by the communist *New Masses* is popular culture but not mass culture; it becomes mass culture, however, when placed within a collection of stories published by the for-profit Bantam Books and is positioned to take advantage of its substantial, national networks. The defining emphasis on "mass culture" thus hinges on production, while my definition of "popular culture" is delimited by audience.[26]

I should also clarify here my uses of "transnational" and "internationalist," which I do not view as interchangeable terms. I use *internationalist* to refer to a global affiliation that explicitly eschews allegiances to any particular nation-state, region, or continent. I employ *transnational* to denote a targeted affiliation to a number of distinct locales that cross extant national boundaries. A transnational affiliation, in my usage, does not foreclose a broader global allegiance but rather implies a kind of subjectivity that, out of political efficacy or the requirements of a viable identity, requires a cross-border affiliation more specific than a generally articulated internationalism. I use the term *internationalist* to describe official Comintern positions—through the Third Period, the Popular Front, and beyond—because, while they often served the needs of the Soviet state, they were articulated as the needs of the people in all nations across the world (or, in the case of the Third Period, viewed anti-imperial nationalism as a mere phase). In these terms, the Popular Front movements within various nations are not internationalist (their nationalist components prevent this), but they are often transnational. In this book I will assert that the work of Carlos Bulosan, H. T. Tsiang, the later Shirley Graham, and, perhaps unexpectedly, Henry Luce exhibited a clear transnationalism, while a very short list of other left and liberal writers of the 1930s and 1940s in this category would include Langston Hughes, Agnes Smedley, Jesús Colón, and Jerre Mangione.

I should also state that this book, unlike much of realism, does not purport to represent a totality. That is to say, I have not set out to cover every last instance of Popular Front, mass-mediated realism, nor even every significant instance. In tracing the diffusion of left-wing realism throughout mass culture, I could have also provided detailed discussions of detective stories, gangster films, evening radio programs such as the Columbia Workshop, Hollywood realism in general, and no doubt much more. With the exception of radio, a large body of research is in abundance in these areas, and I have chosen instead to explore instances much richer, for the sake of this project, or much more overlooked.

This book is guided by the belief that the "People's Century" would be partially incorporated into, yet partly survive, the contending ideal of the "American Century" after the war, and the conclusions of each chapter will meditate on how the subversive force of its realisms were either co-opted or revitalized after 1945. But while the aesthetics of realism are more recognizable in the culture of the 1930s and 1940s than before or since, their impact has been so ground into our expectations of narrative form that they are generally taken for granted in contemporary mass culture. As Stuart Hall reminds us, defeated actors never vanish from the historical stage entirely, and the mass mediated realisms of the Popular Front continue to linger in American culture.

Realism for the Masses

CHAPTER ONE

Taking Down the Great White Hope
The Popular Front Boxing Narrative

In January 1939 *Look* magazine printed a damning exposé of the entire sport of boxing entitled "Prizefights, Pugs, and Profits." Its critique was not particularly original, for it echoed a narrative of prizefighting in wide circulation in the 1930s. *Look*'s writers and photographers focused not on the champions and blow-by-blow accounts of particular fights, but rather on the masses of young men who failed and were crushed in the competition for the title—those who "swung and missed," to use the title of one Nelson Algren story. Its authors write, "For every Dempsey, Tunney or Schmeling who makes a million, 10,000 has-beens are paid off in battered bodies and scrambled minds" (7). Much of the article consists of horrific examples of what happens to the bodies of men who enter the ring, including blindness, insanity, brain hemorrhaging, paralysis, and early death. It even features comparative photographs of two brains: a clean, symmetrical "Normal" brain, and an eerily fragmented, uneven "Punch-Drunk Brain." But the damage to the contenders' bodies and minds is only half the story; the other half is that their suffering is set in motion by greedy gangsters and entrepreneurs. Readers are warned that if a young man takes his fists into the ring, "he is pitting them not so much against another pair of fists as against an industry that thrives on the cheating and ruin of boys" (7).

To illustrate this point, the editors put together a captioned series of photographs describing the rise and fall of a young Italian immigrant named Primo Carnera, whose story was "all the sordid tales of the boxing racket wrapped up in one" (12). When the promoters first found Carnera, *Look* tells the reader, he was working as a strongman at a French carnival. They brought him to America, where he was "cut into four pieces" by four different promoters, each taking a share of the money he generated, then booked in fights across the U.S. Soon gangsters began to demand "cuts" as well, and even fixed fights to ensure his success in the ring. Promoters and gangsters accumulated wealth as Carnera accumulated mental and physical injuries, and once his contract expired he was left penniless. The narrative concludes, "he is just one of many ex-fighters whose own nest was left bare while he feathered the nests of the fight racket's birds of prey" (13).[1]

This story of Primo Carnera is, in short, the Popular Front boxing narrative in its most pervasive form, a realist narrative of rapacious capitalists and ethnic, proletarian outsiders rather than rugged champions and "Great White Hopes." It was told over and over again with various permutations across the films, magazines, plays, radio programs, and novels constituting U.S. popular culture in the 1930s and 1940s, and its popularity attests to the reach of the left at mid-century. Writers, playwrights, and filmmakers such as Clifford Odets, Richard Wright, Nelson Algren, Dashiell Hammett, King Vidor, Robert Rossen, and John Garfield helped formulate the Popular Front boxing narrative, creating their own Primo Carneras in popular theater, literature, and film. As the story of Primo Carnera illustrates, an ethnically marked protagonist was very often at the center of the narrative. Frequently scripted by Jewish American writers, these stories based around white ethnic characters allowed these authors to explore their own positions within U.S. culture and its structures of power, even though their protagonists were generally not of their own ethno-religious backgrounds. The strength of Odets's play and film *Golden Boy*, Algren's popular novel *Never Come Morning*, Rossen and Polonsky's film *Body and Soul*, and Hammett's short story "His Brother's Keeper" lies in their exploration of the position of white "ethnics" in the American racial order. These writers and directors use the stories of white ethnic boxers to launch critiques of white supremacy and American masculinity, situating such critiques as inseparable from class consciousness.

In part, this chapter explores the class, racial, and gender politics of white ethnic, Popular Front subjectivity through an investigation of the realist boxing narrative—a significant but virtually unexplored genre of the movement. Of immediate interest is the extent to which several of the key oppositional writers who used this narrative avoided what David Roediger calls "the public and psychological wage" of whiteness when shedding narrow ethnic affiliations in the name of class consciousness. Algren, Odets, Rossen, and Polonsky largely resist the lure of whiteness that would tarnish many of texts of the "ethnic revival" later in the postwar period.[2] For many ethnically marked European Americans who formed the largest constituency of the Popular Front in Northern cities, the assault on white supremacy was not simple altruism. Matthew Frye Jacobson and David Roediger have shown that the whiteness of those hailing from a score of European immigrant backgrounds was still contested well into the twentieth century, as Southern and Eastern Europeans occupied a liminal position within the dominant culture, not quite deserving of Anglo-Saxon privileges but also not suffering the marginalization afforded to people of non-European heritage.[3] For Popular Front writers of Southern and Eastern European descent, in other words, the quest for class consciousness was intricately bound to acculturation within U.S. society. But as Jacobson and Roediger have argued, the twentieth-century quest of white "ethnics" for social inclusion was not unproblematic—it often stopped short of a general critique of white supremacy and instead settled on the purchase of whiteness for marginalized, European immigrant groups. This tendency was precisely what Odets, Algren, Polonsky, and Rossen attempted to combat in their narratives. Indeed, a critical treatment of race, while definitely not universal, is a more common marker of the prizefighting stories of the Popular Front era than to earlier boxing stories in American popular culture.[4]

But the boxing ring was not a site of crushed hopes for another large, Popular Front constituency: African Americans. While many white Popular Front writers and filmmakers challenged the whiteness of "the Great White Hope," and in so doing called into question the spectacle of prizefighting, most African American cultural production of the period exalted the ring. African American reportage celebrated heroes like the heavyweight champion Joe Louis and the holder of the welterweight title, Henry Armstrong, cheering as these heroes knocked the various Great White Hopes to the canvas. The deeds of Louis in particular were sung by a score of blues and jazz singers, including Memphis Minnie, Joe Pullum, and Cab Calloway, a striking phenomenon considering that virtually no other African American personality of the Depression era was celebrated in a blues song, not even Jesse Owens (Doyle 122). Louis enjoyed a celebrity status in the black press unrivalled by any other African American in the late 1930s and early 1940s. The *Chicago Defender*, for example, with a nationwide black readership and *de facto* Popular Front status by the late 1930s, reported on the champion's every move, creating a cult of celebrity by providing regular updates on his training, his personal habits, his appearances at various events, and his service to the community.[5] *The Crisis*, a decidedly Popular Front journal in the late 1930s, published full-length ads on its back cover through much of 1938 wherein Louis endorsed "Murray's Hair Pomade." Two low-budget independent films helped exalt these champions as well: *The Spirit of Youth* (1938), starring Louis and based on his life, and *Keep Punching* (1939), starring Henry Armstrong.

Realism has never been a genre for the exaltation of heroes, however, and boxing narratives written in any mode by African American fiction writers, poets, and intellectuals are curiously sparse in the period covered in this study. For example, *Negro Story* magazine, a Popular Front literary journal that spanned the years 1944 to 1946 and showcased the work of both established and unknown black American authors, did not contain a single story or poem centered around boxers. The notable exceptions to this intellectual silence were Richard Wright and, to a lesser extent, Chester Himes and Ralph Ellison (in 1947, the latter published his famous story "Battle Royal," the nucleus for *Invisible Man*). Virtually alone among African American writers of the Depression and war years, Wright demonstrated a consistent fascination with boxing and boxing celebrities, a fascination registered in his fiction by the battle royal scene in *Black Boy*, an unfinished novel about a boxer named Tar Baby loosely patterned after Jack Johnson, and, indirectly I will argue, in his best-selling novel *Native Son*.[6] Wright shared the popular fascination with Joe Louis, celebrating the champion in his reportage for *The New Masses* and *The Daily Worker*, and in a jukebox song he wrote called "King Joe," sung by Paul Robeson and put to music by Count Basie in 1941. As I will argue through an examination of his reportage and his famous *Native Son*, as well as through Himes's 1945 novel *If He Hollers Let Him Go*, Wright and Himes attempted to control the "reading" of Louis as a media icon in both the white and black presses, and did so with mass-mediated, realist renderings of Louis's fan-base.

Race and the Commercialization of Boxing

A brief historical account of the sport in the United States will begin to explain the divergent ways of representing boxing among oppositional writers from different Popular Front constituencies. In the early United States, pugilism was rejected on republican grounds as a decadent, British aristocratic spectacle, but it began to gain footing after the War of 1812 when English seamen (along with their cultural practices) were once again allowed in American ports (Gorn, *The Manly Art* 38). Its popularity among urban wage workers and artisans was firmly established by the 1830s, but throughout the antebellum period it continued to be shunned by elites and took place as an underground, illegal spectacle. Boxing was not yet commercialized in the antebellum U.S.: bouts generally were not fought for money but instead grew out of private grudges or local ethnic rivalries. Most fighters were nonprofessionals who fought only one or two bouts, and betting was a show of personal, ethnic, or neighborhood loyalty rather than a quest for private gain (46). Boxing came out from the underworld in the 1880s and 1890s, when middle- and upper-class men increasingly advocated the sport in their search for a more aggressive masculinity, and when the adoption of the Queensberry rules "civilized" the previously bare-knuckle bouts with gloves, timed rounds, and guidelines for sportsmanlike conduct. At the same time, according to Elliot Gorn and Warren Goldstein, American sports at the turn of the century were commodified along with many other leisure activities, becoming "profitable, highly rationalized institutions" (*Brief History* 109). By the 1920s baseball and boxing in particular had become mass culture in the truest sense, with centralized ownership, modern marketing, and elaborate cults of personality around individual sports heroes. Whereas the marketing of heavyweight champion John L. Sullivan in the 1880s and 1890s was limited by the reach of the media at that time, boxing promoters of the early twentieth century such as George Lewis "Tex" Rickard were able to take full advantage of modern media apparatuses with unprecedented sophistication, packaging their fighters with exciting and factually dubious narratives (193).

Boxing has also been a racialized spectacle since the victories of Bill Richmond, nicknamed "the Black Terror," over British troops stationed in the New York area in the late eighteenth century. Other pre-WWII African American boxers to attain fame (or notoriety) in the ring for their bouts with white fighters include the Virginia slave Tom Molineaux (whose career peaked in England in the 1810s), Frederick Douglass's hero Peter Jackson (1870s–1880s), and the enormously influential Jack Johnson (heavyweight champion from 1908–14). The celebrity status of fighters such as Jackson and Johnson among African Americans created the need to destroy them in the white imagination via an equally long tradition of "Great White Hopes." But not all symbolic racial conflict in the ring was African American vs. white. The fight between the Englishman Joe Goss and the Irishman Paddy Ryan in 1880, as well as the fights of Afro-Cuban fighter Eligio Sardinias Montalbo ("Kid Chocolate") and Filipino fighter Pancho Villa in the 1920s and 1930s—to take but a few examples—did not lack social significance for their fans. In the 1930s, Jewish fighters Max Baer, Benny Leonard, and Barney Ross also wore the Star of David on their trunks as emblems of ethno-religious pride. In the early twentieth century, when commodification made American sports increasingly segregated (African Americans often played baseball on professional teams before the 1880s, for instance), interracial competition was more open in boxing than other athletic spectacles (*Brief History* 113). African Americans, for instance, could fight against whites in the lighter weight divisions in the nineteenth century, and Jack Johnson opened the door for African American competition for the heavyweight title in the first decade of the twentieth.

By the 1930s, then, boxing had long been established as a racial performance, but was now a modern mass entertainment as well, with celebrity athletes put forth for emulation and consumption. The unemployment of the Depression also led an unprecedented number of young men to try their hands in the ring, suggesting that these spectacles were guiding the responses of many workers toward their desperate situations (Baker 162). The historical status of the sport up to the 1930s framed Popular Front readings of it in a number of ways. Leftist whites advocating an antiracist class unity could not root for black fighters to go down at the hands of a Great White Hope, nor could they advocate the false consciousness of upward mobility and celebrity emulation that the sport promised. However, both black and white cultural producers with Popular Front sensibilities could more easily root for black boxers, as their victories helped dispel long-standing myths of racial inferiority. To tell the story of a white or probationarily white fighter and stay true to the politics of the movement, the ring as metaphor for capitalism and false consciousness had to remain dominant. But as Wright recognized, the celebration or emulation of African American boxing heroes was also not without its political dangers, and thus the relationship between Richard Wright and "the manly art" was in many ways more complicated.

"They Say Joe Don't Talk Much, But He Talks All the Time"
Reading Joe Louis

Given the central place of Joe Louis in African American boxing narratives in the 1930s and 1940s, it is worthwhile to briefly review his biography. Louis was born into a sharecropping family in Chambers County, Alabama, in 1914. His father was committed to an asylum and died when Joe was four years old; his mother remarried and the new family moved to Detroit in 1926, where the young Louis worked a number of low-paying jobs. He left a position at a Ford plant in the early 1930s to take up boxing full-time, and fought his first professional bout in 1934. The young fighter rapidly gained fame for his success in the ring, knocking out Max Baer, Primo Carnera, and Kingfish Levinsky. His rise was momentarily stalled by his defeat at the hands of the German Max Schmeling in 1936, but he came back to win the heavyweight title in 1937 against James Braddock ("Cinderella Man"). He went on to beat Schmeling in a 1938 rematch and remained undefeated until 1942, when he enlisted in the Army. Not allowed to fight while in the service, Louis returned to the ring in 1946 but with diminished skills. He continued to hold the title until 1948, when he decided to retire after narrowly defeating his opponent Jersey Joe Walcott. In financial distress, he staged an unsuccessful comeback in 1951, losing to Rocky Marciano, then left the ring for good.

As a celebrity icon, Louis and his triumphs held divergent meanings across different sections of the American public in the 1930s and 1940s. In theorizing his reception, semiotics offers a productive frame, one that allows us to think about Joe Louis as a "sign" for his audiences. V. N. Volosinov wrote that all signs are "multi-accentual": different social classes use the same language, and as a result, "differently oriented accents intersect in every ideological sign." Each class, in other words, uses a different accent to enunciate the same signs. In times of crisis, this multi-accentual aspect of the sign becomes more apparent, and the "sign becomes an arena of class struggle" (23). If we decenter class from the analysis, Voloshinov's general idea of semiotic contestation is helpful for articulating the position of Joe Louis within mass culture during the height of his career. While Louis battled opponents in the ring, American popular culture became a much larger arena in which various social groups enunciated him and the significance of his victories in different accents, contending with one another to make meaning of him as a sign.

Louis was known for being taciturn, silent, and highly economical with his words, and this personality trait lent him a particular openness as a sign, leaving writers a great deal of latitude to project what they wanted onto him. Richard Wright observed this quality in his blues song "King Joe, Part I" and identified it as the basis of the prizefighter's power. Paul Robeson sang the lyrics, "They say Joe don't talk much, but he talks all the time / Now you can look at Joe, but you sure can't read his mind." In the mid-1930s, however, the mainstream white press did not even attempt to read Louis's mind. They predictably read his silence as an indication of unintelligent savagery and represented him as a beast from the jungle, viewing his skill in the ring as evidence of a primitive brutality. This reading began to change in the late 1930s, particularly after his victory over Max Schmeling in 1938, whom Hitler had put forth as the representative of the German race and Nazism. Both blacks and whites celebrated this victory, and while he continued to be racialized in periodicals such as *Life* and the *Chicago Tribune*, he also began to be represented in the white press as both a true American and a Horatio Alger success story—proof that any Negro could achieve success if he worked hard and maintained his integrity (Doyle 116–19, Sklaroff 971).

This shift in his reading by the dominant culture was complete after his victory over Max Baer in January 1942, when Louis donated his winnings from the fight to the Navy Relief Society. From 1942 to 1945, instead of making a concerted effort to combat discrimination in U.S. civil society, the federal government attempted to ease racial tensions for the purposes of wartime unity by putting forth Louis as a quintessential icon of Americanness, using him as a poster boy for official claims of American racial egalitarianism. As Lauren

Sklaroff has argued, "In and through the Louis persona, state administrators could advocate an ethos of racial liberalism, while temporarily skirting the issue of discrimination in American life" (959). However, considering the unwillingness of the Creel Committee to put forth any African American as a major symbol of the American spirit during World War I, even this limited move by the federal government reflects a shift in national policy wrought by left-wing and civil rights activism by 1942. This activism arguably helped generate the very tension that led federal officials to see racial unity as a pressing problem.

It was possible for Louis to be read as a patriotic icon, in part, because his managers had cultivated a clean-cut image of him since the earliest days of his professional career. Working to avoid the kind of notoriety that attended Jack Johnson, his manager John Roxborough, an affluent black entrepreneur, instructed him on "proper" manners and dress outside the ring. He even circulated to the press a set of "commandments" that Joe was to follow which ordered him to be sportsmanlike at all times, never gloating over a fallen opponent, and never having his picture taken with a white woman (Sklaroff 969–70). His sportsmanlike, family-oriented, striver persona resonated in black mass culture too, however. For example, in the *Chicago Defender* in June 1938, James Reid synthesized the five traits that defined Louis character as follows: MODESTY, CONFIDENCE, CLEAN LIVING, REVERENCE, AND BALANCED INTELLIGENCE (22). The film *Spirit of Youth* (1938), starring Louis and clearly based on his public persona, followed along these lines as well. Actively promoted by the *Defender*, the film depicted him as the hard-working product of a poor but morally upright family in Alabama.[7] Joe tells his sweetheart Mary before leaving for the big city, "I want to get ahead and be somebody and do things for mama and papa. And for you too, Mary." He keeps his word, sending all of his winnings back home to support his parents and staying true to his small-town sweetheart amid the temptations of the big city.

But for many African Americans, unlike white mainstream press, this clean-cut image of the prizefighter existed alongside and did not necessarily contradict another reading of Louis, that of the racial defender and symbol of bloody revenge. In the same *Defender* article above where Reid praised his upstanding character, he also graphically noted how Louis violently dispelled myths of black inferiority: "Everytime Louis' glove has exploded on the chin of his opponent, he has likewise smashed into smithereens the false prophets of racial inequality" (22). Blues singers in the 1930s and 1940s often emphasized the violence Louis enacted on white bodies in the ring, and even during wartime the black press typically pictured Louis standing tall over a white boxer he had flattened, doubled over, or even caused to kneel before him.[8] As Kegan Doyle has elegantly written, "Louis was, for millions of blacks, a violent savior, who didn't simply raise black pride but enacted fantasies of revenge, by clobbering white men—Braddock, Carnera, Conn, Nova, Schmeling and many more—to their knees" (114).

Communist publications also celebrated Joe Louis as a rebuke the myth of black inferiority, with the *Daily Worker's* sportswriter Lester Rodney praising him for his "courage, speed, and intelligence" ("Brilliant Saga" 8). But they also depicted his fight against Schmeling in 1938 as an epic political allegory of the Popular Front against fascism. Fully in keeping with other *Daily Worker* correspondents, Rodney built up the bout as the struggle between "the spirit of Nazism in person" and the quintessential proletarian, who "was born on an Alabama cotton field [and] worked the assembly line at the Ford River Rouge factory" ("Tonight's Fight" 8). *The Daily Worker* clearly interpreted Louis's triumph as a political one for the Popular Front, with all its reporters stressing the interracial, cross-class, and antifascist nature of the celebrating crowds.[9] While Richard Wright also celebrated it as a communist victory, commenting that "Schmeling must have thought that he was facing one of the Soviet Union's newest army tanks," he emphasized its special significance for African Americans ("Pagan Gods" 1).

Wright was fascinated by Joe Louis; yet, as a writer drawn to realism, his main interest was the lives of ordinary individuals, not superstars. Realists had never placed celebrities at the center of their narratives, a facet of the genre Lukács theorized in his famous work *The Historical Novel*. Here, Lukács lauded nineteenth-century realism for leaving major historical figures at the margins and showing instead how major historical crises and famous figures affected the everyday lives of "middling" individuals. In keeping with this tradition, Wright's main interest in "the Brown Bomber" is the impact of this media icon on ordinary people and their political consciousness. As revealed in his three articles on Louis in *The Daily Worker* and *The New Masses*, the main character in his reportage is not the famous prizefighter, but his audience. Published in 1935, June 1938, and July 1938, these articles were all composed when Wright was a stalwart member of the CPUSA, and only one reveals ambivalence about Louis's African American fans on the part of the author. Instead, they mostly assert that the fighter's black audience is able to read his "talk" with a proper political consciousness.

In the first of these essays, "Joe Louis Uncovers Dynamite," Wright describes the joy of black crowds celebrating Joe's defeat of Max Baer in 1935. He attributes their jubilation to the fact that they "unconsciously . . . imputed to the brawny image of Louis all the balked dreams of revenge, all the secretly visualized moments of retaliation" (34). Yet in Leninist fashion, Wright interprets their celebration as an ephemeral, spontaneous, folk reaction, one that needs to be translated into more organized and political conscious forms. "Say, Comrade," he writes, "here's that wild river that's got to be harnessed and directed. Here's that *something*, that pent-up folk consciousness" (35). In stark contrast, the Harlem crowd Wright describes in his 1938 article "And Oh—Where Were Hitler's Pagan Gods" is marked not by a vague, inarticulate longing but by political surety, and it is able to read Louis's defeat of Schmeling in a politically conscious and organized fashion. He wrote: "The quarter of a million Negroes who live within those narrow confines knew in terms of their daily American life what this fight meant and they gave vent to it in a demonstration, wholly political in character, such as Harlem has never seen" (8). He goes on to specify the nature of their politics by providing a sample of the placards they carried, placards that framed their collective demands quite specifically: "PASS THE ANTILYNCHING BILL, DOWN WITH HITLER AND MUSSOLINI, ALABAMA PRODUCED JOE LOUIS: FREE THE SCOTTSBORO BOYS" (8). This report does not suggest African Americans were trying privately or literally to emulate Louis as a media celebrity. Rather, it implies they had used him allegorically in order to form an internationally conscious, imagined community that subverted his intended reading by the dominant mass culture (and to a lesser extent by the African American press as well: while the *Defender* agreed that "a new race was born" as a result of the fight, it did not report any political placards in the celebrating crowds in Chicago, emphasizing instead that their fun was "clean" [Day 2]). In keeping with the Marxian realist notion of "typicality" (more on this in chapter 3), Wright suggested in his last article on Louis that a revolutionary reading of the fighter was still nascent in the Harlem crowds. In "High Tide in Harlem," he wrote that political placards "appeared on the surface of the sea of people" in the crowds, suggesting that they represented a minority position within the throng that could very well achieve dominance in the future.

Through his writings for the communist press, Wright was trying to shift the revolutionary reading of King Joe from nascent to hegemonic. In other words, Wright was not only reporting on Louis, but also trying to move his interracial audience to read his "talk" correctly. As an author famously hostile to mass culture, who often presented the culture industry as an obstacle to people attempting to map the world after their own best interests, he found it necessary to intervene in order to combat Louis's depoliticization. Yet in only one instance did Wright reject the allegorical possibilities of prizefighting. In "High Tide in Harlem" (1938), he wrote more disparagingly of the spectacle of boxing by labeling Louis and Schmeling as "puppets," and the fight as a "colorful puppet show" (18).

Here, he once again saw Joe's victory as supplying a positive, albeit temporary, liberation from self-hatred among the black crowds. But he also advised his celebrating readers to "Carry the dream on for yourself; lift it out of the trifling guise of a prizefight celebration and supply the social and economic details . . ." (20). His recurrent use of the term "puppet" in this piece was an attempt to make his readers conscious of Louis and Schmeling as mere emblems—and crude, childish ones at that. Unlike Wright's other pieces on the subject, "High Tide in Harlem" suggests to fans that they should not merely reread Louis, inserting him into a more revolutionary allegory, but should wean themselves from him altogether. His song "King Joe: Part I," which fully celebrated Louis, was recorded much later in 1941 and is more typical of his writings on "the Brown Bomber."

But for the project of clarifying his talk, the *Daily Worker* and the *New Masses* had a relatively small reach. With *Native Son* (1940), Wright had the opportunity, in a much more oblique way, to enter the terrain of mass culture in order to prompt audiences to read icons such as Louis politically, and more to the point, to illustrate the dangers of reading mass-culture signs incorrectly. Bigger Thomas is a cautionary tale in this regard, and is the atomized inverse of Harlem's nascently conscious, political crowds.

Native Son is mass-mediated realism in the truest sense. It combined the then critically acclaimed, popular mode of realism with other marketable, mass-culture forms such as Hollywood courtroom drama, "true-crime" fiction, fast-paced melodramatic action, and cinematic characterization (Pudaloff 13–14, Mullen 33). The novel also became mass culture, selling two hundred thousand copies in its first few months of publication to be not only the number one best-seller but, as Bill Mullen noted, "the first African-American blockbuster" (31). Such access of an African American writer to a mass market is anomalous in the pre-1945 United States. Wright's literary success did not immediately open doors for other African American authors—rather, it was white liberals writing on "the Negro question" such as Lillian Smith, Howard Odum, and Earl Conrad who were able to capitalize off his success (Mullen 38–39). The kind of sales achieved by *Native Son* were not followed by a black American author until the publication of Ann Petry's *The Street* in 1946, which sold over a million copies. Nonetheless, the book and magazine publishing market was sadly the *least* restrictive of the culture industries outside of recording. Langston Hughes observed in 1950 that the book publishing market had opened up considerably over the last twenty years and that black cultural producers had gained much greater access to mass magazines such as *The Saturday Evening Post*; but he also noted how Hollywood, professional theater, and radio were still quite restricted for Negro authors in comparison (306–9). In a telling sign of the times, Wright was able to achieve such sales while still affiliated with the CPUSA. It should also be noted that, despite the negative representation of white communists Mary Dalton and Jan Erlone in the novel, Wright did not break with the Party until 1944. *Native Son* received high praise from most communist and leftist critics, and Wright was elected vice president of the Popular Front League of American Writers soon after its publication (Mullen 33).

Kegan Doyle has boldly argued that *Native Son* is a kind of boxing narrative, and that its antihero Bigger Thomas can be read as a nightmare alternative of black masculinity to Joe Louis. Wright, he notes, stated of his novel that "Action follows action, as in a prize fight," and his character Bigger behaves as a boxer, always responding physically to an environment that traps and corners him by compressing time. The narrative begins, furthermore, with a bell (127–29). The purpose of using boxing as a frame for rendering urban black male experience, Doyle argues, is to show the pitfall of revering the black masculinity of icons such as Joe Louis and to illustrate "the danger of setting up famous athletes as role models for the race" (129). A number of critics have also noted that mass culture leads Bigger to his destruction. Lacking any mooring in folk culture, Bigger uncritically patterns his life and values from the movies, magazines, and newspapers. This causes him to evince a tough-guy masculinity that he has borrowed from detective and gangster pictures, to demonize communists and look favorably on fascists, and to find fulfillment only insofar as his life comes to mirror that of a melodramatic hero or villain (he spends his last two cents to read "his" story in the papers, for instance).[10]

If Wright was trying to show his readers that it was impossible for an ordinary black man to emulate media icons such as Joe Louis or Henry Armstrong—and, in particular, the implausibility of violently confronting whites—one could also add that Bigger's fights are tragic, unheroic parodies of these prizefighters' accomplishments. The novel begins not just with a bell, but with a fight—not with Schmeling or Baer, but with a rat that leaps out at him from a corner. His other acts of violence are the antithesis of glamour—he kills two women in their sleep, beats his friend Gus as a way to displace his own fear of confronting whites, and pistol-whips a white pursuer whose back is turned to him. Unlike the Brown Bomber, his confrontations with whites must always be kept hidden, and visibility always works against him. As an ordinary black man, his representation in the white media always shames him, and Wright uses the phrase "making sport of him" a number of times to signal the emasculating nature of his visibility (257, 259, 261). As an unfamous, working-class black man, he desires to rise above the obscure world of his mother and girlfriend Bessie, becoming extraordinary by emulating a kidnapping plot in a cheap story he reads (167). But when he tries to exercise power over whites in the only way he knows how, he becomes, unlike Louis in the 1940s, a monster who ends badly. When he is discovered hiding on a rooftop, it is the white mobs, not adoring black fans, who evince "shouts of wild joy" (247). Bigger serves as a case in point from Wright's boxing reportage, where he wrote that Louis "was respectfully enshrined in the public's imagination in a way [ordinary blacks] knew they would never be" ("High Tide" 18).

While an uncritical distance to mass culture is in large part Bigger's tragic flaw, and *Native Son* can be seen as illustrating the impossibility for a working-class black man to replicate the heroic, public displays of male power like black boxers, the novel is not, as Doyle suggests, a rejection of the spectacle of prizefighting, Joe Louis, nor of mass communication altogether. Wright is not necessarily rejecting mass communications per se in *Native Son*, but rather the dominant mass culture and the way in which his antihero reads it. Bigger watches white-directed Hollywood films, reads detective magazines and (presumably Hearst) newspapers, but nowhere in the novel does he pick up an African American newspaper such as the *Chicago Defender* or the *Pittsburgh Courier*—both of which had an elaborate national marketing network and extensive audience by 1940—not to mention the *Daily Worker*. Consequently, he does not revere black icons such as Louis or Armstrong at all; in fact, Wright gives us no indication that Bigger ever noticed them. When he begins his job at the Daltons, he enters the room set aside for him in their house, a room that had previously been inhabited by a servant named Green. Like Wright, Green had left the service industry to work for the government, a path Bigger wholeheartedly rejects, thinking instead that serving rich whites like those he saw in the movie is "a good job" (32, 36). But Green left behind his pictures on the wall—pictures of Jack Johnson, Joe Louis, Jack Dempsey, and Henry Armstrong. As Wright instructs in his reportage, he had used them, applied their lessons, then moved on. But Bigger looks at them once and never notices them again: they evoke nothing for him one way or the other. Instead of looking to black boxers, he spends the novel trying to build an identity through an uncritical immersion in cultural productions within which blackness is the antithesis of intelligence or character—a tragic mistake.

Chester Himes's novel *If He Hollers Let Him Go* (1945) offers another commentary on how ordinary people read Joe Louis, but it is much more direct in this regard, explicitly referencing the fighter at a number of critical junctures. In doing so, Himes much more directly than Wright, presents Louis as a contested symbol in American culture. Himes was by no means affiliated with the Popular Front by 1945, and his novel did not achieve the sales figures of *Native*

Son. I include *If He Hollers*, however, not only because of its significance as a commentary on Joe Louis and its contrast to Wright's famous novel, but also because it is another instance of mass-mediated realism, one combining proletarian realism with detective noir. The novel is proletarian realism insofar as it is a linear narrative of the life of an African American shipyard worker in Los Angeles, one that leads the reader through the minutiae of the protagonist's labor and his problems on the job; but like the detective noir, it is narrated from a first-person perspective, and the reader is supposed to identify with its cynical, hard-boiled protagonist, Bob Jones, who drinks heavily, is desired by women, and takes pride in his consumer goods (in this case, his 1942 Buick Roadmaster). As a leaderman, Jones holds a minor supervisory position in the yards, and much of the plot revolves around his anger at unjustly losing this position after he hastily responds to the racial taunts of a white co-worker.

Unlike Bigger, Bob Jones is a much more savvy reader of mass culture. Whereas Bigger absorbs the movie *Trader Horn* uncritically—including its degrading representations of Africans—Jones is able to interpret and even subvert the meaning of Hollywood films. After watching a war movie that culminates in the protagonist sinking a German aircraft carrier, Jones reflects: "Just a simple nigger bastard, that was me. Never would be a hero ... If I could just hang on to one [opportunity] and say, 'This is it!' And go out blowing up the white folks like that cat did the Nazis" (74). More in control of mass culture and more conscious of his real enemies, he is able to emulate Louis, albeit in ephemeral ways. After driving fear into a white co-worker by confronting him with a knife, the narrator states "I felt like running and jumping, shouting and laughing; I felt something I'd felt the time Joe Louis knocked out Max Schmeling—only better" (37). Himes's larger critique is not this attempt of his character to emulate the violent spectacle of Joe Louis, the prizefighter who destroys whites in the ring; rather his bigger target is the white reading of Louis that Jones is expected to live by. At the urging of his girlfriend Alice, who has fully absorbed the values of her affluent, accommodationist family, Jones abandons his confrontational ways toward the end of the novel, deciding instead to swallow all the racial injustices he suffers on the job in order to strive for upward mobility. This life choice does not work, however. Soon after he embarks on his new, accommodationist path, working diligently and patiently to show he is "worthy" of being reinstated to his earlier supervisory position, he is falsely accused of rape by a white female co-worker and lands in jail. At the very end of the novel, a company official comes to offer him a deal in jail, throwing the example of Joe Louis in his face: "You were the first Negro to be employed in a position of responsibility by our corporation and you were in a position to represent your race.... We made you a leader of your people, such as Joe Louis, the prize fighter, Marian Anderson, the singer, and others. We had confidence in you. To do a thing like this, at a time when Negroes are making such rapid progress ... is more than a disgrace to yourself, it is a betrayal of your people" (202). It is apparent here that *If He Hollers* comes at a different moment of racial formation from that of Wright's 1940 novel, a moment when the problem of African American writers was to contend with the myth of progress that Louis had been made to embody by the federal government. The novel can be seen as an attempt to resurrect the confrontational spirit embodied by the old Joe Louis—who shattered Schmeling in 1938—from beneath the co-opted "G.I. Joe" persona that only served to mask the suffering of ordinary individuals. In all, Himes's novel shows much more faith in the ability of working-class black men to read mass culture, yet, like Wright, does not turn his back on Louis nor the sport. Politicized white writers would more viscerally reject the ring as a space for the assertion of masculinity, as the lure of boxing for whites in a racially polarized society held quite different implications.

A Dirty Business
Boxers on the Big Screen

Outside of the sport itself, the Hollywood boxing film was undoubtedly one of the primary media through which U.S. audiences encountered boxing narratives during the Depression and war eras. Late-twentieth-century viewers are familiar with the *Rocky* series and more recently *Million Dollar Baby*, but films about boxers were released at a consistent enough rate in the 1930s and 1940s to make them a recognizable genre: at least twenty-eight boxing pictures were released between 1930 and 1948. Only two of these centered on African American boxers, however; the remainder dealt with white working-class prizefighters. In addition, some of these films were converted into radio dramas on *Lux Radio Theatre*, which was among the most highly rated programs on the air in the late 1930s and early 1940s (at its peak, around 30 percent of U.S. households surveyed tuned into *Lux*).[11] Whether or not these films and their radio adaptations were made by Popular Front writers, they bear the imprint of the era's oppositional politics. They also question the cult of celebrity at a different angle from that of Wright and Himes.

In most boxing films of the mid-twentieth century, a number of consistent genre features emerge. First, the narrative almost always centers upon a working-class man, usually white and often ethnically marked, for whom boxing is a means of social mobility. Second, as in the Primo Carnera narrative, boxing is generally a seedy and exploitative world of gangsters, greedy promoters, and fast living that threatens the integrity, innocence, and health of the boxer-protagonist (unless, as in the case of *They Made Me a Criminal* or *The Champ*, he begins the narrative already corrupted). In the 1937 film *Kid Galahad*, for example, the cynical Louise (Bette Davis) tells Galahad, an innocent farm boy, that the world of prizefighting "will knock those clear-cut illusions of yours higher than a kite." The recurrence of fixed fights and double-crosses in this exploitative world ensure that the fight game is rarely a meritocracy. Third, the boxer (or sometimes the promoter) has to overcome the selfishness and individualism that the prizefighting world demands, a selfishness that he often comes to embody. "Help yourself is my slogan," exclaims the protagonist Johnnie Bradfield (John Garfield) before his change of heart in *They Made Me a Criminal*. Fourth, if the protagonist achieves redemption, it is either because he has left the sport behind or he has learned to use it for something more than riches or self-aggrandizement. The exact nature of that "something more" varies greatly: from raising the pride of the neighborhood (*Body and Soul*, 1947), to securing the well-being of family members (*The Champ*, 1931; *City for Conquest*, 1940; *Ex-Champ*, 1939), to saving a children's home (*The Life of Jimmy Dolan*, 1933; *They Made Me a Criminal*, 1939), to winning the money to build an Italian American community center (*Winner Take All*, 1932), or even for the old agrarian dream of owning a farm (*Kid Galahad*). Finally, in terms of plot, scenes depicting actual boxing occupy very little of the narrative, though there is *always* a big fight scene at the end. It is the everyday struggle of the working-class protagonist outside the ring that counts.

Though the protagonist often wins the fight, the whole world of boxing is generally questioned through victory. Either he makes it clear that it was his last fight and says goodbye to the corrupt milieu, or his victory is compromised by some tragedy or pang of guilt immediately following, denying the viewer an unambiguous "happy ending." This general narrative formula was consistent throughout the 1930s and 1940s, from King Vidor's *The Champ* in 1931 to *Body and Soul* in 1947, and could still be found well into the 1950s with films like *The Harder They Fall* in 1956.[12] One caveat, here, however, is that the wartime years saw an almost complete halt in the production of boxing pictures, and the two that were produced—*Gentleman Jim* (1942) and *The Great John L* (1945)—were biographical narratives of famous white boxers. While these pictures preserved many of the traits outlined above, film moguls apparently decided in this interim period that there were bigger fights to be shown on the screen, and that the public needed heroes, not battered workers.

A common metaphorical thread runs through white-authored, boxing narratives of the era, both in and out of Hollywood film. Building on Gerald Early's analysis that boxing is a metaphor for the individual in mass society (54), I would argue that in most cultural productions of the 1930s and 1940s, boxing was also a metaphor for male competition within the world of capitalist production—a competition that exploited one's dreams of the good life and, if one played by its rules, left one disfigured, dead, or spiritually voided. In addition to its critique of capital, the fall of the boxer/worker within the narrative also reflects a realization of the inadequacies of production-based notions of masculinity (though the genre is not free of patriarchy, as I will conclude).[13] If the sport had value, it was in that the stakes of "the fight" could be transformed and redirected toward a more meaningful, redemptive struggle, allowing audiences to enjoy the spectacle of boxing while removing from it the stench of capitalistic masculinity.

But beyond these similarities the shared metaphorical significance of boxing in mid-century Hollywood films breaks down, and a significant part of the breakdown hinges on the ambiguity within the film genre over race. To reiterate, the boxing ring has been openly acknowledged as a symbolic arena of racial conflict since the beginning of the United States, yet the films come to no consensus about the nature of this conflict. In some films, such as *City for Conquest*, race is largely factored out of the metaphorical struggle, while others (*They Made Me a Criminal* and *The Champ*) replicate racial hierarchies by uncritically showing white boxers attaining redemption after beating someone much darker than themselves in the ring. In yet another group of films, such as *Golden Boy* and *Kid Galahad*, the audience gets to see ethnically marked protagonists achieve both financial success in their ascension and spiritual redemption in rejecting that success at the end. As this valorization of the ethnic protagonist does not come at the expense of nonwhite rivals in these two films, it cannot really be considered a bid for whiteness. As I will discuss later, the film *Body and Soul*—written by Abraham Polonsky, directed by Robert Rossen, and produced by John Garfield, all Popular Front figures—offers the most progressive filmic example of the genre, as it explicitly questions whiteness by calling attention to the exclusions that arise from the attempts of a probationarily white fighter to assimilate.

These boxing films, like much of Hollywood cinema in the "classic period," combine the aesthetic modes of realism and melodrama. Conventions from turn-of-the-century realist theater such as individualized characters, linear, continuous narration and editing, and nongestural acting were firmly established in Hollywood cinema by the early 1930s, and prizefighting pictures were no exception. These films were realist in that they focused on ordinary individuals, depicted their vernacular expressions and mannerisms, and often aspired to social commentary. They borrowed from naturalism, furthermore, in that they attempted to show these individuals locked within a harsh and confining contemporary social environment (though unlike turn-of-the-century naturalism, their authors often gave their characters a key to the exit). But insofar as they rejected neither sentimentality nor action, and their plots and characters generally revolved around simple, moral binaries, they possessed elements of melodrama as well. Melodrama is best understood not as a genre such as the Western, the gangster thriller, or the "woman's film," but is rather an aesthetic structure that suffuses all of these genres and more. As Linda Williams defines it, melodrama is a mode that aims to illuminate virtue through a dialectic of pathos and action; in general, it is any drama that works to produce the recognition of virtue, one that forces the dominant order to "yield signs of moral legibility" (42, 53). In addition, it bears out the audience's sense of right and wrong, and is marked by a feeling that the "right" thing will eventually happen (Cawelti 45, Booth 10). It can sometimes share with realism a grounding in everyday life, but uses whatever verisimilitude it carries to impart melodramatic effects (or affects). In contrast to the complex characters drawn by realism, melodrama achieves its effects by presenting a black-and-white world where virtue is ultimately located in some individuals and not others (often cued by dress, manners, or other external features) and wherein formulaic character types are subordinated to plot (Booth 9–12, Hallam 20). Finally, in terms of style, John Cawelti calls it a "drama of intensified effects," wherein the creator uses a whole arsenal of techniques for "simplification and intensification," repeatedly centering the attention of the audience on moments of crisis (at the level of plot, these crises can be produced by violent action, the breakup of relationships, etc.). In this sense, melodrama also splits paths with realism (264).

In the Hollywood boxing film, villainous gangsters and promoters—the capitalists in the allegorical scheme of boxing—are clearly marked by their fancy dress and shifty demeanor, and they contend with virtuous family members and sweethearts for the soul of the boxer-protagonist; meanwhile, dramatic musical scores, rapid plot twists, and violent public spectacles work to produce the intensified effects. Melodrama has historically been at its most powerful when, as in the case of *Uncle Tom's Cabin*, it attaches new social meaning to traditional structures of feeling (Cawelti 46). If the Popular Front was attempting to create a "moral economy" to temper the ravages of capitalism, as Michael Denning and Lizbeth Cohen have argued, then melodrama could be seen as a powerful weapon in the hands of the Popular Front, helping usher in its new, moral economy and allowing oppositional writers to tailor their figures to fit older senses of right and wrong. In terms of the boxing film, the audience's moral code is confirmed when the boxer–social climber either self-destructs in the end or redeems himself by leaving the capitalistic fight racket altogether. The wicked gangsters and fight promoters who try to corrupt him are never vanquished (this is a function of the genre's realism), but they rarely claim his soul either. As illustrated by an examination of Clifford Odets's play *Golden Boy* and Nelson Algren's novel *Never Come Morning*, the melodramatic elements of the Popular Front boxing narrative could be found off the big screen as well, though outside of Hollywood the element of realism was more pronounced and, in general, the politics packed more of a punch.

Versus Whiteness and Capital
The Golden Boy and Never Come Morning

Clifford Odets's play *Golden Boy* shared with Hollywood the conventions of the boxing film, and not coincidentally. Odets decided to write a money-making play for the ailing Group Theatre, the New York–based company of which he was an integral part, and to this end he wrote a play modeled upon the popular film genre. Odets worked for the first time as a screenwriter in Hollywood shortly before he wrote the play, and this experience palpably influenced his dramatic writing. His play *Golden Boy*, for instance, is composed of brief scenes and constantly shifting settings, creating a quick tempo that departed from his earlier works (Miller 70). His plan worked: *Golden Boy* was a rousing popular success as it toured the country in the 1938–39 season, its 250 performances enabling the Group to guarantee annual salaries to its players for the first time in its history (Weales 124–25, Shuman 31). The "golden boy" of Odets's play is Joe Bonaparte, a poor, young, second-generation Italian American. The central dilemma of the play is whether Joe will become a musician or a boxer, which is not merely a career choice, but a choice between two very different value systems. Joe's heavily accented Italian father, Mr. Bonaparte, insists Joe use the scholarship his musical talent has won him and become a professional violin player; to further this desire, Mr. Bonaparte reveals early in the play that he has spent his entire savings to buy Joe a finely crafted violin for his birthday. He knows this career will not bring his son riches, but this does not matter, for as he says, "No millionaire is necessary. Joe love music. Music is the great cheer-up in the language of all countries" (249). Joe, however, is more inclined toward boxing. Despite his love for his father, he strongly desires social mobility. His other talent for prizefighting can afford him wealth, and a host of morally dubious characters from the fight racket pull him toward this decision.

Joe chooses the fast living offered by boxing—with the gangster Fuselli as his manager—and Odets links this choice to modernity and consumerism through Joe's purchase of an expensive sports car soon after. In addition to the working-class status of the protagonist and the element of exploitation by nefarious promoters, the play also joins the chorus of boxing films by making clear that Joe's transformation into a prizefighter is an individualistic one. Lorna tells Joe, for example, that he is becoming "like Robinson Crusoe" with a selfish motto of "me, myself, and I" (265). Later in the play, when his transformation is complete, Joe boasts: "The whole essence of prizefighting is immodesty! 'I'm better than you are—I'll prove it by breaking your face in!'... I don't believe that bull the meek'll inherit the earth!" (305). The metaphorical connection between boxing and individualism was made more clear by the set designs of Mordecai Gorelik. Gorelik turned everyday human interactions into prizefights by having characters come at each other from opposite sides of the stage at the beginning of many scenes, establishing the basis of each relationship as atomized conflict, not mutual understanding (Herr 85).

Not only is Joe aware of his increasing mechanization, yelling at Fuselli, "What do you think I am, a machine?," he is also addled by an obsession with speed—a standard motif of the modern (Odets 309, Herr 84–89). He satisfies his desire for speed with an advertised commodity—a Deusenberg sports car—that he learned to desire from mass culture. "Gary Cooper's got the kind I want," he says to Lorna. "I saw it in the paper" (266). Speeding in his car gives him a false belief in his own transcendent invincibility, for as he states, "When you sit in a car and speed you're looking down at the world. Speed, speed, everything is speed—nobody gets me!" (265). But during the climactic fight at the end of the play, he kills his African American rival "The Baltimore Chocolate Drop" in the ring. Riddled with guilt, he drives off with his sweetheart Lorna at high speed in his expensive brand-name sports car, ending both of their lives as well. The ending of the play, in which he literally self-destructs in his car, thus makes *Golden Boy*, on one level, a morality play about the false temptations offered by modern consumer goods.

The play also shares with the film genre the idea that the "fight" at the core of the metaphor of boxing is only redeemable if channeled into a different, more worthwhile arena. The dichotomies around which the play is based are stated most clearly by a *Daily Worker* reviewer in 1937: "The story is simple. Culture vs. commerce. Music vs. boxing. In this corner Bach, Beethoven and Brahms. In that corner 'Kid Galahad'" (Dexter 7). Music, culture, and some notion of innocence are undoubtedly wedded together on one side of the moral dichotomy, and the fact that the plot pivots around a dualistic moral universe places it within the tradition of melodrama and popular allegory.[14] If these forces alone were pitted against "commerce," Odets would have merely replicated the Victorian moral landscape, which often put forward "high" culture as an alternative to the ravages of materialism. There is much more in "that corner" than Bach and Brahms, however: a purified form of ethnic tradition sits there as well. As outlined above, Mr. Bonaparte, established very clearly as a part of an older, European culture through his accent and his alienation from the "American" world of boxing, is the one who is most wedded to the violin. Also, Mr. Carp, Mr. Bonaparte's close friend and generational peer, largely shares the father's value system. Carp proudly calls the violin "a cultural thing," and shows a predilection for a world beyond materialism by relentlessly quoting Schopenhauer. The fact that Carp is a European Jew effectively locates the resistance to market morality as something not only springing from Italian "roots," but from a number of different (albeit European) ethnic traditions.

However, while it is true that in Odets's world a proximity to the wellsprings of ethnic tradition grants one an advantage in combating the money culture of boxing, it is also important to note that Odets's alternative is not a wholesale retreat to the ethnic margins. The dualism that forms the much larger frame of the play is that of market and nonmarket values; the culture of Carp and Mr. Bonaparte is one wellspring of nonmarket values, but it is not the only one. Joe's brother Frank, a labor organizer for the CIO, represents another. Odets makes it very obvious that Frank's value set, based upon an ethic of political solidarity, is also a clear alternative to the moneymaking, fast-living world of boxing. Mr. Bonaparte had once said that if boxers fought "for [a] cause" the sport would not be meaningless (300). Frank's living example as a political activist personifies a palpable cause outside the ring, a cause that Frank explicitly compares to "music." He tells Eddie, for instance, that his socially oriented path involves being "at harmony with millions of others" (318). Music, then, is not merely a metaphor for cultural refinement and the soul, but for the class-conscious political collectivity embodied by the CIO's industrial unionism with which Frank is clearly identified. The end of the play finds Mr. Bonaparte physically moving closer to Frank as the latter yells to Moody, Roxy, and Fuselli, "You're all killers!" (320), suggesting a parallelism between the values of Mr. Bonaparte and Frank.

If the fusion of ethnic tradition and C.I.O.-style solidarity offers an alternative to the gladiatorial capitalism of boxing, Odets points to an aesthetic way out by suggesting that the commonly reproduced dichotomy of (ethnic) culture vs. commerce is part of the problem. A moment of the play overlooked by critics suggests the possibility of fusing art and boxing to form a new synthesis: a dynamic, realist, political art. In a private conversation with Lorna Moon, Joe explains both his love for music and his sense of its limitations in a passage that bears quoting at length:

> With music I'm never alone when I'm alone—Playing music . . . that's like saying, 'I am a man. I belong here . . . When I play music, nothing is closed to me . . . There's no war in music. It's not like the streets . . . But when you leave your room . . . down in the street . . . it's war! Music can't help me there. Understand? . . . People have hurt my feelings for years . . . You don't get even with people by playing the fiddle. If music shot bullets I'd like it better—artists and people like that are freaks today. The world moves fast and they sit around like forgotten dopes. (264)[15]

Music provides for Joe both a sense of place and a form of masculinity not based upon conflict and fear; its limitation, however, is that is has no practical application "down in the street," and those who make it do not actively engage with the world. What this passage adds to the play, then, is the idea that neither of the culturally constructed options of music (transcendent/private/traditional/ethnically grounded) nor boxing (fast/modern/conflict-based/capitalistic/Americanized) is sufficient in themselves to lead to Joe's redemption. Frank, who in the final scene has bandages around his head because of the labor struggles he has engaged in, suggests the possibility of "fighting" and yet still retaining one's soul, but he lacks an aesthetic counterpart. What he needs, the playwright suggests, is something that draws from and yet transcends ethnic affiliation, something much more like Odets devoted his life to creating: a political art that had the rhythm and beauty of music, but, like a redeemed form of boxing and realism, actively fought social battles outside the artist's garret, battles that affected life "down in the street."

Rather than create a new aesthetic synthesis, Joe aligns himself with American modernity, a tragic plot turn that allows Odets to show the inseparability of class and racial politics. Unlike many mid-century boxing films, the climax of *Golden Boy* (the play and the film) suggests that American modernity is constituted by the binary divisions between races. To embrace its logic, one must embrace these exclusions, along with their fatal consequences. Joe's boxing career in *Golden Boy* is framed by his conflict with a single opponent—the reigning champion named the Baltimore Chocolate Drop. Joe fights Chocolate unsuccessfully at the beginning of the story, yet establishes his career by losing to him only slightly. He then permanently knocks out Chocolate when he meets him again in the climactic fight toward the end. There is no direct representation of Chocolate in the narrative; he haunts the action as an absent presence that Joe must eventually face. After Joe kills him in the ring, Fuselli the gangster along with Moody and Gottlieb (the "legitimate" capitalists) still celebrate the victory, assuring Joe that his success is definitively established now that his last obstacle has been destroyed. For Mr. Bonaparte, on the other hand, the death confirms his belief in the senselessness of prizefighting; in the play, he eschews the victory celebration and merely sobs, "Poor color' boy..." (317).

Odets could have had Joe kill anyone; for instance, his victim could have been an unambiguously white American—and we would have been left with a general moral lesson that boxing/capitalism results in violence against others. But the fact that he killed an African American man carries the social metaphor of boxing further than in many other narratives of the sport, then and now, and yokes it more closely to Popular Front politics. As someone in an intermediate position in the ethno-racial hierarchy, Joe has chosen to move up, and the death of Chocolate implies that there are always consequences of this mobility for those who started even further down the ladder. Joe has achieved financial success in defeating Chocolate, but he has ignored the best aspects of his own ethnic tradition as well as the values of political solidarity in order to achieve whiteness. Odets further suggests that the public and psychological wage offered by whiteness is only short-term, moreover, by not allowing Joe to retain his victory.

A brief examination of the film adaptation of *Golden Boy* (1939) helps illustrate the limitations imposed on the Popular Front boxing narrative by the film industry. It should be remembered that the Hays Production Code, the politically conservative, puritanical guideline for censorship adopted by the motion picture industry to stave off regulation from the federal government, was put into effect in 1934 and was still in operation up until the Second World War. All in all, the film adaptation retains enough of the basic elements of the play to remain a generally progressive narrative: the sport is managed by gangsters and capitalists of low moral caliber, and Joe's Italian immigrant father pits culture against commerce (at one point he angrily shouts at Joe, "Money, money! We've gotta hearts! We gotta souls! Do what is in your heart... In there is a music!"). Further, Bonaparte's obsession with speed is also present, maintaining the link between boxing, consumption, and modernity, and his success is consolidated through the killing of an African American boxer (whose name in the film is Sailor Anderson).

Nonetheless, two main changes to the script undercut its power as a subversive narrative in the screen adaptation. First, the character of Frank is exorcised completely. His absence makes it much more difficult for audiences to see Popular Front solidarity as an antidote to the destructive modernity embodied by boxing. We are left only with a religiously inflected and ethnically based rejection of the capitalist ethos: upon first learning that his son is a boxer, a low-angle, medium-distance shot shows Mr. Bonaparte's worried face next to a large Virgin Mary shrine immediately behind him, establishing a Catholic source for his rejection of market values. Second, the resolution is changed to give the story a happy ending, which necessitated the addition of a few scenes following the death of Anderson. In one of these added scenes, Joe is absolved by Anderson's father in a curious manner. Crying, Joe enters his opponent's dressing room, where he encounters Anderson's father and two brothers. Joe asks the family what he can possibility do, offering to give his life; the brothers reject him entirely, which, to the film's credit, was one of the first times an African American did not give whites what they wanted on screen (Rogin 217). But the father, a sad, gentle, slow-moving man, comforts Joe by saying the following as an orchestral, Negro spiritual plays in the background: "I ain't no stranger to trouble. We's all just lil' people with a burden every one of us. You've got one too, you've got to carry it. Don't try to run away from it." With the inclusion of this scene, the screen writers absolve Joe of his crime by way of a traditional figure from American popular culture—the elderly Uncle Tom who comforts whites through his example of simple, passive, conciliatory suffering. Cleansed of his sins, Joe is able to retreat from the world of moneymaking and return to the loving arms of his father; the final lines of the film are uttered by Joe, who cries, "Papa, I've come home." Thus in the film adaptation, the alternative to crass materialism and racial violence is not a Popular Front cultural revolution, but a return to family and ethnic roots.

    Nelson Algren's *Never Come Morning* presents us with another literary critique of whiteness and capitalism that uses the motifs of the boxing film, albeit with a much more detailed exploration of the role of white ethnic communities in the larger process of U.S. racial formation. However, its nightmarish plot, psychological detail, and the paucity of moral choices it offers its characters lend it a tone more akin to *Native Son* (unsurprisingly, Wright praised the novel) than *Golden Boy*. *Never Come Morning* self-consciously shows the formation of whiteness among Polish Americans and fully explores the psychic devastation of the "public and psychological" wage. Set in the South Side of Chicago, the narrative revolves around a working-class second-generation Polish American youth named Bruno "Lefty" Bicek, who leads a life of crime as he dreams of making his fortune as a champion boxer. Bruno is clearly an antihero, as Algren throws up barriers throughout the novel that would prevent the reader from seeing the course of his development as anything to be morally replicated. A critical moment of the plot comes relatively early, as Bruno succumbs to peer pressure and sets up his girlfriend Steffi to be raped by a group of young men from the neighborhood. He kills a Greek man who tries to participate in her rape, which eventually leads to Bruno's downfall. At the end of the novel, he is arrested for this murder immediately after a victory in the boxing ring that had begun to fulfill his dream of becoming "the Great White Hope" (more on this later). Though Bruno receives the most attention from the author, the stories of other characters in the neighborhood are developed in detail as well. The reader also encounters Casimir Benkowski, or Casey, a slightly older boxer whose career in the ring is destroyed in the opening scene; Steffi Rostenkowski, who becomes a prostitute after Bruno's horrible betrayal; and finally Bonifacy the Barber, a first-generation Pole who controls the criminal activities in the world of the novel, and hence holds immense power over the lives of the other characters.

Like *Golden Boy*, Algren's novel explores the role of mass culture in the process of class, race, and gender formation while stylistically borrowing from that mass culture. Indeed, as a book that sold over a million copies and was marketed in pulp format, *Never Come Morning* (1942) is itself an artifact of the culture industries. In fact, Algren downplayed its significance by suggesting that it was just something people read on the train (Donohue 145). If the novel did serve as casual reading for many people, however, this made it even better positioned to complicate the ways in which audiences read other pop cultural genres, in this case the boxing film. Like Odets's play *Golden Boy*, the narrative structure takes much from the formula of the Hollywood boxing film—a formula that audiences at the time would have recognized—working to comment on the relationship between U.S. class structures and the color line in ways that leftists working in Hollywood could not. The novel also borrows much from the language and motifs of hard-boiled detective noir, drawing upon the genre's frequent representation of police detectives as "clueless," so to speak (though a detailed investigation of this process is beyond the scope of this chapter).[16] But Algren's novel goes beyond Odets's play by serving as a reception study of how audiences read pop cultural genres of the Hollywood boxing films and hard-boiled fiction. *Never Come Morning*, in short, is a realist attempt to illuminate the effects of mass culture while working from a position deep inside of it.[17]

One of the main struggles for transcendence that structures the book is Bruno's attempt to escape poverty through his mass culture–inspired dreams of becoming a heavyweight champion. From the very beginning of the narrative, Bruno is shown to stake his future on prizefighting, and in the fight scene at the very end, he comes very close to success. Like *Golden Boy*, *Never Come Morning* bears much in common with contemporaneous boxing films: it is centered on a white (albeit probationarily white) boxer who tries to use the sport to escape the slums; it makes clear that the events in the ring owe their existence to criminal elements (in this case, the barber, who arranges them); and, to be sure, it ends with a big, public fight. Like his filmic counterpart, Bruno is also highly individualistic. In an argument with one of his cohorts named Bibleback, he states, "I believe I got to take care of number one... That's *my* faith," (46) repeating an expression he had also used earlier in the novel (18). The story departs from Hollywood, however, in the degree to which it makes white racial consciousness a primary theme. Indeed, Algren suggests that whiteness is central to Bruno's route away from pure individualism and into boxing redemption.

The novel also parts company with Hollywood by self-referentially highlighting the cultural power of boxing narratives themselves. While examples abound in the text, one scene in particular nicely underscores how Bruno's desire to become a boxer has been fueled by the realm of mass culture; it also shows his ethno-racial investment in entering that realm. While daydreaming in jail on suspicion of murdering the Greek man, Bruno imagines a "technicolor movie" (89) version of his future that reveals his motives for entering the ring. In the night before the climactic fight in his imaginary "stirring drama of one Powerhouse Bicek," Bruno dreams the following scene, in which he is visited by his hero Tiger Pultoric: "... the night before the fight the good old Pultoric had come to Bicek and shaken his hand, saying that it didn't matter to him who held [the title], so long as it wasn't a Jew or a jig. 'Me'n you 'n Ketchel 'r the best of 'em all,' good old Pultoric had reminded Bicek—and he hadn't had to add that all three were Poles. 'You got the case of a Jew callin' himself th' white hope now,' had been Pultoric's parting words—'seems to me we still need a white hope t' get that title back'" (90). In this passage, as in the whole sequence, monetary gain is neither mentioned nor even alluded to. Much more important is Bruno's desire to publicly place himself—as a Pole—in the position of redeemer of the white race by defeating a Jew. Simultaneously, the fantasy is also about salvaging his own position within the Polish American community, a position that had been severely compromised by his hoodlum behavior. Whereas earlier in the novel, Bruno had brazenly scoffed at the very idea of going to mass, even joking with his peers about turning the neighborhood church St. Bonifacius into a brothel (46), his boxing fantasy ends with him being carried victoriously on the shoulders of Father Francis, the priest of that very same church (94). He imaginarily becomes both a white American and a true Pole, not by mimicking the cultural practices of his parents' generation, but through his achievement within a mass-culture spectacle. The inclusion of Father Francis in the fantasy sequence—and the thrill his victory gives the pillar of the ethnic community—shows that his imaginary achievement has in part been the clearing of the way for Poles to enter the sphere of mass culture as equals. In his fantasy, Bruno had also momentarily become James Cagney ("Bicek, collapsed on his stool, rubbed his jaw reflectively, the way he'd seen Jimmy Cagney do it") and the boyfriend of the starlet Sylvia Sydney (91, 94).

This fantasy is only an imaginary resolution to his poverty, probationary whiteness, and spiritual malaise, and the absence of its realization is a source of constant anxiety. With the one stamp he is allowed in jail, Bruno decides not to mail his Polish mother, but "Kayo: World's Foremost Boxing Magazine" with a series of questions. Most significantly, he asks if his boxing heroes really are Polish, a question he already knows the answer to: "He knew the nationalities of Choynski and Ketchel as well as he knew his own; he merely sought printed assurance that they too were Poles and they too were unbeatable" (135). Viewed within the larger context of the novel, the desire to confirm Ketchel and Choynski's skill reveals less of an ethnic chauvinism than an assurance of Polish assimilability from the dominant culture. By getting the popular magazine to respond to him, Bruno wants U.S. mass culture to acknowledge that Poles are capable of defeating nonwhites in its own public spectacles, and hence actively participate in constructing their white privilege.

The climactic fight at the end of the novel is Bruno's primary attempt to realize his fantasy, and he comes very close to attaining it. After the police temporarily release him from jail on account of insufficient evidence, he competes in the biggest bout of his career—against an African American fighter, "Honeyboy" Tucker. What this fight sequence reveals is not only Bruno's ethnically marked struggle for whiteness, but also Algren's attempt to go beyond most boxing films by calling attention to the entire spectacle of pugilism as a blatant site of racial formation. First, the audience is implicated. The whole crowd is rooting for Bruno solely because of his skin color, causing the phrase "white man's evening" to recur in his thoughts throughout the fight. Algren depicts the spectators as a pan-class assembly of whites, united in the darkness of the arena: "The lights went out all over the house, and down to the cockpit of the ring came the constant and indistinct rumor of voices . . . From the troubled salesman behind the sucker bet and the frayed collar, the housewife getting in secret debt to the dead-pan sheet writer beside her, the jobless youth rejected by the navy . . . the ex-middle-weight from Fargo with a restaurant and a daughter who wouldn't wait on trade . . . the poolroom idler . . ."(263). Despite their differences, the audience achieves a form of cross-class racial unity through their panoptical gaze at Tucker. Algren describes them as "Seven thousand whites in the dark, watching a single brown one in the pitiless glare of the lights," and their unity is expressed in their relentless catcalls of Tucker during the fight (267). The sympathies of the audience ultimately enable Bruno to win with a dubious act of sportsmanship; he knocks his rival out by giving him a surprise upper cut to the jaw while Tucker's back is turned (280). The crowd does not protest, of course, but only "booed happily" after Bruno is announced the winner (280).

Algren also highlights Bruno's racial consciousness in this final match. When the fight is going poorly for him and he is in danger of losing, he regains his strength not by thinking of his family as in *The Champ*, nor of other youth who look up to him as in *They Made Me a Criminal*, but rather an old, anti-Semitic proverb of Bonifacy the barber: "'*Grzmoty zabili diabla*,' he thought slowly, '*diabla zabilia rzyda*' [when the thunder kills a devil, the devil kills a Jew]. He had it now. Now, in this moment, he knew what the barber meant" (277). The one bit of traditional wisdom he heeds in the novel—essentially a call for the oppressed to advance themselves by destroying those lower in racial hierarchy—enables him to win the fight. But only momentarily. Backstage, as Bruno imagines himself the next Ketchel, he is arrested by the police for killing the Greek man during the rape of Steffi. Like the fight against Tucker, this earlier crime had also been an act of racial exclusion. He had attempted to keep the rape "whites only" by telling the Greek, "Beat it, Sheeny, this is a white man's party," and accidentally killed him after the latter refused to leave ("Sheeny" was a slur usually applied to Jews: Bruno's figuration of all "questionable" Europeans as Jews reveals the profound extent to which anti-Semitism mediates his relation to his own identity) (73). The fact that Bruno follows a racial path to redemption allows him to achieve success in the ring, but it also leads to his ultimate downfall. The privilege it gave to him is the privilege to rape, to kill, and to bludgeon, which, as in Roediger's assessment of the public and psychological wage of whiteness, allows short-term power but denies long-term strength.

If the boxing films allowed its protagonists redemption by allowing them to successfully flout the capitalistic "rules" of the sport—if only for a moment—*Never Come Morning* bleakly shows that even the path one takes to redemption can be flawed. The few times, incidentally, when the reader encounters imagery of sunrise—in Algren's world, a metaphor for transcendence—it is during Bruno's successful moments in the ring versus a racially marked opponent, indicating that even his fleeting emergence is predicated on the misery of others.[18] This absence of a valid escape route in the space of the novel caused one critic in the *Partisan Review* to denounce its author as "maudlin" (Buckman 427). This critique is not entirely without justification. Another path to transcendence his author does not lead him to is that of class-conscious political affiliation. Unlike so many left novels of the period, political redemption does not even appear as an option for Bruno—nor does Algren figure into his world a class-conscious mentor figure who Bruno has the luxury of rejecting. Symbols of unions and the New Deal are not used by the characters to make meaning of their lives, but rather appear to them as random objects among the debris of a ruined city.[19]

If all lights at the end of the tunnel are bankrupt, and all symbols of conscious political affiliation are mere debris among the ruins of a forsaken city, what is to be done? In the final analysis, what separates Algren from his naturalist forebears—who tended to use the methods of natural science to place immense distance between themselves and their subjects—is that he shows the very capacity of his Chicago Poles to dream, as misguided as those dreams are, to be a sign of their positive humanity. He writes, "Everyone was alone, trapped in the same vast beer flat forever; making the same endless plans for escape, repeating the same light songs to pass the time . . . Everyone was in on a bum rap; not one would be paroled. 'God has forgotten us all,' Steffi R told herself aloud, 'He has even forgotten our names'" (215). Passages such as this, numerous in the novel, show that if Bruno tries to escape the nightmare of his urban life using mass-culture boxing narratives, or if Steffi uses Ferris wheels or "light songs" for the same end (57), these are not the acts of bugs under a microscope but of human beings with whom the reader is to empathize. Richard Wright thus read Algren's Chicago Poles not as monsters but as embodying "a frustrated longing for human dignity" (Intro ix). And as "frustrated" people with the capacity to dream of the good life, they are capable of redemption—they merely lack a connection to some proper narrative of deliverance. Wright recognized this nascent potential, adding "the Bruno Biceks of America represent those depths of life . . . that periodically push their way into the arena of history in times of crisis, war, civil war, and revolution" (ix).

Body and Soul
The Popular Front Boxing Narrative After the War

Never Come Morning, Golden Boy, and *Native Son* illustrate how Popular Front boxing narratives could offer much grander indictments of American social structures when written for popular theater and the popular fiction market rather than for the film industry. In 1947, however, a box-office hit entitled *Body and Soul*, produced by John Garfield's own independent production company, finally put onto the big screen a subversive linkage between race and class that approached the politics of the Popular Front boxing narrative on stage and in print. John Garfield, born Julius Garfinkle to working-class Jewish parents on New York's Lower East Side, moved to the left in his adolescent years and stayed there for the rest of his life; his politics were well-known to the public, earning him the moniker "the people's actor." He worked with Clifford Odets as part of the Group Theater in the 1930s, and had been drawn to *Golden Boy* from the very beginning. But his relationship to that story had always been marked by disappointment. Though Garfield helped Odets hone the script, director Harold Clurman turned him down for the leading role of Joe Bonaparte, to the amazement of many in the Group, and cast him in the minor role of Joe's brother-in-law Siggie instead (Swindell 94–99). When *Golden Boy* was adapted to film, the rejection was even more cutting: he was turned down by Columbia Pictures for the lead role in favor of William Holden because he looked too ethnic (Rogin 217). The script of *Body and Soul*—written by the leftist Abraham Polonsky—has a narrative structure similar to *Golden Boy*; thus it is generally held that Garfield produced *Body and Soul* to give himself the opportunity to play the long denied role of Joe Bonaparte.

However, the politics of *Body and Soul* were able to go further than those of the 1939 film adaptation of Odets's play, and this has much to do with the postwar moment in which Garfield's production appeared. Despite the fact that the witch hunts of the House Committee on Un-American Activities (HUAC) were beginning to intensify seriously in the immediate postwar years, writers and directors were nonetheless able to raise serious questions about American society in film, in part because of a public appetite for social and psychological depth following the trauma of World War II. Furthermore, issues of race could be explored on the screen in ways impermissible before and during the war, and not only because the Hays Office had been dismantled. The global fight against fascism, as well as agitation by people of color and their allies through the Popular Front, civil rights organizations, and the black press, had raised a greater public awareness and interest in issues of racial and ethnic tolerance.[20] The immediate postwar years gave rise to such films as *Gentleman's Agreement* (1947) and *Crossfire* (1947), which directly confronted the issue of anti-Semitism, as well as *Home of the Brave* (1949), which explored anti-black racism.

The politics of *Body and Soul* reflects this new cinematic and social milieu. The role of the black prizefighter Ben Chaplin, played by Canada Lee, is much more developed than the black boxer character in *Golden Boy*, who did not have a speaking role in either the stage or the screen variants of the script. And in his performance as the boxer Charlie Davis, Garfield was the first Jew to be permitted to play a Jewish character in a leading film role in more than a decade (Rogin

213). Despite the prevalence of Jews on the cultural front of the left in the 1930s and 1940s, *Body and Soul* is also the first major boxing narrative written by a Popular Front author, on- or offscreen, to tell the story of a Jewish prizefighter. Loosely based on the life of the light and junior welterweight champion Barney Ross, the plot follows a familiar Popular Front pattern. Charlie Davis is a working-class youth who becomes a prizefighter to escape the poverty of his parents; but he forsakes his family, his sweetheart, his friends, and even his community as he sells his soul to the double-crossing capitalist promoter named Roberts. Like Bruno Bicek, Joe Bonaparte, and so many others, he signals his shallow naivety early in the narrative by stating, "I just want to be a success. Every man for himself." Like Bonifacy the Barber, the pecuniary ethos of the manager Roberts is also clearly marked. "Everything is addition or subtraction," he bluntly tells Charlie.

But the importance of race to the story is signaled by the opening shot, which shows a guilt-ridden Charlie waking up from a nightmare and crying out "Ben!," the name of the African American boxer he has maimed (as a circular narrative, the film begins toward the chronological end of the events depicted, then tells almost the entire story as a flashback). Ben had been managed by Roberts, who double-crossed him by knowingly sending him into the ring with Charlie without telling the latter that Ben had a blot clot necessitating easy handling in the ring. Such caution would have made for bad entertainment and lower profits, so Charlie almost kills Ben, inadvertently ending his career. Charlie begins to seek redemption by befriending Ben and hiring him as his trainer, and in an African American–Jewish alliance, they work to defeat Roberts's new fighter, an insensitive white Texan whose willing service to Roberts and pronounced southern drawl ultimately make him an incarnation of the racist-capitalist nexus. Knowing that his neighborhood is betting on him as a show of community pride, and that Ben, his friend Shortie, and now himself have all been double-crossed by Roberts, Charlie decides to take the advice of his mother in the climactic scene in the end of the film. She had told him that if he wanted to fight, then he should "fight for something, not for money." He does just that: he knocks out Roberts's Texan and then retires from the sport, telling off his ruthless ex-manager as he makes his way out of the arena.

Jezebels and Uncle Toms
The Limits of White Popular Front Boxing Narratives

While the maiming of the black opponent in *Body and Soul* allows the film to make a critique of American racial institutions, it also illustrates a limitation in the racial politics of white-authored Popular Front boxing narratives, one that had been there all along. On the positive side, for the first time in a boxing narrative of this era, *Body and Soul* depicts a black boxer directly accusing his white boss. Before entering the ring with Charlie, Ben confronts Roberts, saying, "People don't count with you, do they Mr. Roberts?" In his last lines of the film, he screams, "I don't scare anymore!" and "I'm the champ!" while throwing wild punches at his employer. Completely overwrought, he then collapses and dies from his old injuries. Ben's tragic death is the most graphic indicator of Roberts's greed in the film; it also creates the guilty conscience that ultimately drives Charlie to seek redemption. Like *Never Come Morning* and *Golden Boy*, *Body and Soul* is a cautionary tale about the self-destructive nature of whiteness for probationary whites—a moral injunction not to step on those lower than themselves in the racial hierarchy in their quest for assimilation. And like *Golden Boy*, *Body and Soul* questions assimilation too—Charlie's Jewish mother (played by Anne Revere) and his kindly neighbor Schiman the Grocer never leave the neighborhood; untainted by the Americanized milieu of prizefighting, they retain their generosity and moral clarity.

But in the filmic boxing narratives—namely *Body and Soul* and *Golden Boy*—the African American boxer must die so that the protagonist can achieve his redemption, and this raises a number of troubling issues. In melodrama, victimization typically confers moral legitimacy on a character, and these films partake of this mode, establishing Ben and Sailor Anderson's family as "good" people by depicting them as innocent, kind, and long-suffering. As Michael Rogin has observed of *Body and Soul*, this device has a long and not so progressive history in American popular culture vis-à-vis African Americans: Ben, as a kind, suffering "black Christ," dies to save a white man's soul, and this places him in the tradition of the Uncle Tom (218–19). This can also be said of Joe Bonaparte and Sailor Anderson (as well as his father) in the film *Golden Boy*. While Algren's novel and Odets's play avoid this device (their boxers destroy themselves by destroying their black opponents), all of these texts are curiously disconnected from the history of boxing at that time. At a moment when black boxers like Joe Louis, Henry Armstrong, and John Henry Lewis were annihilating whites in the ring, white-authored Popular Front boxing narratives were showing the opposite: whites like Joe, Bruno, and Charlie maimed their dark-skinned opponents, though they lost their bodies or their souls as a result. Unlike his fictionalized counterpart Charlie Davis, Barney Ross never had the opportunity to maim Henry Armstrong and then make him his manager: he lost his title to Henry Armstrong in 1938, then joined the Marines and developed a morphine addiction while recovering from wounds he suffered during the Battle of Guadalcanal.

The spiritual decline or physical destruction of fictional white boxers after their victories over African Americans marks an urge on the part of their authors to frustrate the drive to restore the Great White Hope, to show that nothing is really achieved by taking the title from Louis, Armstrong, or Lewis. But there are troubling consequences here as well. This plot device allowed the fantasies of triumph among white audiences to momentarily come true, which would have left a dangerous semiotic excess. It also made pity and the utter disempowerment of African Americans the precondition for multiracial class solidarity.

Another limitation of this genre is the roles it proscribed for women. Generally speaking, women play one of two "love interest" roles in the boxing narratives of the era: either the innocent sweetheart or the temptress/jezebel. The boxer-protagonist is often romantically involved with the innocent sweetheart before his fame in the ring: his gradual neglect of her serves as an index of his corruption, his reunion with her a marker of his redemption. The jezebel, on the other hand, is a seamless part of the urban world of gangsters, liquor, and money that ensnares the fighter. His courtship with her comes at the sweetheart's expense, and also marks his moral decline. True to the melodramatic mode, neither of these character types is morally ambiguous in the end: if it was ever in doubt, the resolution clearly reveals their innate goodness or innate depravity. Lorna Moon, played by Barbara Stanwyck in the film *Golden Boy*, and Louise "Fluff" Phillips, played by Bette Davis in *Kid Galahad*, were some of the few exceptions to this ubiquitous pattern. They combined both roles into one character who eventually gained redemption along with their man by the end of the narrative. The published script of the play *Golden Boy* also self-referentially questions the exclusion of women from the genre. The male characters repeatedly tell Lorna to "scram"; as a woman, they let her know that she is not welcome in the scene, though she defiantly remains.

But like the female characters in the many other films that fit the formula, the stories of Lorna and Louise are always peripheral to the plot; they exist either to enable or ensnare the boxer at the center of the narrative, and they are never developed as characters. Even the jezebels in films such as *Spirit of Youth* and *Body and Soul* lack the subversive danger often attributed to the femme fatale of the detective noir: while beautiful and glamorous, they are deprived of snappy dialogue by their creators and so weakened by their own vices that it is difficult to construe the threat they pose to the protagonist as real power. Weak or undeveloped women are unfortunately not confined to boxing narratives produced by the film industry: Algren portrays Steffi's desire to reunite with Bruno in a sentimental vein, despite the extreme sexual violence he inflicted upon her. Despite its critical exploration of masculinity as a performance of class and racial identity, the representation of women within the Popular Front boxing narrative reveals its inability extend that exploration to an interrogation of male dominance.

Despite their limitations, Popular Front boxing narratives constituted a laudable attempt to show how the performance of the dominant masculinity could prevent class and racial solidarity. They did not generally represent the abuses of the shop floor, the field, and the home in a way that directly mirrored those faced by their audiences; rather, they intervened by putting forth a "moral economy" that bundled racialization, acquisitive masculinity, consumer culture, and working-class suffering into a tight association. Equally significant, they delivered their punches by creating a new, commercially viable genre—derived in large part from realism—that reached a far larger audience than most of the proletarian literature of strikes and lockouts. While such boxing narratives, in placing division at the center of the American experience, proved ill-suited to the celebratory nationalism of the war years, the culture and aesthetics created in part by the Popular Front allowed other racially and class-conscious films like *Body and Soul* to appear in the 1950s, including *The Joe Louis Story* (1953) and *The Harder They Fall* (1956). The mass-mediated realist genre of the boxing narrative has never repeated its mid-century popularity, but it has seen a cyclical resurgence and decline in later postwar years, notably with the famous *Rocky* series in the late 1970s and beyond, and with the minor resurgence of award-winning boxing films in recent years such as *Million Dollar Baby* and *Cinderella Man*. In many ways, these postwar films bear witness to the decline of Popular Front incarnation of the narrative, as they tend to dilute the critique of U.S. racial formation so prominent in the oppositional 1930s and 1940s variants.[21] Yet only by separating it beyond recognition from the formulas of the 1930s and 1940s, as in the cases of *Cinderella Man* and *Rocky 4*, have postwar filmmakers been able to use the boxing picture as an exaltation of the American spirit.

While the left used the boxing narrative alongside the gangster film and the detective story to interpellate men, other Popular Front writers would attempt to appeal more directly to women using other film genres and popular theatrical modes. But as the next chapter will show, they were not able to gain a critical mass nor become the founding figures within any popular genre created with a female audience in mind. As we will see, however, a number of women writers on the left did make their voices heard in popular culture, breaking the silence of their male comrades.

CHAPTER TWO

Radio Soaps, Broadway Lights

Lillian Hellman, Shirley Graham, and the
Interpellation of Female Audiences

In the 1930s, Eleanor Roosevelt was arguably the most visible woman in the United States. Indeed, by 1940, Gallup polls indicated she was more popular with the public than the president himself. As is well known, she worked for the full participation and recognition of women in public life, and did not merely push this goal for her white sisters. Less well remembered is how she ascribed to literature and the performance stage a significant role in this struggle. In February 1939 she resigned from the Daughters of the American Revolution because they barred the famous African American opera singer Marian Anderson from their Constitution Hall in Washington, D.C., a result of their practice of forbidding black performers on stage at D.A.R. events. In her letter of resignation from the organization, she wrote that "in refusing Constitution Hall to a great artist . . . You have set an example which seems to me unfortunate . . . You had an opportunity to lead in an enlightened way, and it seems to me that your organization has failed." Following her resignation, Roosevelt kept the issue alive by arranging public and official events for Anderson to perform, including her famous concert at the Lincoln Memorial (Black 41–42, 201).

Roosevelt's status as a civil rights ally is often evoked, but her politics here were also informed by the larger structure of feeling created by the Popular Front, in which issues of race were fundamental to the new moral economy many liberals and leftists advocated. In this context, she saw left-wing theater as germane to the issues of exclusion for which she fought. Indeed, she turned to literature for advice on political and ethical dilemmas, according to Eleanor Roosevelt scholar Allida Black (139). Roosevelt was a fan and reader of Lillian Hellman, one of the most famous playwrights of mid-century—and a known communist. Hellman too wrote in the realist mode, and Roosevelt, an avid reader and theatergoer, attended her productions, continuing her patronage long after she was in office and well past Hellman's peak years of fame. Yet her investment in Hellman was not unequivocally positive; there was something unsettling about Hellman's portrayal of women to this famous proto-feminist First Lady. She finally voiced this on 4 November 1949, in her syndicated newspaper column "My Day," when she reviewed Hellman's play *Montserrat*: "Lillian Hellman's women never seem real unless the qualities they portray are rather disagreeable ones. Therefore, the women in this play make very little impression. But the men, as they go out to die, are a wonderful group of characters."

Eleanor Roosevelt's resignation from the D.A.R. illustrates her awareness of the stage as an important site of inclusion for artists of color, and as a vital battleground in the push for showcasing the talents of women, exhibiting their capacity as "great artists." Nonetheless, the dismay she voiced over Hellman's representations also registers a concern that these great artists were not always using their talents in ways that would enable a greater presence in public life for all women. Eleanor Roosevelt's relationship to Lillian Hellman and Marian Anderson illuminates the relationship between the Popular Front, the position of women, and the representational politics of the stage at mid-century. Most basically, her comments on Hellman reveal that mass-mediated Popular Front realism reached the highest offices in the land. Concomitantly, these remarks suggest that even in the hands of its most famous female author, this realism was sometimes seen as insufficient to the task of productively representing women's struggles. Finally, the controversy over Anderson's performance serves as a reminder that while the civil rights work of the Depression era, conducted both inside and outside Popular Front organizations, had helped make race a national political issue, mainstream performance continued to work against the visibility of women of color who in any way defied convention. The road for African American women playwrights with Popular Front sympathies would be a hard one indeed.

Hellman and other female writers in the Popular Front worked at a very difficult moment for authors wishing to openly politicize women's concerns. George Jean Nathan made a prescient point when he observed the kinds of themes deemed as "serious" dramatic fare by his fellow critics in 1941. Nathan was co-editor of *The American Mercury*, author of more than thirty books on the theater, and one of the leading drama critics of his time. Referring to Rose Franken's *Claudia*, he noted that ". . . Miss Franken's play about a young girl's difficult adaptation to the marriage state is, however ably it be done, automatically considered a less worthy achievement than an inferior play which concerns itself with some such subject as the racial problem, the struggle between capital and labor, or the threat of Communism in Scappoose, Oregon" (*Entertainment* 38). One would not expect an observation about the nontopicality of gender in the 1930s to come from a source such as Nathan. He was largely apathetic to the political agendas of the Popular Front, viewing art and politics as antithetical, and was openly dismissive of the abilities of women playwrights. Yet his observation here does speak to a larger truth that did not help the mid-century left in its interpellation of female audiences: that is, the "cultural front" had put issues of class and race on the national political agenda, but often at the expense of gender inequalities.[1]

Yet women were far from neglected by a dynamic, new commercial medium in the 1930s—national network radio—which was speaking to them directly on a dazzlingly large scale. By the onset of the Depression, the commercial radio industry had realized that women formed the vast majority of the medium's rapidly consolidating, national audience, and in 1930 it began airing a new serial genre to capture this female market that remains with us to this day: the soap opera. As the Popular Front had not broken into this medium during the Depression with the same degree of success as in Hollywood or the publishing industry, and, as I will discuss below, its audience was disproportionately working class as well as female, this posed a real problem to its struggle for hegemony.

A fifteen-minute episode of the serial *Brenda Curtis*, aired in September 1939, helps underscore the nature of early soap opera's appeal. The title character is a housewife who is married to attorney Jim Curtis, with whom she has one daughter. Jim is poised to lose the biggest case he has ever handled, which will lead the family to financial ruin, yet he has refused to let Brenda consider an offer to resume her career on the stage. The episode begins with a blissful domestic scene: Brenda tucks her daughter to bed as her African American servant Cleo looks on and laughs, commenting on the child's preciousness in a thick southern dialect. But the tranquility is broken when Jim enters and Cleo exits. Brenda plays her traditional role as housewife by trying eagerly to console him after his long day at work. Since his case is going badly, he is frustrated and irritable, frequently losing control of his emotions. Brenda, meanwhile, is calm, strong, and stable, asking him, "Can't you discuss things reasonably and sensibly?" bringing him under control with her sweet, placating voice. She assures Jim that she has no desire to return to the stage, exclaiming, "How much longer must I try to convince you, darling, that I have no desire to go back to the theater?" At the same time, she tells him she has enlisted the help of an old friend, an engineer named Stacy Gordon, who might be able to save her husband's case and thus the finances of their family. Jim assumes Stacy has designs on Brenda, and the end of the episode finds him deeply distraught with his wife for turning to another man for help.²

This episode of *Brenda Curtis* illustrates the white, middle-class nature of the soap opera, as well as the mixed messages conveyed by the genre about these women's domestic roles. Its opening sequence not only establishes Brenda's happiness with her role as a mother, but also delineates the whiteness and bourgeois standing of the family through the linguistic contrast between Brenda and her servant Cleo. And while Brenda expresses no desire to work outside the home, it is her efforts (her negotiations with Stacy) that have given hope for the economic security of the family. Thus, like many domestic novels of the nineteenth century, the episode does not explicitly challenge the dominant idea that a woman's place is in the home, but it does situate women's agency and strength of character at center. Many other examples could be found of soap operas that questioned women's innate domesticity more directly, with professional or entrepreneurial working women as central characters: Ma in *Ma Perkins*, Myrtle in *Myrt and Marge*, Helen from *The Romance of Helen Trent*. Yet this example from *Brenda Curtis* illustrates the ambiguously empowering nature of the soap opera's appeal to its white audiences even in the more conservative incarnations of the genre.

If radio was a dynamic new medium marketed mostly to women, and the soap opera the genre that attempted to speak to them most directly, culture warriors in the Popular Front who desired to reach female audiences had to vie not only with radio in general but the soap opera in particular. Before the publication of Ann Petry's best-selling novel *The Street* in 1946, the most formidable source of this left-wing challenge did not originate from within commercial radio, nor within fiction or poetry. Rather, it came from popular theater. Judith Smith has argued that an invigorated Popular Front theater competed with and challenged radio formula drama in the 1930s and 1940s, and with some success, instilling in audiences greater expectations of the narratives they consumed (*Visions* 10, 14). Though I view the challenge as an implicit and largely unspoken one, Smith's provocative notion of a competition between Popular Front theater and radio serial drama will serve as a starting point for my own examination of the address to women delivered by Popular Front realism. Far from a washed-up medium by the 1930s, the theater reached millions during the Depression and war, with the Federal Theater Project (FTP) responsible for a great deal of this audience. But theater was much more important, I would argue, as a "feeder" for film and radio. For it was through adaptations from the stage to the screen and the studio, and through the migration of writers, directors, designers, and actors from Broadway to Hollywood, and from agitprop troupes to studios like

NBC's Radio City, that enabled the innovations born of the theater to reach tens of millions. Not coincidentally, the world of the stage was a fantasy space for many a soap opera listener, as revealed by the recurrence of theater careers in the lives of so many soap opera heroines and their men—from Brenda Curtis, to Kitty Kelly in *Pretty Kitty Kelly*, to Myrt and Marge in the serial bearing their names, to Larry Noble in *Mary Noble, Backstage Wife* and others. The stage was hardly without constraints for women playwrights and directors, yet its status as an imagined, symbolic space of female independence suggests a healthy interest in its milieu among women—one that made theatrical performance ripe, in the proper hands, for the interpellation of female audiences.

The work of two playwrights in particular—Lillian Hellman and Shirley Graham—serve as telling examples of both the power of Popular Front theater in the 1930s and its capacity to vie with soaps in order to speak to the concerns of women. Both Hellman and Graham consciously wrote with the mass market in mind, and were particularly adept at doing so. Like the authors of soaps, they put women, their agency, and their suffering front and center; but implicitly, their work in theater, film, and radio took on the limited politics of the daytime serials. They challenged the soap opera on its own ground by setting much of their work in domestic and traditionally female spaces; unlike *Brenda Curtis*, they collapsed public and private by highlighting these spaces as not just reflecting, but as *determining* relationships of social class, and sometimes of race as well. By showing the operation of class hierarchies in the home and in the schoolhouse, they attempted to make such realms legible as political within the public discourse of 1930s and 1940s. Both writers also used a much more unadulterated form of realism than that of the serials, using complex characters and a "historical sense" to represent the formation of class and racial structures in the domestic arena. As such, their work coincided with a shift in CPUSA organizing strategy during the Popular Front period in regard to women, when the Party increasingly tried to address the anxieties of housewives, not just women in the workforce (this effort resulted in a rise of female participation in the organization from 13 percent in 1933 to 40 percent during the Popular Front era [Foley 218–19]). However, Hellman's work in the 1930s ultimately gained visibility, in part, by de-emphasizing conflicts between men and women, providing the origins of Eleanor Roosevelt's unease and placing limits on its ability to form the nucleus of an alternative to the soaps.

Lillian Hellman was the author of the hit Broadway plays *The Children's Hour* (1934), *The Little Foxes* (1939), and *Watch on the Rhine* (1941), two of which were adapted to radio plays, and all to successful Hollywood films. Before reaching the airwaves and the big screen, *The Children's Hour* and *The Little Foxes* had stunning Broadway runs of 691 and 410 performances, respectively, among the longest of the decade for "serious" drama (Rollyson 140; Atkinson 299).[3] Indeed, the work of Lillian Hellman circulated more widely in mass culture than any other woman writer on the left in the 1930s and 1940s.[4] Shirley Graham also had a very impressive career in the theater. She was named the head of the Negro Unit of the Chicago Federal Theater in 1936, where she served as a creative writer, director, and administrator. Her musical entitled *The Swing Mikado*—an update of Gilbert and Sullivan's *The Mikado* using jazz and African American actors—was a bigger box-office success than any other production of the highly popular Chicago FTP, playing to an estimated 154,000 people there before going on tour. FTP director Hallie Flanigan regarded *The Swing Mikado* as one of the "outstanding successes of the entire Federal theater" (Hatch 325–26; Horne 75, 80–81). A versatile artist, Graham also wrote a number of three-act dramas, radio plays, and the pilot for a radio serial in the realist mode, including *I Gotta Home, Elijah's Ravens, The Revolutionists* (cowritten with Selden Rodman), *Coal Dust, Track Thirteen,* and *The Bannekers.*

The work of Hellman and Graham reminds us that women authors have used realism to challenge patriarchy and critically render the lives of women, yet at the same time, the history of their production and reception illustrates the ways in which this aesthetic mode has been associated with masculinity by so many writers, readers, and cultural critics. To have their work produced before large audiences, women writers on the left who fused realism and mass-culture modes had to walk a particularly fine line between being read as too realist (with the consequence of commercial oblivion) and not being read as realist enough (resulting in a lack of support from critics, and, likely, commercial oblivion). Interestingly, the most famous play to critically comment on female labor in the 1930s was Harold Rome's *Pins and Needles* (1937), a musical comedy about young women garment workers that ran for 1,108 performances on Broadway (at the time a record for musicals surpassed only by *Hellzapoppin'*) (Goldstein 205). The musical is as valid a vehicle for delivering politics as realism or any other medium; I raise *Pins and Needles*, however, to contrast the relative difficulty of plays written by women and centering on women's lives to find an audience and critical acclaim in the category of "serious" drama, the exceptional case of Lillian Hellman notwithstanding. As an African American woman, Shirley Graham enjoyed great success in musical theater, but faced tremendous obstacles in being received as a realist, as both her race and her gender were liabilities, in the eyes of the dominant culture, to the narrative authority necessary for the genre. The consequent fate of her work in comparison to Hellman is telling. Her radio serial was not picked up, and her realist work, unlike the musical *The Swing*

Mikado, played in very small venues. Like non–Popular Front, African American playwrights who wrote in a realist mode, most notably May Miller and Georgia Douglas Johnson, Graham's more realist work toured mainly in a circuit of colleges and universities, far removed from the lights of Broadway or the often packed houses of the FTP. Her work was perhaps too realist for daytime radio, and not realist enough for contemporary theater producers.

Before examining the work of these artists, however, an exploration of the discursive field in which they wrote is in order. Their significance is more apparent when measured against the backdrop of mass-culture genres aimed at female audiences in the 1930s and 1940s—the most significant area of which was radio by large measure—and when situating their work within the larger context of Popular Front theater. A consideration of the oft-neglected realm of radio is also essential to the overall argument of this book, as it was the most widely disseminated mode of mass culture in the 1930s and 1940s.

Daytime Serials, the Popular Front, and the Female Audience for Radio

The left helped define the major popular genres catering to men in the 1930s and 1940s, and in no small measure. The detective story, the gangster film, and, as I have added, the boxing genre were shaped in fundamental ways by writers with left-wing and even Marxist politics.[5] There was a discernable impact of communist and fellow-traveling organizations on popular narrative genres marketed to women in the 1930s and 1940s too, though examples are fewer and farther between. In Hollywood, a number of leftists worked within the genre known at the time as "the woman's film," a broadly defined and largely male-authored category that encompassed love stories, maternal melodramas, the Gothic "gaslight" subgenre, and more. Fellow travelers and future blacklistees Francis Faragoh, Donald Ogden Stewart, and Sidney Buchman were just a few of the screenwriters for films tailored to women viewers (Buhle 25–34). King Vidor directed the famous *Stella Dallas* (1937), and before he wrote the infamous *Mission to Moscow* (1943), Howard Koch created the screenplay for *Letter from an Unknown Woman* (1948). In addition, Popular Fronters Edward Chodorov and Marguerite Roberts were part of the team that wrote the gaslight picture *Undercurrent* (1946). In the world of cheap fiction, communist Hope Hale wrote for *Modern Romances*, a story magazine popular with working-class women, and chastised fellow leftists in 1939 for publishing in small literary magazines that no one actually read (Stewart 43).

But the serial genres broadcast on the new media of network radio proved much more difficult for writers and artists on the left to breach, a matter of no small importance to spreading left and Popular Front messages to women audiences. Women formed the majority of radio listeners in the 1930s, the majority by 55 to 65 percent at night and the vast majority in the daytime. Many broadcasters assumed (correctly) that the audience for any program would be mostly female even before reliable audience research methods were available in the late 1930s. Given the social constraints of the time, radio was in many ways an ideal medium for reaching women: it provided a substitute for areas of social life closed to them, such as bars, clubs, union halls, sports, as well as many civic and political organizations. And for the wives of the middle and working classes it could serve as an accompaniment to the household labors of the daytime or nighttime hours. Indeed, radio arguably brought the public into the private sphere much more than any other medium, and this aspect of the new technology did not go unnoticed by advertisers. After advertising agencies discovered during World War I that women were the "household purchasing agents" for 85 percent of new consumer goods, the main economic function for radio gradually became the sale of advertised commodities to women (Hilmes 32–33, 146, 314).

In addition, radio was widely available across class lines, with radio sets a common sight even in the homes and apartments of working-class families and individuals by the 1930s. Less than one in ten households were without a radio in urban areas in the 1930s, and 83 percent of all U.S. residents, rural and urban, owned a radio by 1940 (Savage 6). Indeed, Americans had much more frequent, daily contact with radio in the 1930s than with any other form of mass culture, with the possible exception of newspapers. There are some indications that the poor and working classes tuned in more than those higher on the socioeconomic ladder. This was the discovery, at least, of a 1937 study of radio audiences in Minnesota, which found that the families and individuals it surveyed with an unskilled and or semi-skilled worker as the head of the household listened in for roughly 6.3 hours daily, while those with "professional" or "managerial" household heads listened in around 4.6 to 5.4 hours every day (Baker 102, 115, 143). Thus radio would serve as a new means for corporate America to reach not only women, but also the working class.

According to most scholars of the medium, nonprofit, collectivist visions of the medium imagined by educational, religious, and labor organizations had become marginalized on the airwaves by the late 1920s and early 1930s, clearing the way for the medium to fully consolidate along centralized, corporate, top-down, and commercialized lines (Razlogova 139).[6] A marker of this consolidation was the nationally broadcast serial program. The airwaves of the 1920s were typically filled with music—often light classical or "respectable" jazz tailored to white audiences—or with dramas written especially for the medium. The serial drama and the serial comedy—daily shows with consistent characters, repeated settings, and continuous and often unresolved plotlines—came to dominate the daily schedule in the 1930s, with Gosden and Correll's *Amos 'n' Andy* (1928) and Gertrude Berg's *The Goldbergs* (1929) as the pioneer programs of the genre. Serial program genres, along with the commercialized, institutional structure of radio, would be transferred almost intact to television (Smulyan 114–15, Hilmes xiv–xv, 57). To win the allegiances of women across class lines, the Popular Front would have to contend not only with this new and increasingly commercial medium but also with a new form of programming from which they were largely shut out. Their narratives would need to supply something that the radio narrative genres of the serial drama and serial comedy could not. Most immediately, they would need to seriously compete with the new serial form that spoke most directly to women, one that was generally not taken seriously by social commentators: the soap opera.

The "soap," as it frequently called, was a product of the 1930s. The first serial narrative expressly intended for women to be aired during the daytime hours was Irna Phillips's *Painted Dreams*, which debuted in October 1930 on WGN in Chicago. Many others soon followed in the daytime hours, nationally broadcast every weekday in fifteen-minute time slots. Some of the more highly rated included *Ma Perkins, The Rise of the Goldbergs* (a daily serial in 1931)*, The Romance of Helen Trent, The Guiding Light, Young Widder Brown, Myrt and Marge*, and *Mary Noble, Backstage Wife*. Soap operas were among the earliest texts examined by feminist cultural studies, yet there has been relatively little return to the subject, and virtually no discussion of this genre born of the 1930s in studies of left-wing cultural production of the era. As feminist critics have argued of the televised incarnation of the genre since the 1970s, soap opera content clearly endorses neither patriarchy nor feminism; it registers a discontent with the behavior of men and the roles circumscribing women, yet it fails to provide a radical alternative to existing structures of gender.[7] But whether they examine the soaps of early radio or later television, most feminist critics agree that the politics of soap content are not to be rejected, as their oftentimes female writers put the problems and perspectives of women at center. For this reason, they have also taken issue with the historical dismissal of the genre. Soaps have been consistently dismissed as lacking in political content by mainstream cultural commentators since the 1930s, even though television soaps have regularly explored social issues. While early radio soaps dealt with the power dynamics between men and women within the family and with women's sexuality, television serials since the 1970s have tackled issues such as alcoholism, divorce, abortion, and domestic violence. Meanwhile, the tension between career and marriage in women's lives has been a persistent theme almost from the beginning of the form (Modleski 86, 93; Hilmes 170). Though the resolution of the plotlines generally reinforced the idea that a woman's place was in the home, women were portrayed as having more agency in soaps than in "male" genres or any other serial form on the radio. In contrast to action serials or boxing narratives, it was the man who was the love interest to the woman in the soaps, and women were the strong characters, whether for good or for evil. As Michelle Hilmes has argued, men in radio soaps were generally problematic in some form or another, often "unstable, disabled, or criminal." The radio serial heroine either was unattached to a man—widowed, single, or separated—or she was in a marriage in which the husband was less a pillar of strength than a source of problems and anxiety (171).

Soaps also reflected the changes in the gendered division of labor wrought by the 1930s and 1940s. The husband's role as breadwinner had been challenged by the Depression, as male unemployment skyrocketed while the percentage of women in the workforce actually increased. At a time when more married women had to seek work as a result of the economic crisis, jobs identified as "women's work"—primary education, domestic service, many clerical positions—had not been hit nearly as hard by the Depression as sectors which had traditionally barred women, such as heavy industry (McElvaine 182–83). As is more well known, the war further altered the division of labor. Feminist historians have rightly questioned the degree to which WWII really was the era of female empowerment as suggested by the Rosie the Riveter image; yet it is clear that women of all races and classes experienced expanded employment opportunities during the conflict.[8] These historical shifts were arguably reflected in the "Woman Alone" motif that was ubiquitous in radio soaps of the 1930s and 1940s: serials of the era commonly centered around a woman without a mate who persevered through her own efforts in a hostile world. Derived from nineteenth-century domestic novels and serving as the basis for soaps such as *The Romance of Helen Trent*, *Ma Perkins*, *Girl Alone*, and *Young Widder Brown*, this theme dropped from the later television soaps almost entirely (Cantor and Pingree 21).[9]

But even if they were so inclined, the particular commercial structure of radio made it very difficult for the writers of soap operas to explicitly propose solutions to women's problems that would permanently alter existing hierarchies of gender, even as those hierarchies were being upset by the Depression and the war. Nor did the content of soap operas tie those problems to an explicit critique of racial or class formations. While class difference was not an unusual theme—often in the form of a working-class girl who married into wealth and struggled for acceptance and adjustment in her new world—the plotlines suggested that the domestic virtues of the humble heroines would carry them through (Hilmes 172–73). While such shows exhibited a laudable working-class "accent" by locating a kind of virtue in humble origins, they generally were not critiques of the entire upper class.[10] As with most other serial genres, the world of the soap opera was also solidly white, with the notable exception of *The Rise of the Goldbergs*, centered around a probationarily white Jewish family in the Bronx. Though the settings and characters of 1930s radio soap operas were arguably more plebeian than the generally upscale, professional world of their televised successors, the spaces in which their heroines moved were inevitably middle class or better. For instance, *The Guiding Light*, which first aired in January 1937, was originally set in a slum, and the action of *Ma Perkins* takes place within range of a lumberyard. While viewers reared on TV soaps in the 1970s and 1980s might find such settings unfamiliar fare, the class status of the protagonists would not be. Ma Perkins owned the lumberyard in the town of Rushville Center, and *The Guiding Light*'s Dr. John Ruthledge was a minister and household head of an essentially bourgeois family attempting to spiritually uplift the poor who surrounded them. (*The Guiding Light*, incidentally, is still running: it is the longest continuous narrative in broadcasting.)[11] Published in 1944, Rudolph Arnheim's cross-sectional content analysis of soap operas found a striking absence of working-class characters in the forty-three soap operas he examined; most characters were either professionals or relatively comfortable housewives (Cantor and Pingree 88). This was despite the fact that Kenneth Baker's 1937 survey of radio listeners found that wives of the working class—those of its upper echelons in particular—reported listening to daytime radio more than any other socio-economic group by an overwhelming margin (wives at the very bottom rung of the ladder seldom listened during the daytime, while those in middle and upper-middle also listened a great deal) (142).

However, there were opportunities to represent a broader swath of the American people on the airwaves, and in a Popular Front vein. The Federal Communications Act of 1934 codified more than averted the commercial structure of radio, yet it contained provisions intended to placate influential critics who charged that the medium had become overcommercialized; thus the bill reserved some space for noncommercial, educational, public-interest programming on the dial (Savage 12). The radio industry came to embrace this regulation in its attempt to fashion a public image of respectability and legitimacy, and some of the highbrow, educational, and civic-oriented programming they produced—such as *The Columbia Workshop, Freedom's People, Cavalcade of America, The Pursuit of Happiness*, and Orson Welles's *Mercury Theater of the Air*—provided an opportunity for left-wing and civil rights–oriented writers to put their messages across, albeit in ways amenable to corporate sponsors. In such programs, the scripts and voices of Popular Front writers and figures Arthur Miller, Paul Robeson, Maxwell Anderson, Dorothy Parker, and Irwin Shaw could be heard on the air in the late 1930s and 1940s, while the work of Clifford Odets, Pietro di Donato, Dalton Trumbo, and Guy Endore were all adapted as radio dramas.[12] And as Judith Smith and Barbara Savage have shown, broadcast spaces for the Popular Front and the early civil rights movement expanded further during the war. While national network radio was almost completely inaccessible to African Americans in the 1930s and 1940s, arenas of educational broadcasting and special programming opened up during WWII that offered a few windows for African American self-representation. These shows included *Freedom's People*, broadcast from 1941–42 on NBC and produced in part by black intellectuals such as Alain Locke, Sterling Brown, and Paul Robeson, and also *New World A-Coming*, locally aired in 1944 in New York City (Savage 11–16, Smith, "Cultural Front" 210).

Yet the formula serial programs that constituted the vast bulk of network radio's daily schedule proved much more difficult for Popular Front writers to break into, and daytime serials even more so. The radio industry had created markedly different day and night schedules in the 1930s as a response to critiques of overcommercialization. In dividing their offerings into a daytime schedule of programs for women and children, and a nighttime schedule consisting of public interest programs, male-oriented serials, and comic variety shows for a general audience, the networks attempted to direct its critics to its relatively respectable nighttime fare while simultaneously using its daytime schedule for unrestrained commercial programming (Hilmes 160). Daytime fare was thus more clearly marked as mass culture, all the more so because its overwhelmingly female listeners cemented long-standing associations among social critics between femininity and mass culture. As such, this daytime zone was relatively unimpeded by the demands to serve the public interest—demands that had created spaces for Popular Front voices on the air. As a marketers' playground, writers also had to navigate through additional layers of business interests when writing for serials. By the mid-1930s most soap operas (and many nighttime serials as well) were written by advertising agencies and sold to sponsors, with the network merely supplying the technology to transmit the program. The ad agency functioned as a production company that pitched the show to a sponsor, then sold the whole package to the network (MacDonald 33–36; Cantor 35–36; Hilmes 118–19). The husband and wife team Frank Hummert and Anne Achenhurst, two of the primary founders of the soap opera form, began writing daytime serials for the ad agency Blackett-Sample-Hummert in Chicago, and Irna Phillips, creator of *The Guiding Light* and the other founding figure of the genre, wrote mainly for the Compton agency. Thus a writer of a daytime serial with political inclinations would likely need to write from within an ad agency, and after appeasing this employer, his or her work would need to pass muster with a corporate sponsor, and then with network executives.[13] This was hardly a hospitable arrangement for mounting a direct assault on the dominant order. I have found no evidence that any individual with serious Popular Front leanings played a major role in writing or creating any nationally broadcast daytime serial, though more research needs to be done in this area. Soap opera writers unaffiliated with the Popular Front made isolated attempts to raise troubling issues of race and class, but these were carefully vetted.[14]

Realism and the Left on the American Stage, and Beyond

An examination of Popular Front theater and its adaptations to radio and film begins to illuminate how the left implicitly challenged serial drama; additionally, it shows a key avenue through which it disseminated realism throughout U.S. popular culture in the mid-twentieth century. By the 1920s realism had become the reigning aesthetic of "legitimate" English-language theater in the United States, though American playwrights and directors had been inching in that direction since the 1890s (J. Miller 169; Murphy 86, 133). Melodrama was the dominant mode on the American stage through much of the nineteenth century, but was gradually supplanted by realism as European imports from playwrights such as Ibsen, Shaw, Strindberg, and Chekhov, and innovations from a generation of Americans theater figures such as Edward Sheldon and Rachael Crothers (literary people who were influenced by the substantial corpus of theater criticism written by William Dean Howells and Henry James), came to influence the expectations of largely middle-class commercial theatergoers.

On the stage, melodrama was marked by the use of stock character types who clearly personified either good or evil through their physical appearance, mannerisms, and dialogue. It was also defined by sensationalism in staging and plot as well as contrived, emotional acting that would be recalled as histrionic and "stage-like" by later theatergoers. Attempts at verisimilitude in set design and in dialogue, such as the clumsy rendering of dialect in nineteenth-century local color plays, served to deliver melodramatic effects and conventional plot formulas. Breaking these conventions were a number of innovations, introduced by realism, that audiences—whether for theater, film, or television—now take for granted. First of all, realist plays evoked a sense of time and place: they were not merely set in a particular period or location, but rather were *about* a particular period or location. Second, rather than representing formulaic types, realist characters by the 1920s were complex, psychologically individualized social types; these characters would serve to represent particular groups, but would nonetheless achieve some individuality through their responses to their specific environments. Third, the sets and stage directions established a clear relationship between environment and character. A character's personality, for example, might be reflected in the décor, or might change when the set shifted from a saloon to a respectable home. Fourth, realist acting strove toward verisimilitude, rejecting the contrived, rhetorical mode of delivery that had defined dramatic conventions since Aristotle and instead aimed to capture how actual people talked and behaved. Similarly, in terms of plot and structure, realist playwrights centered their scenes around incidents that would occur in everyday life, and pace the action to resemble the actual flow of events (verisimilitude in terms of acting and structure was essential to achieving the "fourth wall" illusion of theatrical realism—the notion that a play is not heard but overheard). As Jordan Miller and Winifred Frazer have written, "the basic premise of stage realism is the depiction of the lives of ordinary people in ordinary settings, speaking and acting in what the audience will accept as an ordinary fashion" (30). Finally, as with other cultural forms, realism on stage was intended to be of social relevance, to challenge basic ideas about American institutions.[15]

While these realist innovations were firmly entrenched in the commercial theater after WWI, the audience for commercial theater represented a narrow swath of the population. Broadway, the pinnacle of the commercial stage, offered the highly polished, professional Theater Guild productions of realists George Bernard Shaw, Sidney Howard, and Elmer Rice in the 1920s; but with ticket prices starting from $3.30 for plays and $4.40 for musicals even during the Depression (with the exception of some left-wing shows), an evening on Broadway remained out of reach for most Americans (Goldstein 126). The Theater Guild—a company that did not shy away from political plays but was conceived more as an artistic than a political venture—had proven the financial viability of realism on Broadway. Yet it was leftists working through the Federal Theater Project and the new, politically driven companies that opened up the theater—and realism—to a broader audience. In New York, there were the famous Group Theatre (1931–41), the Theater Union (1933–37), the Actor's Repertory

Company (1935–38), the Theatre Arts Committee (1937–39) (which was primarily devoted to raising funds for the Spanish Republic), and Orson Welles and John Houseman's Mercury Theater (1937). In Harlem alone, there were the Rose McClendon Players, the American Negro Theater (1940–50), Rose McClendon's Negro People's Theatre, and Langston Hughes's short-lived companies the Harlem Suitcase Theater (1937) and Negro Playwrights Company (1940). Based in New York but national in scope was the New Theater League (1935–42), the CPUSA's production company during the Popular Front era; through the League, the Party moved away from the agitprop guerilla theater of the early 1930s and toward professional, polished work. With the exception of the Group and the Mercury Theater, most productions of these left-oriented companies were staged in Off-Broadway theaters. But whether off Broadway or on, they typically offered much cheaper tickets than theatergoers were accustomed to. In comparison to the minimum Broadway price of $3.30, events sponsored by the antifascist Theatre Arts Committee featured top Broadway talent like Gypsy Rose Lee, but cost from fifty-five cents to $2.10, and most productions of the Theater Union cost only $1.50. Even the highbrow, Broadway-based Mercury Theater made "popular prices" part of its mission statement (Goldstein 157, 199, 219; Denning 371).

While scholars disagree on the extent to which the new left-wing dramatic organizations reached New York's working class, there is no doubt that it brought theater well beyond the audience of the established commercial stage.[16] For instance, Mordecai Gorelik, set designer for ten of the Group Theatre's productions, identified the company's audience as mostly lower middle class (an expansion in itself), and the Theater Union, not even the most popular or famous of the new left-wing theater groups, had sold 523,000 tickets by January 1936 (Goldstein 81, 218). But the Federal Theater Project more unequivocally brought the stage back to the masses. Established in 1935, with units in New York, Chicago, Los Angeles, Seattle, Newark, Raleigh-Durham, and Birmingham (and Negro Units in all of these locations), the FTP offered amazingly cheap admission. In January 1936 it released its fee schedule for its performances: from ten cents to a dollar, with the underprivileged getting in for free. Even at this rate, FTP box offices took in $2 million nationally (Goldstein 244). Its director Hallie Flanagan saw the FTP as part of a larger movement to create "a national culture by and for the working class of America" (Pells 253). While Congressional oversight ensured that the majority of its productions were not overtly political (the FTP had a wildly popular Circus Unit, for instance, which meant that the New Deal literally provided bread and circuses), a roll call of leftists were either employed by the FTP or saw their work produced there over its four-year lifespan, including Mike Gold, Shirley Graham, Orson Welles, John Houseman, Theodore Ward, Paul Green, Ernst Toller, and Clifford Odets, to name a few.

Of course, left-wing and African American theater movements existed outside New York and the Federal theater; a short list would include the Karamu Theater in Cleveland, the Negro People's Theater in Chicago (1940), the Hollywood Theatre Alliance in Los Angeles (1939–41), and theater departments at colleges across the country (Howard University's theater department alone cultivated the talents of May Miller, Georgia Douglas Johnson, and others). And the most successful plays in New York, to be sure, toured in cities around the country. Yet, then as now, New York was the true beehive of theatrical activity—the only city that offered relentless variety to a large audience who made a night at the theater a staple of their weekend routine. Even the FTP spent 48.9 percent of its budget on its New York unit (Goldstein 256).

This left-wing theater movement inside and outside the FTP was divided between the realism of the fourth wall—most visibly exemplified by the Group Theater—and various strands of experimental modernism, from the Living Newspaper project which revolved around Nicholas Ray and Joseph Losey, to the Mercury Theater, the dramatic projects of Langston Hughes, and to the dramatic theory of Mordecai Gorelik, Bertolt Brecht, and Vsevolod Meyerhold. Denning argues that four major circles of Popular Front theater "left an enduring imprint on American theater and film": the Group, the Mercury, projects around Langston Hughes, and the Living Newspaper (367–68). Of these four, all but the Group eschewed realism.

Yet Denning's assessment downplays the continued and disproportionate importance of theatrical realism as an influence not only on the stage, but on film, radio, and American culture at large. Most of the top left-wing and left-liberal writers of nonmusical drama on Broadway wrote in the realist mode, including Sidney Howard, Lillian Hellman, Sidney Kingsley, Clifford Odets, Elmer Rice, Paul Green, and Maxwell Anderson. (Of course, realism was not the only mode used by all these dramatists, but it was a significant one.) By the late 1930s Hollywood was aggressively courting Broadway playwrights, financially backing productions in expectation of screen rights; it turned to these individuals, who collectively scripted a sizable list of films and saw their work adapted by others.[17] African American playwrights also wrote influential and often popular plays in the realist mode in the 1930s and 1940s, but they found the doors closed to them in Hollywood; these included Theodore Ward, Richard Wright, May Miller, Abram Hill, Georgia Douglas Johnson, and, as I will show,

Shirley Graham. Along with newer experimental works, Shakespeare, and classical drama, the FTP also staged a large number of realist plays and realist classics, including the work of Sinclair Lewis (whose antifascist play *It Can't Happen Here* was one of the big successes of the FTP), Anton Chekhov, Henrik Ibsen, Gerhart Hauptmann, Oscar Wilde, and George Bernard Shaw. Realist work, new and old, also appeared on the log lists of nighttime radio programs much more frequently than texts we would now recognize as modernist. Much of the newer work, moreover, was written by individuals who were based in theater.[18]

Denning's privileging of the modernist influence also elides the singular importance of the Group Theatre, which significantly redefined standards of acting in the United States through its adaptation of Constantin Stanislavski's method acting. Stanislavski's system encouraged actors to draw upon their own emotional memories and to be highly attuned to the details of physical expression, voice, and movement. The goal was to achieve verisimilitude and psychological realism—in short, actors were to speak and to carry themselves like ordinary people. It was first introduced to the United States in the early 1920s by the director Richard Boleslavski, one of Stanislavski's colleagues in Russia, but the modification of his system by the Group Theater and later the Actor's Studio was what came to dominate Hollywood after the war. The Group was founded in 1931 with the express purpose of using this system to reshape the face of American acting; to this end, Lee Strasberg, its chief acting theorist, stressed affective memory as a means of achieving realism, to the exclusion of most other aspects of Stanislavski's system. While actors and directors trained by the Group were actively courted by Hollywood in the 1930s and 1940s—including Elia Kazan and Harold Clurman (the latter became an associate producer for Columbia Pictures in 1941)—former members of the Group achieved an even wider influence after the war. Ex-members Elia Kazan, Cheryl Crawford, and Robert Lewis founded the Actor's Studio in 1947 and, under the direction of Lee Strasberg, this school further developed the Group's Americanized version of Stanislavski that trained a virtual "who's who" list of postwar Hollywood and television personalities (a very short list includes Al Pacino, Anne Bancroft, Montgomery Clift, James Dean, Marlon Brando, Maureen Stapleton, Sidney Poitier, Paul Newman, Jane Fonda, and Dustin Hoffman).[19] While D. W. Griffith adapted from the commercial stage in the 1910s a kind of "subdued" performance associated with realism, left-wing theater in the 1930s and 1940s brought its own mode of naturalistic performance into the age of sound; as such, it has been a powerful and often overlooked force in moving realism into American visual and aural mass culture.

Melodramatic Men and Real Women
Gender and Genre Classification

Nonetheless, a quick glance at the lists of writers and theater figures above reveals a serious overrepresentation of men in the ranks of the Broadway realists who were able to migrate to Hollywood and radio. While women generally had a more difficult time in accessing Hollywood or major Broadway venues as writers, they struggled particularly hard to be heard as realists in such arenas. Much of this difficulty arose from the fact that they inhabited a culture that coded realism as male and melodrama as female, a gendered genre classification that grew out of an older, long-standing, and oft-discussed tendency in American culture to associate women with mass culture. However, women have historically used realism to critique gendered structures of power and to lend visibility and legitimacy to women's perspectives.[20] The problem lies less in the epistemology of realism as a genre than in dominant twentieth-century associations between melodrama/women/kitsch on the one hand and realism/men/art on the other, associations that have fed discourses on women's cultural production as trivial and men's cultural production as "serious." Raymond Chandler made these precise divisions when he distinguished "realist" detective fiction from the classic mystery story in his treatise "The Simple Art of Murder," to take but one example. Chandler praised Dashiell Hammett as a realist because he "took murder out of the Venetian vase and dropped it into the alley . . . He put [hardened] people down on paper as they were, and he made them talk and think in the language they customarily used . . ." (530). While Hammett's realist detective stories should be regarded as "important writing," on par with Hemingway (he even suggests Hemingway might have borrowed from Hammett), Chandler suggests that the antithesis of Hammett's quality is both femininity and consumer culture. Critics of Hammett, he writes, are "flustered old ladies—of both sexes," and the classic mystery story, best embodied by Agatha Christie, can be found any week in "the big shiny magazines . . . paying due deference to virginal love and the right kind of luxury goods." These women's magazines, he adds, contain "more clothes by *Vogue* and décors by *House Beautiful*, more chic, but not more truth" (526, 531).

But if there is nothing innately male about realism—that is, in trying to achieve a historical sense, verisimilitude in the representation of everyday life, transparent form, and so on—scholars of pop culture genres have also been quick to note that there is also nothing innately female about melodrama (Cawelti 44, Williams 50). While I would argue that the male-targeted figures of the detective, the gangster, and the boxer at mid-century were all rendered, in part, through adapted traditions of realism, their stories contained no small degree of melodrama as well. All three genres centered around ordinary, often working-class men whose dialects and environments were emphasized, and who often elided the unambiguous label of "good" or "evil" essential to melodrama, yet they all relied on intensified effects—the gun blast and the knockout—to move the plot along. This fusion of realism and melodrama is just as present in the soap opera, though in different ways. Listening to the old soaps, one is struck by how little happens in the course of a ten- to fifteen-minute episode. They often focus on the minutiae of the everyday, but go the additional step of giving one the impression of overhearing a completely ordinary conversation (in this sense, they are even reminiscent of the pace of the ultrarealist Lumière Brothers films). In a 1934 episode of *The Life of Mary Southern*, for instance, husband Max and wife Mary spend the first half of the show playfully arguing about a missing tie, with Max suggesting that Mary threw it away simply because she didn't like it. Much more extreme in this regard was an episode of *Just Plain Bill*, where it took the lead character Bill Davidson an entire week of episodes to give a haircut to a single customer.[21] Unlike detective or gangster dramas, the soap opera did not need the sensationalism of the murder scene or the tommy gun to move the plot along. One soap opera historian has noted a feature of the genre during the 1930s that points to an additional commonality with realism: that environmental forces strongly affected the dialogue and action of Depression-era soaps (Cox 91). Considering the ordinary nature of the dialogue and slow, lifelike pace of the action, the soap opera should be placed alongside the boxing narrative and the detective story in deriving key formal properties from realism.

Some cultural producers already recognized this in the 1930s, openly challenging the gendered assumptions of genre categorization by claiming women's popular culture as realism. Stung by critics who accused her of producing nothing but trite melodrama, Irna Phillips persistently claimed that her soap operas were in fact realist, not melodramatic, as they handled real issues of significance to their listeners (Allen 18, 24). Likewise, at the 1939 conference of the League of American Writers, Hope Hale argued that the tabloid story magazine *True Story* recognized "the demand for realistic fiction" for the first time. She added that despite the anti-union bias of its owner, "*True Story*, for whatever commercial purpose, did admit that people without food got hungry and sometimes even ill, that babies did not always arrive into a softly bassineted welcome, and that sometimes crime, cruelty, disease, and even the sacred course of true love might be affected by economic problems" (Stewart 44). A very influential woman would also enter the fray, claiming as realism her popular representations of women's lives.

Lillian Hellman and the Politics of Visibility

In theater criticism of the 1930s and 1940s, "melodrama" was by and large a label denoting poor artistic quality, a death blow for the playwright who wanted to be taken seriously.[22] Women playwrights were often assumed guilty of this charge until proven innocent, and many judges were not inclined in their favor. Speaking of women dramatists in 1941, George Jean Nathan wrote in *The American Mercury*, "Give her an emotion, whether tragic or comic, and she will stretch it not only to its extreme limit, but beyond. It is for this reason, I believe, that the drama of most female playwrights, Miss Lillian [Hellman] among them, often resolves itself willy-nilly into melodrama" (35). Most theater critics were not quite so blunt in their associations between women playwrights and melodrama, but Nathan voices a long-standing and unspoken assumption that haunted female dramatists. The special notice he gives to Lillian Hellman reveals much about her place in that milieu. Hellman was not clear of the charges that tainted other women playwrights, yet she was also held above what Nathaniel Hawthorne had infamously called "the mob of scribbling women." Though Nathan brazenly proclaims the superiority of male playwriting, he notes that "Lillian Hellman is the best of our American women playwrights . . . (34)." In another piece in *Newsweek*, he contrasted her play *The Little Foxes* with "the current cheap and squashy family drama calculatedly manufactured by English female pastry cooks," and added that rather than pandering to popular taste, it was "the truest and most honest play on her theme" (26). Though other women playwrights, including Zoë Akins, Rose Franken, and Clare Booth (who married Henry Luce to become Clare Booth Luce in 1935), achieved success on Broadway in the 1930s and 1940s, Hellman was the only one openly affiliated with the Popular Front. And of these, only Hellman and Akins were best known for their "serious" drama. Akins's *The Old Maid*, an adaptation of an Edith Wharton novel, won the Pulitzer Prize in 1934–35, a controversial decision that angered many critics who felt the prize should have gone to Hellman's *The Children's Hour* (the furor led to the establishment of the Critic's Choice Award).[23] Though sometimes faulted for melodramatic "excesses," Hellman was recognized as one of the best playwrights of her day, male or female.

But her politics made her an unlikely critics' choice, especially in journals such as *Newsweek*. She was outspoken in her defense of the Soviet Union in the late 1930s and 1940s, a stance she never fully retracted; and though the FBI never found evidence of her Communist Party membership, she considered herself a member from 1938 to 1940. Shortly after the success of *The Children's Hour* on Broadway, she was hired by MGM as a screenwriter in 1935, where she quickly became one of the highest-paid writers in Hollywood. That same year, she aggressively lobbied for the passage of the Wagner Act, the landmark labor bill. Soon after, despite her own generous contract with Samuel Goldwyn, she joined the effort to unionize screenwriters, and a subsequent trip she took to Spain in 1937 moved her much farther to the left (79). She was unwavering in her activism on behalf of the Spanish republic, which inspired her to coscript the documentary *The Spanish Earth* (1937) with Archibald MacLeish and Joris Ivens. After Finland was invaded by the U.S.S.R. in 1939, Hellman even went so far as to speak out against benefit performances for the relief of the besieged nation, and was quoted as such in the *New York Times*. This position too, she left unretracted in her 1973 autobiography *Pentimento*, in which she suggests the Finns deserved no sympathy (Rollyson 79, 146, 151, 183).

A close look at *The Children's Hour* and *The Little Foxes*, the two most major plays by the most visible female communist writer of the era, yields a story of both political efficacy and limitation, opportunity and constraint. Examining them alongside their adaptations, one can see the extent to which, within theater, radio, and film in the 1930s and 1940s, a white woman playwright on the left could collapse domestic and public realms to highlight the interrelationship between class, race, and gender. Like soap operas, women's struggles and women's agency are more central in these plays and adaptations than in that of almost any male Popular Front writer. Yet her work offers an alternative to the soap operas by showing how class is gendered and gender is classed, and how domestic and traditionally feminine spheres are important sites of class, racial, and even international conflict. In her major plays Hellman emphasizes the conflicts arising from the differences between women, differences of class, race, age, and sexual orientation. This centrality of division in her thinking on women was revealed in an interview as late as 1976: when asked her opinion about how women had progressed over the past fifty years she replied, "I'm not sure young women do have it easier. Yes, there are more jobs available, but for whom? I'm not sure Negro women have it any easier than they did when I was growing up. I'm not sure poor women have it any easier" (Bryer 204–5). While her productions resounded with critics and mass audiences alike, such politics were not easily adaptable to the particular commercial restraints of radio.

While aspects of her politics anticipate third-wave feminism, the ways in which they are rendered in her drama also reflect an unfortunately common political decision in even oppositional work of the 1930s and 1940s. That is to say, in highlighting the differences among women, she sometimes de-emphasizes conflicts between men and women, and even leaves the mediating authority of the father character intact. In *The Little Foxes* and *Watch on the Rhine*, for instance, a father occupies the moral center of the piece, and his absence allows interfamilial conflicts to reach dangerous levels. And her highly problematic treatment of lesbianism in *The Children's Hour* is now well known, as I will soon discuss. The downplaying of male-female conflict in her work is not simply a result of a need to appease the market, for other women writers whose work was produced on Broadway and picked up by Hollywood—Clare Booth Luce and Zoë Akins in particular—foregrounded such struggles to a much greater degree (though Booth Luce and Akins were without a critique of capitalism or race, and their most major works even perpetuated racial stereotypes). Uncoincidentally, neither of these women was affiliated with the Popular Front, except for a brief flirtation in the case of Booth Luce (Shadegg 108–10). Finally, while Hellman laudably strove to make race a significant theme in *The Little Foxes*, her major plays did not stray too far from American mass-culture conventions of the 1930s in their representation of African Americans. It would take African American playwrights like Shirley Graham and later Alice Childress and Lorraine Hansberry to truly challenge mass-culture stereotypes on the stage.

Hellman used a combination of realism and melodrama to deliver her politics—which is what made her work so immanently adaptable to Hollywood and radio—and she indirectly acknowledged this stylistic hybridity in her work. She noted in 1942 that "the realistic form has interested me the most," but also acknowledged that the playwright, unlike the novelist, has to "trick up the scene" with dramatic effects that do not always mimic everyday life ("Introduction" xi–xii). This mixture of realism and melodrama in her plays has been recognized by reviewers and scholars from the 1930s to the present; though with some exceptions, critics then and now have seen her work as leaning more toward the realistic side of the scale, and a number have claimed her as a thoroughgoing realist.[24] Despite her politics her major plays were not seen as overly didactic by contemporary mainstream reviewers, and were generally praised for their truth, fidelity to life, and eye for social significance—in other words, their realism. When critics on the left reviewed her poorly, it was usually her politics, not her artistic abilities nor any inclination to melodrama, that they questioned.[25] Hellman strove to create this sense of her work: as a female playwright, she took special care to distance herself from melodrama in her explicit statements. In the same piece quoted above, she noted that some critics had found her work to be melodramatic, and countered by making clear her aversion to this mode.

While noting that some of its features could be useful if deployed correctly, she defined a melodrama in its usual form as "a violent dramatic piece, with a happy ending ... it uses its violence for no purpose, to point no moral, to say noting, in say-nothing's worse sense" (x–xi).

The Children's Hour (1934) was Hellman's first and most commercially successful play; its rave reviews and Broadway run of 691 performances quickly established its author as a major playwright of her generation. This three-act drama deals with a boarding school scandal in a small New England town. The hard-working, independent headmistresses Karen Wright and Martha Dobie found a school for little girls through years of savings and sacrifice, yet all of their labors are undone as a spoiled and malicious child named Mary Tilford deliberately spreads a rumor that Karen and Martha have a lesbian relationship. The child's grandmother, the wealthy Mrs. Tilford, pulls Mary out of the school, which disintegrates financially after the well-to-do matriarch urges other parents and guardians to do the same. In a plot twist that baffled many of its contemporary critics, Martha reveals in the final act that she actually does have romantic feelings for Karen, who is engaged to a doctor named Joseph Cardin. While the child Mary comes across as a clear villain whose lie is still a lie—the two are never in a relationship, and Karen denies ever having had feelings for Martha—this twist added to a sense of moral confusion and structural disunity for some theatergoers and critics (was the central problem the lie, Martha's sexuality, or both?). At the end, Mrs. Tilford realizes the child's dishonesty and tries to make amends with Karen and Martha, but she is too late—Martha has killed herself out of the shame wrought by her confused feelings.

The Children's Hour was one of the first works on Broadway to treat lesbianism on stage, though this theme was completely deleted from the 1936 film adaptation *These Three*; Hollywood's production code would never tolerate such a topic. In the film Mary's lie is that Karen's fiancée Joseph is having an affair with Martha, making Joseph a much more important figure. With all references to homosexuality gone, *These Three* became one of the highest-grossing films of the year (Steinberg 17). The theme of lesbianism in the play—and its exorcism from the film—has understandably been a central focus for contemporary critics of *The Children's Hour* and *These Three*, and scholars have examined it quite impressively. Though Hellman claimed that lesbianism was incidental to the drama, Brett Elizabeth Westbrook and Jenny Spencer have shown how the politics of sexuality are central to its interpretation.[26] My task here, however, is briefly to show the place of *The Children's Hour* within the left-wing politics of the historic moment from which it emerged. In a move clearly bearing the mark of the 1930s, the author's representational choices make class the central locus of power in the play. But she departs by lending a centrality to women's struggles absent in the work of most male writers, leftist or otherwise. With her all-female cast, she dramatizes class hierarchies among women, and in so doing makes a site of traditional "women's work"—teaching elementary school—a site of class formation. In addition, the title of the play is a reference to radio programming for children; as I will discuss, the title underscores the consequences of ignoring the role of presumably apolitical serials—and the traditionally female job of childrearing—in reproducing capitalist social relations. Perhaps because of its focus on women, however, *The Children's Hour* was not seen as political at all by many contemporary critics, even on the left.[27]

An analysis of Hellman's politics in *The Children's Hour* should begin with the almost complete absence of men in the play—Karen's fiancée Joe is the only one, and though he is entrusted with a key line, he is a marginal character. The lack of men allows Hellman to depict the main conflicts of the play as between women, conflicts that are implicitly classed. In a quintessentially 1930s plot, two hard-working women are brought down by the machinations of the wealthy (Mary and her grandmother Mrs. Tilford) and of those with a pretense to wealth and breeding (Martha's aunt Mrs. Lily Mortar). Martha and Karen were likely never poor—they are college-educated, after all—but their lack of financial support as they try to build their lives clearly marks them as lower on the socioeconomic scale than the Tilfords, and hence objects of identification for most Americans. Martha, it should be noted, was given unequivocal working-class status in the radio adaptation of *These Three* for the evening program *Lux Radio Theater*. Played by Barbara Stanwyck, her class position is established by her tired, unaffected elocution, which stands out markedly from the other characters; added dialogue reveals that she went into teaching because she had a hard time growing up, and this instilled in her a desire to serve others.[28]

Mary's villainy, on the other hand, is closely bound with her class position and her uncanny knowledge of economic power: she is conscious of using her family's class position to bring down the school, telling her friend Evelyn, "I'm going to tell [Grandma] I'm not happy. They're scared of Grandma—she helped 'em when they first started you know—and when she tells 'em something, believe me, they'll sit up and listen" (31).[29] In contrast, Martha and Karen are shown as dignified and hard-working: in bickering with her aunt Lily, Martha snaps, "I'm tired. I've been working since six o'clock this morning" (21). In the pivotal confrontation between the headmistresses and Mrs. Tilford, Joe dramatically underscores the classed nature of the conflict by exclaiming to Tilford in her elegant home: "... they've worked eight long years to save enough money to buy that farm, to start that school. They did without everything that young people ought to have. You wouldn't know about that. That school meant things to them: self-respect, and bread and butter, and honest work. Do you know what it is to try so hard for anything?" (54). This accusation against privilege is preserved in the film adaptation *These Three* as well, but even more so, as it shows Karen and Martha actually building the school, providing a visceral sense of their hard work. But in the film and radio adaptations, Karen delivers this rebuke, intensifying the agency of her character by giving the resistance to class injustice a female voice.

Despite their limitations, both *The Children's Hour* and *These Three* were not without critical and didactic commentary on women's labor and women's roles. Through the character of Mrs. Lily Mortar—the laughable, incompetent teacher of elocution and sewing whose failure to testify on behalf of Karen and Martha seals their fate—Hellman makes clear that training girls for a life of etiquette and domesticity is not synonymous with virtue. Bored by the droning platitudes of Mrs. Mortar, the girls respect the example of Karen and Martha much more, and the audience is clearly meant to identify with their striving for economic independence as well. Also, if one of the main, explicit messages of the play is that children are not innocent—that, like Mary who uses her class position to also bully her classmates, they have hierarchies among themselves—then the world of childrearing and children's education with which women have been entrusted is to be taken as much an arena of class struggle as conflicts in the "male" worlds of manufacturing and raw material production. Indeed, the impossible demands of privileged patrons and customers—in this case, Mary and Mrs. Tilford—is a form in which abusive class power would appear in the lives of the many women workers concentrated in the educational and service sectors. Unlike the famous *Pins and Needles*, *The Children's Hour* does not radically break with convention in order to show the struggles of women in this male-coded world of manufacturing, but it does highlight the significance of traditional "women's work," inside and outside the home, in a way that many 1930s audiences would understand. Though many male critics might not have seen the play as political, the fact that they—and audiences—saw its moral message as important does show that Hellman was successful in ascribing significance to women's labor. The title of the play, a reference to radio, is not incidental in this context. From the early 1930s, many radio stations around the country would advertise a "children's hour" in their schedules, generally between 5:00 and 6:00 p.m., which featured entertainment or educational programming for children. The title of Hellman's play can be seen as an ironic commentary on the assumption of childhood innocence. But more specifically, given the brutal exercise of class power by the child Mary Tilford, it also cautions theatergoers not to dismiss radio programming that evokes the responsibilities of women, as it addresses a juvenile audience that is already waging its own struggles of power under female tutelage, struggles which will be of ever greater consequence as young listeners grow and develop.

Though *These Three* maintains many of the class conflicts that animate the play, its political edge is somewhat blunted, not only by the removal of lesbianism but by the demand of Hollywood and commercial radio for the happy end, which moves the film and radio play much closer to melodrama than its theatrical version.

With even the hint of a lesbian relationship removed as a precondition for its production, the film and radio adaptations—both titled *These Three*—were able to simplify the conflicts of the story even further, and the resulting narrative received even higher praise than the Broadway play on account of its perceived thematic unity. In removing the lesbian plot from the narrative, however, a significant part of its social commentary was lost (albeit a commentary unintended by the author). While Hellman had at best a liberal view of homosexuality in the 1930s—that it was something to be pitied, not criminalized—Brett Elizabeth Westbrook nonetheless suggests that the play offers a valid social critique by linking hetero-normativity to class hierarchies. Mary and Mrs. Tilford, she argues, use their social position to "enforce a sexual norm." Removing this theme not only put the very idea of homosexuality back into the closet, but it also took away a significant, nuanced message about relations of power.[30]

The relatively melodramatic happy end of *These Three* is enabled by plot shifts that alter the role of Mrs. Tilford. On both stage and screen, Mrs. Tilford is never depicted as a villainess (Hellman's stage directions describe her as having "a pleasant, strong face"), but rather as a misguided, naive woman who wants to do "the right thing" according to the standards by which she was raised (35). In the final scene of the play, when she offers to make a public apology to Karen and restore her financially, she comes across as sincerely guilt-ridden and horrified by her actions, but also unproductively sentimental. Karen's cold, tired, and placating response indicates peace between the two characters, but also that there can be no real resolution for the damage that has been done. The ending is a realist one, as it shows not only that virtue does not always triumph, but also that the injustices wrought by wealth do not simply arise from evil individuals. The child's lie was given force not by simple villainy, but by arbitrary power enabled by class privilege, which gave elite testimony greater weight and allowed whispered rumors to spiral into tragic consequences. By contrast, the happy end of the film and radio play holds very different implications. There is no suicide, Mrs. Tilford is allowed to redeem herself more unequivocally, Martha gives

Karen and Joe her blessing, and Mary and Joe are able to go off happily together in a café in Vienna. The evil child has been vanquished and virtue triumphs. One the one hand, the wealthy are still shown as an obstacle to hard-working, independent women; on the other, the root problem becomes more localized in the child, and those in power are ultimately able to keep deceit in check. Thus, as in the adaptation of Odets's *Golden Boy*, the accentuation of the melodramatic by Hollywood and commercial radio does not negate the political implications of the theatrical piece, but they do blunt its social critiques.

Written after her radicalizing trip to Europe in 1937, the subject matter of both stage and Hollywood versions of *The Little Foxes* (1939) were more recognizably political—and realist—than either *The Children's Hour* or *These Three*, despite a rather melodramatic plot (though, once again, Hollywood accentuated the nonrealist elements). Also a hit on Broadway, *The Little Foxes* was adapted to film in 1941, and its screen adaptation remained much closer to the play. It was adapted for radio much later; in 1951 it was aired on *Philip Morris Playhouse on Broadway*, a popular evening program similar in structure to *Lux Radio Theatre* (Grams 381). The historical sense is fundamental to the play, a family drama set in a small Alabama town in 1900. *The Little Foxes* is most remembered for the scheming Hubbard clan—brothers Oscar, Benjamin and their sister Regina Giddens (played by Bette Davis in the film), *nouveau riche* members of the town's merchant class whom Hellman modeled after her mother's family in New Orleans. The play is set almost entirely in the home of Regina and her husband Horace. As it begins, Ben, Oscar, and Regina are trying to convince a visiting investor from Chicago to finance their plans to open a cotton mill. In order for their venture to get off the ground, Regina's husband Horace, a wealthy and respected banker, must contribute funds. This is a serious catch, however, as Horace is not only seriously ill in a hospital in Baltimore, but is also estranged from his wife. After he is brought back to Alabama by their daughter Alexandra, he refuses to pitch in the necessary capital, largely out of his world-weary disgust with exploitative schemes, which leads Oscar and Ben to steal the money from him in the form of bonds. After a series of plot twists, Regina deliberately triggers a heart attack in her husband Horace then kills him by refusing to give him medicine, and blackmails her brothers for a 75 percent share of the mill. Hellman suggests that her victory is not complete, however. In the last scene, her daughter Alexandra confronts her, vowing to run away and fight "her kind," then exits the stage.

Hellman reportedly typed 115 pages of notes researching the New South period from 1880 to 1900, particularly on the system of tenant farming, in order to recreate the specific social dynamics of the historical moment as accurately as possible. Film director William Wyler explicitly strove to avoid melodrama in his adaptation, and his *Little Foxes* was nominated for nine Academy Awards in the attempt (Rollyson 179–80). But Wyler also took a big step away from realism with one of the film's opening placards, which universalized the setting. "Little foxes have lived in all times, in all places," it read. "This family happened to live in the deep South in the year 1900." Though this move seriously dilutes the realism of the narrative, it does not manage to negate its politics. Both the film and the play strove to retain realist characterization, as the scheming Hubbard family was not intended as a group of villains by Hellman nor Wyler. Tallulah Bankhead's performance as Regina Hubbard on Broadway did justice to this intention, conveying a moral ambiguity that made one reviewer compare her character to "a figure who might have stepped out of the pages of Balzac" (qtd. in Rollyson 139; Barlow 159).

Thus the realism of the play emerges not only from its historical sense, but also in the complexity of Regina's character and Hellman's clear desire for social significance. Regina is an impressively shrewd businesswoman who will lie, steal, or murder to achieve her dream of an independent life of luxury in Chicago. But her easy status as villainess is complicated by the environmental factors that produced her; namely, she was wronged in her youth on account of her gender. As a girl, she was cut out of her father's will. All the money went to her brothers Oscar and Ben, thus she had to struggle more than anyone else in the family (233). And while the other characters do approach the melodramatic, coming across as either essentially "good" or "bad," their motivations, individual histories, and analyses of each other are multilayered and complex. The social relevance of the play is made apparent mostly through the lines of the "good" characters—Horace, Alexandra, the maid Addie, and Oscar's abused wife Birdie—who call attention to the destructive effects of the Hubbards' business practices on the town's multiracial working class. Ben tells Horace, for instance, that he interested the Northern investor in their mill venture by promising cheaper wages than in Massachusetts, smiling as he asserts, "Why, there ain't a mountain white or a town nigger but wouldn't give his right arm for three silver dollars every week, eh, Horace?" Horace responds: "Sure. And they'll take less than that when you get around to playing them off against each other. You can save a little money that way, Ben. And make them hate each other just a little more than they do now" (212). Regina's African American maid Addie states more bluntly of the Hubbards, "they got mighty well-off cheating niggers" (225).

Written after Hellman's radicalization, *The Little Foxes* not only goes farther than *The Children's Hour* in explicitly linking class and race, but in connecting class and gender hierarchies as well. Women are "bought" and "sold" in both play and film, and their exchange on the market traps them in abusive marriages. Hellman illustrates this process most clearly through the cruelty of Oscar Hubbard toward his wife Birdie, which she highlights in the very first scene of the play. Birdie, a woman from an old-money family whom the stage directions describe as "usually nervous and timid, but now . . . gay and excited," is happy because their out-of-town visitor Mr. Marshall has shown interest in her music album (168). But alone together, Oscar rapidly deflates her, calling her "a child" and a "fool" who has merely bored their guest with her wine-driven chattering (169). This emotional abuse is repeated throughout the play, and at the beginning of the third act Birdie reveals its absent cause: Oscar only married her for her family's land. Likewise, Regina also attempts to "sell" her daughter to Oscar and Birdie's son Leo in order to gain control of her brothers' property. As Judith Barlow has argued, in setting the Hubbards' business schemes in a domestic space, and highlighting the buying and selling of women for land, Hellman comments on "the gender relationships spawned by capitalism," demystifying the relationship between the economic and the domestic (161–62).

Hellman makes this connection more complex and nuanced by refusing to represent the perpetrators of these gendered transactions as male and those who stand against them as female. The perpetrators are Regina, Oscar, and Ben, and those who voice resistance are Horace, Alexandra, Birdie, and Addie—with the resistance led by Horace. Regina attempts to gain control of the system by playing by its rules, subjugating workers and other women, namely her daughter and her black servant Addie, whom she also demeans. The final conflict crystallizes between Alexandra and her mother Regina, who refuses to be "sold" as part of her mother's game. Hellman suggests an alliance between the maid Addie and Alexandra at the very end of the play. With Alexandra present at the beginning of Act Three, Addie had spoken against those who stand by and watch injustice. At the end of the act, when Alexandra heeds her call, vowing to fight Regina and people like her rather than idly watching them carrying out their greedy designs, Addie "smiles" as she puts out the lamps, ending the play (more on this in a moment).

While this division among women in the play is an analytical subtlety on the author's part, the way in which it is deployed also becomes a problem. The two most prominent women in *Little Foxes*, Birdie and Regina, fall into one of two categories—pitiable, abused, and weak on one side, and shrewd, independent, yet utterly malicious on the other. The daughter Alexandra provides the synthesis to their thesis and antithesis, yet she is an undeveloped character who only makes a striking appearance at the very end. Horace provides the real moral center to this domestic space. The most poignant political and moral critique of the Hubbards' plans comes from his mouth; he is consistently calm, sincere, and understanding; and it is he who devises a clever means to foil Ben and Oscar's theft (checked only by his poor health). His absence from the household is what has allowed wickedness to flourish, which is precisely why the good-natured characters Alexandra, Addie, and Birdie view him as a savior upon his return. In a convention Hellman borrows from melodrama, his physical weakness gives him added moral authority.

Hellman's attempt to clarify the role of southern merchants in exacerbating racial tensions and in fueling divisions between poor blacks and whites is highly laudable. Like *Watch on the Rhine*, the play also opens with a conversation among two servants, calling attention to the racialized domestic labor that enables the comfort of the bourgeois family. *The Little Foxes*, like so many other Popular Front cultural productions, helped make race and class inextricable in the political discourse of the late 1930s and 1940s. But despite these strengths, and the fact that Addie voices a clear sense of injustice, Hellman's depiction of African American servants (particularly male servants) does not stray far from the standard mass-culture stereotypes of her day. During the 1930s the casting of blacks almost exclusively in comic servant roles prompted Thomas Bogle to label that decade of Hollywood history "the age of the Negro servant" (35–36). The servant Cal in both the stage and film variants of *The Little Foxes*, and to a lesser extent the servant Joseph in *Watch on the Rhine*, unfortunately replicate the stereotypical figure Bogle labels "the coon," which he concisely defines as "an amusement object and black buffoon" (7). Like Stepin Fetchit, the highest-paid black actor in Hollywood during the Depression, the servant Cal is used for comic effect to create this very stereotype, though to a much more egregious extent in the film. In Wyler's picture, when asked by Horace to deliver a message, Cal slowly drawls "I'm not good at totin' messages. My memory gets confused." It is hardly surprising, then, that Alexandra is the one who must lead the future battle against greed.

Hellman offered an alternative to the soaps by situating the agency, labor, and oppression of women (particularly white women) in the home and in the schoolhouse as essential to capitalist hierarchies, and *The Little Foxes* provided another example of a mass-mediated realism that posited the inseparability of class and racial formation, albeit in a limited form. At the same time, the compromised and sometimes conflicted nature of her gender and sexual politics assured that her early plays and their adaptations are not generally regarded as proto-feminist. As a female playwright, Hellman was able to fly under the radar of gender-coded assumptions surrounding realism and melodrama precisely because her plays were not seen as being "about" the subjugation of women. Rather, reviewers held their central themes to be ethics, capital, race, and, in the case of *Watch on the Rhine*, antifascism—all indelibly associated with realism in the 1930s and 1940s. But if access to realist authority in the mass market carried strict terms for Hellman, for African American women before 1945 such access was sealed off completely. And the representational politics of Hellman and so many other writers on Broadway and Hollywood dramatically illustrated the need for their presence.

Realism Deferred
Shirley Graham, African American Women's Playwriting, and the Mass Audience

It is well known that African Americans had scant access as writers or directors in the culture industries of the 1930s and 1940s—particularly film and network radio—and I have noted such barriers at a number of points in this book. At the beginning of the Depression, this utter lack of access was true of Broadway as well, where most white playwrights rehashed the same racial stereotypes as Hollywood without fear of censure (Goldstein 132). As the 1930s wore on, however, there were halting signs that things were beginning to open up: Langston Hughes's *The Mulatto* (1935) was a hit with 373 performances on Broadway, and Hall Johnson's folk musical *Run, Little Children* (1932) was also well-attended downtown. Produced by the Negro Unit of the Newark FTP, Hughes Allison's murder mystery *The Trial of Dr. Beck* (1937) moved to Broadway where it ran for four weeks to rave reviews (Hatch 310, 313, 330). The war facilitated a much larger opening for African American playwrights and black-themed plays at this pinnacle of the U.S. commercial stage. Richard Wright's *Native Son* (1941) and Abram Hill's rewrite of *Anna Lucasta* (1944), both realist plays starring Canada Lee, were Broadway hits, the latter with a phenomenal run of nearly a thousand performances, unprecedented for a black-authored play (Hatch 352). Wartime audiences flocked to see the play *Carmen Jones* (1943) by Oscar Hammerstein II, and also to see Paul Robeson as the first black man to play Othello on Broadway. His performance set a record run for any Shakespeare production there, one that held until 1998 (347). Immediately following the war, the ever louder and more frequent attention to civil rights in American culture was echoed on the professional stage. From 1945–50 twenty civil rights dramas were produced, nine of which played on Broadway (338). Federal and off-Broadway theater also saw the rise of a constellation of black production companies and works by black authors and directors, mostly based in New York. Most notable were the Negro Units of the FTP (1935–39), which were a component part of every major branch of the organization; the American Negro Theater (1940–50), which produced Hill's *Anna Lucasta*; the Rose McClendon Players, founded in 1936 and which launched the career of Ossie Davis; the short-lived Negro People's Theatres in Chicago and New York; the Negro Playwright's Theatre (1940); Langston Hughes's short-lived New Negro Theatre and Harlem Suitcase Theatre (1938 and 1939, respectively); and finally the continuing work of drama departments at black colleges around the country.

But whether they worked off Broadway or on, the serious theater was not the same gateway to Hollywood for black writers and directors. While Langston Hughes cowrote the musical *Way Down South* (1939) for RKO, his was an exceptional case for black playwrights before 1945. It would take the postwar agitation for civil rights to increase the flow of this generation of black artists from stage to screen, and much of that was in the form of actors (notably Sidney Poitier, Harry Belafonte, and Ruby Dee, who trained at the American Negro Theater's drama school in the 1940s). Even *Anna Lucasta* was not picked up by Hollywood in its black-cast adaptation until 1959. By way of contrast, Hellman's work, with a much smaller run, had been seized by Samuel Goldwyn almost immediately. And if it was difficult for black male playwrights, it was virtually impossible for black women to enter mass culture in this role: not until the production of Lorraine Hansberry's *A Raisin in the Sun* (1959) did a drama written by an African American woman appear on Broadway (Perkins 1). Before this landmark achievement, black female playwrights of serious drama such as May Miller, Georgia Douglas Johnson, and Eulalie Spence had seen their work produced, but mostly at high schools, public libraries, black colleges, and other relatively small venues around the country.

Between 1936, when the directing career of actress Rose McClendon at the FTP tragically was cut short by cancer, and 1949, when Alice Childress rose to prominence in off-Broadway theaters in New York, one notable African American female playwright and director was able to produce for sizable audiences: Shirley Graham. As I have noted, her play *Swing Mikado* (1938) was one of the biggest successes of the FTP, actually turning a profit of $35,000 for the government with its Chicago run before moving to Broadway. There in New York, it would have fared even better were it not for competition from a white-authored commercial imitation, *The Hot Mikado*, that was not constrained by FTP budget limits. Graham also composed *Tom-Tom* (1932), an opera that narrated the journey of Africans from slavery to freedom in the New World through a celebration of African music and its American transformations.

Playing before twenty-five thousand people at the Cleveland Stadium and aired over CBS Radio, it was the first all-black professional opera in the U.S. Like many African Americans in the theater arts in the early twentieth century, Graham's background was in music, a pathway to the stage less strewn with obstacles for blacks at that time (though far from obstacle-free, as the case of opera singer Marian Anderson illustrated). She studied music at the Sorbonne, Howard University, and Oberlin College, and headed the music department at Morgan State College in Baltimore from 1929 to 1931 (Perkins 209–10). She wrote for the theater and for radio in a variety of modes, however, including realism. Composed approximately fifty years before Toni Morrison's *Beloved* (1987), her one-act play *It's Morning* was about a slave woman who kills her daughter rather than allowing her to be sold into slavery. Its slave characters spoke all of their lines in dialect, yet the structure of the piece was modeled after ancient, Aristotlean tragedy. Graham's more realist works were her three-act plays *I Gotta Home* (1940), *Elijah's Ravens* (1930), her dramatic rendering of a mine disaster *Coal Dust* (1930) (revived in 1940 as *Dust to Earth*), her cowritten drama of the Haitian uprising *The Revolutionists*, a short story in *Negro Story* magazine entitled "Tar" (1945), her radio play *Track Thirteen*, and her unaired radio serial *The Bannekers* (ca. 1944).

But despite the quality of her realistic plays—*I Gotta Home* in particular—her musicals were her most celebrated work, and gave her access to much larger audiences. Other African American female playwrights of Graham's time wrote in the realist mode, including May Miller and Georgia Douglas Johnson in the 1920s and 1930s, and Alice Childress and Lorraine Hansberry after the war. And the constitution for the American Negro Theater, a vehicle for male and female playwrights, was definitively realist in tone.[31] However, it was the black male realists in the 1930s and 1940s who saw their plays produced on a grand scale, including Richard Wright, Abram Hill, and Theodore Ward. When Shirley Graham directed Theodore Ward's serious and overtly political family drama *The Big White Fog* for the Chicago FTP in 1938, the harsh responses of the black elite to its preview taught her a lasting lesson about the dangers of realism—as compared to the praise for lighter, more celebratory musical fare—for a female writer or director.[32] Likewise, when Johnson submitted her anti-lynching play *Safe* to the FTP, a play written in decidedly realist mode, its readers were openly dismissive of its veracity (Fletcher 54–55). Clearly, if realism was often understood to be masculine, and access to large audiences difficult for any black writer, then black female playwrights desiring exposure as realists faced a double bind. But an examination of Graham's realist work shows that African American women not only used realism to highlight their struggles, but also intervened in the creation of class and racial formations through innovative representations of domestic space. Given the audiences for Graham's realist work as opposed to her musical theater, her reception also reveals that most theatergoers of the 1930s and 1940s were not ready for a black female realist, an unfortunate fact that would have dire consequences for black women in film and radio as well.

Like Hellman, Graham was increasingly drawn into Popular Front circles in the late 1930s, but she took the additional step of joining the Communist Party during the war. She remained openly supportive of the Party in the late 1940s, when it was becoming more dangerous and less acceptable to do so. In the 1950s, she increasingly yoked her socialist politics to the cause of global anticolonialism. She and her husband W. E. B. Du Bois, whom she married in 1951, moved to Ghana in 1961 to escape harassment from U.S. officials. In Ghana, a nation that held global symbolic significance as the first African colony to declare independence from Europe, she helped develop the national educational curriculum, was named director of television, and became a close friend of President Kwame Nkrumah. Like Hellman she never recanted her socialist beliefs. Her commitment to the Soviet Union began to waver in the 1960s, largely because of what she saw as its insufficient support of the Third World, but rather than becoming anticommunist she became an avid booster of communist China. She died in Beijing in 1977 (Horne 7, 115–16, 225).

In her domestic play *I Gotta Home* (a revision of her *Elijah's Ravens*) and in the unaired pilot for her radio serial *The Bannekers*, her politics are present, though strategically muted. Graham wanted mass culture's audience, for her own sake and for the advancement of other black artists as well, and she relentlessly tried to make connections to lead her to Broadway or Hollywood. After her contact with a Broadway producer in April 1940, she optimistically wrote to Du Bois: "Gradually I believe I can break through the barriers. And this is the only hope for real development of the Negro in the theatre. Some one of us must be in a position of authority. Until that happens we get no plays produced and most of our acting is turned into a burlesque." She had reason to be upbeat, for as her biographer Gerald Horne writes, "if anyone was in a position to say what worked with audiences, it was Shirley Graham" (81). She knew that a somber, frontal assault on entrenched American power, such as *The Little Foxes* or *Native Son*, would be unlikely to bring production funding or grand audiences to an African American woman. *Coal Dust*, her three-act play about black coal miners in Illinois and their exploitative white boss, was called a "melodrama" and dismissed as "sensationalized" by the *Cleveland Plain Dealer* when it played in that city at the Karamu Theatre in April 1939 (Pullen). With the notable exception of her deeply tragic play *It's Morning*, much of her work was positive, celebratory, and slightly comic in tone, whether her mass-culture operas or her more realist dramas. At this point in her career, her choice of lighter fare was clearly driven by her concern to reach a broader audience. In another letter to Du Bois from December 1939, she contrasted her new play *I Gotta Home* with *Coal Dust*. Having realized that *Coal Dust* was "too heavy for immediate production" in New York, she was taking a different tact with *I Gotta Home*. "It is a comedy," she wrote, "frankly written to lighten people's hearts and make them laugh. I have high hopes for it" (Letter, December 1939).

She was critiqued for this strategy by Richard Wright and Theodore Ward, both of whom saw her politics as tepid at times. Ward felt she had insufficient nerve to pursue realist projects when she refused to continue directing his play *The Big White Fog* after its controversial preview, and Wright saw musicals like her *Swing Mikado* as "a waste of talent" (Horne 73, 76–78). But Graham questioned their approach as well. In yet another example of how Wright was not the penultimate embodiment of the African American left, a case Bill Mullen has made quite persuasively, Graham saw Wright and his *Native Son* as bad representatives of the African American cultural front.[33] She questioned the efficacy and veracity of his heavy-handed realism, writing that "to people who do not know the Negro 'Native Son' offers a very one sided picture." She noted of his famous novel: "That book turns my blood to vinegar and makes me weep for having borne two sons. They say it is a great book. Why?" (Letters, March 1940, March 1942). But even Graham's more cautious strategy was not enough to land her the audiences she desired, and as a consequence, her correspondence with future husband Du Bois exhibits recurrent financial anxiety. Yet an examination of the domestic comedy *I Gotta Home* illustrates the political efficacy of her "lighter" brand of realism, which could have illustrated a very different side of African American life had it received the proper support.

Graham's three-act comedy *I Gotta Home* was written in late 1939 while she was on a Rosenwald Fellowship at Yale University. It ran for two weeks in February and March 1940 at Western Reserve University in Cleveland. It was performed by the Gilpin Players of the Karamu Theater, who used the university's Eldred Hall because the Karamu's own space had been damaged by fire. It also played for one night at Oberlin with funding from the Oberlin Alumni Association. *I Gotta Home* is a revision of her earlier domestic comedy *Elijah's Ravens* (1930), which also played at the Karamu, and was briefly revived for two nights at Ohio State University in 1941 and at Dillard University in New Orleans that same year. *Ravens* also may have been produced in a number of other venues across the South.[34] Both works, as I will note, can be seen as her alternatives to *The Guiding Light*.

I Gotta Home is about the Cobbs, an African American family who live a threadbare existence in a church parsonage. The action is set entirely in this domestic space. The father, the Reverend Elijah Cobb, is an idealistic and slightly naive preacher with sincere devotion to the needs of his flock. But in his diligent service to his cash-strapped congregation, he is not good at collecting the church revenues demanded by its Presiding Elder. So as the play begins, his children E.J., Mirah, and Lilacs nervously discuss how their father is "behind with his dollar money again," and how they will probably have to move to a different parsonage for yet another time (228). In this sense, the play is autobiographical for Graham: her father was a minister for the African Methodist Episcopal Church whose politically inflected sermons mixing religion and civil rights, as well as his placement of self-sacrifice over bourgeois respectability, got him in trouble with its bishops. Thus the young Graham also had to move from place to place, from Seattle to Louisiana to the industrial cities of the Midwest, as the bishops kept sending her father away to unenviable parish assignments (Horne 39–40). The Presiding Elder in the play is Dr. Calab Green, who is referred to in the character list as "One of those hierarchical left-overs from the days of overseers." He is overweight and gluttonous, making bombastic proclamations as he devours all the food served to him by Mrs. Cobb out of her own family's budget, and it becomes clear that he and his entourage of deacons and stewardesses only care about money and the maintenance of their own class privilege. The children conspire to bail out their father without his knowledge, and the son E.J. temporarily spares the family the headache of once again having to move by drumming up money for the church and delivering it anonymously in an envelope. But the financial woes of the family are definitively resolved by Rev. Cobb's sister Mattie, reputedly a Hollywood heiress, who drops in from out of town. As it turns out, Mattie is a firebrand and a drunk who attacks white reporters, but no heiress. She is resourceful and good-hearted, however, and after she talks her friend Jasper out of an expensive horse-racing sweepstakes ticket, her horse wins, earning her and the Cobb family $50,000. *Elijah's Ravens* contains a quite similar plot and almost the same character list; the main differences is that in *Ravens*, Mattie does not win money for the family by gambling, but through an elaborate scheme to convince churchgoers that Elijah is an actual prophet (Graham Du Bois Papers, Box 42, folder 4).

I Gotta Home contains elements of realist theater, melodrama, and entertaining comedy at the same time (as the local color genre illustrates, realism and comedy were never antithetical, as evidenced by William Dean Howells's preference for comic figures in nineteenth century theater). Borrowing from melodrama, its nonvirtuous characters are clearly marked as such: Green and his entourage are transparently callous, and the wife of the local doctor, Mrs. Swan, is snobbish to an extraordinary, comic degree. Their physical attributes are likewise meant to clarify their repulsive personalities: Deacon Perkins is "a sour-faced little black man," and Calab Green has a ministerial garb "that encases layers of fat" (232, 234). But like realism, the play emphasizes the dialect of its characters; it centers on the trials of an ordinary family; its language is clear and non-self-referential; and it aspires to be a commentary on its place and time (listed in the stage directions as "1938," in "a large, Midwestern town"). Its alternate *Elijah's Ravens* brought together these elements as well, which earned it the label "The Play of Negro Life" (Du Bois, Letter to Graham, July 1941). But one key intertextual consideration also would have made this play legible as entertainment. Through *I Gotta Home* and *Elijah's Ravens*, Graham arguably drew upon her own experiences to offer an African American, left-wing alternative to one of the most popular soaps on the air at that time, *The Guiding Light*. First aired in 1937, two years before Graham wrote *I Gotta Home*, Irna Philips's famous soap also revolved around the troubles and joys of a reverend and his family. Reverend John Rutledge, its focal character, earnestly ministered to his congregation in a fictionalized "small Midwestern town" called Five Points; as in Graham's two plays, many of the episodes centered on the women around him, and much of the dialogue was set in his home.

Though a comedy, its social critique comes through quite clearly: the play highlights the class divisions among African Americans, and particularly the corruption of black clergy's upper echelons. Graham shows this not only through the money troubles of the Cobbs in relation to the gluttony of the elders, but also through those of Rev. Cobb's friend Brother Pugh. Pugh is a poor preacher lacking in education but, like Cobb, wholeheartedly devoted to his parish and short in his revenue collections. He sadly tells Cobb: "Ah ain't up wid dese new times ... Hit ustta be all right cause Ah knows 'bout sorrow an' sufferin'—knows 'bout da love o' Jesus," adding "Nobody wants to hyear dos things no more. Ah can' raise money" (246). Cobb naively disagrees with Pugh about the priorities of the church elders, but then offers to help by giving his friend one of his old coats. The decidedly nonrealist end, in which the family's woes are solved by a winning sweepstakes ticket, was arguably Graham's attempt to compromise with her audience, delivering a definite social critique, but in terms not so heavy as to ruin their entertainment. In contrast to *Native Son*, *I Gotta Home* balances out its portrait of "negro life" by representing both admirable and dishonorable figures within the community, and uses a much less sensational plot to do so. Her domestic setting and family plot provide an established arena for the emergence of virtue, facilitating the positive representation of black character and creating less potential for misreading by white audiences.

But like Hellman and the soap operas, Graham directs attention to the women characters, particularly the Reverend's wife Mrs. Cobb and his sister Mattie. The Reverend is largely absent until the end of the first act, which instead focuses on his wife's frantic attempts to keep the house in order, marshal the children, and serve food to the church elders. She furiously works to maintain the parsonage throughout the play, and is constantly distracted as her attention is diverted to some new household crisis, like a broken window or a leaky faucet. While illustrating Rev. Cobb's genuine virtues, Graham also suggests that Mrs. Cobb has had to pay for his idealism through her ceaseless labor and worry. In no way a comic character, Mrs. Cobb loses patience with her husband, telling him: "For twenty years I've listened to you tellin' me why other people should have so much and we should have so little—for twenty years I been seein' other men pass you by one by one—while you talk, talk, talk. These other men think about their families ... their wives can have something—their children can be somebody" (264). In short, Graham shows through Mrs. Cobb how the capitalist ethos of the church elders enters domestic space and takes its greatest toll on the women who work to maintain it. Women's labor is also shown to enable the male idealism of her son Toussant. Like his namesake, Toussant aspires to be a leader, praising Paul Robeson and Paul Lawrence Dunbar to whoever will listen (239–40). In the hands of the early Richard Wright, Toussant likely would have functioned as the dialectical negation of his churchgoing father, forging a Marxist consciousness out of the best qualities of his father's religion. But in stark contrast to Richard Wright's "Bright and Morning Star," in which the mother Sue sacrifices herself to save her communist son and the Party he holds dear, Mrs. Cobb and her daughter Mirah merely clean up around Toussant as he makes lofty speeches. He remains a minor character who merely annoys his mother by asking her intellectual questions as she works.[35]

These domestic women are juxtaposed with the Reverend's sister, Mattie Cobb—a character Graham uses to comment on the position of black women in the culture industries and to frustrate the appeal of extant soap operas. The Cobbs and the elders learn of her coming arrival from a tabloid paper the *Chicago Watchtower*. This tabloid has reported that Mattie has inherited a fortune from Sadie Kessler, the "beloved star of stage and screen" for whom she worked as a maid, and they anticipate her appearance as if a visit from royalty (236). As it turns out, Sadie was indeed a close companion of Mattie, but she died broke, and Mattie is trying to work every trick she knows to get to New York, where her connections have promised her a job (259). Mattie is an unequivocally confident, powerful woman who makes her entrance on stage by punching a white reporter who tries to take her picture (251). Immediately before this brash introduction, Calab Green wrongly predicts she will be a "broken an—Poor, lonely little thing" who will need someone to take care of her (Green wants to marry her and live off her fortune) (250). Clearly, Mattie needs the charity of no man, and as I indicated above, it is the deal she cuts with her friend Jasper that saves the day. As in so many soap operas, it is the agency of a female character that spares the family. At the same time, the character of Mattie dispels a recurrent fantasy perpetuated by the soaps. If the frequency of Broadway or Hollywood careers among soap opera characters capitalized on the allure of the stage and screen among daytime radio listeners, Graham frustrates this fantasy by suggesting that there can be no Hollywood glamour for black women (which proved to be the case for her as well). She compromises with mass-culture convention by including a character with some connection to the glamour of the theater and the motion picture industry. But she exposes as delusional the belief of ordinary African American characters that the riches of Hollywood and Broadway might somehow come to them. Through Mattie, Graham suggests that Hollywood is an empty fantasy for black women, but in contrast to their degraded representations by that industry, African American women are not lacking in strength or resourcefulness.

The author keeps the tone of the play relatively light, not only through its happy end and comic interactions but by showing a family who, despite its troubles, is genuinely devoted to each other. In all, *I Gotta Home* avoids overt critiques of whites, exposes class hierarchies among African Americans as they play out in the domestic realm, highlights the labor of women that enables male leaders, and positively celebrates the strength of the black family. It does so, moreover, using an entertaining hybrid of theatrical realism that would have been perfectly suited to the mass-culture milieu of its day. The play was well received in the Cleveland press, both black and white, as was *Elijah's Ravens* in the venues in which it appeared in the South and Midwest.[36] Her brand of domestic realism might have fared quite well if given the opportunity of a national tour, or even filmic adaptation, but this was not to be. While Graham enjoyed the success of *I Gotta Home* and *Elijah's Ravens*, her satisfaction was tempered by her acknowledgment that it was merely playing in "the hinterlands," as she put it (Letter, April 1940). The Theater Guild in New York considered a revised version of *Elijah's Ravens*, but nothing came of it (Letter, May 1941). A range of papers discussed Graham as an up-and-coming playwright, including *Variety*, the *Atlanta World*, and *P.M.*, yet she never managed to fully "break through the barriers."

Graham's attempt to reach a mass audience a few years later was successful, but once again not with her realist material. She stopped writing about the lives of ordinary individuals and began writing a series of popular and critically acclaimed biographies of famous African Americans, the first of which was *George Washington Carver, Scientist* (1944). As this intellectual labor earned her far more money than playwriting, she continued turning out such books for decades, writing biographies on Fredrick Douglass, Phyllis Wheatley, and Paul Robeson in the 1940s, and figures as divergent as Gamal Abdul Nasser, Julius Nyerere, and Booker T. Washington much later (with a few exceptions, all of these books were on men). She began writing radio dramas around 1944, two of which were broadcast on CBS to wide acclaim. Both of these were dialogue-driven narratives of the lives of famous black Americans—one on Phyllis Wheatley and the other growing out of her recent book on George Washington Carver. If, as Barbara Savage has argued, the 1930s and 1940s were decades in which African Americans had virtually no direct influence and control on national network radio, this should be regarded a rare moment indeed (12). Graham was greatly excited when a movie producer expressed interest in her Carver project, but no such film came to fruition (Horne 104). Her success did encourage her, however, to venture into virtual terra incognita for a female Popular Front playwright, black or white: the radio serial.

Graham's earlier work for radio was aired locally on WICC in New Haven, Connecticut, in 1940. *Track Thirteen* was a blend of mystery and realism centering around a sleeping-car porter hassled by demands of white passengers; although light in tone, the play presented the demands of white mothers in particular to be unrewarding labor for black workers—a response to the harmonious, domestic scenes presented in shows like *Brenda Curtis*.[37] In 1945 she decided to take her work for this medium to a larger and more ambitious level, writing and promoting a prospectus and a pilot episode for a radio series about an African American family entitled "The Bannekers." According to *Variety*, the entertainment-industry newspaper, this serial was "making the rounds" in New York City in March 1945. *Variety* noted, "It's generally thought that some all-Negro broadcasts may come after the war when time eases up" ("Another All-Negro Serial"). But while a number of black-cast soap operas were aired much later in the 1950s, a result of increasing civil rights agitation and the decentralization of radio ownership triggered by television, this was not the moment for Graham.[38] I have found no evidence that "The Bannekers" was ever broadcast, especially not on national radio.

In stark contrast to the famous individuals in her biographies, the pilot and the prospectus stress the ordinary nature of the Bannekers, yet optimistically acknowledge their potential for fame. The Announcer of the pilot introduces them as "just another family living on the edge of Harlem—nothing special about them—no celebrities—no heroes, that is, not *yet*. Never can tell what might happen these days" (1). Like so many soap operas, the pilot is set almost entirely in the family's home. Unlike the protagonists of many soap operas, the Bannekers do not speak boarding school English; however, only the lines of the Grandmother from South Carolina are written in thick dialect. Though ordinary individuals, they are, like Mattie in *I Gotta Home*, remotely tied to fame through their possession of a clock made by Benjamin Banneker, a famous African American clock-maker, astronomer, and mathematician who lived in eighteenth-century Maryland (and the subject of one of Graham's biographies). The family got the name Banneker when one of their slave ancestors came into the possession of one of the eighteenth-century artisan's clocks and decided to name himself after its maker. The grandmother brings the clock—the family's prize heirloom—with her from South Carolina to Harlem, where it sits in the family's living room. The link to black achievement via Banneker underscores the author's emphasis on the potential, untapped talent within ordinary African American families and marks the author's attempt to create a hybrid serial genre drawing not only upon realism but also on popular autobiography—another mode with which she was well acquainted. Graham indicates that she will use the clock to create a usable past for African Americans, and to show the intersection between northern and southern black cultures. As she writes: "These people—living in today's exciting, pulsing Harlem, in the city of New York—will be projected upon a warm and human background rich with the past of two blending cultural patterns" (5). This cultural blending is to be reflected in her desired musical introduction for the show: "a medley of the old South, blending into tunes from Gershwin and Ellington, with a bit of boogy-woogy" (1).

The overall spirit of the pilot and prospectus is contributionist; that is to say, the author mentions nothing about racial oppression, and instead stresses the family's positive, middle-class typicality and its contributions to the war effort. Pa Banneker is a "good provider" who works for a black-owned life insurance agency; Ma Banneker is active in the Abyssinian Baptist Church and has "lots of civic pride"; their son Dan is serving in the South Pacific, and their daughter Sally is a good-natured young woman who "flits about" from job to job but still does her part by serving in the U.S.O. Finally, their son Sam Banneker is an Army Air Corps pilot trained at Tuskegee who has just earned his wings, as the family discovers in the first episode; Graham depicts them beaming with pride. The only white man in the pilot episode, Mr. Wentworth, is a good-natured, friendly neighbor of their grandmother from South Carolina who has accompanied and assisted the old woman on her journey from South Carolina to New York. Wentworth tells Pa Banneker, "You know, Banneker—our folks have lots in common. We're not so bad down home as lots of people seem to think" (15). His gentlemanly aid to the grandmother leaves no reason to doubt this claim. Issues of racial justice may have cropped up as the theme of individual episodes had the series been allowed to continue—Graham no doubt had to be super-conservative in her initial pitch to radio executives—but we will never know.

Graham was certainly masking her own wartime experiences in this contributionist radio serial. Unlike Sally Banneker, Graham was forced out of the U.S.O. in Fort Huachuca, Arizona, after fighting the widespread discrimination against black soldiers there; and while she expressed great pride when her youngest son Graham became one of the Tuskegee Airmen, she reacted with horror when he was initially drafted in 1943 at a mere eighteen years of age, writing to Du Bois, "I was somewhat prepared for Robert's going in, but not at all for Graham. I know too much about this United States Army!" (Letter, June 1943). Yet despite all the punches she pulled in writing the pilot of "The Bannekers," even this ultra-cautious, celebratory attempt to promote black humanity—one expertly conceived to arouse no controversy among the guardians of the airwaves—was not aired. In 1945 it was still virtually impossible for women of color to break into the heavily vetted world of the serial drama.

African American women writers would reach a mass audience as realists more frequently after 1945. Not only did Ann Petry's 1946 novel *The Street* sell over a million copies, but the realist plays of Alice Childress and Lorraine Hansberry were produced on a grander scale than those of any African American female playwright writing before the war. Graham, meanwhile, in the 1960s finally found an audience larger than she had ever enjoyed before—but in Ghana. As with Carlos Bulosan, who I will discuss in chapter 4, Graham's work would move in more obviously transnational directions after the war, and would find sizable audiences outside the United States as the Cold War took shape. Nevertheless, during the Depression and war the Popular Front valiantly aided, but was unable to complete, the creation of a culture that would expand the narrative authority of African American women into new aesthetic arenas within the United States.

The Popular Front writers Shirley Graham and Lillian Hellman were both quite adept at navigating the restrictive demands of U.S. culture industries. Yet the limited representational politics of soap operas such as *Brenda Curtis* would go unchallenged on the genre's home turf of daytime radio until after the Popular Front disbanded. This is not to say that women writers on the left failed to speak to a mass audience at all—works such as *These Three* and *Swing Mikado* prove otherwise. That the work of Hellman and Graham made it onto the airwaves, even in politically compromised form, marks a significant breakthrough. But the difficulties faced by women in obtaining employment as writers within the culture industries, the particularly restrictive corporate structure of daytime radio, and the deprioritization of women's concerns in public, political discourse prevented women on the left from directly defining whole genres targeted to women as did male Popular Front writers with the male-coded boxing, gangster, and detective narratives. For audiences, the persistent appearance of serial forms and recognizable popular genres turns narrative consumption into everyday ritual; intervening in this ritual affords authors an indispensable opportunity to create a new common sense. Offering a more sustained narrative of domesticity theoretically would have engrained Popular Front sensibilities even more deeply into the daily lives of many female audiences. As the next chapter will suggest, the inability of the Popular Front to define mass-culture genres for women would help ensure that the most widely received female realist of the 1930s and 1940s was not a writer on the left at all.

CHAPTER THREE

Realism with a Little Sex in It
Erskine Caldwell's Challenge to *Gone with the Wind*

While the major dramas of Lillian Hellman took place all over the national map, mass-mediated boxing narratives were almost always set in urban centers in the Northeast or Midwest. True to the "local color" tradition of American realism that marked the genre in its earlier phases, these stories of troubled prizefighters eschewed universality in order to announce their precise location. *Golden Boy*, for instance, was set in New York, *Native Son* and *Never Come Morning* took place on the South Side of Chicago, and *Body and Soul* began in the Bronx. A standard feature of the Hollywood boxing film was a montage of fight posters and falling opponents that telegraphically established the rise of the protagonist's career; almost without fail, these posters advertised fights above the Mason-Dixon Line and east of the Mississippi. And the wisecracking, tough-guy dialects of the boxers and their entourage, like those of their counterparts in detective and gangster films, definitively evoked the urban cultures of the Northeast. While it can be said that the cultures of Northern cities were overrepresented in mass-mediated realism of the 1930s and 1940s—particularly in film—rural life was far from invisible. Indeed, these Northeastern and Chicago tough guys appeared alongside a range of increasingly familiar rural characters in the mass culture of the era. In the publishing industry, a look at U.S. bestseller lists from the 1930s and early 1940s suggests that the inclusion of an agrarian theme was almost a prerequisite for major literary success in the Depression decade and beyond. If one considers Pearl Buck's *The Good Earth* (bestseller in 1931 and 1932), Margaret Mitchell's *Gone with the Wind* (1936 and 1937), John Steinbeck's *Grapes of Wrath* (1939), and Richard Llewellyn's *How Green Was My Valley* (1940), one finds that some degree of rural nostalgia suffused the novels in the number one best-seller slot for six of the ten years between 1931 and 1940 (Hackett, *70 Years* 143–61).

In fact, the two most widely read novels of the 1930s and 1940s were set not only in the countryside but in rural Georgia: Margaret Mitchell's *Gone with the Wind* and Erskine Caldwell's *God's Little Acre*. Their authors benefited from the widespread longing for agrarian life wrought by the Depression and the war; they responded by using realism to present the "true" rural South to national and even international audiences. Significantly, their portraits contested one another, a result of their authors' diametrically opposed political positions. Mitchell's response to a piece of fan mail in September 1936 is quite revealing in this regard. The fan, a doctor from Ohio, had apparently asked if she was familiar with the work of the other famous southern writer at the time, Erskine Caldwell. "I did not see 'Tobacco Road' but I read the book," she replied, referring to Caldwell's famous Broadway play and novel: "When I read it I thought it was intended for a grand parody on the gloomy Russian novelists and I laughed almost as much as I did over 'Gentlemen Prefer Blondes.' Shortly afterwards, I learned it was supposed to be stark realism and must admit I was somewhat bewildered!" (Harwell 66). The exact contents of the original letter from Ohio are unknown, but the fan's reference to *Tobacco Road* confirms that Mitchell's portrait of the region was contested by a rival narrative of the South in the national arena. Her flippant dismissal of Caldwell's status as a realist hints at their divergent politics, but it also reveals a great deal about the relationship between aesthetics and narrative authority in the 1930s. Pitting "stark realism" against popular entertainment, Mitchell's response is yet another reminder of how the label of realism was necessary to authorize any ontological claims among her generation of writers, even if one was writing for a mass audience.

Mitchell had good reason to be flippant. Her novel and its cinematic counterpart had already begun to cement a comforting image of the South and its history in the national imagination during the 1930s and 1940s—one of bucolic plantations and fertile cotton fields, charming planters and docile slaves. *Gone with the Wind* was number one on the best-seller list in 1936 and 1937 and would sell more than 8.6 million copies to become one of the best-selling books of the twentieth century.[1] Its film adaptation was perhaps even more of a critical and popular success; in 1939 it won four Academy Awards, including Best Picture, and is still hailed as a cinematic classic. To this day, *Gone with the Wind* (hereafter, *GWTW*) has been held as *the* epic narrative of the South and its history among many people both inside and outside the region.

It would be easy to conclude that the representation of the South put forward by *GWTW* achieved complete hegemony in U.S. popular culture, and further, has been hegemonic for quite some time. But the truth is much more complicated. While the popular diffusion of *GWTW* is widely acknowledged, much less well known is that the novel was outsold by *God's Little Acre* for several decades. Published in 1933, Caldwell's story of poor white Georgia farmers and mill hands eventually sold more than 8 million copies, making it not only the most commercially successful novel on the South through the 1960s, but also the third best-selling work of fiction in the United States for the first seventy years of the twentieth century. Unlike Mitchell's novel, Caldwell's popularity took off more slowly, his sales not exploding until the 1940s when his work was marketed in cheap paperback editions. But by 1965 *God's Little Acre* had still outsold *GWTW*, and Mitchell's novel only surpassed Caldwell's sales a decade later (and only slightly at that).[2] Compared to *GWTW*, however, the transition of *God's Little Acre* from page to cinematic stage proved much less remarkable. Released in 1958, the success of the film adaptation among both critics and audiences was relatively limited.

The challenge posed to Mitchell's epic by *God's Little Acre* (hereafter, *GLA*) and by other popular novels of Caldwell is significant; for, despite the flaws in Caldwell's work, the portrait of the South he constructed for national audiences placed his novels within the cultural project of "the People's Century," as it would come to be known. Mitchell, in contrast, came to see her work as a rebuke to the very notion of "the people" increasingly popularized by Caldwell and others. The setting of *GWTW* within a sanitized slave economy provided its Depression-era audiences with an Edenic past to look back upon, while its ruthlessly practical heroine offered a moral model for survival after the Fall. Its depictions of African Americans as simple and helpless, as well as its portrayal of poor whites as criminal and treacherous, revised both the slave past and the need for continued planter-class control in the present. Not surprisingly, Mitchell was explicitly conservative in her politics. The appeal of *GWTW*'s general message of "survival" to Depression-era audiences has already been established by critics (Morton 52–56, Pauly 164–76). Generally overlooked, however, is how Mitchell came to view her novel's significance within the battle over class and racial formations of the era, both domestically and abroad. The extent of Mitchell's conservatism is illustrated by one of her literary associates, who claimed, "I practiced silence during Margaret's vituperative denunciations of F.D.R. and all his works" (Pyron 438). In a letter to archconservative psychologist Dr. Henry Link in 1941, she could not contain her pride that he had used her character Scarlett to illustrate his individualist, anti–New Deal philosophy. Referring to *GWTW*, Link had written, "Ten million readers! Ten million nostalgic gasps from the victims of a machine concept of social security, a people still faintly protesting against the loss of personal responsibility" (Harwell 342).[3]

Georgia-born Erskine Caldwell was, by contrast (and despite his later claim to be "a writer, not a reformer"), heavily involved with the various social movements for economic and racial justice in the 1930s and 1940s, and he intended his work to further these movements. Caldwell sat on the national advisory board of the communist Film and Photo League, supported the Communist Party's presidential candidate in the 1932 election, wrote for the Popular Front tabloid *P.M.*, and tirelessly agitated for southern sharecroppers in print and in touring lectures with his second wife, Margaret Bourke-White (Alexander 30). And despite his postwar claims never to have been a Marxist or even a fellow traveler, he traveled to Sofia as late as 1984 to receive the Bulgarian Ministry of Culture's Medal of Merit and a standing ovation from the assembled audience (Klevar 410). Given these politics, his work eschews the planter class to focus on the attempts of poor whites to make ends meet in the decaying Georgia countryside, impoverished South Carolina mill towns, and Gulf Coast industrial centers of the Depression and war years. Unique among proletarian realisms of the decade, however, Caldwell's novels possess a humorous side that makes it easy for readers to both empathize with *and* laugh at his highly flawed characters—at their own notions of racial superiority, at their bizarre attempts to get ahead, at their sexual relationships, and more. As a result, while in both film and novel *GWTW* is littered with African American stereotypes and was boycotted by civil rights organizations in the 1930s and 1940s, the racial and class politics of Caldwell's work were praised by no less than Richard Wright and NAACP president Walter White (Klevar 231, McDonald 114).

Considered in the context of the proletarian novel, the sales figures of Caldwell's work are even more intriguing. Most class-conscious literary works about factory workers, mill hands, and downtrodden farmers did not achieve a mass audience in the United States. Of all the anticapitalist stories of working-class life, only John Steinbeck's *Grapes of Wrath* made the American top ten list during the 1930s. But while the work of literary leftists Mike Gold, Jack Conroy, Josephine Herbst, and John Dos Passos achieved critical praise but modest popular recognition, seemingly everything Caldwell put to print broke sales records. Out of the top forty best-selling works of fiction in the United States between 1895 and 1965, six were written by Erskine Caldwell (Hackett, *70 Years* 12–14). I hope to illuminate the reasons these southern stories of social conflict did so well in the arena of mass culture, an arena where so many other proletarian novels did not make their mark.

Addressing the popular appeal of Caldwell's work will require an exploration of the politics and aesthetics of his novels, a look at their reception by critics on the left, and a brief consideration of their marketing and textual history. It must be noted that his aesthetic was not legible to most critics on the left as realism, a label necessary for a work to be considered viable, political art at midcentury. In an era when this term was rather broadly applied by modern standards—granted to works as far apart in form as the experimental *U.S.A. Trilogy* by Dos Passos and the classic naturalist novel *The Jungle* by Upton Sinclair—it is worth wondering why Caldwell's work did not merit the label (Foley 54–57). I will argue here that it was difficult for many critics to see Caldwell as a realist writer not only because of how his work was marketed, but also because of his departure from the kind of novel advocated by many among the mid-century left. In so doing, I will use this chapter as an opportunity to explore notions of realism common among left-wing critics in the 1930s and 1940s, with particular attention to their amenability to mass-mediated realism. Caldwell's success came as a result of his blend of realist, southern, and mass-culture aesthetic elements—namely, realism, the southern grotesque, the pleasures of humor, and (particularly for his heterosexual male readers) sexual allure. This brand of mass-mediated realism, formulaically deployed in most of his novels in the 1930s and 1940s, may illuminate the reasons for his popularity as well.

The discomfort of many left and liberal critics toward Caldwell is reflected in more recent scholarship on the 1930s and 1940s in which, despite his immense diffusion throughout popular culture, he receives scant attention at best. Barbara Foley's *Radical Representations* and Michael Denning's *The Cultural Front*, both seminal works on the proletarian novel and left cultural politics of the 1930s, give him only passing mention, and few of the many articles emerging from the revived interest in the 1930s left over the last ten years have dealt with his work in a sustained manner.[4] This is not to say that Caldwell's politics were so avant-garde as to be beyond the register of contemporary scholars; indeed, as I will attempt to show, his politics were deeply flawed. It *is* to say that Caldwell's work provides us with an excellent opportunity to reflect on the conditions under which a proletarian novel could become mass culture, an opportunity yet to be explored. And while far fewer young people in the United States are familiar with the story of *GLA* in comparison to *GWTW*, it is difficult to say whether the tenacity of Caldwell's image of the South within U.S. popular culture has been less profound. Caldwell has undoubtedly left subtle marks on U.S. popular culture that have not been examined to date, and while the precise impact of Caldwell's southern figures on U.S. and international audiences is beyond the scope of this book, I hope this will serve as the beginning of an inquiry.

In using the Marxian criticism of the period to frame the work of Caldwell, my intention is not to paint him as some kind of "dissident" writing from the margins of the left after being shut out by its gatekeepers at the *New Masses* or the *Daily Worker*. As James Murphy, Barbara Foley, Michael Denning, and Alan Wald have shown in their respective ways, the idea of a Moscow-driven "core" of communist cultural producers effectively disciplining a larger body of leftists and left sympathizers with a uniform political aesthetic is a construction of the Cold War.[5] The "center" of the left at this time was exceedingly difficult to find; more than this, the attempt to find it is futile, as it exercised little real power to control the larger cultural movement on the U.S. scene. For example, Caldwell did not see eye to eye with Mike Gold, the influential editor of the *New Masses* from 1926 to 1933 and also a lifelong columnist at the *Daily Worker*. Caldwell stated in a letter that Gold "doesn't think so much of my Communism ... and he devoted most of our conversations to harangue. I tried to argue my special brand of communism with him, but I had little success" (Klevar 107). But this "harangue" did not prevent Caldwell from being an active and influential participant in the mid-century left—even in communist organizations such as the Film and Photo League. Rather, my interest in using mid-century Marxian criticism as a frame stems from an engagement with that criticism, and its successes and failures in comprehending the audiences for cultural production unfolding around it.

To establish the image of the South that Caldwell and Mitchell wanted to project in the national eye, we first should look at the politics within their most famous novels, as well as their contemporary critical reception. In my section on Caldwell, I will be basing my assertions on his six best-selling novels, all of which were published between 1932 and 1944 and contain roughly the same representational dynamic. These six novels are *Tobacco Road* (1932), which sold 3.4 million copies; *God's Little Acre* (1933), 8 million; *Journeyman* (1935), 3.9 million; *Trouble in July* (1940), 3.5 million; *Georgia Boy* (1943), 3.5 million; and *Tragic Ground* (1944), 4.8 million (Hackett, *70 Years* 12–14). I will devote special attention, however, to his most famous book, *GLA*. In examining the politics of these novels, one positive pattern that emerges is their affront to the American exceptionalism implicit in the popular idea of the yeoman farmer.

Margaret Mitchell and the Politics of "Gumption"

What made *GWTW* an organic cultural narrative to so many white Southerners is not only how it vindicated the historical record of the South within a compelling romance plot, but also, ironically, how it "updated" the South to a national audience. The story shows its protagonists to be the masters of both modernity and capitalism—the very forces to which the South was supposedly antithetical. Mitchell was not the first to link the region to modernity; this linkage had been central to the ideologues of the first "New South." Rather, the political significance of the novel lies in its reassertion of this linkage at a moment of intense social and political crisis. Mitchell wrote all but three chapters of the novel's first draft from 1926 to 1929, but as Pyron's biography of Mitchell has shown, she relentlessly revised it during the 1930s up until its publication in 1936, adding significant new material on the Ku Klux Klan around 1933 which will be discussed later in this chapter (280, 288). The constant revisions during the 1930s make the novel as much a product of the 1930s as the 1920s. By imbuing Scarlett O'Hara with the spirit of modernity, *GWTW* articulated the kind of heroic subjectivity necessary to restore the class and racial formations threatened by left social movements of the Depression era.

A coalition of working-class whites, middle-class liberals, and working-class blacks was indeed forming in the South as Mitchell was revising her novel in the 1930s; the most well-publicized "front" upon which this coalition labored was the Scottsboro trials, begun in 1931. As Robin D. G. Kelley has shown, many African Americans in Alabama saw the arrival of the Northern-based Communist Party in the South as a second Reconstruction come to liberate the region, and received it enthusiastically. Kelley argues that many southern black radicals attracted to the party even regarded the Soviets as "the New Yankees" (*Hammer* 99–100). Whether or not Mitchell revised her novel with this coalition consciously in mind is purely speculative. What is clear, however, is that Mitchell was increasingly aware of the role her narrative played in the emergent political coalitions after its publication in 1936. In a 1937 article in the *Crisis*, George Schuyler had written of Mitchell, "Some of her malicious outbursts are unparalleled in the worst cracker diatribes" (2). He caustically added, "It WOULD be a best seller" (3). On the same page was a plug for an article in the next issue, wherein John Davis of the National Negro Congress (a Popular Front organization) would explain the multiracial organizing of the CIO. The CPUSA, the *Chicago Defender*, and the rest of the organized left banded together to boycott the film *GWTW* when it opened in Chicago's theaters in 1939 (Mullen 4). Cognizant of this organizing opportunity that her work was providing, Mitchell slid revealingly between the 1930s left and the post–Civil War Northern occupation when she wrote in 1939, "The Radical press tried to use 'Gone with the Wind' as a whip to drive the southern Negroes into the Communist Party somewhat in the same manner that 'Uncle Tom's Cabin' was used to recruit Abolitionists. Of course, you know how happy it made me to have the Radical publications dislike [it]" (Harwell 273). Darden Ashbury Pyron suggests that the constant attack from the left on *GWTW* helped solidify and define Mitchell's political thinking. After the war, she quite consciously placed her novel in service of the fight against international communism, linking the reviews of her work in the Soviet bloc to the reviews in *Daily Worker*, and serializing *GWTW* in a Gaullist publication in France to increase its readership. Her agent, George Brett, signed the permission to use the novel with the phrase "Yours for the death of Communism" (436–43).

Much has been written about Mitchell's famous narrative, and the scholarship to date has been essential in enabling this study. Amazingly, however, very few of the scores of essays written on her work examine the convergence of its class and racial politics.[6] As some critics have already argued, the novel *GWTW* is not really guided by nostalgia, though this was not because Mitchell was highly critical of slavery or the antebellum South. The novel presents slave labor as essentially humane; Scarlett's father, Gerald, we are told, "could not bear to see a slave pouting under a reprimand, no matter how well deserved, or hear a kitten mewing or a child crying" (19). The southern world enabled by slavery is represented throughout the early part of the novel as a site of abundance, with lavish barbeques and elegant parties. Mitchell suggests, however, that there is no turning back the clock to this golden age. Though the antebellum South may have been a wonderful place, the war destroyed that society, and Scarlett must repress its memory as much as possible in order to function in the present. Commenting on Scarlett's return to Tara immediately after the war, Mitchell writes: "Throughout the South for fifty years there would be bitter-eyed women who looked backward to dead times, to dead men, evoking memories that hurt and were futile, bearing poverty with bitter pride . . . But Scarlett was never to look back" (283).

The novel posits the destruction of antebellum southern society as a historical rupture, like others before and since, which allows for the individual's raw talents and inner fortitude to emerge through the course of social regeneration. As if the course of events in the novel were not enough to convey this notion, Mitchell articulates it for the reader in the words of Rhett Butler. In a conversation with Scarlett, he reasons,

> This isn't the first time the world's been upside down and it won't be the last. It's happened before and it'll happen again. And when it does happen, everyone loses everything and everyone is equal. And then they all start again at taw, with nothing at all. That is, nothing except the cunning of their brains and the strength of their hands. But some people, like Ashley, have neither cunning nor strength . . . And they go under and

they should go under. It's a natural law and the world is better off without them. But there are always a hardy few who come through and, given time, they are right back where they were before the world turned over. (514)

The recurrent word that Mitchell uses to signal her heroines and heroes to the reader is "gumption," a quality that encompasses the classic bourgeois virtues of energy, ruthlessness, and business acumen. Those lacking in gumption are not simply the traditional have-nots; Ashley Wilkes, to whom Rhett's commentary is aimed, is the quintessential southern gentleman. Those with "neither cunning or strength" in the face of adversity are plentiful in the ranks of the old southern elite as represented in the novel—Cathleen Calvert (471), the McRae family (478), Hugh Elsing, Frank Kennedy, and Suellen O'Hara, to name a few.

Nonetheless, the theory of history espoused by *GWTW* vindicates the old planter class. Despite the leveling effect that Mitchell describes via Rhett, no character in the novel who was poor before the war actually rises substantially in the years that follow. Those with gumption, the raw quality that allows one to be on top when the world turns right side up again, all hail from the antebellum elite: Mrs. Merriwether (514), Grandma Fontaine and her son Alex (478), Rene Picard (514), and, of course, Scarlett O'Hara and Rhett Butler. Former slaves remain in states of servility, helplessness, or debauchery after the war, and the only way blacks or poor whites rise to any position of real authority is through the system of criminal graft enabled by the "bayonet rule" of Reconstruction. Upon close inspection, we find that gumption, though at first glance a properly bourgeois quality accessible to anyone regardless of caste or privilege, is actually an innate quality of certain unique bloodlines within the *ancien régime*. When Scarlett returns to Tara after the war, she realizes that her ancestors, "whose blood flowed in her veins," always had the will to conquer, as they had endured Napoleon's throne, English landlords, and the Haitian revolution, always recovering their fortunes (278). Grandma Fontaine relates the same narrative of ancestry to Scarlett; her lineage was also comprised of aristocrats thrust out of France, England, Scotland, and Haiti by popular revolutions (both class- and race-based), but they always emerged victorious through the force of their will. Thus rather than enabling a full meritocracy, the Civil War according to Mitchell purged the old elite of its less capable elements while providing opportunities for some of the women within its ranks.

It is important to note that the recovery of wealth, enabled by the possession of conquering blood, involves the recomposition of hierarchical class and racial formations. In the novel, turning the world right side up again fundamentally involves putting blacks and poor whites back "in their place," a place that has been destabilized by the war and Reconstruction governments imposed on the South. Significantly, the foundational act of Scarlett's agency is her striking of the slave Prissy, a character Mitchell uses as a marker against which Scarlett's gumption is measured. The siege of Atlanta, during which Scarlett must deliver Melanie Hamilton's baby as the battle rages outside, provides the first real test of the heroine's character, as it is the first time she must truly fend for herself without the advantages of her privileged upbringing (241). While Prissy is reduced to "teeth chattering idiocy" (217) and the repetition of the famous phrase "Ah doan know nuthin' 'bout bringin' babies" (241), Scarlett rises to the occasion, taking command of the scene to deliver the child successfully. She has learned to dominate others in this moment of self-definition, as demonstrated by her striking Prissy for her cowardice. Mitchell writes, "She had never struck a slave in all her life, but now she slapped the black cheek with all the force in her tired arm." Immediately afterward, Scarlett speaks "with authority in her voice" for the first time in the narrative (242).[7]

But as Mitchell demonstrates, the larger social transformations of the South were much more difficult to control. The Northern occupation of Georgia, as rendered in the novel, has allowed "no account" poor whites of the old regime, like Hilton, Jonas Wilkerson, the MacIntoshes, and the Slatterys (the latter Mitchell described as "shiftless and whining," possessing "little energy"), to take positions of power via the Freedman's Bureau (32). There, the author relates, they "stir up" former slaves with false atrocity stories in order to consolidate their new power over their former betters, ultimately endangering white womanhood. To Scarlett, Reconstruction means "The negroes were on top and behind them were the Yankee bayonets. She could be killed, she could be raped, and very probably, nothing would be done about it" (430). The remedy lies in the conquering blood of the planter class: "Gerald's blood was in her, violent blood . . . Violent blood was in them all, perilously close to the surface, lurking just beneath the kindly courteous exteriors. All of them, all the men she knew, even the drowsy-eyed Ashley and fidgety old Frank, were like that underneath—murderous, violent if the need arose. Even Rhett . . . had killed a negro for being 'uppity to a lady'" (431). This violent blood, essentially masculine in its manifestation, congeals politically in the Ku Klux Klan, represented in the novel as a "tragic necessity" that attempted to restore the class and racial lines blurred by Northern rule (435).

Given this context, it is not a coincidence that when Scarlett is assaulted in the shantytown, it is by two attackers: an ex-slave and a poor white man. The fact that one of her attackers is white prompts Pyron to suggest that *GWTW* is a subversion of the older Lost Cause romance, as it helps deracialize the incident (585). Mitchell's move, I would argue, is not so much a subversion as an updating of the older narrative à la Griffith, Dixon, or even its antebellum incarnation. In the antebellum plantation novel, according to Susan Tracy, the climax of the plot almost always depicted a heroic planter and his faithful, desexualized slave defending a virtuous planter-class woman from a poor or middle-class white villain (9). In response to emancipation, *Birth of a Nation* modified this formula in its pivotal scene by making the attacker of the planter-class woman a black sexual predator, not a low-born white. Thus, while some form of attack from below on an upper-class white woman was a standard feature of conservative southern literature, the nature of that attack in *GWTW* marks a rupture with the past. By figuring the attack on Scarlett as a class-based, multiracial one, Mitchell imagines the assault on elite white womanhood to be constituted by an unholy coalition of freed blacks and dispossessed whites, a coalition whose acts are given political authority by progressive Northerner occupiers.

In sum, *GWTW* created a usable past through which affluent Southerners could rediscover the gumption in their veins and reassert their power—a power threatened by a dynamic new political movement. Significantly, one of the few chapters composed from scratch by Mitchell in the 1930s depicted a crisis surrounding the death of Scarlett's husband as he performed his "duty" as a Klansman. His death occurred during a Klan raid that was intended to restore the heroine's honor vis-à-vis blacks and poor whites (Pyron 280, 288). The social movements of the 1930s, with their attendant notions of "the people," challenged white supremacy and capitalism with an intensity not seen in decades. Their official incarnation—the New Deal—was seen by Mitchell as a second Reconstruction that threatened to decompose established hierarchies. Like Reconstruction in the novel, "It wasn't to be bourne" (430).

Erskine Caldwell's Departure from Dialectical Realism

The gumption of Caldwell's southern characters is of a totally different sort: it is directed toward short-term gains, or toward some failed strategy to find a way out of their desperate situations. Their peculiar agency formed part of what one critic called a "Caldwellian pattern," which by 1940 had become clear in the author's work (Ivy 122). While the formulaic nature of Caldwell's novels was a disappointment to many contemporaneous critics, it fortunately allows the scholar to discuss them as a piece. This section will attempt to define the Caldwellian formula, and more importantly, to assess its politics.

To begin, his six most famous novels center around poor or lower-middle-class whites in the South, most often in his home state of Georgia. The setting is always either a farming community or a small industrial town, and whether they reside in the town or the country, the characters are never far from their agricultural roots. Caldwell also populated his stories with his own set of stock characters: the selfish but comical patriarch guided by instrumental reason is the most ubiquitous (Ty Ty Walden in *GLA*, Jeeter Lester in *Tobacco Road*, Spence Douthit in *Tragic Ground*, Morris Stroup in *Georgia Boy*, Clay Horey in *Journeyman*, and Sheriff Jeff McCurtain in *Trouble in July*). There is also the gullible utter simpleton, who sometimes doubles as the patriarch and is often overweight (Pluto Swint in *GLA*, Jeff McCurtain, Clay Horey). Then there is the wife or daughter who escapes the family and "runs off" to a mill or a town (Pearl Lester in *Tobacco Road*, Mavis Douthit in *Tragic Ground*, Lorene Horey in *Journeyman*, Rosamond Thompson in *GLA*). Not all of Caldwell's characters neatly fit into a pattern, however. The lusty preacher Semon Dye in *Journeyman*, the headstrong labor organizer Will Thompson in *GLA*, and the innocent young African American Sonny Clark in *Trouble in July* are unique to their particular stories.

Two main critiques of Caldwell's work emerged from the 1930s left. The first was that the poor southern whites in his novels were overly simplistic "caricatures." Edwin Rolfe wrote in the *New Masses* that even the most well-developed character in the story is "a complete caricature, developed through a series of witty exaggerations of description and action, and not through any synthesis of his character with the unfolding situation" (Rolfe 32). Jack Conroy added that "the characters fail to emerge full-blown," while Kenneth Burke noted Caldwell's dirt farmer figures appeared as "subnormal mannequins" (Conroy 27; Burke, "Caldwell" 49). The second critique leveled against Caldwell's work by the 1930s left was that it was too erotic. Norman MacLeod wrote: "Caldwell, is first of all interested in sex," adding, "He should go left" (21). Burke simply commented: "Caldwell has yet to learn that the revolution begins above the belt" (50).

Caldwell's work is undoubtedly sexualized. No other proletarian novel comes close to the level of sexual desire depicted in stories such as *Tobacco Road* and *Journeyman*. *GLA* in particular is filled with scenes of bawdy flirtation, passionate kissing, and direct and indirect references to sexual intercourse. The charge of "caricature" is implicitly linked to this sexual aspect, as Caldwell's primary "exaggeration" is his characters' sexual drive. In the tradition of naturalism, both male and female characters are driven by their basic desires (particularly sex), though unlike naturalism, sexual matters are often narrated suggestively by the author so as to create a clear, libidinal connection between (heterosexual male) reader and text. The repetitive nature of their lusts, combined with their poverty, racism, and lack of education, make the characters appear simplistic on first glance. It is important to note that Caldwell comes dangerously close to the pervasive stereotype of poor white Southerners—a stereotype that has long held poor southern whites to be lacking in both intelligence and character. This limitation is particularly underscored by Caldwell's subject position. Not only is he a male author writing a novel that allows the opportunity for men, both as characters within the story and as readers, to gaze incessantly at eroticized women, but he is also a Southerner from a middle-class background producing degraded representations of those lower than himself on the socioeconomic ladder.

Nonetheless, the way Caldwell renders the class difference between his characters and his readers is more complicated than the charges of his 1930s critics suggest. Overall, while Caldwell's characters generally have a comic side, they are not simply caricatures, as implied by 1930s critics, nor are they merely "white trash" stereotypes. Their otherness is somewhat necessary given their racial politics, in which complete empathy would be dangerous (though countercurrents in Caldwell's writing work to produce some level of empathy, which I will explore momentarily). Caldwell deploys what are at first glance caricatures to draw the reader into a critical exploration of the complex class and racial formations in the South that have generated those caricatures. In regard to the stereotype of the lazy poor white, for example, the characters in *GLA* do not work as those in a farm family should, yet they are far from slothful. Though Ty Ty and his sons dig for gold instead of planting cotton, they dig frantically and diligently, sometimes into the night (67). And though Will is unemployed, his consistent refrain of "I want to turn the power on" expresses a clear desire not only to go back to work, but also to take over the means of production. Jeeter Lester in *Tobacco Road* obsessively tries to find a way to continue farming, and his ill-fated attempt to sell wood in Augusta is a means to that end. In *Tragic Ground* the jobless Spence Douthit walks constantly in search of work (9). Consequently, we are led to believe that the unemployment or seemingly irrational work habits of the men in these stories are not so much the product of laziness or ignorance, but the only option available (allegorically speaking) in a social system that does not pay farmers or workers enough to make ends meet. Caldwell underscored this very point explicitly in his nonfiction work *You Have Seen Their Faces*, a joint project with his second wife Margaret Bourke-

White. At the very beginning, he writes, "Twice a year [the South] takes it easy . . . The rest of the time it works harder than anybody else, chopping its cotton from dawn to dusk" (1).

Further, Caldwell uses several means to lessen the distance between his characters and his readers so that his poor white creations are not completely othered. As I will show below, Will's eventual idol status by the end of *GLA* could have endeared him to many male readers. But in a more positive example from the same novel, it is not the narrator who "explains" the flaws of the mill and farm people; rather, poor white characters point out each other's flaws within the dialogue. Rosamond and Will laugh at Ty Ty's attempt to get rich by digging for gold, Ty Ty chides Will for his drunkenness and infidelity, all laugh at Pluto's sloppy flirtations with Darlin' Jill—forming an incomplete circle of critique in which no character stands completely on the outside. The circle closes in a speech at the end of the novel that lays bare the meaning of the social structure, and this moment of metaphysical wisdom is uttered not by the narrator, but by Ty Ty and Griselda. In *Tobacco Road* and *Tragic Ground*, the analysis of the suffering in the novel is also disclosed by a poor white character at the end, Lov in the former novel and Jim Vance in the latter (237, 137). Further, though it is clear that the characters lack a formal education, Caldwell actually deemphasizes this fact in the dialogue. In the tradition of "local color" fiction, he could have made their southern dialects much more pronounced and still remained relatively accurate to the realities of southern life. While he removes high vocabulary from their speech, he also eliminates many local speech patterns and idiomatic expressions, such as "goin'" and "'em" (as opposed to "them"). Echoing Victorian fiction, for example, Rosamond says to Pluto as she sets up the dinner table in *GLA*, "The cream is stiff by this time, Pluto . . . Take off the top while we're getting the dishes and spoons. And be careful of the salt" (58). The relative lack of a recognizable southern accent could be seen as Caldwell's way of lessening the gap between the poor white southern characters and national readers, helping bridge a gulf created by the characters' actions.

There does need to be a partial gulf, however—one necessitated by Caldwell's racial politics. Some leftist novels written by white authors in the 1930s and 1940s avoided a critical treatment of race by either relegating racism to the words and actions of the bourgeois and their allies (Robert Cantwell, Myra Page, Jack Conroy), or by not even attempting a critical treatment of race (John Dos Passos). Others offered a more complex look at U.S. racial politics by placing a racist antihero at the center of the story (James T. Farrell, Nelson Algren). Caldwell takes a unique path by creating characters whose lives are clearly predicated upon white supremacy, but who possess values we are not supposed to wholly reject either. African Americans are peripheral figures in his most popular books, even in his anti-lynching novel *Trouble in July*, which devotes only one full chapter to the hunted Sonny Clark. But their presence, and their status of dependency on figures as flawed as Ty Ty Walden, Pluto Swint, Clay Horey, Morris Stroup, and Jeff McCurtain ultimately serve to critique racial privilege by highlighting white pretensions to supremacy. At the beginning of *God's Little Acre*, for example, Ty Ty tells his son Buck: "I wish you had more sense than to listen to what the darkies say. That ain't a thing in the world but superstition. Now take me here. I'm scientific. To listen to the darkies talk, a man would believe they have got more sense than I have. All they know about it is that talk about diviners and conjurs" (2). His "scientific" method, we soon learn, is capturing an albino to help him divine the location of gold—a quest that occupies a significant portion of the plot. Clearly, the joke is on him.

The selfish patriarch figure in the Caldwellian formula, as well as the comic simpleton figure, often rely on the labor of black tenants, field hands, and in the case of *Georgia Boy*, even black children. Clay Horey in *Journeyman*, who combines both figures as owner of a small farm and as a hapless victim of Semon Dye's schemes, laments the shooting of one of his workers by stating: "I sure do hate to see one of my hands passing away on me right at this time. It's planting time . . . I'd have to get out and do some of the work myself" (25). Ty Ty's gold dig, a central facet of the story line in *God's Little Acre*, is also predicated on the exploitation of the black sharecroppers on his land; it is their labor that enables his futile project. Caldwell writes of the patriarch's tenants: "Ty Ty always managed to keep an eye on them, because he realized that if they didn't raise any cotton or corn, there would be no money and little to eat that fall and winter" (11). Despite this fundamental dependence, Ty Ty angrily balks at Black Sam's request for a food advance, a traditional facet of the sharecropping relationship, stating, "I ain't going to have darkies worrying me for rations at a time like this" (7). Pluto Swint, another simpleminded, comical figure, is also a small landowner who exploits black sharecroppers. He is running for sheriff, we are told, because the "colored share-cropper" on his land does not provide him with enough to eat, and he has not figured out what else he can do (71). If Scarlett's whiteness is constructed in relation to the blackness of Mammy and Prissy, the whiteness of Pluto, Horey, and Walden is constructed through their relationship to their black tenants—with very different results. Whiteness, following David Roediger's reading of W. E. B. Du Bois, is a "public and psychological wage" that enables its downtrodden beneficiaries to claim certain short-term advantages while ultimately denying them the class consciousness necessary to recognize the real social forces holding them down (12–13). The characters of Ty Ty and Pluto illustrate this theory quite well. Although the exploitative sharecropping relationship confers a degree of power to Ty Ty, Clay, and Pluto, the reader can clearly see that this power does not ennoble them; rather, it makes them tyrants and/or fools. It should also be noted that patriarchs without black labor—namely Spence Douthit and Jeeter Lester—are the most desperate of Caldwell's characters, and they are secretly mocked or spurned by people of color. In *Tobacco Road*, three African American men hide and watch as Jeeter allows Lov to have sexual relations with his daughter in exchange for a bag of turnips. "The negroes were laughing so hard they could not stand up straight," Caldwell writes (46). In a similar vein, it is revealed on the first page of *Tragic Ground* that Chinese grocers have refused credit to Spence Douthit: "There had been a time when he had never bothered to go out of his way to trade with a Chinaman, and now the Chinamen would not go out of their way to trade with him" (1). Significantly, however, Douthit and Lester maintain pretensions to racial superiority, holding firm to their white identities and casually dropping racial epithets whenever thoughts of African, Chinese, or Mexican Americans enter their minds. Lester and Douthit never get politically organized or in any way transcend their dismal situations; as with Ty Ty and Clay, we are left to assume that the false pride provided by their racial identities is part of the reason.

While Caldwell's novels were intended first and foremost as portraits of a region, not the nation as a whole, his representations of farmers and ex-farmers undermined American exceptionalism by dispelling the aura from a central icon of U.S. nationalism at that time: the hearty yeoman. The 1930s was a decade in which the yeoman farmer—the symbol of virtue in Jeffersonian agrarianism and much of U.S. republican thought—was resurrected by Steinbeck, Pare Lorentz, and other aestheticians of the New Deal and popular literature as the symbolic victim of the Depression. The redemption of the nation hinged upon his fate, and the pluralist iconography of "We're the people" valorized his image at the expense of others. But the sexual lusts, racial politics, and general tragicomic attributes of small farmers such as Clay Horey, Ty Ty Walden, or Jeeter Lester make them stand out among this cultural backdrop, disrupting the ideological work implicit in the beatification of the yeoman. Particularly in his early novels, Caldwell explicitly praises farming as a noble calling and sees the drive to make it sustainable once again as a national moral imperative. At the same time, however, it is abundantly apparent in his work that "the people" of the land are just as likely to be tools of fascism as vanguards of leftist social change, and that their closeness to the earth does not necessarily clarify their consciousness. This is particularly apparent in *Journeyman* and *Trouble in July*. In *Journeyman*, none of the rural characters is able to resist the rhetoric of the nefarious preacher Semon Dye, least of all the small landowner Clay Horey. When Dye uses the word "anticipates," Horey exclaims "That's it! That's the big word! I never can think to say it myself, but what's the use anyhow? You're always there to tell it to me" (58). Similarly, when the country people enter the schoolhouse to hear Semon preach, they enter "like a flock of sheep," and hang on his every word even though his sermon is incoherent (105). He leaves the community having cheated and exploited many of its members, yet the end of the novel finds Clay pining his absence.

The consciousness of the small farmer is perhaps rendered most disturbingly in *Trouble in July*, an anti-lynching novel Caldwell began writing in May 1939 shortly after the publication of *The Grapes of Wrath* (Klevar 218). Caldwell's literary star was in a temporary decline in the late 1930s; he had not written a single novel between 1933 and 1939, and his reputation was rapidly eclipsed by John Steinbeck at the end of the decade. *Journeyman*, written in 1933 and published in 1935, had been a critical and popular failure, and this discouraged the author from writing for the remainder of the Depression years. Caldwell intended *Trouble in July* to be his "comeback," and its appearance in 1940 made him yet another white author to capitalize on the success of Richard Wright, who had popularized of the theme of black/white relationships via *Native Son*. (It should be noted, however, that *Trouble* was completely overshadowed by *Native Son* in critical praise and popularity in 1940 [231].)

Trouble is essentially a story of inaction in the face of monstrous injustice. Its main character, Sheriff Jeff McCurtain, spends the entire novel desperately looking for a way to do nothing as a mob of white farmers and farm tenants hunt down an African American youth named Sonny Clark, who has been accused of raping a white woman. Always fearing for his reelection, McCurtain vacillates and ultimately chooses inaction as the path of least resistance, and Sonny is murdered by the crowd. In stark contrast to *The Grapes of Wrath*, the values of "the people" appear as a nightmare in this novel. The members of the lynch mob are mostly tenant farmers, and McCurtain justifies his inaction in their murderous affairs by stating, "I've always believed in not going against the will of the common people" (47, 48). While these white tenant farmers enact terrible violence upon black tenants and field hands, they also passively cower before the authority of the large landowner Bob Watson. Small landholders are shown to be as bad as tenant farmers in their racial politics. In a lengthy interchange toward the end of the narrative, McCurtain argues with one of the electorate whom Caldwell gives the archetypical name "the farmer." As if to illustrate the irrationality of the people and the bankruptcy of public debate, the farmer chides McCurtain only on the particulars of the case: it would have been more effective and less costly for the taxpayers if the sheriff had used bloodhounds to track down Clark before the mob got to him, argues the yeoman (133–37). It is also a cotton farmer named Harvey Glenn, finally, who makes a decision to hand Sonny over to the mob. Caldwell's representations of the tiller of the soil, whether tenant or small landowner, were clearly out of step with the aesthetics of "We're the people." Interestingly, Richard Wright urged readers to see *Trouble in July* as a mirror of reality in his praise of the novel. He reminded them that the crazed and seemingly outlandish character Narcissa Calhoun, who wanted every white voter in the county to sign a petition to send all blacks back to Africa, was no mere hyperbole: "Caldwell was serious, no matter how fantastic it sounds, for such notions are being aired in the halls of Congress today" ("Lynching Bee" 115).

However, many critics on the left did not see realistic social commentary in Caldwell's writing—in large measure a result of the premium they placed on the representation of "whole individuals" and on the avoidance of its inverse, caricature. What united the critique of caricature for many left critics of the 1930s was adherence to a dialectical Marxist realism that predominated aesthetic theory in the 1930s, even in the critique of the "fellow traveling" Kenneth Burke. A sophisticated theory of proletarian realism came together in the work of the Revolutionary Association of Proletarian Writers (RAPP), the leading group of Marxist literary critics in the Soviet Union from 1928 to 1932. This theory was exported to the United States and Germany through the Soviet-based journals *International Literature* and *Literature of the World Revolution*, as well as through the translations of the work of Georg Lukács and RAPP forerunners Franz Mehring and Georgi Plekhanov in the *New Masses*, *Partisan Review* (U.S.), and *Linkskurve* (Germany). According to this aesthetic, the novel should ideally be a space where "typical" (i.e., emergent) character types are shown in a process of becoming within a complex and shifting social environment. The major conflicts of the age were to be represented through a story of everyday characters, who should be flawed yet capable of change, and whose positive traits would find full expression in the new historical formation charted by the novel. In order to achieve this effect, characters could not be represented as simplistic, placardlike caricatures but rather as individuals depicted with enough psychological depth to convey the contradictory and dynamic nature of their emergent consciousness. Such an individual, so portrayed, was referred to as "the living man."[8]

Though RAPP was disbanded by the Soviet government in 1932 to make way for the theories of socialist realism, one sees its influential ideas used to evaluate literary texts in the United States both before and after that date, albeit often in diluted form (arguably, they entered a ground made fertile by earlier American strands of realist literary and drama criticism from the likes of William Dean Howells and Henry James).[9] The reviews of Caldwell were no exception. Most of Caldwell's reviewers on the left evaluated him using established RAPP parameters: namely, the psychological complexity of characters, the ability to convey dynamic individuals in changing, fluid contexts, and the capacity to select the most relevant set of social forces as the central theme. In most all of these attributes he was found lacking. For example, Edwin Rolfe noted in the *New Masses* in 1933 that Caldwell "must go beyond mere sympathetic depiction into the higher sphere of dialectical development of characters placed in situations that clamor for treatment today." Remarking on the character Pluto Swint, he added, "the sense of growth or change is conspicuously lacking" (32–33). Similarly, Jack Conroy wrote in 1932 that "somehow his characters fail to emerge full-blown," and added that he lacked the proper "sociology" to put them in motion (27). In the *New Republic* in 1935, Burke very lucidly compared Caldwell's treatment of his characters to a scientist who removes the higher centers of a frog's brain to simplify its responses to stimuli. The frog jumps or croaks when prodded, but loses its free will in the process. Revealing his preference for psychological complexity and holistic representation, he concludes, "What the decerebrated frog is to the whole frog, Caldwell's characters are to real people" ("Caldwell" 51). Later in the same essay Burke contrasts the automatons created by the southern writer with the "complex realistic texture" of the social novels of nineteenth-century realism (52). A later *New Masses* reviewer revealed a penchant for the layered, fluid settings of dialectical realism, writing in 1938 that although Caldwell's short story collection *Southways* "lacks power," its author "has developed a more dynamic control of the setting" than in his earlier works (Shukotoff 24).

Judged by such standards, Caldwell's novels are not really proletarian, and definitely not dialectical in the sense outlined above. His characters are placed within social contexts; the problem, all of these critics agree, is that, within the terms of dialectical realism, the characters lack the dynamic qualities necessary to change (by contrast, one thinks of Alexandra in *The Little Foxes*). Curiously, Caldwell did represent the social relationships most relevant to 1930s left-wing critics. Caldwell's third-person narrator is generally not explicit in its references to the southern social structure, with the exception of his early novel *Tobacco Road*, wherein the narrator outlines the precise relationship between creditors, landlords, and tenant farmers (228–29). But the sociohistorical context of class and racial exploitation is always present. In *GLA* it appears in the narrator's references to the effects of mill work on male bodies (60); in Ty Ty's son Jim Leslie, a cotton broker who Will authoritatively states has become rich off the farmers' destitution (64); and in the recurrent exploitation of black labor. In *Tragic Ground* culpability for exploitation lies in the absent hand of the military-industrial complex, which lured southerners away from their small towns and into wartime defense work in the city of Poor Boy, where it promptly abandoned them. But it is true that Caldwell's characters do not develop or grow within these oppressive contexts. Rather, each maintains his or her particular relationship to their social environment, a relationship apparently developed before the narrative began. In *GLA* we see Will's class consciousness from our first encounter with him, so that his defiant act at the mill at the climax of the novel appears inevitable. Darlin' Jill and Griselda remain underdeveloped objects of male desire, and Caldwell leaves Ty Ty exactly as the reader found him at the beginning—digging for gold. This facet of his characterization deeply dismayed his left-wing critics, so much so that they saw his chosen social themes as irrelevant.

Not only is Caldwell undialectical, but it is also questionable whether or not he is even a realist in the classic sense. Kenneth Burke explicitly distances him from nineteenth-century realism and instead places his outlandish plots, exaggerated characters, and sometimes bizarre depictions of mill work in the category of the fantastic, the grotesque, and the magical. As examples he cites the women in *GLA* who kiss the factory walls with their lips, Will's simplistic scheme to "turn the power on," and the bizarre death of the grandmother in *Tobacco Road*, concluding, "All this is magic, not reason; and I think we are entitled to inspect it for the processes of magic" (McDonald 52–53). With this observation, I find that Burke, more than any other 1930s critic, hits closest to the mark in his analysis of Caldwell. But whereas Burke faults the author for not matching the complexity of nineteenth-century realism, I find the presence of the "magical" in Caldwell's work to be the basis of its didactic value for those interested in the relationship between politics, aesthetics, and audience.

His most famous novel *GLA* ultimately shows the failure of magical transformation, as both the divination for gold by Dave the albino and the mythical "God's Little Acre" itself do not bestow good fortune on the Waldens. But the fantastic reveals itself in more subtle ways in his fiction—in the uncanny mixture of eroticism and revulsion evoked by his scenes, in his surrealistically gendered representation of mill work that critic Laura Hapke rightfully deplores, and in the bawdy nature of Caldwell's writing, which draws as much from *True Confessions* as it does from William Dean Howells. In part, the magical qualities of Caldwell's work derives from his attempt to evoke pleasure in his readers—both in the form of humor and eroticism—and to do so he employed devices that were much more commonly found in mass culture than in the "serious literature" of the cultural moment from which he was writing. At the same time, the nonrealistic quality of these novels resides in their incorporation of the grotesque, a mode increasingly favored by southern writers in the twentieth century. What the 1930s critics lambasted as "exaggeration" is part and parcel of both mass culture and the grotesque. As Lillian Hellman recognized, the realist writer often had to depart from a strict realism to achieve commercial success.

In addition to the bawdiness I have already enumerated, a key trope these six novels share in common with mass culture is repetition (interestingly enough, repetition was cited by a number of critics, including Burke, as a sign of Caldwell's simplicity as a writer). On one level, repetition in dialogue gives the characters a comic quality. Ty Ty repeatedly says, "What in the pluperfect hell?"; we know Pluto Swint by his phrase "And that's a fact," and Sheriff Jeff McCurtain works the phrase "frazzle-assed" into his every other sentence. Such use of repetition for comedy has a long history in popular culture. From George Aiken's popular adaptation of *Uncle Tom's Cabin* to the TV series *The Simpsons*, characters in pop-culture narratives have often been marked by a peculiar phrase that, when uttered, marks the character for a comic reading and lightens the scene. Whenever Aiken's Phineas exclaims "Teetotally!," whenever Matt Groening's Homer utters "D'Oh!," or when Pluto asserts "And that's a fact!" we are immediately signaled to read the scene as entertainment (in part), not as dialectical realism.[10] This comic repetition furthers the race politics of these novels, as it allows readers to laugh at the characters' presumed racial superiority. As Ty Ty digs for gold, for example, he incessantly distances himself from blackness by repeating, "I'm scientific all the way through. I wouldn't have anything to do with conjur" (5). His scientific method, one recalls, is to capture Dave the albino.

Other forms of repetition drive home the class politics of Caldwell's work. The repetition of diction within the narrative voice drives home the class politics of *GLA* by making certain images stick in the reader's memory. For instance, Caldwell uses a variant of the phrase "the bloody-lipped men spitting their lungs into the yellow dust" multiple times in his description of the mill workers, a reference to their work-related illnesses and the vitamin deficiencies resulting from their inadequate diets (60). He also advances his class politics by describing repetitive thought patterns in the minds of his characters. Jeeter Lester of *Tobacco Road* obsesses about getting guano, which would enable him to plant his crop, but no creditor will lend it to him and no moneymaking strategy he devises brings in the capital he needs to buy it. As with Spence Douthit, who obsesses about moving back to Beasley County, repetition here conveys a mind hellishly repeating a failed strategy, looking for a way out in a social structure that has provided none. Such thoughts form a "signature" for these characters, a device that (as in popular narratives) clearly marks them for their audiences; but in the service of proletarian literature, it also illustrates their desperation.

Caldwell also departs from realism in his use of the grotesque, a mode that, while not unique to the South, has been chosen often enough by writers of the region so as to become a staple of southern literature. The grotesque has been defined in many ways, and a review of these myriad definitions is beyond the scope of this book: suffice to say here that scholars agree on the fact that it is not a realistic mode, even though it is grounded in the real. It is signaled by an unsettling combination of elements—oftentimes congealed within a single character—that defy existing categorization and thus produce conflicting emotions in the reader, such as pity/disgust or empathy/revulsion. This generally startling transgression of existing categories has caused some critics to view the grotesque as a subversive mode; one could add that, in the context of southern literature, it is particularly subversive of the tradition of the plantation novel out of which *GWTW* arises. Burke found the deliberate incongruities within Caldwell's characters to be the essence of the grotesque in his work: for instance, in their animalistic lack of agency one moment and capacity for profound wisdom the next (353–57). However, Burke does not discuss the prevalence of the grotesque in southern literature, a prevalence Flannery O'Connor attributed to the mysticism and religiosity of the region.[11]

Although instances of the grotesque in Caldwell's best-sellers are too numerous to detail, perhaps the most instructive example for the author's politics is the character Dave the albino in *GLA*, who simultaneously illustrates Caldwell's humor. As an albino, Dave represents a type of whiteness that is unsettling, and thereby confuses the racial binaries around which southern culture is constructed. Ty Ty attempts to create a new racial category for Dave by repeatedly referring to him as an "all-white man," and he inscribes this new category with the rigid boundaries of the familiar, historical, black/white relationship of Jim Crow. Ty Ty had abducted Dave from his cabin in the swamp, and when he tells the story of the abduction to his son-in-law Will, he reveals his disgust upon finding that Dave was married to a white woman. He says, "It's a good thing we brought him away. I hate to see a white woman taking up with a coal black darky, but this is just about as bad, because he is an all-white man" (70). After the kidnapping, Dave is forced at gunpoint to work on the Walden farm in the absurd quest to find gold. As can be seen in the assertion "It's a good thing we brought him away," Dave's presumed racial difference forms a shallow justification for this enslavement to Ty Ty. But despite his abduction and enslavement by the patriarch of the Walden farm, as well as the expressed need to keep him from "mixing" with a white woman, Dave's ultra-white racial position is not equivalent to blackness within Ty Ty's racial hierarchy. As an albino, we are told, "He was said to possess unearthly powers to divine gold. In that respect, Ty Ty held him above all other men" (75). However, the reader quickly sees that the "purity" of his whiteness does not grant him any special powers, and that he is guided by the same flaws and lusts as everyone else in the novel. He and Darlin' Jill have a brief fling, and as a result, he stays on the farm of his own free will, joining the quest for gold so that he can see her further. He eventually disappears, however, when her affections are diverted elsewhere. Again, the joke is on Ty Ty—and on his faith that whiteness grants one any innate abilities. Caldwell's inclusion of this grotesque character can be read as a satire on the arbitrary, self-serving, and economic dimensions of racial categorization. Dave is read as a racial inferior to justify his forced labor at one moment and then as a wonderful idol in the next: his status ultimately hinges upon Ty Ty's immediate needs.

Humor, and the pleasure that derives from it, often relies on the repetition of recognizable character traits for its success, but in doing so takes us away from the holistic representation required by realism. The challenge, politically, is to place the character's actions in a clearly oppressive social context *and* to anchor them with enough humanity so that we ultimately laugh with them, not at them. Caldwell largely succeeded in this endeavor by couching his humor in the grotesque mode, and in doing so he produced something more than "de-cerebrated frogs." He created characters that have too much agency to feel sorry for, too many kernels of wisdom to dismiss as stupid, too many flaws to fully identify with, and too much humanity to reject outright. As is common with grotesques, the contradictory feelings they evoke leave open the possibility for empathy.

Aspects of this empathy are also the source of the novels' primary political limitation, however. The overly libidinal nature of the characters in these books does afford a major critique of Caldwell that was missed by his contemporary critics: his repressive politics of the gaze. Laura Hapke insightfully notes that Caldwell's most famous novel *GLA* betrays a fear of women in the workplace, as the narrator repeatedly depicts downtrodden male strikers impotently looking on as energetic female "scabs" take their jobs at the mill (22). Details from Caldwell's biography support Hapke's critique of his gender politics; he generally wanted his female companions to devote themselves not to employment in the public sphere, but to providing him solace on the domestic front.[12]

The thrill of "looking"—often erotic looking—is a recurrent motif within Caldwell's novels. The reader is often inscribed into sexualized scenes in the form of another character who watches the erotic action unfold; in *GLA*, for example, Pluto watches Darlin' Jill in the bathtub, Will looks at Rosamond and

FIG. 3-1. Paperback cover, 1946 Penguin edition of *God's Little Acre*

Darlin' Jill asleep, Darlin' Jill ogles Dave for an extended period, and Rosamond and Darlin' Jill watch Will ravage Griselda. The thrill of looking is even more pronounced in *Tobacco Road*, where virtually every sexual moment happens with other characters watching, whether from behind a tree, outside a window, or in plain sight. This is taken to a truly fantastic level in *Journeyman*. In one of the more bizarre moments in Caldwell's work, male characters take turns staring through a hole in a cow shed which affords a view of absolutely nothing; despite the fact that they are only looking at trees, the act of viewing provides a feeling of complete euphoria. As Tom exclaims, "it's just the sitting there and looking through it that sort of makes me feel like heaven can't be so doggone far away" (103). Jonas, the artist who illustrated the book covers for the 1940s Penguin editions of the novels, captured this spirit of Caldwell's work. His design for the 1946 cover of *God's Little Acre* positions us as viewers through a knothole looking onto a barren landscape and a little house, the element of eroticism suggested by a heart punctured with arrows carved into the fence wood in the foreground.

Caldwell valorizes a kind of controlling gaze for men, though in a manner not so clear-cut as in Laura Mulvey's famous template, partially because social class complicates the interpretation of visibility. In these novels the highly flawed nature of the male characters, in addition to their unenviable class positions, leaves most male readers without any solid ego ideals with which they can identify. And as often as not, male watching is an act that exposes the impotence of the watcher. One example is when the men watch the women take their jobs at the cotton mills in *GLA*. As the women run joyfully to their work, Caldwell writes that "the men stood in the streets looking, but helpless." Even though the working women are "firm-bodied girls with eyes like morning glories," the men cannot enjoy their beauty. Rather, they merely "stood on the hot streets looking at each other" (59).

In Caldwell's world, young women are particularly prone to "run off" to the city and to the mills. In *Tobacco Road* Lov unsuccessfully tries to tie down his young wife Pearl with plow lines to prevent this from happening (218). In this case the author does not blame Pearl for escaping to the town: though we never meet her, the narrator states that "Pearl had more sense than any of the Lesters" (40). Such is not the case in *God's Little Acre*, however. As if aware of the tenuousness of their scopophilic power, both Will and Ty Ty must insist that Griselda "sit still" while being looked at. Ty Ty tells her, "Now you just sit and be quiet while I praise you mightily" (103). Later, Will also commands, "I told you to stand there like God intended you to be seen" (135). The anxious insistence on the women's motionlessness, the passivity necessary for them to become proper objects of desire, should be contrasted with their frenetic activity as mill workers. Caldwell generally depicts them as "running" to their jobs, and in one particular instance, writes that the girls "ran in and out [of the mills] endlessly" (60). Presumably, they would "sit still" if the men were able to attain justice and go back to work. Indeed, at the end of the novel, Will's agency is fully reestablished—as is the power of the male gaze—after Griselda stands passively before his eyes (135). He "takes" her as she stands still and submits to his ogling, and this reconnection of male watching to effectively controlling action gives him the strength to finally confront his employers. In the final analysis, the main limitation of Caldwell's politics is that he binds class emancipation to the reestablishment of patriarchy, since the agency of the men vis-à-vis their employers is predicated upon women's ejection from the realm of wage work as well as their motionless visibility.

Paperback Dialectics and the Politics of Dreaming

Caldwell's work did not achieve its massive sales figures during the Depression itself. As Barbara Foley has noted, book sales during the Depression were generally very bad (103–6). The popularity of his novels did not really take off until the early 1940s, when two things happened: they were released in twenty-five-cent paperback editions, and, as important, they were aggressively marketed. Caldwell actively promoted his books in collaboration with mainstream publishers, giving lectures that were also billed as book-signing events. He also consented to pulp-fiction paperback covers (Klevar 270–71, 279).[13]

Immediately after World War II, paperback covers became more lurid, colorful, and sensational. Drug and department stores—major retailers in the book market at that time—had less room to devote to the display of books, as they suddenly were flooded with stock items unavailable during the war. Publishers responded with more eye-catching cover designs that could better draw consumers' attention away from other commodities in the room (Schick 81). But what is most revealing about Caldwell's 1940s paperback covers is that they advertised his work as cheap entertainment and social realism at the same time, as if guiding the reader to expect a mixture of realism and titillation inside the jacket. The cover artwork for the 1948 Penguin edition of *Tragic Ground*, for example, shows an attractive woman smoking a cigarette in the foreground; behind her we can see rundown row houses through a hole in a tattered curtain,

FIG. 3-2. Paperback cover, 1948 Penguin edition of *Tragic Ground*

suggesting that the reader will be afforded a curious mixture of pulp eroticism and Popular Front sociology. The cover of the 1949 Signet edition of *Sure Hand of God* features a man, hidden by the night, looking through a window into a well-lit room at an attractive woman in a nightgown; amazingly, the writing on the back cover begins, "Literary recognition comes slowly in this country for writers who don't cater to best-selling formulas." It goes on to tell us that Caldwell studied sociology at the University of Virginia and had lectured on southern tenant farmers at the New School of Social Research. The fact that social realism remained part of the marketing strategy speaks volumes to the diffusion of Popular Front aesthetics in U.S. mass culture. The literary world saw more of the pop culture and less of the sociology, however, and Caldwell was consequently shunned by many literati in the 1940s and 1950s for what was deemed the blatant commercialization of his work.[14]

The incredible marketability of his mass-mediated realism raises the question as to whether it was necessary for the proletarian novel to depart from dialectics to achieve popular success. It would be too easy to deduce from Caldwell's popular appeal—and from the low sales of other left-wing novelists whose work was more well-received in the *New Masses*—that dialectical realism has been an alien language to most U.S. audiences. To the contrary, I would argue that dialectical realism and America popular culture are not mutually exclusive. A consistent critique leveled at naturalism by most all varieties of twentieth-century Marxist literary criticism was that the genre was too bleak, its dark resolutions ultimately denying the characters agency and hence the possibility of social change. Anatoly Lunacharsky, the Soviet Union's first commissar of education, represented this tendency best in a 1933 lecture on socialist realism. Naturalism, he argued, was essentially an aesthetic form of the petty bourgeois, a class unsatisfied with life under the "big bourgeois," and described only the negative side of capitalism without offering any model of redemption. Consequently, Lunacharsky labeled it "negative realism" and opposed it to the "affirmative realism" of the pre-1848 bourgeois (329). Lukács furthered this notion in *The Historical Novel*, where he argued that grim naturalism locks the reader into the immediacy of events, thus denying him or her a window into rich contexts, dynamism, and transcendence (212). The Marxist notion of typicality, on the other hand, was preferred by left critics because it entailed a sense of transformation, which carried with it a hope for a better world (one is reminded of Sturges here: it is doubtful that a film ending with two grappling men falling to their deaths would have ever won accolades by a leftist critic in the 1930s). The Marxist discomfort with the "unhappy end" of negative realism in favor of more hopeful narratives ironically placed Marxian critics on common ground with those in the culture industries, a common ground that can be seen most clearly in the shared use of the "conversion narrative." The dialectical process of "becoming" could be and sometimes was fitted to the conversion narrative, a structure familiar to U.S. audiences from Protestant traditions. In the narrative of conversion, the protagonist comes to "see the light" of God or class consciousness after traveling down a number of false paths. All of this is not to say that the increasingly upbeat tone of American consumer culture (embodied by the happy end) made American consumerism properly dialectical, nor that all proletarian novels were conversion narratives. Rather, it is to point out the ways in which dialectical realism could be fitted to cultural forms that were familiar to U.S. audiences.[15]

Ironically, *GWTW* illustrates how a dialectical novel could achieve popular success in the United States, as it is much more in line with Marxian literary forms than anything produced by Caldwell. Mitchell's narrative followed most of the conventions of nineteenth-century realism that Lukács advocates in *The Historical Novel*, which, though it was not available in English until after the 1940s, synthesized in elevated form aesthetic standards in use by U.S. critics of the 1930s. In line with Lukács's ideal historical novel, Mitchell's story shows major historical crises in terms of how they affect the everyday lives of the main characters. It leaves major historical figures marginal; it foregrounds the conflicts of the age by showing the opposing parties (in this case, the nostalgic antebellum elite, the forward-looking new elite, and the villains associated with Reconstruction) so that dialectical negations are made visible; it shows the nobility of past social formations while highlighting the necessity of their decline; and it sets its characters within a shifting, concretely articulated historical context. Finally, it ends on a hopeful note. Perhaps most important, it places at its center Scarlett, a flawed, dynamic, "middling" figure, whose gumption, not allowed to express itself in the antebellum social formation, is allowed to find full expression in the new historical epoch the novel chronicles. As such, Scarlett embodies an emergent "type" that rises from the negation of the previous era. Incidentally, Mitchell was irritated that the film drew upon conventions from the plantation romance that the novel did not, such as the famous long shot of Scarlett running down the steps of the lawn with the vast, beautiful plantation house in the background.[16] That a novel with such politics could come close to Lukács's aesthetics should come as no surprise; his model for realism is Sir Walter Scott's *Ivanhoe* (ironically, very popular among southern slaveholders) and a host of other reactionary novels whose explicit politics he found abhorrent. Left critics were less forgiving of their contemporaries, however. Had Scarlett aligned her gumption with Reconstruction—if she possessed, to quote Conroy, the "right sociology" to put her portrait of the South in motion—we may very well have had a novel receiving high praise in the *New Masses* and in the writers' congresses of the international left. But then it most certainly would not have held the organic place in the dominant culture of the South that it has managed to cling to for more than half a century.

Though grounded in Popular Front sociology and, in part, realism, I have argued that Caldwell's novels took a different aesthetic path from dialectical realism—that of the magical. If it is true, as Burke suggests, that Caldwell's plots "are guided by the logic of dreams," we should ask ourselves about the efficacy of deploying dream logic toward political ends. Ultimately, Caldwell's dream aesthetics came as close to Bertolt Brecht as to Georg Lukács and proletarian realism, but not simply because Brecht represented the opposite pole to the latter in the aesthetic debates of the mid-century left. Rather, Brecht and Caldwell departed from RAPP-inspired ideas of political art in parallel ways. Brecht's critique of "realism," as the term was employed in Soviet circles, was that it was too narrow, reserved only for works that resembled the nineteenth-century realism of Honoré de Balzac and Leo Tolstoy. To the contrary, Brecht argued that "realism is not a matter of form," but a function of the work's ability to lay bare causal networks and expose the dominant ideology. The title of realism, in other words, was to be bestowed upon works with a particular political affiliation, not with a particular structure. The aesthetic that could most effectively enact these politics was one that met the audience halfway, "taking over their own forms of expression and enriching them," which in Brechtian practice meant couching one's critiques within familiar forms of popular culture, and popular musical theater in particular. This newer, more flexible realism was to preserve the fun and enjoyment of popular culture, while self-reflexively calling attention to the function of entertainment under capitalism. The means of performing this critique of both capitalism and its cultural apparatus was the famous "alienation effect," in which the audience was prevented from identifying with the characters through a variety of techniques of script writing and stagecraft.[17] When deployed on stage, the alienation effect often presented theater audiences with individuals who were more like cartoon characters than deep psychological portraits, albeit cartoon characters who exposed real social contradictions through their words and actions.

Caldwell definitely was not the theoretician of his craft that Brecht was, nor did the mass-culture qualities of his work form a self-reflexive critique of the culture industries. Caldwell's unselfconsciousness of the method he created is nicely illustrated in his biography by Harvey Klevar, which revealed his deep anger toward critics who claimed that his work was not strict realism. These critiques drove him to document his narratives of the South with the naturalistic authority of the photograph in *You Have Seen Their Faces*, a photo-essay collection with his second wife, Margaret Bourke-White (159, 169). And one gets the distinct sense that some of the mass-culture qualities of his work—particularly the sensational sexuality—are there not as part of a larger social critique, but because of the author's own desires. But despite the lack of self-reflexivity in Caldwell's novels, his incorporation of mass-culture modes and the grotesque within his self-described "realism" does produce a kind of alienation effect between character and reader, generated by the contradictory traits within each character, humor, the avoidance of deep characterization, and the absurd scenes in which he sets his figures in motion. And though his use of humor and sexual pleasure did not show the constructed nature of desire under capitalism ("productive enjoyment," as Brecht might call it), it could nonetheless draw readers into a critique of capitalist social relations and southern racial formations. As I have argued, the humor Caldwell projected onto Ty Ty's absurd quest for gold, when juxtaposed with Will's class-conscious battle with mill owners in the city, works to produce this critique. Ty Ty's ogling of Griselda does not.

While their politics were decidedly limited, the best-sellers of Erskine Caldwell offered an opportunity to establish a reading of southern society within American mass culture that was generally in line with the mid-century left. A suitable context for his reception had been paved by the social struggles of the 1930s and 1940s, which had established a "common sense" for both understanding and using the novel's positive politics, particularly in Northern cities. Perhaps most uniquely, his eroticism and grotesque brand of humor yoked *pleasure* to these politics, particularly for straight male readers, with very mixed consequences to be sure. Strikes, racism, lynching, misery in both town and country—all the themes a political novel of the 1930s and 1940s was expected to cover—seemed to demand the most serious tones imaginable. In this milieu, a story that covered these themes *and* attempted to be entertaining stood out; one could argue that Caldwell's best-sellers marked a unique attempt to strike a compromise between proletarian literature and consumer culture. The fusion of realism, comic repetition, exaggeration, and the southern grotesque within Caldwell's novels called into question many of the class and racial structures of the United States, particularly those of the South. Yet it is uncertain whether Caldwell's dangerous dance with stereotypes of poor whites made audiences any wiser in gauging southern social relations. Perhaps the real value of Caldwell's best-sellers, like so much of Popular Front culture, rests in our hands as we examine the kinds of authorial subjectivity and aesthetic compromises necessary for a politically didactic work to appear before the largest of audiences.

CHAPTER FOUR

Asian Yeomen and Ugly Americans
Carlos Bulosan, H. T. Tsiang and the U.S. Literary Market

> In November, 1942, when there was too much pain and tragedy in the world, I found the story ["My Father Goes to Court"] in my hat. I sent it to *The New Yorker*, a magazine I had not read before, and in three weeks a letter came. "Tell us some more about the Filipinos," it said. I said, "Yes, sir."
> —CARLOS BULOSAN, from Afterword to *The Laughter of My Father*, 1944

> Poor Wong Wan-Lee, who had made no ten thousand fortunes, was a failure; but his cousin Wong Lung [*sic*] had made a million and had become the hero of *The Good Earth*—Horatio Alger!
> —H. T. TSIANG, *And China Has Hands*, 1937

The case of Erskine Caldwell and Margaret Mitchell illustrates how the label *realism* was necessary to confer narrative authority and literary respectability in the 1930s and 1940s. Far from being a hindrance in the mass market, socially committed authors who deployed realism in a way that earned the label could gain access to the mass audience they desired. But as I have argued with the case of Shirley Graham, not everyone had equal access to the profession of writer or screenwriter within the culture industries, nor to the badge of narrative authority granted by realism. While critical treatments of the black/white color line were visible in the mass-mediated realisms of Erskine Caldwell, Lillian Hellman, Nelson Algren, Clifford Odets, and John Garfield, writers of color had an incredibly difficult time actually crossing this line into the mass market, gaining recognition as realists, and thus framing social critiques on their own terms. And though Richard Wright achieved huge commercial success with *Native Son* in 1940 and again with *Black Boy* in 1945, he was the exception to the rule.

This lack of access was more severe in regard to Asian American authors during the Depression. White writer Pearl S. Buck had proven without a doubt that there was an interest in Asia within the U.S. literary market of the 1930s that went beyond the Yellow Perilism of Sax Rohmer's *Fu Man Chu* series. Her realist novel about the common Chinese farmer Wang Lung became a number one best-seller in 1931 and 1932, but this interest did not automatically translate into a widespread desire to hear Asian American voices representing either Asia or the United States. As the Chinese American, Popular Front writer H. T. Tsiang lamented above, his novel *And China Has Hands* (1937), about a Chinese laundryman in New York, remained obscure while Buck prospered.

But while writers of Asian descent on the U.S. scene had the smallest of audiences in the 1930s, the situation changed somewhat around the time of Pearl Harbor. America's entrance into World War II provided authors of Chinese and Filipino descent in particular with access to an unprecedented literary audience in the United States. Christina Klein writes, "The emotional bond that Americans felt with the people of China and the Philippines as allies in the Pacific war created a greater awareness of and sympathy toward Chinese and Filipinos living in the U.S., which translated into a national audience for the stories they had to tell" (227). The turn-of-the-century Yellow Peril nightmare of Sino-Japanese unity—that of Japanese technical acumen directing Chinese coolie labor—proved illusory. Thus according to Robert G. Lee, "For the first time, being able to tell one Asian group apart from another seemed important to white Americans" (*Orientals* 147). The war did not represent a generalized wave of tolerance toward people of Asian descent, but rather a lessening of the Yellow Peril discourse historically directed at the Chinese and Filipinos and an intensification of this discourse in regard to the Japanese and Japanese Americans. Betrayed by the CPUSA, forced into internment camps, and falling to the very bottom of the U.S. racial hierarchy for the duration of the conflict, Japanese American authors and illustrators such as Toshio Mori, John Okada, Mine Okubo, and Hisaye Yamamoto would have to wait until after 1945 even to find a publisher.[1] But from within this national scene where intra-Asian difference was increasingly recognized, Filipino American author Carlos Bulosan and Chinese-born Tsiang were able strategically to use the rise of fascism abroad to articulate a transnational political aesthetic, one that struggled for class-conscious, anti-imperial liberation for their countries of origin and a viable space for Asians living in the United States. Bulosan's nationalistic deployment of both "America" and the Philippines, as well as Tsiang's nationalistic deployment of China, are central to their unique configurations of global and national within the Popular

Front—configurations that evoke the tropes of "We're the people" while simultaneously exposing their limits. One of the aims of this chapter is to examine the nature of these configurations in order to highlight the kind of Asian American transnational politics that were possible within the U.S. literary market in the 1930s and 1940s. For writers Bulosan and Tsiang, to be legible as a "realist" was a major prerequisite for visibility.

The differences between Bulosan and Tsiang in actually achieving an audience for their transnational projects were profound. Tsiang arrived in the United States in 1926, after having been forced to flee China on account of his left-leaning political activities. He had grown up in poverty in Jiangsu Province but had nonetheless earned a university degree after years of struggle. He continued his education at both Stanford and Columbia, and also became a writer for Chinese-language and communist presses in the late 1920s and 1930s. His political activities at this time earned him the ire of both the U.S. and Chinese governments, but despite the attempts of Chinese officials to extradite him and American officials to deport him, he remained in the States for the rest of his life. He published poetry in the *Daily Worker* and the *New Masses*, wrote two plays and three novels, and was an actor on both stage and screen. His works have been praised by more recent scholars for their historic, political, and aesthetic significance. Of Tsiang's legacy, his 1937 novel *And China Has Hands*—a book that linked racial tolerance in the U.S. to the liberation of the Chinese people from Japanese imperialism—has been regarded as his best work. Commenting on this book, Floyd Cheung has written: "Adapting form to purpose, Tsiang deftly blends Chinese and Western literary modes and, at times with comic pungency, captures the bicultural dissonance integral to the Chinese-American and, more broadly, the Asian-American experience" (10). In contrast to such recent praise, Tsiang's published work was largely ignored by the public in the 1930s and 1940s; reviewers in left and mainstream presses scarcely noted it, and his book sales were unimpressive even by 1930s standards.[2]

Bulosan, on the other hand, had consistent access to mainstream newspapers and journals, where he was warmly received until a plagiarism case destroyed his literary reputation in 1946 (the plagiarism charge was later struck down in court, but only posthumously). Bulosan grew up on a destitute farm in Northern Luzon and migrated to the U.S. in 1931, where he was thoroughly marginalized on account of his race as he migrated from job to job along the West Coast. Like Tsiang, he never returned to his country of origin (San Juan Jr, *Cry* x, Kim 46). Between 1942 and 1946, he published three collections of poetry and two fictionalized autobiographies, *Laughter of My Father* and *America Is in the Heart*, all of which met general acclaim from journals ranging from the communist *New Masses* to the (then) conservative *New York Times*. In addition to his essay in *Saturday Evening Post*, his stories also appeared in the *New Yorker*, *Town and Country*, and *Harper's Bazaar*. Excerpts from *Laughter of My Father* were broadcast to U.S. troops during the war to create greater sympathy for their Filipino allies, and *America Is in the Heart* was named by *Look* as one of the fifty most important books ever published (Kim 45). A sketch of Bulosan's face even appeared on the front cover of the *Saturday Review of Literature* in March 1946.

If the Pacific War (1937–45) pitted the home countries of Tsiang and Bulosan against the Japanese, giving both authors potential access to a sympathetic U.S. audience, and both used that access to promote a homologous, transnational political project, what accounts for the vast differences in their reception? It is tempting to answer this question simply by looking at their publication dates: Tsiang published most of his major works in the 1930s, before U.S. interest in Asia peaked with the bombing of Pearl Harbor, while Bulosan published his works after 1941. The issue is much more complicated, however, not least because Tsiang's highly anti-Japanese *And China Has Hands* could have easily been reissued after the U.S. entrance in the war, which was only four years after its initial publication in 1937. Indeed, many books initially published in the 1930s were republished in the 1940s, when a heavily enlarged market for books—triggered by the development of inexpensive paperbacks, reduced wartime leisure opportunities, and rising incomes—tempted publishers to reprint books that had met with only modest success the first time around (*God's Little Acre* serves as a perfect example).

I will argue, to the contrary, that Bulosan achieved such a wide audience for four main, interconnected reasons that have not been explored in the criticism to date. First, because of his rhetorical deployment of the yeoman farmer, a figure that, in his most "successful" work *America Is in the Heart*, Bulosan placed within a popular narrative of agrarian decline that had enabled the novels of John Steinbeck, Pearl Buck, Erskine Caldwell, and Margaret Mitchell to achieve best-seller status. Bulosan caught the attention of American readers by inscribing Filipino peasants with the virtues of the republican yeoman, and in so doing, he attempted to correct the blindness of even American leftists like Edgar Snow to an oppressive history of American imperialism, a history both referenced and elided by the pluralism of "We're the people." Second, his work was more recognizably realist than that of Tsiang, though the nature of that realism would shift considerably from *Laughter of my Father* to *America Is in the Heart*. Though the yeoman farmer has enjoyed mythic status in the history of American republican discourse, the agrarian narrative in which he moved was read as more real than romantic in the 1930s and 1940s; Bulosan's use of this figure in *America* greatly helped enable his reception as a realist writer. A third reason for his U.S. literary success resulted from a complex, shifting relationship he creates between his Filipino characters and modernity, as I will elaborate. Finally, much of Bulosan's work was immediately legible within the emergent Cold War hegemonic order in a way that Tsiang's literary work was not—a Cold War order that, in part, grew out of World War II–era antifascist and antiracist discourse. Tsiang's visibly communist major work implicated American novel readers to the extent that the very possibility of their culture fostering genuine cultural pluralism was thrown into question. In part, this chapter addresses the issue of relative U.S. appeal through a literary reading of these authors' most popular books: Bulosan's *Laughter of My Father* and *America Is in the Heart* (hereafter, *Laughter* and *America*), and Tsiang's *And China Has Hands*. But I will closely explore the contemporary critical responses to these works, an exploration essential to moving the question of their impact on readers beyond abstract speculation. A close reading of the reception of Bulosan in particular is largely missing from contemporary scholarship, and its inclusion here is essential to my final argument: that although Bulosan's work was more amenable to the emergent postwar order, it resisted full co-optation. Both Tsiang and Bulosan dramatically avoided the exceptionalism of "We're the people," the pluralism embodied by *The Grapes of Wrath* and much of the New Deal. They serve as the some of the most transnational expressions of the People's Century.

Rather than signaling a general breakthrough, the case of Carlos Bulosan signals an ephemeral window of access for oppositional Asian/Asian American authors to the culture industries. And though Bulosan can be considered the first Filipino writer in the States with a definite readership, his work did not reach nearly as many people as the representations of Asia by white authors Pearl Buck or Edgar Snow, nor even the readership of *Black Boy* or *Native Son*. Nonetheless, the peak years of literary output for Bulosan and Tsiang should be seen as interventions within an important moment in the history of American Orientalism. A number of seminal works in the field of Asian American studies have held the 1930s and 1940s as a crucial transitional time in the representation of Asians and Asian Americans by the dominant U.S. culture. In their own respective ways, David Palumbo-Liu, Robert G. Lee, Christina Klein, Elaine Kim, and more recently Colleen Lye have seen these decades as a bridge between the prevailing pre-WWII view of Asians/Asian Americans as the Yellow Peril and the reigning postwar discourse of Asian Americans as "model minorities." Domestically, the shift involved a legal and cultural imperative to assimilate people of Asian descent living in the United States as citizens, while in international affairs, the shift was marked by an image of the U.S. as a friendly, noncoercive partner to decolonizing nations.[3]

The most important reason for the shift, these scholars agree, was the increasingly unavoidable U.S. relationships with Asian countries brought about by the rise of fascism, increasing U.S. investments in the region, and the emergent Cold War, in which the Yellow Peril discourse was ill suited for creating the alliances across the Pacific essential to pursuing new economic partnerships and military conflicts. Scholars disagree on what constitute the crucial years of the transition from Yellow Peril to model minority discourse. But what collectively emerges from these studies is the link between official World War II–era antifascist narratives and the rhetoric of the Cold War consensus, a link that the study of Asian racial formation reveals.[4] The realm of culture was crucial in creating the new images of Asia and Asian America necessary to meet these U.S. policy goals; but, for oppositional Asian Americans, it was also a crucial sphere for contesting them. By examining realist representations of Asia in the popular culture of the 1930s and 1940s, the following sections will illustrate how Popular Front writers both contributed to and contested this transitional phase of Asian/Asian American racial formation. Bulosan, in particular, effectively took advantage of the instability of Orientalist discourse at this historical moment to promote his class-conscious, anti-imperialist politics. Using realism as a site of inquiry, this chapter will ask: what was usable to the postwar hegemonic bloc within Popular Front renderings of Asia and Asian America, and what needed to be silenced? As such, this chapter and the next will be looking forward in time, interrogating the usability of mass-mediated realisms for Cold War ends. I will begin with influential white Popular Front readings of China and the Philippines, because in many ways they defined the cultural milieu in which Asian/Asian American writers could operate.

From Yellow Peril to Brown Republican
The East Asia of Pearl Buck, Edgar Snow, and Edward Dmytryk

In the last chapter I noted the abundance of agrarian-themed novels at the top of the best-seller lists in the 1930s. Moreover, the class-conscious novels from 1930–45 that had the greatest sales—*The Grapes of Wrath, Tobacco Road,* and *God's Little Acre*—contained some degree of agrarian nostalgia. *The Grapes of Wrath* and similar narratives of the New Deal era—John Dos Passos's *USA Trilogy,* the photo narratives of the Farm Security Administration, and the documentary films of Pare Lorentz, to take a few examples—often imagined a preindustrial republic of virtuous small farmers or artisans as a way of gauging how America and its people had gone astray. In an oppositional variant of republicanism which Michael Denning has called "the Decline and Fall of the Lincoln Republic," this virtuous world is betrayed by robber barons and gilded dreams of empire (168). But because of the generally white homogeneity of this imagined past, the pluralism of much of this work is more in line with "We're the people" rather than "The People's Century" (barring Caldwell, as I have argued).[5]

It is also important to note that this agrarian nostalgia intersected with extremely popular representations of China in the 1930s and 1940s, particularly in the work of Pearl Buck and Edgar Snow. It should come as no surprise that two of the key writers who "translated" Asia for U.S. audiences deployed such yeoman figures as well. Buck's best-sellers *The Good Earth* (1931) and *Dragon Seed* (1942) centered on common Chinese farmers deeply wedded to the soil, while the reportage and topical nonfiction of Edgar Snow, a Popular Front journalist for the *Saturday Evening Post*, turned Chinese communists into Jeffersonian icons. Both of these authors avoided representing the Chinese in terms of the absolute difference necessary to Yellow Peril discourse. In a U.S. mass culture permeated with the hard, anti-Chinese racism inherent in the figures of the coolie and Dr. Fu Man Chu, they participated in shifting public discourse on the Chinese away from such images. The results were quite significant. As Colleen Lye has written, the mid-century narratives of Buck and Snow "inscribed Asian politics into the very heart of American national identity" (143). But in doing so, they problematically—and unrealistically—elided any substantive cultural differences whatsoever.

At the very top of the best-seller list in 1931 and 1932, Buck's *The Good Earth* was tremendously influential. In his 1958 study of American views toward Asia, Harold Isaacs claimed that this novel defined the impressions of influential Americans toward the Chinese more than any other text, adding that all interviewees who spontaneously cited Buck as the main source of their images of the Chinese viewed them as "a wonderfully attractive people" (155). In the 1930s and 1940s, Buck's work was hailed by mainstream and left critics for cutting through the Yellow Peril racism of novelists like Sax Rohmer, the creator of Dr. Fu Manchu, and she was often considered a goodwill ambassador between China and the United States. However, her stories of Chinese life were increasingly placed alongside Rohmer's mysteries in the dubious canon of Orientalist literature after the Yellow Power movements of the late 1960s enabled a greater space for Asian American literary self-expression (Allmendinger 361, 370, Lye 204–5).[6]

The Good Earth centers on the character Wang Lung and his wife O-Lan, who begin the story as small farmers in northern Anhwei province in China. Through hard work, frugality, and tenacious devotion to the land, they overcome all obstacles and accumulate a fortune, surpassing the decadent landowners of the House of Hwang in which O-Lan began as a slave. Wang Lung becomes as decadent as the family he surpassed, however, turning his back on the moral clarity of farming to pursue the luxury symbolized by a concubine named Lotus. The simple, hard-working O-Lan dies after his long neglect, and he moves into town with his sons to reside in the former House of Hwang. Meanwhile, all his children have become estranged from the land in various ways. Eventually, he forsakes this affluent yet alienated existence to return to his original house, spending the rest of his days as a simple farmer. But the novel ends on a bitter note, for Wang Lung overhears his sons discussing a plan to sell the land he loves so dearly after his death.

The story is both agrarian and republican in that it creates a polar opposition between plain living, frugality, small landownership, and virtue on the one hand, and a frivolous, unscrupulous, and urban culture on the other. Holding the producerist values of the yeoman farmer, Wang Lung rejects the values of both the landless proletariat below him and the decadent aristocracy above; he instead favors the simple pleasure of tilling the soil, a pleasure not reducible to financial gain. During a famine that temporarily throws his family into the ranks of the urban proletariat, Wang Lung reflects: "He belonged, not to this scum which clung to the walls of a rich man's house; nor did he belong to the rich man's house. He belonged to the land and he could not live with any fullness until he felt the land under his feet and followed a plow in the springtime and bore a scythe in his hand at harvest" (123). His connection with the earth is so intense that at times it becomes literal, even approaching the surreal. Buck writes, "And if he grew too weary in the day he laid himself into a furrow and there with the good warmth of his own land against his flesh, he slept" (145). This literal connection to the land is also racial; as Lye has noted, Chinese tillers of the soil have dark skin in the novel, while those who become estranged from the earth (including Wang Lang and his children) turn yellow in complexion (216). Thus, in Buck's universe Chinese farmers have lost the quality of absolute difference which made them a Yellow Peril in Western eyes, not only because they are essentially hearty yeomen of the American republican tradition, but also because they have literally shed their yellow skin.

Buck became a harsh critic of American foreign policy during the Cold War, arguing that it marked a continuity with European imperialism and thus could never hope to win the loyalties of the Third World. She was also active in antiracist campaigns that were transnational in scope (including the Citizen's Committee to Repeal Chinese Exclusion), pursuing a politics that linked U.S. militarism abroad to the oppression of women at home (Shaffer 152–53). But neither American communists nor the People's Republic of China embraced her most famous work, though her ambivalence about communism in the 1930s was largely overlooked during World War II. It was hard for the left to claim *The Good Earth* because of the individualistic qualities of Wang Lung, who eschews all community and collective organization in his single-minded quest to keep his plot of land (it is not by accident that a number of critics, including Tsiang, noted a Horatio Alger quality in *The Good Earth*).

Despite its rather far-fetched conflations of the United States and China, *The Good Earth* could be taken as a serious portrait of China because of its realist form, which Buck employed with great effectiveness. This realism lay in a combination of elements the book brought together: focus on an ordinary individual in a specific (albeit misrecognized) social context, lack of ambiguity in the prose, clear linearity of the plot, and intended social significance. Buck saw this form as befitting her subject, as she found the Chinese to be "realistic [and] practical, rather than artistic" (Isaacs 158). While elite critics did not always see Buck as a serious artist, the interviewees of Isaacs's 1957 study saw Buck as replacing "fantasy images of China" with a "a more realistic picture of what China was like" (156). And while the American left largely ignored the publication of *The Good Earth*, she was retroactively embraced by the communist press as a realist with the publication of *Dragon Seed* in 1942. Re-dubbed by a reviewer in *The New Masses* as "The Good Earth's Warriors," her novel of antifascist resistance was praised for its "unflinching realism," while *The Daily Worker* praised it for its "rich detail" and the "realist psychology" of its complex characters (Sillen 27, Morison 7). "The Good Earth's Warriors" was an apt retitling of *Dragon Seed*, as it contained a quite similar cast of rugged, soil-loving, small farmers, albeit now engaged in a collective struggle to repel the Japanese fascist invader. In addition to the greater tolerance afforded to noncommunists after the Third Period, *The New Masses* now embraced Buck's work because the missing link of collective action had been restored to her portrait of China. As its reviewer wrote, "If *Dragon Seed* is the firmest and most convincing of Pearl Buck's novels, it is in large measure because the author has imaginatively participated in a crucial phase of anti-fascist struggle" (Sillen 27). That such a yeoman figure could be read as an authentic representation of the Chinese, both inside and outside the left, shows the unfortunate capacity of realism to sometimes naturalize conventional ideological signs. It also illustrates how, for many critics and ordinary readers in the 1930s, there was nothing "romantic" about the hearty yeoman, particularly if located in a land far way.

Edgar Snow's topical, nonfiction books of China and East Asia had far fewer readers than Buck, but they also were stunningly influential among intellectuals and shapers of public opinion (Isaac 163). Unlike Buck, however, Snow was more consistently embraced by the left during the 1930s and 1940s, and one quickly sees why when reading his work. In *Red Star over China*, he told the story of Chinese "Reds" from the perspective of what we would now call an embedded reporter. Writing from within Chinese Soviet districts, he interviewed communist leaders (including Mao Tse-Tung), covered Red Army clashes with Nationalist troops, and reported on improved conditions for peasant farmers in communist-controlled areas. Despite the fact that Snow was not a communist—to the contrary, as a staff writer for the *Saturday Evening Post* he was a quintessentially mainstream journalist—*Red Star* was glowingly favorable to the communists and highly critical of the Nationalist government. Not only did it heavily influence U.S. views of China but, unlike Buck's work, it had a material effect on anti-imperial movements in East Asia. Many Chinese youths learned of the Soviet districts for the first time from *Red Star*, and it was used by the Huk guerilla movement in the Philippines as a training manual for military operations. At a time when most of the world thought the Chinese Red Army was finished, the book not only confirmed its existence but substantially built up its worldwide image (Lye 224–25).

The book arguably endeared American readers to the Chinese communists because it also translated their struggles using the terms of agrarian republicanism. In contrast to the Nationalists, the Red leaders are consistently depicted as self-sacrificing: Mao is described as "plain-speaking and plain-living," and is shown not to live any better than ordinary soldiers. Snow even calls him "Lincoln-esque" (70). Like their American counterparts, Chinese farmers are squeezed by wealthy landlords in a "share-crop" system that is causing the decline of "independent farming" and the accumulation of wealth in fewer and fewer hands (84). In the Red-controlled areas, by stark contrast, the communists have granted tenant farmers ownership of the land they work on, abolished taxes, and have established universal suffrage and a kind of representative government (230, 234–35). These land reforms, we are told, have given Chinese peasants the will to fight both Nationalist troops and the Japanese. Snow's choice to represent China as a clear-cut yeoman democracy helps explain why his work spread so widely in U.S. culture, while Agnes Smedley's glowing reports of the Chinese communists, by contrast, were not as influential outside of left-wing circles.

Colleen Lye has brilliantly examined how Snow, in his description of his first glimpse of one of Mao's soldiers, inscribes the Chinese Red Army with the virtues of American frontiersmen. In this vein, his rendering of his first encounter with a "Red" farmer is equally telling, as it reveals his attempt to counter Yellow Peril discourse while also buying into its underlying assumptions. Shortly after entering communist territory, he describes this first meeting: "A young farmer, wearing a turban of white towelling [sic] on his head and a revolver strapped to his waist, came out and looked at me in astonishment. Who was I and what did I want?" Snow goes on to write: "He did not seem to belong to the race of timid peasants of China elsewhere. There was a challenge in his sparkling merry eyes, and a certain bravado. He slowly moved his hand away from his revolver butt and smiled" (34–35). His subsequent account of Chinese politics explains that bravado, which questioned Snow's right even to be there: that is, the Reds made timid coolies into brave, self-governing men willing to defend their land. Throughout the book he presents the Chinese Reds as eliminating the qualities that made the Chinese a "peril" to U.S. labor within its narratives of exclusion, chief among them passivity. Through his travels in Soviet territory, he writes that "I began to understand a little bit why the Chinese communists have fought so long, so uncompromisingly, so un-Chinese-like" (63), and thus partly assumes that prerevolutionary China conformed to its Yellow Peril reading by U.S. exclusionists. Other practices that had made the Chinese a "peril" were also banned in Red territory, as Snow reveals: "Foot-binding and infanticide were criminal offences, child slavery and prostitution had disappeared, and polyandry and polygamy were prohibited" (241). *Red Star* also emphasizes how the communists banished opium from their China. Revealingly, one of the few small farmers in the book who protests against Soviet reforms does so because the Reds will not allow him to smoke opium (261–63).

While Snow tries to make clear to his readers that "traditional" Chinese passivity arose from oppressive social conditions and not innate racial traits (228), his republican dualism between prerevolutionary dependents versus revolutionary independents, applied to the Chinese context, partly assumed the problems besetting Chinese society as defined by Yellow Peril discourse. That said, Snow's overall work did not simply and easily facilitate official U.S. foreign policy agendas. In contrast to Pearl Buck, Snow's work was officially sanctioned by the Chinese government as an accurate account of prerevolutionary China. Mao assaulted critics who challenged the veracity of Snow's version of events, and years later, one of Snow's former comrades, Xiao Qian, remarked, "At a time when most foreigners treated Chinese as cows that could produce milk for them, Snow took us as equal partners who co-operated with him for the same cause" (Farnsworth 316, Wang 56). While such praise would have been potentially palatable in the U.S. after Nixon's visit to China in 1972, during the early years of the Cold War it led to a rapid decline in Snow's journalistic influence. But in gauging the dissonance Snow (and to a certain extent Buck) created for official policy, what was perhaps more important than their official favor in an "enemy" nation was the way in which they exposed the United States as not living up to its yeoman, republican ideas abroad. Colleen Lye has astutely noted that Snow and Buck presented U.S. readers with a "satisfying escape from insurmountable agricultural failure" at home, and that Snow's account of the Long March in *Red Star* was a "thrilling counter-epic to the troubling phenomenon of mass migration in the 1930s" (233). One can read *Red Star* as more than an "escape" from the nation's failure of its commitment to the American farmer, however. In the elision of cultural difference it enacts by representing the Red Chinese as hardy yeoman of the republican tradition—painting the communist Chinese as more American than Americans, as it were—it poses real problems for American exceptionalism not only in suggesting that so-called "American" virtues are not unique, but also by illustrating how the contradiction within its own ideals are resolved by its political and racial antithesis. And while *Red Star* largely absolves the United States from its complicity in China's woes (according to the author, Mao is a fan of George Washington and mostly has Japan in mind when using the word "imperialism" [91–92, 134]), his subsequent books *Battle for Asia* (1941) and *People on Our Side* (1944) do not. Like Buck's wartime writings, these later works explicitly indict U.S. foreign policy for aiding the repressive Chiang Kai-shek government rather than the communists. To Snow, the American support of Chiang marked a failure to live up to the promises inherent in the Four Freedoms and the wartime rhetoric of the "people's war."

But Snow's brand of anti-imperialism did not lead him to question the broader American record of empire. In *People on Our Side* one finds the following description of a national demonstration in the Philippines commemorating the fortieth anniversary of the U.S. occupation: "Millions of humble Filipinos marched out under banners of the infant republic to pay tribute to the United States 'for the boundless blessings bestowed upon us,' the first time in history any people ever spontaneously offered thanksgiving to its own conquerors" (42). This anecdote was intended to underscore the differences between the British imperialism he witnessed in India, based on racial prejudice and the solidification of ancient hierarchies, and American intervention, which built schools, scientific achievement, and, more fundamentally important, a sense of liberty (42).

Such a view was echoed in the contemporaneous film *Back to Bataan* (1945), directed by Edward Dmytryk and cowritten by Ben Barzman, both Popular Fronters at the time (Dmytryk later became one of the Hollywood Ten). The film attempted to achieve a documentary quality. Its opening text asserted that "This story was not invented . . . The characters are based on real people," and then cut to ennobling, FSA-style shots of actual GIs liberated by American and Filipino forces, accompanied by captions giving their name, rank, and home town. Dmytryk and Barzman presented Filipinos as a friendly, brave, and likeable people, but also implied that their American parentage had enabled them to rediscover their innate courage and their will to resist. *Back to Bataan* achieves this effect by combining its realist cinematography with popular allegory. The allegorical American "father" in the film is military tutelage, embodied by Colonel Joe Madden (John Wayne), while the "mother" is American education, embodied by the schoolteacher Ms. Barnes (Beulah Bondi). Their status as parents becomes clear in one pivotal shot, where they are framed together cradling the dying Filipino child Maximo, who had embodied the spirit of liberty by sacrificing himself to save his guerilla unit.[7]

While these white Popular Front representations allowed for a more sympathetic reading of Asian peasants to take hold in the United States, potentially creating a larger audience for authors of East Asian origin, they were clearly inadequate for a critique of American imperial designs in Asia and their links to Asian American racial formation within the U.S. Tsiang and Bulosan took up these critical tasks but, in the case of the latter author, entered the symbolic language of these earlier Popular Front writers in order to do so. Bulosan, in particular, would reinscribe the agrarian tropes of Buck and Snow in his own realist vein to win an American audience for his transnational politics.

The Forgotten Literary Interventions of H. T. Tsiang

Like Bulosan's work, *And China Has Hands* (hereafter, *Hands*) weaves together various left nationalisms of the 1930s, imaginatively adapting them to Tsiang's own diasporic location to form a class-conscious anti-imperialism. The plot centers mainly on the character of Wong Wan-Lee, a Chinese immigrant who, at the beginning of the story, has already moved to New York City to make his fortune. He works as a waiter in a restaurant, then buys a laundry to become a small proprietor. In his stint as a laundryman, Wan-Lee meets Pearl Chang—the second major character of the novel. Pearl, a young, biracial woman who grew up in the U.S. South, had moved to New York in the hopes of achieving stardom. Pearl is half black, yet she is drawn to images of beautiful white movie stars and a notion of Chinese authenticity that she has gleaned entirely from U.S. mass culture. The middle portions of the novel detail the attempts of Wan-Lee, an ardent Chinese nationalist, to exorcize Pearl's mass-culture baggage and teach her what it means to be "authentically" Chinese. The laundry on which Wan-Lee had pinned his hopes of prosperity is eventually bankrupted, however, by a combination of nefarious white competitors, corrupt officials, and Chinese American con men. The end of the narrative finds him back in food service again—albeit at an even lower level, as a busboy in a highly exploitative Chinese cafeteria, alongside Pearl. It is in his return to wage labor and food service that both he and Pearl attain a political consciousness fully in line with that of the author: they take part in a multiracial strike against his Chinese American employer, and Wan-Lee is killed on the picket line by a Japanese agent.

Hands was ignored by both mainstream and leftist presses, despite the fact that it was published at the height of its topicality: it appeared in 1937, the year Japan launched its full-scale invasion of the Chinese mainland and when the Second Sino-Japanese War was regularly in the headlines. As if predicting its obscurity, Tsiang inscribes himself into the novel in the form of a marginal, unnamed character who is a writer of proletarian literature. This character tells Pearl that he wrote *China Red* and *The Hanging on Union Square*—two titles that Tsiang actually authored. He says to her that despite the fact his work was praised in the Soviet Union, "the fakers here in America condemned it," and they had added "'he is not much of a writer'" (35). But neither the communist *Daily Worker* and *New Masses* nor the "dissident" *Partisan Review* responded to this novel, despite the fact that the former periodicals had published Tsiang's poetry in the late 1920s. Given a similar silence on the U.S. left in regard to Bulosan's major prose works, one explanation for the oversight lies in the overwhelmingly black/white frame the left used in interpreting domestic racial relations, a frame that allowed it to overlook a great deal of Asian American self-expression.[8] Tsiang's cold reception by the mainstream press—which reacted very positively to Bulosan—is slightly more complicated. One reason is the form, which, as Floyd Cheung has noted, is more in line with experimental modernism and draws on Chinese literary structures unfamiliar to U.S. readers. In the 1940s and 1950s, several narratives of Chinatown circulated widely within American popular culture, namely C. Y. Lee's *Flower Drum Song* (popularized by Rodgers and Hammerstein's musical adaptation), Jade Snow Wong's *Fifth*

Chinese Daughter, and Pardee Lowe's *Father and Glorious Descendent.* The reasons for the "success" of these stories helps explain why *Hands* fell on deaf ears, but the explanation does not lie exclusively in terms of aesthetic form.[9]

Christina Klein sees these later tales of Chinatown as helping integrate the Chinese in the U.S. by showing their difference to be a matter of culture, not race. However, they deny essential realities of the Chinese American experience in the process. Their focus on the family, with an emphasis on generational conflict, helped make the Chinese seem "just like" other Americans; but this family frame erased the overwhelmingly male demographics of Chinese communities in the U.S. created by nativist legislation. The Rodgers and Hammerstein musical in particular stressed the ease with which the Chinese were assimilating into mainstream American life, but it did so by denying the history of racialization (228–29). Significant for their pluralistic ends, these Chinatown narratives also had a "touristic quality," with narrators who "guide[d] their readers like privileged tourists through the inner workings of Chinese families, businesses, social relations, and customs" (228). Whereas earlier tourist excursions into Chinatown had represented the place in terms of absolute foreignness—often serving exclusionist ends—these 1950s tours of Chinatown were displays of "ethnic" culture designed to promote cultural awareness.

Like Wong, Lowe, and Rodgers and Hammerstein, Tsiang in *Hands* can also be seen as guiding the non-Chinese reader through Chinese America; he does so, furthermore, for the purpose of undermining assumptions about its spaces that had been implanted by earlier narrative excursions there in literature, film, and popular reportage. But unlike the popular postwar narratives, Tsiang responds to pre-WWII constructions of an exoticized Chinatown by frustrating the tourist impulse altogether. For him, the cultural encounter provided by tourism is inherently hierarchical and commodified.

In contrast to most Popular Front nationalisms, *Hands* maintains a thorough rejection of the culture of the imperial core, particularly its tendency to commodify the cultures of those it colonizes. Although Wong Wan-Lee comes to embrace a different form of nationalism at the novel's conclusion, his observations of white crowds in Chinatown and Chinese museums during what Palumbo-Liu calls his "naive" stint as a laundryman reveal a critique of cultural commodification not negated by the resolution of the novel.[10] A key component of this commodification, to Tsiang, involves the way in which most Americans have constructed Chinese culture through food—particularly chop suey and chow mein. In response, both Wan-Lee and Pearl attempt to construct an identity partially based on the consumption of "genuine" Chinese dishes. For instance, Wan-Lee repeatedly tells Pearl that chop suey and chow mein have no basis in a genuine Chinese tradition. When Pearl naively asks Wan-Lee to serve her the Chinese "national dishes" of chop suey and chow mein, he defiantly replies "I am no American. I eat no Chop Suey. I eat no Chow Mein" (53). Wan-Lee shows Pearl authentic Chinese food by taking her to dinner at a Chinese club; in this dinner scene, Tsiang describes the content of their meal in great detail, thereby describing (and performing) in his status as author a corrected version of Chinese culture to non-Chinese readers (and/or to Chinese readers in the U.S. who, like Pearl, are in danger of losing their cultural heritage) (62). If, as Klein wrote, chop suey was "a witty ode to American pluralism" in the Rodgers and Hammerstein musical, here it is a symbol of cultural contamination and a means of shaming those who have taken part in ethnic tourism.

Thus, from his location within the U.S., a pressing task for Tsiang is stripping Chinese labor and culture of its Orientalist baggage so that its role within the global context can begin to be recognized by his readers there. This project is also predicated on the complete demystification—even banalization—of the Chinese community. To this end, the author takes one of its hallmark spaces, the Chinatown backroom, and renders it mundane, altogether frustrating the lure of the exotic. The Chinatown backroom had been the site of an exocitized, exclusionist narrative about Chinese workers since the late nineteenth century. According to this narrative, the back of a Chinese-owned business—often a laundry or restaurant—was a mysterious and sinister place into which young, innocent white girls were often lured and brought to ruin through opium addiction and slavery. Though as the following passage from the infamous American Federation of Labor tract "Meat vs. Rice" illustrates, "any building in Chinatown" held such backrooms:

> Now, follow your guide through a door, which he forces, into a sleeping room. The air is thick with vapors. The atmosphere is tangible ... Tangible to the sight, tangible to the touch, tangible to the taste, and oh, how tangible the smell! You may even hear it as the opium smoker sucks it through his pipe bowl into his trained lungs ... It is a sense of horror you have never experienced, revolting, and to the last degree, sickening and stupefying ... Before the door was opened for your entrance every aperture was closed, and here, had they not been thus rudely disturbed, they would have slept in the dense and poisonous atmosphere until morning. (Gompers 16)

In *Hands* the protagonist's movement through his laundry, which includes a front area for dealing with customers and a back area for his private use, forms much of the plot. In direct contrast to the titillating horror offered by the authors of "Meat vs. Rice," Tsiang bluntly exposes the banality of the "secret" space behind the curtain generally off-limits to whites:

> In the doorway, between [some] wooden shelves, was a curtain.
> Behind the wooden shelves and the curtain was a drying room.
> Behind the drying room was a bedroom (24).

The narrator goes on to describe the daily routine of Wan-Lee as a laundryman, a routine marked by never-ending labor from dawn to dusk. At the end of the day, Tsiang writes, "Pulling the curtains down and putting out the light of the outer room, he retired to the back room, washed, cooked, ate, and slept. Day in and day out, year in and year out, that is the life of a Chinese laundryman, and Wong Wan-Lee was one of them" (27). The space behind the curtain of the Chinese laundry is thereby stripped of its dangerous exoticism for white readers and is instead exposed as a humdrum site of recuperation from endless and unnecessary toil. The message to would-be Chinatown tourists is also clear: there is nothing here to see.

For Tsiang, the American tourist gaze is part of a larger Orientalist popular culture that works to prevent revolutionary agency. He develops this position mainly through his character Pearl Chang. She demands that Wan-Lee prepare her chop suey and chow mein because her Chinese identity has been mediated by American radio, tabloids, and Hollywood film. She also expects Wan-Lee to have a "pigtail," since all Chinese she has seen in the movies have queues, and is disappointed when he does not (37). Pearl has a photo of a movie star by her bed, and her nightly reading of tabloids both deepens her love of film stars and deludes her into dreaming she can actually become a star herself (51). So while Wan-Lee's early naivety revolves around his faith in upward mobility and his investment in a bourgeois form of Chinese nationalism, Pearl's naivety wholly revolves around her investment in U.S. mass culture. Given that Tsiang wrote at a moment in which the most well-known Chinese individual in American popular culture was still Dr. Fu Manchu, created by Sax Rohmer over a series of novels dating from 1913 to 1959, and made into film with *The Mask of Fu Manchu* in 1932 (starring Boris Karloff), and that Chinese men had been consistently represented as a sexual threat from the very beginning of American film in titles such as *The Cheat* (1915) by Cecil B. DeMille and *Broken Blossoms* by D. W. Griffith (1919), this investment in U.S. mass culture by a person of Chinese descent could only be self-destructive (Lee *Orientals* 117–20). But unlike his character Pearl, Hollywood was not a complete abstraction for Tsiang. Though little is known about his biography, his experience as an actor in Hollywood—in which he was always relegated to minor roles—must have fueled the frustrations with mass culture as rendered in *Hands*.[11]

Thus, unlike many 1940s and 1950s narratives of Chinatown, *Hands* does not skirt troubling issues of exclusion to make its case for Asian inclusion. For almost a century leading up to its publication, a string of nativist bills had limited the Chinese presence by thwarting their attempts to form families in the U.S. The Page Act of 1875 made it very difficult for Chinese women to enter to country, while the Expatriation Act (1907) and the Cable Act (1922) removed U.S. citizenship from American-born women who married Chinese men. These laws helped ensure that Chinese communities in the U.S. would remain "bachelor societies." It is significant, within this legislative context, that Wan-Lee is never able to establish a family in the U.S. His union with Pearl occurs only at the moment of his death, and his passing on American soil with only a symbolic union reflects a reality of anti-Chinese legislation. Wan-Lee's desire to save money as an independent businessman is also repeatedly handicapped by the machinations of whites: namely, the building inspector who demands exorbitant bribes (80–83) and the white laundrymen who spread vicious rumors about their Chinese competitors (107). Indeed, there is not a single positive white character in the entire text; more than this, apart from the building inspector and a waiter named "Butcher Face" mentioned only in passing (21), there are no white characters in the novel at all. Whites exist as an otherwise menacing and faceless force that threatens to either co-opt Wan-Lee's culture or drag him into poverty.

This "white peril" is also part of a much larger threat that crosses national borders: fascism. The other characters who seek to destroy Pearl and Wan-Lee are fascistically aligned Chinese. Tsiang tells of a Chinese loan shark who exploits the protagonist: "He had recently finished his Ph.D. thesis—'How to Sell China More Profitably'—and he had also made great progress in studying Japanese" (88). The cafeteria's Chinese American owner, a self-proclaimed member of the "Chinese Nationalist Party," fires the multiracial Pearl, bluntly telling her, "I have to respect the national race purity . . . You have scorned my racial theory! Get out!" (102).[12] The mutual desire to thwart the ambitions of Wan-Lee and Pearl aligns whites and Chinese fascists within a common bloc.

The novel's equation of domestic racism and international fascism are standard Popular Front fare. So is its antidote to domestic racism. The song of the picketers in the final strike scene, for example, tellingly rebukes the cafeteria owner's intolerance of racial hybridity:

> They were marching on, singing their song:
> The song of the white,
> The song of the yellow,
> The song of the black,
> The song of the ones who were neither yellow nor white,
> The song of the ones who were neither yellow nor black,
> The song of the ones who were neither black nor white,
> And the song that knows nothing of white, yellow, or black. (124)

Though "the song" goes beyond the black/white frame common within U.S. Popular Front racial vision and shows an unusual accommodation of in-betweenness, it remains along the same basic continuum, as Tsiang replaces fascist "racial theory" with a multiracial class solidarity.

However, it is also unlike both the Popular Front and later Chinatown narratives in another important sense. To be sure, the strike shows the possibility of multiracial unity in the U.S. But Tsiang's indictment against the culture of the imperial center, reflected in his condemnation of cultural co-optation and the U.S. culture industries, is too strong to be neatly resolved by picket-line unity. In combination with the narrator's death at the hands of the Japanese agent, the novel disavows the U.S. as a space where genuine cultural pluralism is possible. Wan-Lee's final dream is consequently of a China that has achieved unity in diversity—one that only the Chinese Red Army can achieve. In the final pages, Wan-Lee is cheered to hear that the Chinese communists and Nationalists have put their differences aside to unite against the Japanese (122). But the figure of the racist Nationalist boss, whose nationalism left no place for the hybrid Pearl, implies that the Nationalists will only perpetuate the injustices he and Pearl have experienced in the U.S. after the Japanese have been defeated. Thus the dying words of Wan-Lee to Pearl are unambiguous longings for a communist victory: "My dear angel . . . the Chinese Reds now have one fifth of the whole Chinese population and one sixth of the whole Chinese territory. In the years to come they shall have more, more, and endlessly more" (127).

This resolution rested uneasily with "the Four Freedoms" because of the clear antithesis, residing in the imagination of most Americans, between communism and just about every form of freedom. And, as I will discuss later, the idea that communism was the true facilitator of racial tolerance was the exact notion that Cold War rhetoric was obsessed with combating. In addition, the novel's experimental form did not give its author the narrative authority of realism (though as the case of Shirley Graham illustrated, using realism would not have been sufficient in itself to grant such authority). In the following sections I will show how Bulosan, for better or worse, worked within the reading practices of most mid-century Americans to a much greater degree, creating clear, positive spaces for whites within his narratives. As will hopefully become apparent through the contrast with Bulosan's fictional autobiographies, a final reason that *Hands* failed to gain a wide American readership is that its protagonist's life began almost as a tabula rasa in New York. An easier way for an Asian American author to "succeed" in the American literary market in the late 1930s and 1940s was to set their stories in Asia, and more specifically, an imaginary Asia that spoke to frames of reference familiar to most American novel readers.

Folklore, Local Color, and the Misreadings of *The Laughter of My Father*

Both *Laughter of My Father* (1944) and *America Is in the Heart* (1946) responded to the demands of a U.S. readership eager to learn something about Filipinos, wartime allies whom Americans encountered in the news with much greater frequency after Pearl Harbor. The overwhelmingly favorable reviews revealed that many readers saw Bulosan's books as their first introduction to the people of the Philippines. A critic of *Laughter* from the *Saturday Review* expressed her ignorance by writing, "My intimate acquaintance with anyone resembling Father boils down to a Filipino named Ernest who cooked for us one summer" (Littledale 22). Another reviewer wrote of *America* that "I hope it is read by all the people who have a lot to learn about the Philippines *and* America" (Gissen 422). The *New York Times* responded to the Filipinos in *Laughter* by simply stating, "It is a joy to meet them" (Sugrue 7). But while critics enjoyed meeting the people of Luzon through his stories, Bulosan was deeply disturbed by the early nature of the encounter. In many ways, his disgust over the reception of *Laughter* informed the revision of his life found in *America* two years later. *Laughter* has received less critical attention to date than *America*, partially owing to problems with its reception that has plagued the text from the beginning. Written in a way legible to U.S. readers as local-color realism, this earlier narrative deserves revisiting, and not only because its reception impacted the representational choices Bulosan made in his later *America*. It illustrates the dangerous ground trod by authors of Asian descent as they used notions of the modern and "the folk" in the realm of American popular culture.

Unlike the latter work, *Laughter* is set entirely in the Philippines. This very different fictional autobiography is composed of a series of short tales about the author's upbringing in the countryside of Pangisanan, most of which center around the narrator's father, Simeon. Each tale is essentially a story of his father's cunning in the face of various threats to the family and the rural community—threats in the form of jazz age consumer culture, the incursions of U.S. agribusiness, new legal codes imposed by the national government, and the local bourgeois. The sources of conflict are not always external to the village, however; as often as not, the father employs his cunning against rapacious neighbors and family members who at times represent these larger forces. In the framing story, "Father Goes to Court," the family of the narrator is sued by a rich neighbor who accuses them of depressing his spirit, as the sight of their constant laughter and happiness (despite their poverty) has driven him nearly mad. Father/Simeon wins the case in court by winning over the judge with his wit. This story and the others in the collection are purportedly modeled after folktales of the northern Philippines. As such, in conflicts with the rich and the powerful, the protagonist—in this case the father—always emerges the victor at the end. And like the other stories in the collection, the rich and powerful men who fall victim to Father's wit are almost always the local, Filipino bourgeois, not Americans.

"My Father Goes to Court" and "The Tree of My Father" serve as coded critiques of American colonization. In the later story, the narrator relates how Filipino peasants lived for centuries in a system in which "We made our own laws and obeyed them willingly," but when "men of a new type came to our village and settled among us ... they started questioning our unwritten laws [and] began a series of serious controversies over the ownership of land" (32). What Bulosan references here is the historical centralization and expansion of government power resulting from American rule, which differed from the less intrusive system of the Spanish that was reliant on the consent of the peasantry in much larger measure. A key facet of this centralization was the "cadastral survey," in which the central government finally surveyed and titled all land in the Philippines in a manner that privileged the claims of large landlords. In disputes, landlords could much more easily use the legal system to support their cases, and thus by the 1920s and 1930s the new, standardized legal system of American rule constituted a form of enclosure, destroying the peasants' traditional right of landholding (Kerkvliet 22). Bulosan does not cite the United States as the source of these changes, and in both stories, Father successfully uses his wit to stave off the attempts of newly affluent Filipinos to manipulate the legal system at his expense. But Bulosan was certainly aware of both the impact of American rule and the tragic effect of such disputes he references in *Laughter*.

Nonetheless, Harcourt Brace (and later Bantam) marketed the book as humor, which infuriated Bulosan. The cover and insert literally render the

FIG. 4-1. Paperback cover, 1946 Bantam edition of *Laughter of My Father*

book's Filipino characters as cartoons, and to leave aside any possible ambiguity as to how one is supposed to read the text, the label "HUMOR" appears at the top.

Its marketers and contemporary reviewers did not see *Laughter* as serious literature because they read it as an "introduction" to unthreatening, carefree primitives. The *New Yorker* wrote, "Mr. Bulosan's impoverished Luzon peasants have a quality of aimlessness, gaiety, and inconsequence that is refreshing when there is so much 'significant' fiction about" (89). *Booklist* described it as covering "the experiences of [an] uninhibited, unself-conscious, and happily amoral Philippine family" (300). The *Saturday Review* observed that the family in *Laughter* acted with "perfect spontaneity," adding "They felt what they felt and they acted on it. No repressions!" (Littledale 22). As these responses illustrate, *Laughter* unfortunately facilitated a long-standing Orientalist practice of using the culture of the other to escape the repressiveness of European life.

Yet *Laughter* could be placed along the same U.S. literary continuum as Charles Chesnutt, who used seemingly quaint folktales to "trick" predominately white readers into a critical reading of U.S. racial formations. Though it draws upon Filipino folklore, the collection can also be read as part of the American local color genre that Chesnutt both worked within and subverted. Emerging shortly after the Civil War and enjoying a popular readership into the twentieth century, local color marked an early wave of American realism. Popularized by writers such as Mark Twain, Bret Harte, Harriet Beecher Stowe, and Joel Chandler Harris, a local color piece was typically a short story that sought to capture the speech and the folkways of rural people in particular regions; its realism derived from avoidance of classic, highbrow literary tropes in favor of the speech and culture of the unlettered. As in *Laughter*, the pretensions of sophisticated, urban people were often mocked in the course of the narrative, with the apparent "rube" emerging as the wiser character. Local color stories were often "light" and even humorous in tone, yet they were part of a serious post–Civil War effort to define the dialects and cultures that constituted the United States. For William Dean Howells, as for Bulosan in *Laughter*, the ultimate purpose behind capturing dialects and specific cultures in literature was to unite different peoples, to "widen the bounds of sympathy" by illustrating universal humanity in the local and the particular (Nettles 68). In the twentieth century the continued marketability of this form can be seen in the sales of Erskine Caldwell's *Georgia Boy* (1943), a series of light, purportedly autobiographical short stories about the author's father in rural Georgia. The structure of Erskine Caldwell's collection bears an uncanny similarity with *Laughter*, and the plots of Bulosan's stories "The Education of My Father," "My Father and the Fighting Ram," and "My Father's Political Appointment" in *Laughter* have rough counterparts in *Georgia Boy*.[13] Unlike Howells and most nineteenth-century local color authors, however, Bulosan was of the people he was representing, and his writing was not tinged with the same elite cultural assumptions about rural peoples. His use of the genre was strategic, an attempt to "widen the bounds of sympathy" using a form that American novel and magazine readers heartily consumed.

But while I agree with the extant criticism that *Laughter* can be seen as a subtle critique of U.S. imperialism and not simply the storehouse of stereotypes it was marketed as, I believe it would also be a disservice to Bulosan to leave him merely in the role of trickster, as some of his critics have done.[14] He clearly had no intention of playing that role and did not see himself as even entertaining quaint stereotypes. In the very same edition that rendered Bulosan and his father as cartoons on the front cover, the publishers schizophrenically registered the author's voice in a postscript on the back, in which he was allowed to signal both his intent and his intended audience: "For the first time the Filipino people are depicted as human beings," his statement reads. "I hope you enjoy reading about them." In response to the marketing and reception of his book, Bulosan wrote the essay "I Am Not a Laughing Man," in which he stated: "I am mad because when my book, *Laughter of My Father* was published by Harcourt, Brace, and Company, the critics called me 'the manifestation of the pure Comic Spirit.' I am not a laughing man. I am an angry man" (138).

The features of *Laughter* that enabled an Orientalist reading bear scrutiny, as Bulosan's departure from them led to a more unequivocal literary success in *America*. Much less explored is the fact that the intent of *Laughter*—the depiction of Filipinos as human beings—was achieved in a way that made it easy to deny the Philippines a capacity for full-blown modernity, a modernity necessary to construct a valid national narrative on par with that of its Euro-American counterparts. While *Laughter* did help white readers to recognize their common humanity with Filipino peasants in certain ways, it was insufficient to the task of leading its audience into a more thoroughgoing critique of American Orientalist discourse, mainly because the relationship Bulosan constructed between the Philippines and modernity did not place its "folk" within an established, nostalgic narrative of the people coded as "serious" within American culture.

As revealed in his essay "The Growth of Philippine Culture," Bulosan saw himself as part of an emerging national movement in the Philippines that looked back to the "native" traditions as a source of strength necessary to overturn both capitalism and empire. Thus Bulosan adapted a view of folklore in keeping with the Popular Front and as old as Johann Gottfried von Herder and romantic nationalism: that is, folk culture as a site of the genuine national culture, the official diffusion of which serves a political renewal. However, a usage of the preindustrial figure of the "folk" within an American context—whether for exceptionalist or transnational ends—is complicated when that figure is Filipino, mainly because it intersects with a racial form constituted by a troubling relation to the modern. As Bulosan himself has shown in *America*, Filipinos in the U.S. were held to be "sex-crazed" and "animalistic," and their supposed inability to control their impulses served as the justification for their exclusion. (As my next chapter on *Life* magazine will show, Filipinos abroad were represented in similar terms.) These traits were the antithesis of the disciplined persona prerequisite for whiteness and, as such, placed Filipinos within a familiar pattern of American racialization.[15]

In Bulosan's experience of the U.S. in the 1930s and 1940s, then, the lack of modernity attributed to Filipinos was a rationale for their dehumanization, while at the same time, as Colleen Lye has noted, an adeptness at modernity at that point in the history of American racial formation was more often than not a basis for excluding other East Asian groups.[16] Bulosan was in danger of replicating the dominant racial hierarchy if he imbued his Filipino characters with either too much or too little of a modern sensibility. Thus, in his argument for

Filipino humanity in *Laughter*, he compromises with the prevailing discourse on Asia in general and the Philippines in particular by showing Filipinos as capable of mastering modernity but, like Pearl Buck's famous Wang Lung of *The Good Earth*, ultimately rejecting it. The demonstrable ability to master the modern is necessary for them to be seen as having the same innate abilities as Westerners, and hence to read as fully "human"; yet at the same time, by playfully choosing to reject modern incursions into village life (some of which are, ironically, of Western origin), they nullify the potential threat they may pose as rivals to the West. This is not to say that this was either his conscious intent or an achieved goal—rather, it is a process visible in the text.

The story "The Capitalism of My Father" illustrates this process most clearly. The narrator's brother, Osong, has become an agent for a multinational tobacco company jointly run by American and Filipino investors. As an agent for this company, Osong buys the tobacco crop from the farmers of the region, including his father, and cheats them mercilessly when weighing it. There is potential here for a critique of capitalism and empire, but Bulosan undercuts this critique by not stating that the exploitation of peasants is a general company practice; instead, he implies it to be a moral failing of Osong. Also undercutting a critique of empire, he writes that the villagers, like the company's agent, are all liars and cheaters too: "[The farmers] were also expert in cheating and lying . . . They cheated themselves when they could not cheat their neighbors. It was like that in our town when I was growing up. You had to be a good cheat or nothing at all" (41). Since everyone is guilty of lying and cheating, from the highest company official to the poorest villager, no one is really guilty. Father (Simeon) uses his inherited expertise in cheating to one-up his son Osong; when the elder man goes to sell his crop, he puts iron into his bags of tobacco, drastically increasing their weight and hence fleecing the company in turn. With his earnings from the weighted tobacco, it momentarily appears that Father is breaking from the traditions of the village by accumulating capital. Bulosan's child narrator complains, "You don't need any money in the village . . . The peasants don't sell anything. They just give anything away. Why do you accumulate so much money?" (42). But Father reveals his trick to the other farmers too, and when they all start cheating the company, Osong loses his job and Father's true intention is exposed—that is, to get Osong fired from the company and bring him back to the land. When Osong protests that Father has ruined his career, Simeon replies to his son that he bought him a plot of tobacco land with the money he stole, ironically adding, "There is nothing better than honest work" (44).

As in the other stories of the collection, Father is represented here as an enterprising, clever man more than capable of playing the game of capitalism;

his peasant ethos, however, prevents him from using this talent for anything more than happiness for himself and, sometimes, his family. American mass culture, it should be added, is similarly mastered and rejected. In "My Mother's Boarders," the men of the family learn to dance quite well to some jazz music brought to their village by "loose women" and played on a phonograph from "the city"; yet the narrator labels the music "goofy," and while he and his parents hold no great love for the tunes, they use them to make money selling alcohol. This short-lived venture dies as soon as the women are expelled from town, leaving the family in their same nonthreatening state as before their skillful manipulation of American pop culture (17–19).

For Bulosan, masculinity also mediates the relationship between Philippines and modernity, and it too is an important basis for his interpolation of U.S. readers. Viet Thanh Nguyen has argued that in both *America* and in the posthumously published *Cry and the Dedication*, Bulosan fashioned a "pre–Yellow Power Asian American masculinity" designed to keep emasculation and feminization at bay (63). Moreover, according to Nguyen, *America* was "an attempt to recuperate the wounded bodies of Asian American men, speaking to American society in terms that it could understand . . ." (62). *Laughter* can also be seen as a struggle to recuperate Asian American masculinity, one that presents them to U.S. audiences as "men" based on a template they understand.

Bulosan tries to bridge the distance between Filipinos and their American readers with a family frame of male bonding, one that shows the men of Luzon evading modern discipline, yet evading it in a way that makes them legible within the terms of American masculinity. For instance, the plot of "My Father Had a Father" is centered around Father, Grandfather, and the narrator (as a boy) getting drunk around a fire together. Late in the night, Grandfather says to his son, "It is good to be a man, Simeon . . . You can stand by a fire at night and drink wine with a little boy. You can talk all night with another man whose likes and dislikes are similar to yours, while a little boy sits and drinks with you all night long" (54). At the end of the story, after Grandfather has reminisced about his own father's "way with women," has outlasted Father in their all-night, drinking bout, and has even carried Father to bed, the narrator concludes: "Then I knew why my brothers admired Grandfather. He was a man to the last ounce of his strength" (59). Though in the U.S. experience, drinking to excess has been viewed as a breach of capitalist discipline since the mid-nineteenth century, American masculinity has, as often as not, been exercised in opposition to capitalist forms of discipline as well.[17] The idealized space of the fraternal campfire in "My Father Had a Father" would have been familiar to Americans by the 1940s, serving to bridge a cultural (and racial) divide by positing a universal form of male release.

In general, the men of the narrator's extended family are consistently shown gambling, drinking, and womanizing, often to excess (a recurring image in the stories is that of Father or another male relative passed-out drunk with flies buzzing around their mouths). And in the stories where Father does all these things, a great deal of his ingenuity is used hiding his illicit activities from Mother. The narrator, more often than not, is his coconspirator, and their mutual concealment of reckless activities from the more practically minded Mother cements their father-son bond. The fact that all the gambling, drinking, and womanizing in the collection goes on without genuinely tragic consequences would make it relatively easy for American men to affirmatively identify with its characters from inside the bounds of American masculinity—a "rough" rather than "respectable" American masculinity to be sure, but masculinity nonetheless (perhaps this was why the U.S. military broadcast the story via radio to its troops).[18]

Yet, while the characteristically male evasions of discipline in *Laughter* may have endeared its figures to some American readers, and the playful Filipino rejection of modernity that Bulosan constructs may have made its culture less threatening, these representational moves simultaneously foreclosed a "serious" reading of the Philippines in the U.S. Bulosan's ludic peasants in *Laughter* could not be taken seriously because they could not be fit into honorific narratives of the folk that had already been established in the minds of American readers—neither Jeffersonian agrarianism nor its 1930s oppositional variant, "the Decline and Fall of the Lincoln Republic," as Michael Denning calls it.

Whatever its intentions, *Laughter* does not convey the fundamental sense of tragedy and loss that animates the Lincoln Republic narrative. The family's severance from the land and subsequent migrancy do not come across as tragic; indeed, in the first story, which emphasizes the family's unshakable happiness, the author reveals that they had lost their farm prior to the narrative and were now living in a town (1). The loss of the ancestral farm, fundamental to the Lincoln Republic narrative, is also never really final in *Laughter*; the family moves on and off the land as their luck ebbs and flows, implying that dispossession is merely a temporary state. And given their ingenuity and their ability to laugh in the face of hardship, one gets the sense that they will turn out okay in the end. The final moment of the collection solidifies this sense: Father has lost his main draft animal (a *carabao*) as a result of his antics, and he tells his son, "Forget the carabao, I'll farm without one. I've done it before" (152).

In sum, the slippery relationship to modernity that Bulosan inscribes into his figures in *Laughter*, wherein the stereotype of the libidinal Filipino was never far away, as well as the Orientalist reading practices his audiences were grounded in, kept his "folk" from being read as the virtuous protagonists of U.S. agrarian narratives. Given the deeply engrained nature of American Orientalism, it is hard to fault Bulosan for this. And, to be clear, the overall literary value of *Laughter* is not reducible to how most Americans read it in the 1940s; as recent scholarship has shown, its critique of empire can be more easily seen with the passage of time. Despite his frustration with the reception of *Laughter*, Bulosan continued his daunting, maddening project of bringing white readers into an awareness of their own Orientalist practices. In *America*, he came much closer to his goal.

The Transnational Pluralism of *America Is in the Heart*

Reflecting on his boyhood in the Philippines in *America Is in the Heart*, Bulosan wrote: "Whenever I saw a white person in the market with a camera, I made myself deliberately ugly, hoping to earn ten centavos. But what interested the tourists were the naked Igorot women and their children ... They were not interested in Christian Filipinos like me. They seemed to take a particular delight in photographing young Igorot girls with large breasts and robust mountain men whose genitals were nearly exposed, their G-strings bulging large and alive" (67). Like Tsiang, Bulosan disrupts the popular racist images directing the American tourist gaze, but in a self-referential move. Given the exaggerated sexuality of the peasants in *Laughter*, published two years prior, as well as Bulosan's narrative persona in the earlier collection—who had long hair, drank wine constantly, and was called "Igorot" by everyone in his community—this anecdote can be read as a self-reflexive commentary on the U.S. audiences for his earlier work, particularly the way they interpreted its narrative strategy for making Filipinos visible. It signals a very different means of pursuing his transnational politics, one marked by a relationship to modernity more recognizably "American" to his U.S. readers.

Published in 1946, *America* is Bulosan's second autobiography, one that covers his bitter childhood as the son of an impoverished farmer in the Philippines, his immigration to the west coast of the U.S. to start a new life, the marginal employment and racialized violence he encounters there, and his development as a reader, writer, and political organizer. Bulosan's political project, involving rights for Asians living in the U.S. on the one hand and the true liberation of the Philippines on the other, is much closer to the surface in this text than in *Laughter*, and this transnational project paradoxically relies upon the signifier

"America" for coherence. His seemingly nationalistic deployment of "America" in the text, a point of contention among literary critics, has vastly different implications from those of other Popular Front writers.[19] A basic reality separating Bulosan from most other major authors in the U.S. left was that, as a Filipino, not only had he experienced U.S. imperialism firsthand, but he was also ineligible for citizenship until 1946. In this context, his use of patriotic language is both practical and strategic; it is a form of agitation for citizenship, more in the cultural than the legal sense, directed at predominately white readers.[20]

Like other Popular Front literary nationalisms, Bulosan's investment in "America" is not to the extant nation but to the potential, multiracial workers' state which would arise if new traditions were absorbed and the ghosts of its past liberated. He tells a crowd of Filipino laborers, for example, that "America . . . is our unfinished dream" (312).[21] His commentary on the imperfections of the existing United States highlight the ways in which Bulosan has revised the earlier relationship between Asia, modernity, and the U.S. he put forward in *Laughter*. In *America*, for example, Bulosan also depicts Filipinos fighting, gambling, drinking, and womanizing in bars and dance halls along the West Coast. He makes explicit, however, that they did not bring this behavior with them to the States. Rather, the narrator consistently remarks on the brutalizing nature of American culture—how the new country brought out a moral decay among those he knew that was unheard of in the Philippines. In a rhetorical reversal of *Laughter*, he writes of his fellow Filipino workers, "I knew our decadence was imposed by a society alien to our character and inclination, alien to our heritage and history" (135). In a further contrast, the true primitives in this narrative are white. He calls attention to (and neutralizes) the stereotype of the "sex-crazed," "animalistic" Filipino rather explicitly by placing it in the mouths of numerous crass, violent, and even drunken white people over the course of the story. Thus in stating "America is our unfinished dream," Bulosan implies that the traditions he and others bring with them from the Philippines have the potential of rejuvenating the violent, hedonistic culture of the U.S. Asian modernity, in other words, is put forth as something neither to be feared nor denied, but embraced as part of a powerful new force for social equality.

In the most basic sense, the transnational nature of his project in *America* is signaled by Bulosan's choice to set his narrative in the Philippines for the first third of the book. Despite the fact that dozens of immigrant novels and autobiographies emerged from the Depression generation—novels that often articulated class and ethnicity in compatible terms—very few included lengthy depictions of the author's country of origin. The left, or left-leaning, ethnic American novel and autobiography of the 1930s and 1940s was by and large a second-generation phenomenon that had an abstract relationship to the "old country" at best, and, moreover, ultimately revealed a national allegiance to the U.S. in many cases.[22] By contrast, when Bulosan patriotically refers to "the nation" in this first section, he is, as often as not, referring to his country of origin. His account of a homologous system of class oppression in both the Philippines and the U.S. allows the reader to connect systems of power across national borders. Thus even though Bulosan never lived longed enough to return to the country of his youth, the "America" he constructed in his autobiography did not foreclose affiliations elsewhere; viewed within the context of his unending dedication to the Philippines, "America" appears as less of a bounded entity and more as a self-conscious fiction allowing Bulosan to address one front within a global network of power.

America Is in the Philippines? Bulosan and the Virtuous Yeomen of Northern Luzon

Viet Thanh Nguyen noted that in *America*, Bulosan withheld a critique of American imperialism from his account of poverty in the Philippines. Partly because of this, Nguyen adds, his criticisms "were muted, distorted, or marginalized" by his readers (81, 85). It is very true that Bulosan's 1946 narrative did not go nearly as far as *Cry and the Dedication* in its exploration of the hierarchical relationship between the Philippines and the U.S., and that his criticisms were in many ways "distorted" by his white audience. Surprisingly, however, the contemporary reviews of *America* illustrate that mainstream liberal American readers *did* in fact register a critique of empire in the book, a fact that has not been explored in the scholarship on Bulosan to date. A commentator from the *New Republic* observed, "What [Bulosan] tells of those early years [in Luzon] will be a shock to any number of people who have always imagined a land of little, happy brown brothers being helped toward independence by handsome Americans like Paul McNutt and Douglas MacArthur" (Gissen 421). William Lynch of the *Saturday Review of Literature* expressed a similar sentiment, but did so in a way that revealed how Bulosan managed to enable such a critique: "To most of us the Philippines means only Manila, legends of the Spanish American War, the promise of independence, and the feeling that there must be good roads and schools since American occupancy always means good roads and schools. Bulosan's Philippines knew few of these benefits. It did know a people whose capacity for work and whose ambition for their children bestow on them the heroic qualities of Pearl Buck's peasants" (7). On one level these responses to the novel show how the putatively "sympathetic" representations of East Asians by Buck, Snow, and Dmytryk had in no way prepared American readers for the basic realities of American imperialism in the Pacific. Thus the mere revelation of discord in the Philippines by Bulosan would come as a "shock" that was subversive in itself. But the last passage also highlights the terms of that shock. I have already noted that Bulosan depicts Filipinos as ideal candidates for U.S. citizenship. But as illustrated by the comparison to "Pearl Buck's peasants," Bulosan similarly enabled U.S. readers to see the inadequacies of their foreign policy by showing Filipinos across the Pacific as hardworking and ambitious, and thus equally fit for self-government. Since Pearl Buck's realism formed the template for "serious" American readings of much of Asia, *America* worked its subversive effect by its recognizable redeployment of that realism, employing some of its motifs in a way that underscored the silences they enacted. After reading *America*, a writer for the Catholic journal *Commonweal* simply noted of the Philippines that "the people are good" (Monaghan 149). As such, they could also be wronged.

An important way in which Bulosan tries to unite both sides of his political project—Filipino national liberation and Asian American inclusion—is through his representation of the people of Northern Luzon in the first section of *America*. An examination of this first section—the section to which contemporary reviewers were overwhelmingly drawn—reveals that the Philippines are able to rejuvenate American institutions precisely because its pre-modern "folk," as represented by Bulosan, contain the seeds of that modernity. In *America*, the "folk" of the Philippines are not represented in their ludic incarnation (i.e., in terms of the undisciplined, pre-industrial figures of the minstrel or of some folklore studies), but in the virtuous, proto-modern terms of the American agrarian and republican ideal.[23] In this representational choice and in the overall aesthetic structure of his *America*, Bulosan uses a form akin to the most popular realisms of his era.[24] He expressed his preference for realism in *America* itself, writing that the Russian writer Maxim Gorki attracted him more than any other writer. He reiterated this appeal in a 1949 letter, in which he stated a desire to write a fifteen-hundred-page novel of Filipino history combining the best qualities of Tolstoy and Gorki in particular (*America* 246, "Letters" 180).

The first section of *America* can be read as agrarian, in essence, because it nostalgicizes life on the predispossession family farm. Despite the narrator's expressed horror at certain village practices, and his observation that their tiny plot was "barely sufficient to keep our family from starving" (5), he fondly remembers his boyhood labor of working the land. He writes, "In the village, life was a simple peasant lullaby; we had our animals and we had our house" (60). Similarly, he notes, "The work on the farm was heavy and every hand was needed until the harvest was over. But there were gratifying compensations in the depth of my childhood" (10). These "gratifying compensations" are the virtues arising from life on the farm; having established the village as a space of hard work (and thus, avoiding the representational dynamic of *Laughter*), he can go on to narrate the more idyllic aspects of his life there. A recurring motif in his description of village life is the kindness of villagers, and particularly his father, to animals. Watching his father in the fields, he writes, "He took the rope again and flipped it gently and suggestively across the *carabao*'s back, and the two of them, the patient animal and my father, walked slowly and industriously away, the sharp plow blade breaking smoothly through the rich soil between them" (4). This gentle work relationship between his father and animals establishes the fields, when controlled by the common farmer, as a space without exploitation; further, the non-coercive nature of the labor that takes place there, as this passage reveals, does not prevent "industrious" work.

What enables this kindness in the sphere of production are the "inborn qualities" of those who do the work, of which the narrator's father is the chief representative. Bulosan catalogues these qualities in the following way: "He was an honest simple man, who went about his work hoping for an ample reward at the end. He was also a strong man when his deep convictions were at stake. Illiterate as he was, my father had an instinct for the truth. It was this inborn quality, common among peasants, that had kept him going in a country rapidly changing to new conditions and ideals" (23). Similar to Steinbeck's Okies, Pearl Buck's Wang Lung, and the protagonists of most Americans agrarianisms, these values of work, honesty, and simplicity, are shown to be "rooted" in a close and long-standing relationship to the land. The narrator writes of his father's "love for the earth" (76) and notes, "A stubborn peasant like his ancestors before him, my father had always believed that life should be rooted in the soil" (58). In common with U.S. agrarian narratives, terms such as "land," "earth," and "soil" serve as symbols for a set of social relationships arising from a system of small farms. Relationships based on wage labor and large-scale agriculture threaten this virtuous world, existing in opposition to it. Thus when the peasant farmers are dispossessed of their land, Bulosan writes, they go to work on "vast haciendas" (24). This is very difficult for them, for as the narrator illustrates, wage labor is something alien to peasant values: "... my father was a farmer, not a hired laborer. It humiliated him to hire himself out to someone. Yet he was willing to swallow his pride and to forget the honor of his ancestors" (29).

Rootedness, a quality necessary to sustain the peasant values of hard work, simplicity, and honesty, is tragically destroyed in the book by the dispossession wrought by "usurers" (23), the harbingers of modernity and villains of 1930s agrarian narratives. Their displacement by the usurer also places Bulosan's peasant farmers within a common discursive continuum with Steinbeck's Okies and the Dust Bowl refugees of F.S.A. photography. Also in common with these emplotments, the presence of the usurer posits removal from the land as a social rather than a natural disaster and, as such, the beginning of political consciousness for both the narrator and his father. Referring to their loss of land, Bulosan states, "This family tragedy marked the beginning of my conscious life" (29). Similarly, his father expresses his emerging political consciousness by saying, "There is something wrong in our country when a man can take away something that belongs to you and your family" (55). That the narrator registers dispossession as an injustice is important within the context of American labor and reform discourses, which had figured Asians as quiescent, and hence unfit for democratic participation within their corresponding social movements. In contrast to the stereotype of the complacent coolie, the author writes that his father "struggle[d] to hold onto the land he knew so well, fighting to the end and dying on it like a peasant" (27).

Unlike Simeon in *Laughter*, who is confident in winning his land back at the end of the book, the story of the narrator's father in *America* thus shares the tragic nature with American agrarian narratives of the 1930s. That is to say, the Joads, Jeeter Lester, the O'Haras, and Wang Lung all either lose their land or see the idyllic life associated with it come to an end. It suited Bulosan's political ends with American readers much better to use the more familiar, tragic variant, wherein the "lullaby" of rural life is inevitably swept away. Thus Bulosan attempted to make visible his struggles as a Filipino immigrant in America by tapping into a narrative that had made the suffering of Steinbeck's Okies a national metaphor for the ravages of capitalism, and that had already made East Asia intelligible to Americans in the writing of Pearl Buck and Edgar Snow. The rootedness of his narrator within a culture of small family farms; his farmer heritage of hard work, simplicity, and honesty; his family's dispossession by usurers, as well as their noble struggle against that dispossession—all of these plot elements rendered Filipino diaspora in a way legible to American readers in the 1930s and 40s. Regardless of whether or not this emplotment was intended by Bulosan, it came through to many of his contemporary mainstream reviewers. The *Commonweal* wrote: "The roots of [the narrator's] life are in the hills of home; and the land," adding that "their father loved his land" (Monaghan 149). The reviewer for the *New Republic* noted that Bulosan "witnessed and shared in the tragedy which of all tragedies is the greatest that can come to workers on the land—loss of ownership of that land" (Lynch 7). Both the narrator and these commentators remarked how this agrarian background allowed Carlos to "survive in the west coast hell he found in the vestibule of America" (Monaghan 149).

As yeomen, the folk protagonists of *America* (particularly the narrator's father) embody the disciplined personalities necessary for civilization, yet are uncorrupted by the degeneracy often associated with the modern world. Their migration to America, then, could serve to re-implant the values of the old Lincoln Republic onto American shores, values that had long ago been lost by its "natives." In *The Grapes of Wrath*, published seven years earlier, Steinbeck's virtuous Okies were shown to have reached the "natural" limit of westward expansion in California; unable to reestablish a republic of small farms there, Steinbeck suggested they would express their old, yeoman virtue in new collectivist impulses that would reshape American culture along the lines of the New Deal. Bulosan's narrator and his dispossessed yeoman compatriots also arrive in California, but from the other direction. Arriving from a different yet uncannily similar landscape, they bore the scars of a westward expansion that had stretched across the Pacific and far beyond the vision of Steinbeck. Unlike the Okies, the earlier beneficiaries of territorial expansion, they called into question whether U.S. colonial impulses ever rewarded the virtuous. In pushing their integrity eastward, they reminded American readers that true social renewal lies not in the conquest of literal space but in embracing the collectivist values of racial outsiders who embody "the heart" of their nation.

Finally, the narrator's constructed agrarian heritage, along with the tenacious ability of the Filipino characters to hold on to this heritage in the U.S., makes them eligible to write themselves into the American landscape. In the oft-discussed conclusion, the narrator Carlos rides in a train alone, traveling along the West Coast and reflecting on his strong bond to the American soil:

> ... I heard bells ringing from the hills—like the bells that had tolled in the church tower when I had left Binalonan. I glanced out of the window again to look at the broad land I had dreamed so much about, only to discover with astonishment that the American earth was like a huge heart unfolding warmly to receive me ... It was something that had grown out of my defeats and successes, something shaped by my struggles for a place in this vast land, digging my hands into the rich soil here and there, catching a freight to the north and to the south, seeking free meals in dingy gambling houses, reading a book that opened up worlds of heroic thoughts. (326)

The narrator's claim that "the American earth was like a huge heart unfolding warmly to receive me" was certainly premature; Bulosan died in poverty, alcoholism, and obscurity in a Seattle street in 1956, apparently after collapsing there in a drunken stupor (Kim 45–46). Yet his use of American landscape imagery in this passage is significant. Denning identified one of the central problems of the Lincoln Republic narrative as "Whose lives embody the Lincoln republic? Whose voice can tell its story?"; and this formal problem applies to other nostalgic narratives of the people as well (169). As I have argued, Ma Joad's famous statement "We're the people" was a white Anglo-Saxon claim to universality. Bulosan expressed a disappointment with Steinbeck, Erskine Caldwell, and Margaret Mitchell—Mitchell for her overt racism, and Steinbeck and Caldwell for failing to craft "a weapon strong enough to blast the walls that imprisoned the American soul" ("My Education" 128, *America* 238). His frustration with them suggests an awareness that his story, or anything useful to him, was missing from their portraits of the land. The conclusion of *America* does not stake a claim to a fixed location in the U.S. ("America" is to be viewed as a sensibility, after all), nor does it position the narrator as the quintessential American. But its use of agrarian and landscape images—the "American earth," "digging my hands into the rich soil," the "broad" perspective—is important in that Bulosan, as a Filipino author, is declaring his right to the authorship of a conventional, naturalized aesthetic of U.S. nationalism. In essence, he is positioning himself not only as a constitutive part but also as a master narrator of the American West Coast landscape, a landscape that, as Don Mitchell reminds us, had been predicated upon the silence of working-class and nonwhite people for its aesthetic value (20).

While it created a momentary questioning of American intervention and formed an effective rhetorical call for Filipino inclusion in the U.S., the way in which Bulosan rendered visible Filipino migration to the U.S. posed dangers for co-optation within the discourse that Christina Klein calls "Cold War Orientalism." After World War II, Klein argues, Cold Warriors put forth an image of a racially and ethnically diverse U.S. in order to appeal to decolonizing nations and legitimize American global expansion. Firmly rejecting the racial theories that had fallen out of favor with the defeat of fascism—and that were associated with European colonialism—Cold War rhetoric in regard to Asia tried to create a sentimental, empathetic relationship between American and Asian peoples, one based upon non-coercive "exchanges" and the acknowledgment of a shared spirit of independence rooted in their mutual histories (11–12). Significantly, this rhetoric grew out of both left- and right-wing internationalisms of the 1930s and 1940s, as it combined "the left-liberal ideal of international integration with the right's fierce opposition to communism" (32). Middlebrow culture—the primary site in which this discourse was produced—offered didactic lessons instructing Americans in the proper, empathetic relationship to Asia. One of the most important middlebrow, narrative forms taken by Cold War Orientalism was what Klein calls the "people-to-people narrative." As she writes, "... people-to-people narratives ... served as a cultural expression of the principle of international integration: they depicted politically engaged individuals communicating across racial and national boundaries, recognizing their shared interests, and working together to solve the root problems that provided a breeding ground for communism" (85). The most emblematic example Klein uses is the 1958 novel *The Ugly American*, which drew clear lines between "ugly" and "non-ugly" Americans in Asia: the former were racist and refused to mingle with locals, while the latter were tolerant cultural pluralists who integrated themselves into local cultures and thus won the friendship of Asians (88).

While it is not entirely reducible to this narrative form, Bulosan's *America* definitely held the potential of serving as a people-to-people narrative. Like the 1940s and 1950s stories of Chinatown that Klein describes, *America* "introduce[s] Americans to a people whose integration has become a geopolitical imperative" (228). And like the people-to-people narratives, it teaches American readers how to be tolerant, inclusive, "non-ugly" Americans using a sentimental mode of address that keeps open the possibility of an empathetic relationship. Not coincidentally, the journal most enthusiastic about *America* was the *Saturday Review of Literature*, which, along with *Reader's Digest*, was one of the two main periodicals that produced and advocated people-to-people narratives (Klein 63). On 9 March 1946, the *Saturday Review* placed a drawing of Bulosan's face on its front cover (the same image used on the front of the contemporary reprinting of *America*), making the story the main attraction of the issue. The reviewer registered Bulosan's desire to maintain an open, empathetic exchange by comparing him to other proletarian authors: "He never shrieks with the stridency of many of our other proletarian authors who confuse comradeship with shrillness and who solve all problems by calling the other fellow a Fascist" (7). Unlike Bulosan, these other, presumably communist authors resolve their differences in an intolerant manner, and thus, like communism itself, fall outside the "American Way." Bulosan, by contrast, appears as the "model minority" for a model system.

America's proximity to a people-to-people narrative also resides in how its author shows the global negative consequences of American insensitivity toward Asians. At several points in the story of his childhood he reveals that the flames of violent revolution in the Philippines were fanned by Filipinos who had immigrated to the U.S. and had returned after experiencing ill treatment there. The Colorum Party, for example, which Bulosan describes as a "fanatical organization of dispossessed peasants that terrorized Luzon," was a "vengeful sect of anarchistic men led by a college-bred peasant who had become embittered in the U.S." (60). Similarly, one of the narrator's boyhood teachers, who had apparently been mistreated as a houseboy in America, returned to the Philippines after fifteen years only to find that his parents had died. As a result, he becomes an advocate of violent class war (83). Discrimination against Filipinos in the U.S., in other words, creates a bitterness so deep that any empathetic relationship between Asia and the U.S. becomes impossible. These cautionary tales of what happens when Filipinos are mistreated in the States are contrasted with the positive example of Miss Strandon. Strandon is a "non-ugly" American the narrator meets in the small city of Baguio; through her generosity, she wins him over to the idea of America for the first time. Not only is she kind to the young Allos, she also teaches him that the U.S. has a history of racial tolerance through the story of Abraham Lincoln. Though there were "vicious men" in America who owned slaves, she tells him, Lincoln died to free them, adding, "He was a great man" (70). Like her subsequent Cold War counterparts, Standon draws an image of America, for Third World consumption, as a space where racial animosity can eventually be resolved. Carlos takes her lesson to heart, so to speak, and his narrative of America, initiated by her kindness, serves as an object lesson to middle-class readers in how an ex-colonial subject can be steered toward an affiliation with America—a "loyalty in spite of all," to use the title of one review.

But while *America* was usable within the middlebrow project of Cold War Orientalism in many ways, the thoroughness of its indictment of American racial violence and its portrait of the inadequacies of U.S. "tutelage" undermined its full co-optation. John Fiske has argued that once cultural texts have done their ideological work for the hegemonic order, there is often a "semiotic excess" that stays with its audience, haunting their reception and scrambling their ideological effects for the purposes of the dominant culture. One famous example is that of the female lead in classic *film noir*; though she is "put back in her place" by the end of the story, what viewers remember is a strong, powerful woman, and this memory undermines the patriarchal resolution (403). Unlike Rodgers and Hammerstein's production of *Flower Drum Song*, which Klein sees as a narrative of Asian inclusion fully serving the U.S. Cold War agenda, *America* does not deny the history of racialization and Asian exclusion to make its case (236). Bulosan's relentless accounts of beatings, mob violence, job discrimination, and verbal abuse of people of color by whites constituted a "semiotic excess" that curbed his book's employment as an exportable narrative of American pluralism. Despite the enthusiasm of *Saturday Review* and other mainstream newspapers and magazines, neither Bulosan nor *America* was touted (like Dong Kingman or Jade Snow Wong) by the U.S. government (241–42). The faint critique of empire that haunted its reception, as well as its explicit endorsements of international class solidarity, was enough to make Cold Warriors shy away from using it as a tool for winning hearts and minds in decolonizing nations for U.S. global interests.

If *Hands* was primarily concerned with winning the war against fascism, it can be said that *America* was intended to win the peace. In "Freedom from Want," Bulosan had mentioned neither his race nor his country of origin; apart from a fleeting reference to lynching, his essay addressed race-specific forms of oppression in a coded manner. He had introduced himself and his ambiguously othered "people" to the family in the Rockwell illustration more in class than in racial terms, but the absence of race within the essay made it even easier for *Post* readers not to visualize any new faces at the dinner table, faces different from those evoked by long-established American nationalism. While *Hands* worked outside the paradigm of "The Four Freedoms" altogether, *America* can be seen as a long, narratival attempt by Bulosan to specify new faces even further, breaking the imposed silences within his earlier definition "Freedom from Want." More than this, it was a reminder to readers of the wartime promises embodied by the Freedoms and an attempt to sustain the "People's Century" and prevent a postwar return to normalcy.[25] Given that the material troubles facing migrant workers could not be resolved within the text, his hopeful conclusion left it up to the reader, ultimately, to help solve the problem of "want" for those who had done their part to defeat fascism. As the fate of the author illustrates, his readers did not live up to this responsibility.

The short-term nature of Bulosan's visibility in the U.S. reveals that both transnational projects—those of Bulosan and Tsiang—had little place within the Cold War order, regardless of whether the authors worked from inside or outside of dominant wartime discourses. But despite his relative literary obscurity, Tsiang lived a much longer life than Bulosan. Bulosan died a broken man at age 43; Tsiang died in 1971, at age 72, after pursuing an active film and theatrical career into his older years. Bulosan once voiced a desire to write for Hollywood, and his recently published detective noir novel *All The Conspirators* illustrates his versatility with popular U.S. forms, as well as the adaptable talent that went untapped by the film industry (Hau xv). As illustrated by the posthumously published *Cry and the Dedication*, about revolutionary Huk guerillas in the Philippines, Bulosan was perhaps beginning to realize something both Tsiang and Shirley Graham had seen at different points in their lives—that an unfettered, anti-imperialist "freedom" had to be sought outside of popular American culture altogether. The fate of his work after the war would have borne out such a conclusion, as it achieved its widest readership not in the U.S. but in the Philippines, where the author gained "a legendary aura," as E. San Juan Jr. has written (38). Unlike other authors in this study, the civil rights and Yellow Power movements of the 1960s and 1970s, not the white-dominated culture industries, gave his work its greatest visibility and current canonical status in North America. Ethnic studies, born of those struggles and institutionalized in college and university systems, has revived and defused the work of this author whose name is still to date an unfamiliar one in mass culture. Ironically, even though Tsiang made it to Hollywood and worked within the culture industries (albeit in minor roles), he generally did not reproduce U.S. mass-culture forms in his own writing, even strategically. Though not a formula for success, maintaining a narrative voice radically autonomous from this milieu was, for a Popular Front writer of Asian descent, perhaps a surer form of personal survival.

CHAPTER FIVE

The Popular Front in the American Century

Life Magazine, Margaret Bourke-White, and Partisan Objectivity

When Vice President Henry Wallace first articulated the idea of the People's Century in 1942, it was in direct response to a vision of globality already in wide circulation—that of Henry Luce's "American Century." Before his assembled audience in New York City, Wallace exclaimed, "Some have spoken of 'the American Century.' I say that the century on which we are entering—the century which will come out of this war—can and must be the century of the common man" (193). That the vice president of the United States would have to struggle against a media baron such as Luce in a battle of the "centuries" should come as no surprise. By 1942 the culture industry was far better positioned to influence the public than the state, even amidst the emergency atmosphere of wartime. The magazines, radio programs, and newsreels of Time Inc. were no exception.

By early 1941 Luce commanded a media empire with unprecedented reach—and it had become clear to many that his success had finally gone to his head. His first magazine, *Time*, founded along with partner Briton Hadden in 1923, had revolutionized the news magazine by developing a narrative mode of news reportage that covered its subjects with both wit and concision. *Time*, with its unprecedented short news stories aimed at "the man on the go," quickly eclipsed its stodgy, genteel rival the *Literary Digest* and established Luce as a public figure. *Fortune*, begun in 1930, extended his influence by providing a highly affluent readership with a more in-depth and even intellectual magazine of business and world affairs. And with the *March of Time* radio program and newsreel, founded in 1931 and 1935 respectively, Luce's reach extended into exciting new media. But it was an innovative picture magazine—*Life*—that took his company Time Inc. to new heights after it first appeared in November 1936. Whereas *Time*'s readership had been approximately 780,000 in 1939, and *Fortune*'s much smaller—around 130,000 in the same year—*Life*'s circulation was truly startling to contemporaries. By 1940 it had a circulation of 2.86 million and a high "pass along rate," multiplying its actual audience (qtd. in Baughman, *Luce* 73; Baughman, *Life* 44). With his influence now firmly secured, Luce began to see himself as a man of destiny, imbued with both the power and the responsibility to mold the national mind single-handedly. Though he had laid claim to such powers before, many contemporaries saw Luce's ego spinning out of control with *Life*'s success. A *Time* staff member recalled that he "began to entertain the delusion common among press lords: that he could control and direct the enormous influence his magazines exerted on public taste" (qtd. in Baughman, *Luce* 113).

With his newfound sense of purpose, Luce sat down to write his famous editorial, "The American Century," in February 1941. In what came to be the most influential essay of his career, Luce synthesized a political project he had been developing since the late 1930s. Breaking through the contemporaneous political dichotomy over foreign policy that pitted a conservative isolationism against a leftist internationalism, Luce articulated an expanded leadership role for the United States that could be dubbed a corporate transnationalism. The United States had a mission to assume world leadership, he wrote, a mission that most Americans had yet to realize. Prefiguring the Cold War, this mission involved the spreading of American ideals of freedom and democracy around the world, and differed from the global vision of both Hitler and the left in that it was based on liberal "freedom and democracy" rather than "one-man rule." But this transnationalism would be grounded neither on politics nor mere military might, but on a more subtle level—on the culture of consumption. According to Luce, "Once we cease to distract ourselves with lifeless arguments about isolationism, we shall be amazed to discover that there is already an immense American inter-nationalism. American jazz, Hollywood movies, American slang, American machines and patented products are in fact the only things that every community in the world, from Zanzibar to Hamburg, recognizes in common" (65). Immediately generating almost five thousand letters, many of them glowing praises from influential citizens, the essay provided a foundation for those Americans who wanted to actively intervene in world affairs but who were looking for a different model than that offered by the Popular Front. Ultimately, it came to embody corporate America's blueprint for the postwar world. Michael Denning sees it as the manifesto of what he calls "The Advertising Front," a historic bloc of conservative forces opposed to the New Deal and the Popular Front (43-44).

But this imperial consumer ethos would not create itself. To Luce, it had to be constructed—and constructed using specific representational strategies that Time Inc. had already been developing. In a speech given at the American Association of Advertising Agencies in 1937, he had already denounced the prevailing consumer model guiding the media, which he dubbed "Press-that-gives-the-people-what-they-want"— a philosophy employed by media professionals who rewarded a passive, uncritical audience with "vulgarity," "tripe," and "triviality," consequently leaving audiences open for "the barbarous domination of the mass mind" (38, 41). Luce urged advertisers to instead take a position of cultural and moral leadership by supporting quality journalism (like his own) and by keeping out of editorial departments so that culture workers could fulfill their mission unimpeded. Ever conscious of fascism and communism, he instructed them, "You are the Commissars, you exist as an alternative to the People's Commissariat of Public Enlightenment" (40). An unqualified faith in the common man would be misguided, he argued, as the "crowds" of modern society are irrational and impressionable. A mass media that gives them "what it wants and whatever it wants and more of it" might ironically deliver them to the first demagogue who came along (41). To counter this threat, not just any consumerism would do, but one that would accompany a political and cultural project designed to lift these crowds from the dangers of the modern world. The speech reveals Luce's strange dance with fascism by the late 1930s, in which he abhorred it while proposing a rival form of elite leadership in its stead. But more essentially, it was one of Luce's early calls for a new "common sense" antithetical to that offered by the left at the time.

While the articles in *Time*, *Life*, and *Fortune* did not collectively form a mirror image of their founder's beliefs, Luce's stated views were reflected in his publications to a stunning extent. In *Life* they would be translated into images of the people and its other that would rival both the New Deal and Popular Front pluralisms of "We're the people" and "the People's Century." What was at stake in the battle of the centuries was not only the nature of American participation in the world, but also the more subtle contours of American globality: Who would be the agents in the twentieth-century world? Who was "us" and who was "them"? Luce's call for American leadership involved a constantly shifting vision of American global citizenship that did not stop at U.S. borders. This chapter will outline the parameters of this political project within Time Inc. by focusing on *Life*, primarily from its founding in 1936 to the United States' entrance into

World War II. I have chosen *Life* for a number of reasons. The magazine's virtually uncontested status as a source of visual news in its early days, its innovative uses of photography, and its massive diffusion within the upper and middle classes (far more so than *Time* or *Fortune*) placed it in a unique position to transform modes of vision within the more privileged sectors of the United States. I will first investigate the representational strategies by which this mass magazine tried to forge the class, national, and consumer consciousness of its "people"—the agents of the American Century—as well as the explicit politics it yoked to its new way of seeing.

Much like its nemeses in the Popular Front, the representational strategy the magazine employed was an attempt to mediate the political and economic crisis of the 1930s for its readers. Yet, as a form, the modern magazine was born of crisis, and *Life*'s attempt to manage unrest for its audience placed it squarely within the history of magazines stretching back at least fifty years. Since the "magazine revolution" of the 1890s, magazine readership had been overwhelmingly middle class, and *Life* was no exception. Throughout its history, *Life* readers tended to be middle and upper middle class (Baughman, *Life* 44). But the world of the fledgling *Life* was quite different from the world of the first magazine revolution. By the 1930s, corporate managerial structures had long since been established and Americans were even more deeply entrenched in mass consumer culture than they had been at the turn of the century. At the same time, this entrenched corporate power was in the midst of a profound economic crisis of much longer duration than the crisis of either the mid-1880s or mid-1890s. Just as significantly, corporate power was threatened from the left by the dynamic new social movement of the Popular Front.

To the magazine reader of 1940, radical alternatives to bourgeois democracy such as socialism, communism, or fascism were quite tangible and to some seemed, under the demagogue F.D.R., to have found expression in the highest office of the land. The social upheavals of the 1930s and 1940s were palpable in a variety of forms in mass magazines of the period, and the authors of the articles generally pitted themselves against this newfound working-class power. Broadsides against the president and his policies were prevalent in their writings, the Popular Front social movements were parodied with regularity, and the rich were often presented as an embattled class fighting to preserve its way of life.[1] Newspapers exhibited similar trends, with Roosevelt receiving less and less favorable coverage with each election cycle. In 1932 he had the editorial support of 41 percent of American dailies while enjoying 57 percent of the popular vote; when he coasted through the 1936 election with 60 percent of the popular vote, he received the support of only 37 percent of dailies and approximately 40 percent of weekly papers. In 1940, in the largest gap between newspaper and popular approval since Thomas Jefferson, he won 55 percent of the popular vote yet received the backing of only 25 percent of daily newspapers (Winfield 127–28).

Life was no exception to this conservatism, and even gloried in being part of a larger, united press effort to unseat this popular president.[2] Before the war it is difficult to find a single word of support for F.D.R., and the left social movements of the day are usually presented in its pages as a joke. Thus the innovative aesthetics *Life* deployed in its early years, which made intriguing connections between crowds, the Popular Front, friendly versus unfriendly peoples, and advertised commodities, were an attempt to forge a solution to the contemporaneous political crisis.

Significantly, this solution involved the incorporation of leftist aesthetics into the magazine format, aesthetics in which realism played no small part. The second intention of this chapter, then, is to suggest that the Popular Front and the so-called "Advertising Front" were not fully separable. Although the explicit politics of *Life* by and large followed Henry Luce's imperial, capitalist formula presented in "The American Century," the aesthetics of the magazine were stamped by those on the left, not least because Popular Front personnel were involved in its production. While some studies of *Life* have commented on various aspects of its conservatism, no study to date has looked at the influence of the left on the epistemology of Luce's favorite child.[3] My investigation of this influence will revolve around *Life*'s use of the photographs of Margaret Bourke-White, a Popular Front figure who played a seminal role in defining the aesthetic of the magazine—a pioneer who stamped her brand of realism onto its pages. But while the presence of realism in *Life* is undeniable, I will also argue that when examining its photo-essays in the overall context of the magazine—the ads, the illustrations, the endless juxtapositions—it is hard to claim that *Life* is unequivocally realist. Rather, *Life* constitutes a mass-mediated realism, and thus an opportunity to explore the politics thereof, not only in an arena of visual popular culture unique to mid-century, but also one in which the Popular Front did not fully control its shape. Tracing the strands of realism within the pages of *Life* is one way of addressing the extent to which Popular Front modes of vision were absorbed into the dominant culture that would emerge after World War II. As with the previous chapter on the Popular Front and Asia/America, this chapter adds to the scholarship exploring the ways in which Popular Front and New Deal "structures of feeling" were incorporated (and left behind) within the Cold War consensus.[4]

Trouble in Louisiana
An Introduction to *Life's* Political Aesthetics

In the 29 January 1940 issue of *Life* appears a fascinating three-page photo-essay on Louisiana politics. It deals with the electoral battle between Earl Long (brother of Huey) and a slew of other candidates opposing him. The layout of page 1 is dominated by a single photograph in which Long, with the sharp gesticulation of a fascist leader, speaks before a sullen crowd. The crowd faces us—it is they who seem to be the real subject of the photograph. The viewer is challenged to look into their faces, discerning whether or not the magic of the demagogue has taken hold.

But by reading the text at the side of the page, introduced with the headline, "Long Machine Crippled in Louisiana Primaries After Twelve-Year Rule," we find that Long's magic is not working that well after all. In prose both dramatic and entertaining, the article tells us that the "corrupt and tyrannical rule" of the Long machine has been finally challenged by the erstwhile "submissive electorate." In this three-paragraph block of text—the longest, most sustained verbal narration the article provides—we hear the curiosities of the election: how Long was cut off the air for the "hells," "damns," and other profanities that filled his speeches; how another candidate named Noe broke his fist in a fight; and how Long was parodied by a spectacle of parade floats. But it halts the curious anecdotes to latch on to one thing its authors take seriously: the candidacy of Sam Houston Jones, a conservative lawyer with the backing of the business community. We read that, "barring vast chicanery," he would be elected imminently.

A true visual explosion begins, however, when we turn the page over. The two-page spread immediately following consists entirely of photos, ordered in three neat rows, with brief, scarcely noticeable captions underneath. The top row shows masses of people gathered around parade floats satirizing Long; the middle consists of three photos, each illustrating the activities of an individual political candidate; while at bottom are close-ups of individual floats, their clearly legible messages allowing us to take part in the entertainment vicariously. The photos immediately communicate one central message: action. The photos of candidates eschew the static conventions of portraiture to show their subjects in motion, and the massive crowds suggest that, someplace where we are not, something big is happening. More basically, we are dimly aware that this whole spectacle is a political election.

Skimming the small captions, which the reader may or may not have done, we find that there is a vague logic to the layout, even a narrative of sorts. The

FIG. 5-1. "Long Machine Crippled in Louisiana Primaries After Twelve-Year Rule," *Life*, January 29, 1940

captions, in tandem with the photos, paint the political candidates as if good and evil characters in a melodrama. At left is "Candidate Jones," resembling Eliot Ness with his fine suit and noble bearing, who the caption tells us is the "white hope of reformists." At right, the "boyish and versatile" candidate Morrison is on his feet, seemingly yelling into a telephone while his campaign staff around him look exhausted (a staffer in the background looking at photos spread out on a bed seems to invite a self-reflexive comment on the use of photography as a means of political persuasion, but no such analysis follows). Both of these men oppose the corrupt, villainous Earl Long and seem to form a united front. Together, they appear as stock heroes in an exciting, melodramatic narrative with very clear boundaries between virtue and villainy. Given identities with streamlined and easily digestible language, these oppositional candidates provide order, hope, and humanity to the otherwise menacing and visually overwhelming images of crowds.

I describe at length this moment of coverage because it contains a whole constellation of representational strategies in *Life* highly significant to the formation of American mass culture and the reproduction of middle-class consciousness in the 1930s and 1940s: (1) Luce's concept of *partisan objectivity*, a fundamentally realist practice in which blatantly partial claims are embedded in the seemingly unauthored, "real" nature of the photograph; (2) a sensational, melodramatic mode of address (both visual and verbal) that bears witness to the decline of the great genteel project of the nineteenth century; (3) a mode of reading amenable to consumerism, based on simultaneity, titillation, and what Raymond Williams calls "total flow"; and (4) a political project that attempts self-consciously to intervene in the formation of crowds, altering the ties that bind them together. This project only slightly modified an older Anglo-Saxon consensus on who constituted "the people" and was linked to a transnational worldview in which fascists, communists, and populists, at home and abroad, were essentially united by the mindless crowds they drew together. Sometimes racialized, such crowds became the synecdochal representations of much larger political bodies united against American bourgeois notions of freedom, democracy, and property. None of *Life*'s major competitors in the world of magazines approached such a combination. Neither *Collier's*, *Ladies' Home Journal*, nor *Saturday Evening Post* featured photography as a central part of their content, employed realist representational strategies as intensely as *Life*, nor offered significant news coverage. The bulk of the content in *Collier's* and *Saturday Evening Post* consisted of light fiction illustrated by drawings, while *Ladies' Home Journal* featured short stories, tips on everyday life, and lots of ads. At the time of its birth, *Life*'s only real rival in the visual presentation of news were the newsreels (the largest of which, *March of Time*, was also part of the Luce empire), and even these presented news less in terms of realism and more through the obvious artifice of dramatic re-enactments.

Partisan Objectivity and the Nature of *Life*'s Realism

A look at *Life*'s partisan objectivity is in order, for it illuminates the brand of realism the magazine employs. Through her insightful book *Life's America: Family and Nation in Postwar Photojournalism*, Wendy Kozol asserts that *Life* merged traditions of documentary objectivity with sentimental modes of address to give its photographs the authority to transparently represent "reality." She labels this process—visible even in the early days of the magazine—*realism* (10). While her work remains a groundbreaking study of the aesthetics of the magazine, it relies on a poststructuralist critique of realism to challenge *Life*'s representations, and in doing so misses much of what is historical specific to its form. Kozol at times conflates realism and objectivity, two terms that are not synonymous. The desire for objectivity was not a consistent goal of the realism of the late nineteenth century, but rather of naturalism in particular.[5] Further, her primary grounds for labeling *Life*'s news practices realist is that they produce a "transparent" visual language that does not call attention to its status as representation. In other words, its articles are not self-referential; they offer a picture of reality by obscuring the fact of authorship from a definite subject position. This claim is true; *Life* does not call attention to authorship and rarely provides hints that photographs are constructions (by contrast, its Popular Front competitor *P.M.* regularly instructs its audience on how to "read" photographs).[6] But again, there is much more to realism than this. It is much more helpful to ask, "What kind of realism does *Life* create, and how does it differ from the realism of its political opponents (if at all)?" Insisting too much on *Life*'s tendency to employ unauthored discourse—i.e., representations that appear as objectively "real," with no author putting them forward—avoids a central feature of *Life*'s philosophy and practice: blatant and conscious partisanship. Its photographs most definitely lay claim to the real, and may have received the authority to do so by the documentary traditions Kozol traces, but when viewed in context of the layout, text boxes, and captioning, we find that *Life* is making no attempt to conceal its position. This has important implications for its hybrid brand of realism, which I will discuss momentarily.

My description of *Life*'s coverage of the Louisiana primaries attempted to demonstrate that the magazine was quite open in its endorsement of Sam Houston Jones over Earl Long. But one does not have to look far for other examples of partisanship. Popular Front social movements receive a blatant, dismissive form of scorn throughout the magazine. An article from 23 September

1940, entitled "Young Pink," provides a suggestive example. The article is an exposé on a young "radical" activist named Bud James. Bud is depicted as a spoiled dilettante from a well-to-do Protestant family. The author relates: "Bud belongs to and helps lead the celebrated Youth Congress whose members, many conservatives scathingly insist, are a rebellious pack of malcontents, whiners and complainers with a bad case of the 'gimmes'" (the radicals are not allowed a rebuttal to this charge). Bud James is as dangerous as he is comical, however, because he has the power to mobilize the gullible mob. Recounting a speech he gives before a crowd of largely African American munitions workers, the article states that the mass "believes him because he is convincing . . . and they punctuate his address with cries of 'Yas Suh, Yas Suh, Sho' is right' and 'That's just beautiful!'" (82). This portrait thus represents the Popular Front as constituted by spoiled leaders and a sheeplike rank and file, the latter of whom are all the more dangerous for their racial difference (it also positions the reader as an independent thinker not subject to mass thinking). A head shot of Bud takes the depiction a step further. In the photo he appears stiff and unshaven, mouth firmly closed and eyes darting away from the camera, making him look both cowardly and slightly deranged.

Equally dismissive is the coverage of Popular Front culture. Brett Gary has argued that *Life* was relatively easy on the left during the Popular Front period and even "progressive" in its coverage (particularly in relation to its coverage of fascist movements), but shifted to a more unequivocally negative treatment with the signing of the Hitler-Stalin pact in August 1939 (79). My own examination of the periodical, to the contrary, has found negative portrayal of the left fairly consistent even before that event. For example, a review of an exhibition of Mexican art touring the U.S., appearing on 14 March 1938, fires a number of barbs at now canonical Mexican artists with left sympathies. Under a reproduction of a Diego Rivera painting a caption instructs the reader, "Notice the small meticulous signature of this big fat artist who is now host to Leon Trotsky." The caption next to a Carlos Orozco Romero painting reveals its creator as a man "who does not always practice what he preaches," and we learn that in order to make a living, the artist Jesus Guerrero painted tanks, billboards, and railroad cars "like Adolph Hitler."

Life's partisanship was aimed not only at the left but also at the most mainstream representative of the New Deal—Franklin Roosevelt. With the exception of its first issue, which featured an optimistic photo-essay by Bourke-White and Luce on the government's construction of the Fort Peck Dam, the magazine's portrayal of both F.D.R. and the New Deal is consistently negative (writers even declared the dam project a failure in a 1941 follow-up article).[7] On 4 April

1938, a photo-essay entitled "The President's Album" begins: "Whom or what does Franklin Roosevelt blame for the 1938 Depression? He does not blame himself—although he might, because for five years he had more power than any other peacetime President, and he took all the credit for rising prosperity in 1936 ... He [instead] blames 'selfish' businessmen." An incredible example of the magazine's treatment of F.D.R. comes from 18 April 1938. Entitled, "Speaking of Dictators ... ," it juxtaposes photos of Hitler, Stalin, Roosevelt, and Mussolini all engaged in similar types of activities. A photo of Roosevelt holding his arm outstretched with his hand cupped during a speech is placed next to a photo of Hitler and Mussolini in an almost identical pose. A text box at center reads, "Dictators charm the opposite sex and shake their fingers at audiences. So does President Roosevelt ... Dictators make dramatic gestures, shake hands with their admirers, pat animals. So does Roosevelt." Such depictions comport with Luce's personal views; he was supportive of much of the legislation of the more cautious "First New Deal" (1933–34), but broke with the President after his rhetoric became markedly hostile to business in 1936 (Herzstein, *Portrait* 79–82).

Bud James with his gullible mob, Jesus Guerrero painting like Adolph Hitler, F.D.R. as totalitarian dictator—in all of these examples, *Life* anticipates the Cold War conflation of fascism and socialism, wherein both appear as structurally equivalent threats to a pluralistic "American Way." But there is a slight difference in the magazine's treatment of the right and left. On 22 May 1939, for example, *Life* farcically portrayed the Communist Party's attempt to appear more "American" in an article covering a communist-organized swing dance. Entitled "Young Communists 'Get in Groove' at Party Rally," it reads, "Lest anyone confuse them with sobersided Nazis, [the communists] turned jitterbug and continued to stomp vigorously even after the jitterbug began to decline in public favor." Earl Browder, head of the CPUSA, is shown scowling in a photo directly underneath; we read that "he watched the young antics solemnly." The representation of the Communist Party, then, is not that of a genuinely fun-loving organization as opposed to solemn Nazis, but rather, the comic spectacle of a grim organization attempting to be "fun" and in tune with American popular culture—and failing miserably. *Life*'s captioneers deflate the attempts of the Popular Front to be American by displaying those attempts as a joke for middle-class readers. The caption underneath a young woman held up by a man during a dance reads, "Marxist interpretation of dance tableau below: the woman symbolizes capitalist society, supported by the worker, who in turn is crushed in scissors-grip of greed." If the magazine presents fascists as grim and brutal, it presents the Popular Front as grim and comical—a difference to be sure, but

FIG. 5-2. "Young Communists 'Get in Groove' at Party Rally," *Life*, May 22, 1939

one that makes it clear that neither constellation is a valid part of the nation. This article thus registers a war over popular culture in the 1930s and implicitly underscores the stakes of that war for Time Inc. Those who are able to claim the latest pop-culture trends—who know the difference between a jitterbug and a

Lindy Hop, and have the privilege to laugh at those who do not—can feel themselves a part of the imagined community of the American Century.

I am not attempting to claim here that impartiality is somehow possible, and that *Life* has erred simply by straying from constructed notions of journalistic objectivity. I do claim, however, that its partiality is quite brazen. When one looks at the most widely circulated newsmagazine before the explosion of the Luce press—*The Literary Digest*—one sees a conscious attempt to stay above the fray by not taking sides in areas marked as culturally contested.[8] The fact that *Life* strays from this impartial structure is not coincidental. Henry Luce and his partner Briton Hadden defined themselves against the journalistic standards of the *Digest* as they conceived *Time* in the early 1920s. Unlike the *Digest*, Hadden and Luce imagined the articles of their fledgling publication not as quoting from various voices but as authoritatively speaking from a single voice. They would not merely break from the dry, distanced tone of the *Digest*'s prose; they would overturn its entire pretense to objectivity. "The *Digest*," they wrote, "gives little or no hint as to which side it considers to be right. *Time* gives both sides, but clearly indicates which side it believes to have the stronger position" (Baughman, *Luce* 31–32). The promise to give both sides was never followed up; but aversion to the ideas of impartiality and objectivity within journalism stayed with Luce his entire career and was implemented in his subsequent publications *Fortune* and *Life*. Defending the practices of his press at a convention for *Life* staff in May 1939, he stated: "Never, at least with my knowledge and consent, did *Time* ever claim impartiality ... Impartiality is often an impediment to truth. *Time* will not allow the stuffed dummy of impartiality to stand in the way of telling the truth as it sees it" ("Causes, Causes!" 56–57).

Objectivity was not a long-established standard within journalism when Luce was railing against it in the 1920s and 1930s. Michael Schudson has persuasively argued that the modern notion of objectivity within journalism is a relatively recent phenomenon that began to take shape after World War I; it was born of journalists' frustration over state and corporate attempts to control the flow of "facts" through governmental propaganda agencies during the war and the new public-relations agencies emerging in the 1920s. In the view taking shape in the 1930s, facts did not speak for themselves and were increasingly seen as something separate from value judgments; as such, they required some authoritative form of interpretation and evaluation to give them validity. Interpretive reporting was one path to objectivity beginning to take shape in the 1930s, and partisan objectivity shared some of the epistemology behind this style of reportage. Interpretive reporting acknowledged that facts had to be contextualized via an evaluative framework in order to speak the truth, but held that this truth had to be approached through an admittedly subjective lens. Reporters who practiced this kind of journalism sometimes acknowledged their subjectivity but, at the same time, often possessed a specialist's expertise in the area on which they were reporting that gave them some authority to speak. Interpretive reporting, in short, was primarily available to those whose authority had been already established in some sense (Schudson 144–49).

But what gave these photographers, writers, and editors the authority to make interpretive claims on the world? *Life* did not advertise itself as possessing a specialist's knowledge, nor did it attempt credibility by placing its claims in the mouths of established journalists (such journalists did in fact work for *Life*, but since bylines were either difficult to find or nonexistent, authorship was murky at best). Instead, it grounded its authority on the mimetic quality of the photograph. The credibility of a *Life* photo-essay resided not in its authors' overt claims to objectivity, nor in its flouting the expertise of its authors, but instead, as Kozol has shown, in the constructed notion that the photograph had the power to transparently represent the real. However partisan the captioning of a photograph might have been, however blatantly subjective the text might read, partiality would always be anchored by the presence of photographs—and more specifically, by the sense that the subject within the photo frame actually existed on some level (the "indexical" quality of the photograph). As I mentioned above, the photo-essays lent themselves to a transparent reading by refusing to call attention to the constructed nature of photographs. Additionally, *Life* would often caption its photos with phrases such as "Here is . . . ," "Here are pictures . . . ," or "These are . . . ," as if it were the mere exhibitor of found objects.[9]

The realism of *Life*'s photo-essay resides not in the lack of self-referentiality within their photos; rather, it lies in the relationship of photo, caption, and text. It is ultimately the captions, not merely the photographs themselves, that make *Life*'s photo-essays approach something akin to realism. But how can realism be defined in a manner relevant to journalism, and to *Life* in particular? Much of twentieth-century journalism shares some of the traits common to realism that I identified in the beginning of this book—an attempt to use a transparent, accessible form, an impulse toward social significance—and *Life* is also known for its focus on "ordinary" individuals in specific, contemporary contexts (or for making public figures into ordinary individuals through its innovation of the "candid" shot). Terry Lovell's *Pictures of Reality*, which outlines the tenets of realism as both an epistemology and an aesthetic, elaborates a quality of the form quite germane to journalism and objectivity. As Lovell argues, realism shares with science the belief that representations of reality should be grounded in empirically observable facts, but breaks from empiricism in holding the immediately observable to be an insufficient picture of reality. A larger social network exists beyond what we can immediately see and hear; and since a language of observation unmediated by theory does not exist, some kind of theory must inevitably accompany one's observations if one is to effectively articulate reality (18–20). Realism does not allow theory to encompass reality entirely and push out any place for the empirical, but at the same time does not privilege the empirical to the extent that empiricism and positivism do. As William Dean Howells asserted in his famous manifesto "Criticism and Fiction," "When realism becomes false to itself, when it heaps up facts merely . . . realism will perish too" (15).

If, as Lovell argues, realist epistemology holds that reality is to be apprehended through an inevitably subjective interpretive frame, but one with an empirical grounding, then the realism of the photo-essays within *Life* actually derives from the relationship between the captions and the photos. The photos represent the immediate—they provide the empirical base for the partisan observations in the text. But without the captioning they are nothing, for the captioning provides the larger theory that ultimately leads us to reality. This realist relationship between caption and photo was stated rather clearly in *Life*'s famous prospectus, in which the layout of the magazine was definitively theorized:

> Pictures are taken haphazardly. Pictures are published haphazardly. Naturally, therefore, they are looked at haphazardly. Cameramen who use their heads as well as their legs are rare. Rarer still are camera editors . . . And almost nowhere is there any attempt to edit pictures into a coherent story—to make an effective mosaic out of the fragmentary documents which pictures, past and present, are.
>   The mind-guided camera can do a far better job of reporting current events than has been done. And, more than that, it can reveal to us far more explicitly the nature of the dynamic social world in which we live. (Luce, "Prospectus" 35)

To construct a coherent narrative out of seemingly transparent fragments, to believe that such a narrative can and should transcend the immediacy of fact, and to hold the goal of representation to be the unraveling of a larger social matrix using both the mind and empirical document—these ideas embody most incarnations of the realist spirit. *Life*'s prospectus was in effect a blueprint for realism within visual mass culture, and, at times, the photo-essays it engendered remained loyal to these founding intentions to the best of their creator's abilities.

A People on Top of the World... and Above the Crowd

The imaginary community Luce cultivated in *Life* through partisan objectivity—his version of "the people," as it were—was highly complex. I have noted how the writers and editors showcased photographs of crowds, and how they often depicted the crowd as a passive body directed by a malign, irrational head such as Bud James, Earl Long, or President Roosevelt. An examination of the body politic that Luce attempted to create should begin here because, through the representation of crowds, *Life* invited its readers to imagine themselves as part of certain collectivities, and to exalt themselves above others. *Life*'s representation of the masses, in other words, viscerally attempted to define the form of collectivity appropriate to the transnational ideal of the American Century.

Luce was deeply influenced by José Ortega y Gasset's book *The Revolt of the Masses*, which held that modern technology and media had created a barbaric "mass man" who was naturally drawn to the totalitarian systems of fascism and communism. To Ortega y Gasset, the only hope rested with people of "excellence and superiority" whose agency was most pressingly needed to counter this new threat to civilization (Herzstein, *Portrait* 83). Luce explicitly referenced this book in his speech to advertisers in 1937, suggesting to them that, thanks to consumerism, the crowds epitomizing mass man were to be found not only overseas: "[Ortega y Gasset] begins by making you face the great new physical reality in society—crowds. Not merely Hitler's crowds, or Mussolini's, or Stalin's, or Hirohito's, but the crowds on American beaches, the crowds in the movies—the even vaster crowds you advertisers yearn for—mass circulation. These crowds, he says, will destroy civilization" ("Address" 41).

But the crowds displayed in *Life* photographs were not always presented as fearful. They could be composed of slavish mass men gathered around the likes of Earl Long, but they could also be rational or harmless expressions of a democratic/market culture. The synopsis of the 25 July 1938 issue underscored the varied nature of crowds by announcing, "Crowds made the picture news of the week—crowds which varied in mood and appearance with the sights and the heroes which brought them forth" (14). The issue depicted essentially harmless crowds gathered around the spectacles of major league baseball, Wimbledon tennis, and the landings of the aviator Howard Hughes. In all of these stories, photos of fun-loving crowds were used to underscore the newsworthiness of an essentially benign event, even though these assemblies seem little different from the sinister masses at American beaches and movie theaters that Luce cautioned against. In general, the magazine's editors presented all manner of nonpolitical consumer spectacles as harmless, and by passing on celebrity gossip the captioneers even positioned *Life* as part of the fun.[10] Some of the apparent disconnect lies in the fact that Luce did not control every day-to-day choice made by his editors and staff. But the coexistence of Luce's deeply held belief in *The Revolt of the Masses* and the innocent representation of cheap amusements in *Life* is not completely contradictory. If the "American Century" essay posited American consumer culture as an important basis of U.S. global leadership, linking people in Chicago with people in Zanzibar and Hamburg, then Americans could and should be conversant in the mass-culture language that defined them and enabled others to recognize their leadership. More specifically, recurrent readers of *Life* had earned the right to be part of such crowds: they implicitly consented to the magazine's global agenda by repeatedly coming back to it, and thus were inoculated from a devolution into mass man.

Articles featuring political candidates endorsed by Time Inc. also showcased crowds, but these photo-essays offered *Life* readers, through words and images, the acceptable terms under which they could belong to a mass. The magazine's ten-page article on the Wendell Willkie campaign offers such an example. Like Luce a moderate, interventionist Republican, Willkie tactfully slipped through an isolationist Republican Party apparatus to become a major contender against Roosevelt in the 1940 presidential election, and *Life* supported him wholeheartedly. Robert Herzstein has even suggested that Willkie got through the primaries because of Luce (*Crusade* 4). *Life*'s coverage of the campaign in its 30 September 1940 issue featured a two-page spread with panoramic shots of massive crowds at Willkie rallies in Illinois and Kansas. Shot from the perspective of the speaker and looking down into the countless faces of the assembled throng, these photos are virtually indistinguishable from other *Life* images of crowds. One notable difference, however, is that in two photos the speaker has his arms outstretched in an open, embracing gesture, rather than the sharp, up-and-down gesticulations *Life* associated with dictators. But other, more significant differences make these crowds acceptable compared to those assembled to hear Long. First and most obvious are the explicit politics of the speaker, which are clearly spelled out by the magazine's partisan objective writers. "I Shall Go Up and Down This Land Preaching the Doctrine of Democracy" is the headline over the crowd shots, and the adjacent text blocks specify that "democracy" means intervention, a faith in self-reliance, and an opposition to centralized executive power, especially in regard to the regulation of markets. Second, and linked to these explicit politics, is that crowd shots are de-emphasized, occupying only two of the article's ten pages. As in literary realism, ordinary individuals are used to tell the story of a larger social movement. Seven of the ten pages focus on the selfless, devoted work of individuals—campaign professionals, leading citizens, and ordinary people working through "Willkie Clubs"—who were volunteering their time and money to propel the campaign. Most of the photos are framed around single individuals whose names are given in captions, such as the smiling "Willkiette" Bess Weiner whose job is to pass out buttons, and the serious, determined campaign advisor Harold Stassen. The individual volunteers all appear affluent, and are disproportionately female. While a few men in suits strategize over the selection of images, a larger number of attractive women are engaged in making signs and handing out buttons—the grunt work of the campaign. There is a surprising moment of inclusion: in a movement otherwise rendered as completely white, one Willkiette—Rosetta Burton—is black, and her photo occupies the center of one page. The real "other" in the article is two white workmen (one of them dirty, with muscular arms exposed—a classic Hugo Gellert proletarian icon) who hassle a fresh, smiling Willkiette.

This piece is emblematic of the kind of collectivity *Life* invited its readers to create and share. Members of this community are animated by an unambiguous set of interventionist Republican politics. They come together in crowds, but are not defined by crowds—rather, they are active, individual citizens with names. This body of agent-citizens is affluent and well dressed, consists of both men and women with clearly defined roles, and is ever-so-slightly racially diverse. If Luce began to dislike Roosevelt for making it seem as if industry was "not part of America," this article put images of the managerial class and its devoted allies squarely back into the national frame (82). But *Life*'s imagined community was not always constructed around images of crowds, nor did it lie exclusively within U.S. borders. The boundaries of this community, shadowed by the image of the dirty workman, could be rigidly drawn, and in drawing such boundaries an image of individuals could just as easily suffice to exclude whole groups.

The inclusion of an African American in the vaunted Willkie campaign signifies the baby steps taken by *Life* toward a more positive role for African Americans in the American Century. As a moderate, Northern Republican, Luce detested the repeated blocking of anti-lynching legislation by southern Democrats, and was supportive of attempts to abolish Jim Crow. In the 1950s and 1960s, *Life* would become generally favorable to the civil rights movement. But while the magazine exalted a number of "exceptional Negroes" like George Washington Carver and, surprisingly, Paul Robeson, ordinary African Americans were largely missing from its photo-essays before 1945.[11] When they did appear, it was most often in the advertisements, where they were depicted as comical rubes or smiling servants, as was typical in other mainstream media at the time. Sometimes, this racism could work its way into the photo-essays too, as in a light story on the southern watermelon market from 9 August 1937. Here, a caption reading "Nothing makes a Negro's mouth water like a luscious, fresh-picked melon" appeared beneath a photo of an African American woman in a shanty, a baby nursing in one arm and a watermelon in the other (52). More often than this, in a tentative nod toward civil rights, black Americans appeared in the photo-essays as lynched or incarcerated bodies. But they were at best pitiable victims, not agents, within articles that refrained from condemning the perpetrators with *Life*'s usual partisan bluntness.[12] In addition, the magazine employed no African Americans as full-time researchers, writers, or photographers until Gordon Parks came on staff in 1948. Even then, Parks recalled that when he came to work he felt like "a pepper seed in a mountain of white salt" (qtd. in Doss 233). But if African Americans were underrepresented, other American people of color were virtually absent from both the professional staff and the pages of the magazine. So while *Life* at least acknowledged the existence of ordinary African Americans within the American Century, it generally reserved a marginal or downright inferior place for them, and thus constructed the real agents of its political project as not only affluent but white.

But if Americans were to intervene in world affairs to an unprecedented degree as called for by Luce's most famous essay, they had to have a sense of connectedness to peoples across their borders—an investment in their fate, as it were. This connectedness could not be achieved by representing other cultures in terms of absolute ethnic or racial difference, especially if a shared mass culture was to be an important basis of hegemony. *Life*'s photo-essays thus tried to bridge the gap between its American readers and those others around the world whom Luce perceived as willing, capable participants in the American Century. In its representation of certain overseas populations, Time Inc. was thus a forerunner of what would become a more pervasive Cold War strategy identified by Christina Klein: the middlebrow project of getting Americans to shed outmoded notions of racial superiority in order to forge sentimental bonds across borders. But *Life* erected as many barriers as bridges. According to its photo-essays, peoples who subscribed to leaders or ideas deemed threatening to U.S. interests did so out of some cultural or racial deficiency, while others were depicted as lacking the innate capacity to effectively participate in the American-led global order envisioned by the magazine's founder. In both cases, *Life* fell back on vicious, long-established stereotypes to render such people in terms of absolute difference.

Who was "like us" and who was utterly alien was rarely stable in the pages of the magazine; they shifted depending on Luce and his confidants' perceptions of U.S. foreign policy needs. Providing a detailed map of all of its cultural representations is beyond the scope of this chapter, but a synopsis with a few emblematic examples will impart a sense of Luce's pluralism. From its founding in 1936 up until the bombing of Pearl Harbor, *Life* notably singled out Jews across the world and the Chinese (particularly Chinese nationalists) for sympathetic treatment, and also generally sided with the British in its struggles with its subject peoples. In this same period a larger number of cultures were written off as hopelessly backward: the Arab world, the cultures of the Philippines, and Latin and South America. The peoples of Japan and the U.S.S.R. were cast in a sinister light, but were not yet seen as credible threats. After Pearl Harbor, the U.S.S.R. and the Philippines were portrayed with much less hostility, though Luce's alliance with the Soviet Union was short-lived. Shortly after the war, the Soviet Union and the Chinese communists would emerge in the pages of *Life* as the greatest threat to the American Century, and its assaults on them would be relentless and shrill.[13]

When building bridges across cultures, *Life*'s photo-essays enacted a number of consistent strategies. Its partisan objective writers claimed a power to generalize entire ethnicities, regions, nations, and cultures with a degree of un-subtlety that is stunning to the uninitiated (for example, a sub-headline in the watermelon article referenced above reads "All Southerners Like Watermelons"). When using such generalizations to form bonds, one strategy (more commonly used with European allies) was to elide cultural difference altogether and to stress that another people was almost "just like us." For example, in its remarkable special issue on the U.S.S.R. from 29 March 1943, *Life* stressed that the diverse people of the Soviet Union were brought together in a "melting pot" by "the race of Great Russians, a prolific, gregarious, talkative, aggressive, and friendly mass of blond Slavs who have conquered and colonized a sixth of the earth's land surfaces." In case the reader did not catch the allusion to the rugged frontiersmen of American mythology, the writer added: "To a remarkable degree, they look like Americans, dress like Americans, and think like Americans" (23). A more common strategy, however, and one used most often with regard to Asia, was to acknowledge some degree of cultural or racial difference, but to posit the people in question as becoming more "like us" through Western tutelage and the teleology of progress entailed by that tutelage. This was the case with the Chinese and, after Pearl Harbor, the people of the Philippines as well.

China occupied a particularly special place within the media of Time Inc., a fact that has not gone unnoticed by scholars. Henry Luce's parents were both missionary educators in China, and he was born in a missionary compound in the Shandong peninsula, where he lived until his teenage years. From this upbringing grew a sense that the United States had a Christian responsibility to help build Asia, a notion that formed one of Luce's core beliefs (Herzstein, *Crusade* 1). The media baron developed a blind adoration for Chiang Kai-shek and the Nationalists in particular, and in 1942 was dismayed that Americans were paying too much attention to Europe and not enough to the war in China and the Nationalist efforts against the Japanese (39). Almost since its founding, *Life* had been trying to redirect the American gaze away from the Atlantic and toward the Pacific, and it did so by depicting a courageous ruling family in China leading a nation at war with itself toward the American way of life. An article from 16 August 1937, titled "Mei-Ling ('Beautiful Mood') Helps Her Husband Rule China" emphasizes the American education of Soong Mei-ling, who was dubbed Madame Chiang by the American press. A prominent photo shows her holding hands with a white American classmate at Wesleyan College for Women in Macon, Georgia, and noted how Methodist Mei-ling "thoroughly charmed" her later Yankee classmates with her "Georgia accent" (18). Readers were told that this Christian woman with an elegant southern twang married the "crude, brash warlord" Chiang Kai-shek in 1926, setting up a narrative of a virile despot tamed and civilized by the influence of his Christian wife (a predecessor to the Cold War musical *The King and I*, with Madame Chiang in the role of Anna). Thus Americanized, subsequent articles demonstrate how these leaders, working along with their Western allies, were in the process of making the rest of China more American.

Unlike Edgar Snow and Pearl Buck, however, who converted the Chinese into Americans through the trope of the yeoman farmer, *Life* used modern Western market culture to enact this transformation. (Standing on opposite sides of the Chinese civil war, Edgar Snow and Henry Luce also selected very different groups within China to Americanize.) *Life*'s exposé of what it considered an emblematic Chinese town demonstrates its editorial view of market modernity as agent of Americanization. Published on 24 November 1941 and titled "A Chinese Town: Little Market Towns Make China Unconquerable," the article suggests that the Szechwan town of Lung Chuan I is "unconquerable" because the government of Chiang Kai-shek has linked it to Western culture and innovation. It is emblematic not because it is the statistically average Chinese town, but because it is typical of a larger, nascent process of social struggle and transformation—in other words, it is typical in the Marxian realist sense of "typicality." Lung Chuan I is shown to be in the midst of a cultural war between new and old values: the "old" is visualized as quaint handcrafts, a primitive medicine man, and decrepit elders who oversee an outmoded, Confucian "family system." This China, readers are instructed, lacked "the Western man's drive to become the master of his environment," which explains its crippling lack of technology (86).

Other captioned photos illustrate the "new" as a Chinese Christian pastor and his wife, an "able" Nationalist officer, smiling women who use Western medicine by weighing babies, and a government-sponsored reading room that connects the townspeople to a world outside their "Confucian morality." A photo of an athletic club director holding a basketball is most striking, however. The text reads, "The educated Chinese shown at right with a basketball is actually a revolutionary apparition in China. . . . What he teaches, even more than physical exercise, is team effort, to a China now engaged in the greatest team effort in its history" (89). Whereas the pluralism of Snow and Buck conflated China and America, but in doing so at least assumed the spirit of resistance to come from the Chinese themselves, *Life* makes clear that the Chinese will to fight has been cultivated from the outside. It is not class warriors who make the Chinese fight so "un-Chinese-like," but rather the agency of the West, embodied by the education of Madame Chiang, technology, the spirit of ambition, and last but not least, U.S. popular culture. The Chinese are embraceable, *Life* instructs its American readers, not because they *are* you, nor the noble agricultural heritage you have lost, but because exemplary American institutions have helped them lift themselves to your level.

But *Life*'s coverage of China and the Philippines also shows how its imaginary imperial project of cultural assimilation was never far from hard racism and the construction of absolute difference. Its representation of Filipinos serves as a case and point. After the bombing of Pearl Harbor, Filipinos were portrayed as embraceable, like the Chinese under Nationalist governance: as in the previous example, this was because of their willing acquiescence to Western cultural and military leadership. Appearing shortly after Roosevelt's declaration of war, the photo-essay "We Shoot Down the First Japs" pictured Filipino troops, trained by General MacArthur, operating sophisticated radio equipment with a caption describing them as "bright, capable, willing soldiers" (30). A prominent photo atop the opposite page visualizes American tutelage even more clearly; it shows a white American woman carrying a Bible and marching at the head of a Filipino infantry unit. However, when the editors of *Life* did not deem the Philippines to be acquiescent to American leadership (or, did not give priority to the creation of sentimental bonds), their representation of Filipinos emphasized the very same racist stereotypes of tropical primitives Bulosan combated in his work. In its report from the colony on 13 February 1939, for example, it announced that American colonization had made its people "the luckiest in the Orient," yet depicted them as so backward as to be unable to appreciate U.S. beneficence. Its two-page spread on the culture of the archipelago used the Igorot highlanders as the quintessential Filipinos, and its most prominent photo presented a quite literal image of their partial assimilation: it exhibited a group of Igorots wearing Western shirts and hats, but completely naked from the waist down. The accompanying text stated that Filipinos "are still incredibly lazy and incompetent, spoiled and quarrelsome. Accustomed to nakedness, the Igorots, like those below, put on shirts and shoes when they come to town, but no trousers. For all the fond belief that the Filipinos have learned democratic ways, they will inevitably slide into dictatorship" (53). Like so many other peoples it deemed fundamentally deficient, *Life* saw no reason to include Filipinos in the American Century in 1939, nor to move its readers to a more positive view of them. A similar fate would befall the Chinese after the revolution of 1949.

Thus *Life*'s American Century reached beyond American borders to include some of those formerly held to be racial aliens, and took very tentative steps to highlight southern injustices against black Americans. But it was not guided by a consistent antiracist philosophy, nor did it generally put forth a relationship of equality between white Americans and "the darker races" at home and abroad. At its worst, *Life* perpetuated the hard racism within American culture; at its best, it exhorted its affluent white readers to recognize their agency, to lift themselves out from the crowd and embark on a global mission of capitalist uplift, one that sometimes brought them into imaginative contact with racial others whom they had been reared to view as threats.

The Dangerous Playground
Life and Fetishized Reading

The consumerist basis of Luce's imagined global community—visually rendered by the Chinese athletic director holding a basketball—meant that the cultivation of consumer desire among readers of *Life* was fully in keeping with its political project. In its drive to generate a culture of consumption—and, more immediately, to remain viable as a profit-driven publication—the magazine and its advertisers turned to aesthetics other than realism. Realism was not the only means of bringing about the American Century within the pages of *Life*; while it was a powerful force within the photo-essays, it was not the only representational mode within the magazine. The photo-essays were only a part of *Life*—they were wedged between mazes of advertisements that grew more complex as the magazine aged. The overall layout defined the way in which the reader would experience the realism within the photo-essays; as a result, it cannot be conveniently bracketed off. When we examine other elements of the magazine, we find that the overall effect of *Life* can hardly be described as realist, for juxtapositions between advertisement and photo-essay undermine the ideological coherence (necessary to realism) the essays work to create. Some of the advertisements, when viewed independently, do operate under a realist mode, as they tell stories of ordinary people with everyday problems, using a linear, frame-by-frame technique reminiscent of comics (sometimes the frames are even numbered to make the sequence abundantly clear), and they tell such stories with photographs to boot. Much more often, however, they are nowhere close to realism, and instead display an advertised object within a stylized setting using a single image, often a drawing—a classic instance of commodity fetishism. But whether creating linear narratives or not, the ads were generally in keeping with the hard-boiled advertising style of the 1930s, when copywriters rejected the elegant lines and colors of the 1920s in favor of a more ugly, blunt aesthetic (Marchand 300–306). This made the ads more seamlessly blend with the black-and-white, photograph-based layout of *Life*.

In a magazine reading experience familiar to the modern reader, one must navigate one's way through a maze of advertisements in order to find the articles. In my investigation, the proportion of ad to article in the early days of the magazine hovered around 43 percent. For instance, of the ninety pages in *Life*'s 22 May 1939 edition, thirty-nine pages are composed of ads.[14] Whereas the news articles are bracketed off relatively clearly, its lifestyle, culture, "women's interest," and curiosity articles are not. In these categories, photo-essays are juxtaposed with advertisements featuring photos, often on the same page, which has the effect of blurring the line between article and ad. Furthermore, *Life*'s innovations of the oversized photo and the photo-narrative are employed by both article and ad, making the line even less clear. A photo-essay about the movie star Joan Wanger in the 9 September 1940 issue, for instance, is juxtaposed by a facial soap ad providing a linear photo-narrative of a glamorous, feminine world much like that of the movie star herself. The woman in the ad resembles the actress in the article—both are brunettes with the exact same hairstyle, both have patrician features and wear luxurious clothing. Both article and ad are set in elite social worlds: the article tells us that the actress has a personal secretary and a daughter who attends the same school as Shirley Temple, and the ad relates through both captioning and photos that its protagonist attends fancy debutante balls. Further, both photo-essay and ad are laid out using the standard *Life* formula in which a large, prominent photo is followed by a series of smaller ones that tell a narrative. In this instance, ad and article reflect each other on the level of both form and content.

Sally Stein studied the implications of this reading experience in her essay "The Graphic Ordering of Desire." Looking at middle-class women's magazines

FIG. 5-3. Juxtaposition of article and advertisement, *Life*, September 9, 1940, page 126

from 1914 to 1939, Stein argues that the magazines played a significant role in forging a new kind of reading practice amenable to consumerism. In the magazines she investigates, reading is no longer a linear, continuous, reflective, or even textual experience. Rather, the new magazine creates a text in which reading is scattered, discontinuous, and mediated by ads, wherein readers "freely" negotiate their own individual paths through the "magazine labyrinth." Photographs have a primary role here: not only do they make reading an increasingly visual experience, they also intensify the pleasure and the uninterrupted flow of the new reading practice (both vital elements in a consumerist project). The color in the photographs increases the pleasure, while the "endless juxtapositions" of photographs to text produce the uninterrupted flow. Juxtapositions of photo and text take place within articles, within ads, and between articles and ads, forming an endless web of play in which advertised commodities are inescapable.

This scattered, discontinuous reading experience is not only a function of the overall layout in *Life*; it seeps into the photo-essays as well, undermining their realism. Though the essays use photographs in a series to create a narrative, seldom does this narrative attain anything resembling linearity. In the exposé of Louisiana politics, the photo of Earl Long that spans almost the entire first page establishes a kind of beginning by providing us with a villainous backdrop soon to be heroically transcended by the conservative opposition. But as one turns the page, all sense of beginning/middle/end is lost: the top and bottom of the two-page spread illustrate different aspects of the same event (the satirical parade), while the middle depicts simultaneous political bids against the same opponent. Similarly, in a two-page photo-essay in the 6 September 1937 issue covering the court battle between the C.I.O. and Weirton Steel, the layout does not lead us down a chronological path in which X happens, then Y, then Z; rather, it shows us simultaneous shots of the same event. An enlarged photo on page 1 shows us the courtroom from the perspective of the balcony, while a smaller photo underneath shows us the façade of the courtroom from the outside. Flipping the page, one sees a total of four pictures representing the inside of the courtroom: on top, a relatively large photo of the balcony shot from the perspective of the courtroom floor; in the middle, two smaller photos of the attorneys; and at bottom, a photo of the spectators on the floor level. Rather than choosing to represent various moments of the trial, the photo-essay provides us with different visual perspectives of what seems to be the same slice of time.

It is tempting to reach into the world of film and apply the label of "suturing" to *Life*'s storytelling mode. A practice already common among filmmakers in the 1940s, *suturing* creates a narrative by shooting roughly simultaneous fragments of the same event and splicing them together in a series (the shower scene in Hitchcock's *Psycho* stands as a famous example). The layout of *Life* is even more radical than this, for even though suturing works with seemingly disassociated fragments, it ultimately depends on linearity. In a film we see one shot follow the last, and the nature of moving pictures forces us to view them in the order the director desires. In the magazine, however, no one can tell us where to

FIG. 5-4. From "The New Deal Dispenses a New Brand of Justice to Labor and Industry," *Life*, September 6, 1937

begin and where to end, and more to the point, the creators of the photo-essays do not even try. Rather than through suturing, its layout operates by a kind of radical simultaneity.

As a reading experience, simultaneity is not necessarily bad—poststructuralist critics have pointed out how the older, linear modes of reading produced within realism can work to reproduce oppressive systems of thought, and how more synchronic, playful modes of reading and analysis can work to undo these oppressive systems.[15] But the simultaneity within *Life*, unanchored by a discourse that could help us navigate a world with less hierarchy—and consequently without articulation along the lines of a genuinely emancipatory mode of desire—forms a dangerous playground, ultimately creating the disassociated, chaotic reading experience Stein describes. I would argue that it consequently works to create a fetishized mode of reading.

If we agree that a fetishized reading experience is one in which pleasure is attached to commodities, and in which the layout works against our attempts to imagine a world with less privilege and hierarchy, then *Life* certainly works to create such a reading experience. Advertisements relentlessly work to attach pleasure to commodities, which should come as no surprise. Not only was *Life* a for-profit part of Time Inc., but if one thinks back to Luce's "American Century" essay, the building of global recognition for American consumer goods was tied to the political project of the magazine. And as I have argued, an anti-Popular Front ideology provided the larger organizational principle driving the quasi-realist photo-essays, one that imagined affluent white Americans as leaders of a new global order. Meanwhile, endless juxtaposition of these conservative photo-essays with advertisements creates a flow of information that works against any attempt by the reader to question the emerging capitalist culture. Hence *Life* works to push the explicit politics of Luce's "American Century" using semi-realist photo-essays, but the overall thrust of the magazine is to create a more subtle agenda of the American Century—consumerism—in a manner that undermines the realism used to convey its explicit politics. Viewing *Life*'s realism within the larger context of the magazine ultimately points to the fate of realism within the new mass culture Time Inc. was creating in the 1930s and 1940s. In the emerging mass-culture template designed by Luce and *Life*'s editors, realism was unable to continue serving the oppositional function it had often served in the past (more on this in a moment), and had severe limits placed on its ability to act as the emancipatory force desired by its proponents in the Popular Front.

Margaret Bourke-White, *Life*, and the History of Realist Journalism

I have attempted to describe in detail the representational strategies *Life* used to further the political intentions of its founder and to create a bulwark against the

Popular Front. But the question remains as to how these strategies got there. Of all the elements *Life* brings together, realism is the key to tracing the paradoxical presence of the Popular Front in the magazine. To reiterate a foundational assertion of this book, realism had been the form of choice for several generations of cultural producers who wished to uncover social contradictions, and in the 1930s, Popular Front writers and artists displayed a clear preference for the genre. The presence of trace elements of realism in *Life*'s pages would not be sufficient evidence of a Popular Front influence—earlier mass publications had employed the form as well, and *Life* arose from an earlier relationship between realism and journalism. The possibility of a Popular Front presence here rests on *who* was bringing realism through its door.

In the late nineteenth century, realism had a stronger foothold in journalism than in other areas of mass culture. Three transformations took place in and around American mass periodicals in that century's last two decades that were relevant to the relationship between realism and journalism: the innovations of the Pulitzer press; the aforementioned magazine revolution of the 1890s; and the realist turn in still photography. Beginning in the 1880s, the innovations of the Pulitzer press were increasingly diffused throughout American newspapers, dramatically expanding the use of illustrations, advertisements, and even realism in journalism through what has been labeled "sensationalism." Sensationalism, often held to be the use of emotionally laden and stimulating appeals in order to sell stories, had been around since the penny press of the 1830s and 1840s. The Pulitzer press revolutionized the style rather than the content of sensationalism by dramatically increasing the number of ads, increasing the type-sizes of headlines, and expanding the number of illustrations in order to achieve sensational effects. Realism would seem to be far removed from such publications, but according to Michael Schudson, the reigning ideal among journalists working at this time was a realist one. He suggests that reporters in the 1890s saw themselves as scientists discovering the facts of industrial life more "realistically" than anyone who had come before them, and notes that most of the famous turn-of-the-century realist authors wrote for newspapers, including Dreiser, Crane, Cather, London, Bierce, and Norris. Not only did they bring their styles into the pages of the newspapers, but their experience of working for newspapers helped define their fiction (70–71, 95–96). If this is the case, then the boundaries between literary and journalistic realism had always been somewhat blurred; each facilitated the emergence of the other.

The first magazine revolution also occurred at the turn of the century, when circulation figures increased so dramatically that magazines for the first time merited the label "mass." These magazines published the stories of now canonical realist authors, albeit to a relatively small middle-class audience, and did so as they changed in the 1890s from a genteel to a consumerist orientation. Christopher Wilson has argued that, even in their consumerist reincarnation, realism was fundamental to the form of turn-of-the-century middle-class magazines, and could be seen in their use of everyday, accessible language, their "practical" content, their attempt to convey authority and expertise, and through its editorial intervention between reader and content.[16] Also at the turn of the century, a decisive realist trend developed within American photography, which was significant for periodicals in that they were using an ever increasing number of photographs. While the less politically inclined photographers of the turn of the century were drawn to pictorialism—an attempt to turn photography into a fine art, in part by eschewing everyday subjects—more socially conscious camera artists such as Jacob Riis and Lewis Hine emerged who were drawn to the realist mode. Riis and Hine were among the first in American photography to break with the deliberate artifice of portraiture and art photography, and they used their work to critique the public neglect of the nation's underclass (however misguided Riis's critiques could sometimes be). In the 1930s, Popular Front photographers such as Dorothea Lange, Walker Evans, Russell Lee, Ben Shahn, and—most important for my purposes here—Margaret Bourke-White drew upon this brief history of photo-realism with renewed attempts to make the nation's forgotten subjects visible, reversing the 1920s tendency toward abstract modernism embodied by Edward Weston and Edward Steichen.

The newsmagazine as developed by Luce and the personnel at Time Inc. was a new form that built upon, deepened, and made more visible the long relationship between realism and journalism. I have argued that *Life*'s format was novel among its predecessors and competitors in that it brought together the increasing use of photographic images within journalism, the disconnected reading experience of an ad-driven publication, a content devoted predominately to news, and a partisan objectivity aligned against the Popular Front. I have also noted how Luce's partisan objectivity, which in *Life* was grounded in the indexical quality of the photograph, was a kind of realist revolt against the emergent goal of objectivity within the profession of journalism. As such, its presence in the publications of Time Inc. meant that the new form of the newsmagazine was stamped with a significant aspect of realist epistemology. But this novel form was not exclusively the brainchild of Henry Luce. Others also developed and implemented the founding ideas of his news empire, and they transmitted into the magazines the aesthetic ideologies of the period in which they were grounded.

Henry Luce maintained friendships with a number of individuals who did not share his politics, and it was no secret that he hired people with left and liberal sympathies at Time Inc. At least in part, his hiring decisions were driven by a practical impulse to capture the best creative talent available, and in the 1930s at least, much of that talent had aligned itself away from the established order. When asked why he employed "Reds" at his business magazine *Fortune*, he responded on a number of occasions with "damned Republicans can't write" (qtd. in Herzstein, *Portrait* 80). Accepting the basic principle of collective bargaining and even endorsing the landmark Wagner Act, he was also tolerant enough to offer no major objections when his editors, writers, and researchers at Time Inc. organized through the A.F.L.-affiliated Newspaper Guild in 1936, though he voiced concerns about individual contract demands. (In general, *Life*'s coverage of labor disputes was not as anti-union as one might expect.) By 1939, there was a critical mass of actual communists at Time Inc., enough to publish their own anonymous broadside called *High Time* which thrashed the positions put forth by the Luce press. Luce's tolerance did not extend this far, however, and after he hired a private detective to find the source of this dissident publication, it simply vanished after three issues (86–87).

Unlike at *Fortune*, however, the sympathies of trade unionists and communists at *Life* were prevented from consistently congealing into cohesive Popular Front narratives within the photo-essays. But significant elements of their aesthetic were incorporated into the magazine, particularly in its initial phases. And, at moments, they did win narrative control. While evidence of the political sympathies of most managing editors reveals little in the way of Popular Front sensibilities, it is clear that major figures in the early conceptualization and operation of the magazine were deeply steeped in the left social movements of the day. Left-liberal playwright and poet Archibald MacLeish helped write the famous prospectus in which *Life*'s use of photography was definitively theorized. Though the extent of his contributions are unknown, the prospectus was a product of collaborative writing between Luce and MacLeish; and while he was never employed on *Life*'s staff, the poet remained a friend of Luce, retaining a warm respect for him into his later years (Wainwright 32–33; Drabeck 122).

An even more foundational influence was Ralph Ingersoll, general manager of Time Inc. in the mid-1930s. Though a shrewd corporate manager, Ingersoll had clear Popular Front sympathies, as manifested by his staffing of *Fortune* with a talented left-liberal crew, a "curiosity" about communism that led to his membership in a communist reading group in the mid-1930s, and his later establishment of the decidedly Popular Front tabloid *P.M.* in 1940. Ingersoll biographer Roy Hoopes persuasively argued that the idea for a "picture magazine" within the Luce press was hatched by Ingersoll. The left-leaning general manager pushed the idea of a photographic newsmagazine to Luce as early as 1934, and persisted so relentlessly that Luce finally gave in. Ingersoll was heavily involved in designing the layout as well. Office memos reveal that Ingersoll was largely responsible for the final decision on the size of the magazine and helped craft the layout formula. The layout of the famous first photo-essay in *Life*'s premiere edition in November 1936, which enthusiastically covered the New Deal public works project the Fort Peck Dam, was personally put together by Luce, Ingersoll, and MacLeish out of photos supplied by Margaret Bourke-White. This layout would serve as a rough blueprint of photo-essays to follow. Although Luce was managing editor of *Life* in its early days, Ingersoll's position within Time Inc. gave him the power to choose editors of all sorts, and his proposed tree of managing directors was approved in 1937. His persistent appeals to Luce on behalf of the Spanish Loyalists even carved out a space for a Popular Front, antifascist position on the Spanish Civil War within the pages of *Life* (Hoopes 96–97, 136–40, 145, 148, 155; Goldberg 177; Herzstein 98).

But perhaps the most dramatic Popular Front influence at *Life* was photographer Margaret Bourke-White, who made a name for herself in the 1920s in advertising, shooting highly aestheticized pictures of heavy machinery. She underwent a major shift in her political consciousness in the mid-1930s, however, and soon was producing documentary photography for countless left-wing political groups. She was intimate friends with *New Masses* editor Joseph Freeman, made murals for the Soviet consulate, worked with the communist Film and Photo League, and actively promoted aid for refugees of the Spanish Civil War. Her political activities gave her the honor of being cited by the House Committee on Un-American Activities thirteen times (Goldberg 155, 157, 328). Bourke-White was hired at *Life* as one of the original four photographers on its staff, and saw her position in the new picture magazine as a continuation of her political activities. She wrote to a friend in 1936: "People don't realize how serious conditions in this country are ... The new job [at *Life*] will give me more opportunity to work with creative things like this ... I am delighted to be able to turn my back on all advertising agencies and go on to life as it really is" (183).

Her enthusiasm for the political promise she saw in *Life* continued well past the first edition, and in her time on its staff she influenced *Life*'s photographic practice enormously. Her biographer Vicki Goldberg argues that Bourke-White effectively "set up the *Life* labs, practices, and standards" (185). She hired the magazine's first film editor, Peggy Sargent, and taught her how to define a quality photograph. Sargent, in turn, was put in charge of editing all the photographers' film, which meant that any film shot by a *Life* staff member had to first pass her approval before being sent on to the layout editors. Bourke-White's direct influence on the others on staff was recalled by *Life* photographer Carl Mydans: "her effect on all of us is incalculable. It was from her that I learned to workshop the quality of a photographic print" (qtd. in Goldberg 185). Her impact seemed to be acknowledged by her superiors as well, for she remarked in her autobiography that it always made her proud when editors referred to a photo-essay as "the Bourke-White kind of story" (*Portrait* 147). Bourke-White had become famous immediately preceding her employment at *Life* by the publication of *You Have Seen Their Faces*, a now classic work of photo-realism that marked a decisive shift away from the abstract modernism of her earlier advertising work, and she is generally known as one of the great social documentary photographers of the United States. One can conclude that all of those hours of training and teaching by example was showing her colleagues how to edit and shoot as realists.[17]

But what was the fate of Bourke-White's brand of Popular Front realism within the pages of *Life*? To what extent was her desire to show "life as it really is" rewarded? I have already traced a definite move away from Popular Front sensibilities within the photo-essay template she established, so to reveal that Bourke-White eventually left the magazine in deep frustration should come as no surprise. Political and professional disillusionment over the promise of *Life* caught up with her by 1940, when she quit Time Inc. and began work at a new Popular Front tabloid, the New York–area *P.M.* A brief survey of her photo-essays within *Life* helps illustrate the roots of her frustration; in addition, a comparison of how a specific set of Bourke-White's photos were edited within *Life* to their editing in a publication in which she had much more control—*You Have Seen Their Faces*—fully brings out the ways in which *Life* co-opted Popular Front journalistic realism.

Published in 1937, *You Have Seen Their Faces* (hereafter, *Faces*) was a collection of Bourke-White photographs depicting southern life, punctuated by narrative interludes of about five pages in length written by her then-husband Erskine Caldwell. The captions underneath her photos—all of which were fictionalized quotes from the people represented—were also written by Caldwell. The bulk of the photos were of destitute tenant farmers and farm workers, both black and white, and of the environments in which they lived. At moments the book replicates stock images of the region and its people; the second photo in the book, for instance, shows four African American men quietly reclining on a bench by a river above a caption that reads, "Just sitting in the sun watching the Mississippi go by." Reminiscent of Caldwell's novels, another photo shows an old white man contentedly smoking his pipe from within a shanty that has only three walls. He appears to enjoy the view provided by the absent wall, and this is confirmed by a caption reading, "I spent ten months catching planks drifting down the river to build this house, and then the flood came along and washed the side of it off. Doggone if I don't like it better the way it is now."

Taken alone, these images would convey a stereotypical shiftlessness and comic fatalism; but they are juxtaposed with a much larger number of images that clearly contradict them. We are shown angry faces such as the close-up head shot of an African American man with a grim expression, shot at eye level, accompanied by a quote through which he relates his exploitation in the fields. We also see evidence of a strong work ethic, as in the head shot of an African American independent farm owner coupled with a quote revealing the relative affluence of his family's "homestead." The southern work ethic is also highlighted in the first photo of the book, which shows a white child pushing a plow alongside a caption stating he must work rather than go to school, since his father insists that the family do all the labor of the farm by themselves. It must be added that almost all of Bourke-White's photos in the collection are shot either at eye level or from underneath the subject: the latter is a classic method of exalting the person photographed, and the former a way of creating empathy by putting the viewer on the same plane. Despite this unifying technique, no single image sticks as one flips the pages—the faces are alternately pitiful, proud, grotesque, angry, stunned—nor do the captions attached to these faces point to a single sentiment that unifies the exploited.

Taken together, the captioned images of the book suggest to the reader that, if one wants stereotypes when looking at the South, one can find them. But—much like W. E. B. Du Bois, who decried the view of the "car window sociologist" that saw only "shiftlessness" when looking at Black Belt tenant farmers—*Faces* reveals idleness or comic fatalism to be mere moments within a much larger, more complex reality of suffering, grueling labor, and exploitation (314). The text definitively announces on the first page that "Twice a year [the South] takes life easy.... The rest of the time it works harder than everybody else, chopping its cotton and sawing its wood from dawn to dusk." The narrative interludes by Caldwell thread together the seemingly fragmentary images in order to link class and racial formation: they illustrate how the unholy merger of the sharecropping system and the southern racial order are the absent causes behind the various expressions represented in the photos. The people of the South have reacted to their condition, the reader is told, in ways both revolutionary and self-destructive, with both racism and righteous anger. The system is to be removed through both government intervention and the militant action of the sharecroppers themselves. If the text makes one thing clear to the reader, it is that a storm is brewing among the oppressed, one that may wipe away the suffering on the faces you have seen. But the photographs by Bourke-White take the politics of the text a step further to reveal a tension within *Faces*. They depict women as often as men, supporting Paula Rabinowitz's argument that Bourke-White, despite her class difference and the problematic means by which she sometimes obtained her photos, at least made the suffering of poor women visible (*Represented* 73–74). The text, on the other hand, consistently examines the problems of the South from the perspective of the male household head, obscuring the visibility of working women within the master narrative that ties the work together.

But in its re-editing of *Faces*, *Life* elided the gendered nature of working-class suffering by avoiding suffering altogether. The editors of *Life* constructed a photo-essay out of these same photographs and captions for the 22 November 1937 issue, but with a very different effect. Photos and text from *Faces* were excerpted and arranged in a five-page spread that distinctly recast their meaning in the *Life* magazine style. The first page is dominated by a single Bourke-White photo showing a poor woman and her child sitting among the massive columns of a ruined plantation house, suggesting a southern gothic narrative to follow. Instead, what comes after is a series of photos and captions representing the southern poor as comic or irrational simpletons. The main text block announces that of the two motifs animating *Faces*—bitter exploitation and "strange sardonic humor"—*Life* has decided to reproduce the latter, as the misery of the sharecroppers has already become "tiresomely familiar to the U.S. public." Consequently, the excerpted photos depict what the editors describe as "the sharecroppers' peculiar fatalism and bitter laughter." A photo showing two men picking a guitar in a shanty is accompanied by a caption reading, "It never felt like Sunday until I plucked the guitar some." Beneath this is the photo and text described earlier of the man enjoying the view from within his three-walled home. Turning the page, one sees a full spread depicting a very emotive, backwoods religious ceremony in a tiny wooden church with singing and dancing. The caption underneath one of these images reads, "Religion, Mr. Caldwell finds, is to the sharecroppers a 'release and escape' from drudgery, often takes [*sic*] the form of hysteria" (in actuality, Caldwell presented their religious faith not as pathology, but as an understandable choice that anyone in a culture without usable political discourses would make).[18] Comic primitivism develops into its close cousin minstrelsy on the final page, which shows an old African American woman cooking something in the fireplace of another decrepit house, with a caption reading, "What my menfolks have a powerful gnawing for right now is a slab of sowbelly to eat with this cornbread."

FIG. 5-5. From "Caldwell and Bourke-White Look at the Cotton Country," *Life*, November 22, 1937

A number of contrasts stand out between this article and the collaborative book from which they were taken. First, absent Caldwell and Bourke-White's juxtaposition of these images with more numerous figurations of social conflict and anger, the lives of the subjects become local-color entertainment for a middle-class readership. The presentation of white tenant farmers is not dissimilar from that of Snuffy Smith in *Barney Google*, a popular comic strip in circulation since 1934. And the image of the African American woman presented on the final page creates an association between African American women and "home-style" cooking consistent with the advertisements of the magazine. The lives of the subjects, in other words, are reformatted to be amenable to consumption. Second, whereas *Faces* often attempts to bridge the distance between viewer and subject by shooting the faces from close range, and many times with the subject looking directly into the camera, the effect of the *Life* issue is to create distance. Not a single one of the Bourke-White photos selected by the editors of *Life* features rural southerners looking directly into the camera, nor do any of the images contain faces in close-up. What we find in the *Life* article, to the contrary, is a set of subjects fundamentally othered, whose "hysteria" marks them not only as comical but as potentially susceptible to totalitarian ideologies. Like many of their brethren abroad, they cannot be true citizens of the American Century. The same issue features a piece on fascism in Brazil, which not only conflates Roosevelt with the fascist Brazilian president Vargas, but also represents the Brazilian people as unfit for resistance. It shows a poor man sleeping atop sacks of coffee beans under the shade of an umbrella, with the caption "Taking It Lying Down."[19]

Finally, on the level of form, *Faces* is based on linearity, as there is only one photograph per page that the reader must digest before proceeding to the next. The bulk of the *Life* article, however, presents the readers with a collage of multiple images per page, creating the fragmented reading experience described earlier in this investigation. Also, *Faces* foregrounds its fictional quality. The opening passage of the book reads: "The legends under the pictures are intended to express the authors' own conceptions of the sentiments of the individuals portrayed; they do not pretend to reproduce the actual sentiments of these persons." The *Life* article, however, stays consistent with the magazine's practice of exhibiting its photo subjects as found objects. Nowhere does it clearly state that the captions are fictionalized, and its editors add an original caption underneath one of the religious revival photos stating, "Dancing such as this is a common form of worship." It is not enough that we are to see the culture of the rural South as entertaining and consumable; we are also not to question the referentiality of the images that convey this presumably self-evident viewpoint.

Some of Bourke-White's very early pieces for *Life* are linear narratives that exhibit the Popular Front politics of her work in *Faces*. This can be seen in the editing and captioning of a photo-essay on the "Common Steel Worker," which appeared on 15 March 1937. Mirroring the form of *Faces*, the photo-essay begins with a single close-up shot of the smiling face of Andy Lopata (the title character) enlarged to take up almost the entire page. The editing constructs a chronological, visually simple story of Andy Lopata as he wakes up in the morning, walks to work, and comes home exhausted. His wife appears in almost every photo—preparing his meals, helping him rinse off in the backyard, seeing him off—which establishes her role in the reproduction of his labor. He and his wife are identified as "Slavic." Both text and photos place his life in a concentric ring of larger and larger contexts—from his simple (positive) image, to his daily routine, to the local labor politics that have affected this routine, to the national politics of labor-management relations. Rather than a Popular Front praise of union power, the piece is a tribute to responsible labor-management cooperation: it instructs that the organizing of the C.I.O. as well as the "far-sighted statesmanship of steel tycoons" have improved Andy's life. Nevertheless, in its praise of the C.I.O., its linear form, its placement of the ordinary individual in social context, and its positive image of a probationarily white worker and his wife as emblematic Americans, the piece comes rather close to many Popular Front realist representations.

Her early work for *Life*'s pieces on Muncie, Indiana (10 May 1937), and Jersey City's despotic Mayor Frank Hague (7 February 1938) also remained relatively close to the politics and form of *Faces*. By 1939, however, the editing of her work for *Life* reflected the consumption-oriented editing that was coming to mark the magazine's photo-essay format as a whole. The earlier co-optation of her work in *Life*'s 1937 piece on the rural South was now consistent. In addition, she was given less serious sociological topics and apolitical fluff assignments such as "Aerosol Makes Even Ducks Sink" (27 February 1939) and "Life Cycle of the Praying Mantis" (21 August 1939). But those knowledgeable of her work can still detect a coded critique in her photographs even in this final phase of her employment at Time Inc. This can be seen in a laudatory piece on A.T.&T. in July 1939 that used her photos. The article defended the "fair, benevolent, and public-minded" telecommunications company from meddlesome New Deal attempts to castigate and regulate it. The text states that "people run its machines," not "robot" equipment, and that most of its workforce is composed of young women. A girl hired by A.T.&T., notes the writer, must not be "more than 10 percent lighter or heavier than normal weight for her height and age" ("Telephone" 61). A reader familiar with the context of Bourke-White's work, however, might recognize her attempt to visually undermine the idea that such practices are "benevolent." The only image of the young female employees that actually shows their faces depicts them as grim and emotionless, undermining the text's claim that the company is not run by robots. In the other images of the women, shot from behind and above their heads, they appear small among mazes of wires and office directories, a classic photographic means of emphasizing alienation. And her close-up shots of telephone equipment stand in contrast to the modernist industrial photography of her pre-political period, which de-familiarized industrial sites to make them appear futuristically beautiful. Accompanied by text explaining how the telephone is a "marvelous mechanical instrument," these close-ups instead render the machinery as a bewildering, ugly, and sometimes even dirty labyrinth of wires and gadgetry. Most *Life* readers were not familiar with Bourke-White's oeuvre; thus, while dimly perceptible, her attempt to make the alienation of working women visible here, as in the Popular Front *Faces*, stands as a message in a bottle.

I have argued that *Life* put in motion a conservative bid for hegemony at a moment of history when the left was making deep inroads into American common sense, and that these leftist inroads made their way into the form of even this anti–Popular Front magazine. *Life* put forward its way of seeing using realist photo-essays lost within a confusing maze of advertisements, and its ad-heavy layout undermined even the attempt of its pro-business brand of realism to construct a coherent and transparent portrait of the world. Its incorporation of oppositional forms could also be seen, in many ways, as reflective of the political syntheses of its founder. The particular conservatism of Luce—based on an unevenly inclusive form of transnationalism—was a new ideological amalgam (which very likely grew out of conversations with his many Popular Front friends and associates) combining the left's politics of international integration with the culture of consumption.

Life was indeed a magazine, and as such, it boasted of its circulation figures within a medium that had the smallest audience of all mass media. Even when figuring in pass-along rates the reach of newspapers, radio, films, and, later, television went much further than that of magazines (Baughman, "Who Read" 43). That said, however, the novel blend of representational practices *Life* brought together carried great weight well past World War II. Its high circulation figures made it one of the main sources of visual news for mass audiences well into the postwar years. It is tempting to conclude from this, and from the death of the New York left's great picture tabloid *P.M.* in 1948, that conservative forces simply hijacked Popular Front aesthetics and used them to dominate the world.

In this reading, Popular Front modes of vision merely linger on as ghosts in the machine through decades marked by McCarthyism and consumer euphoria.

But it is too easy to close the matter here. A brief reflection on *Look* magazine, *Life*'s copycat that began publication in 1938, casts a whole new light on the evaluation of *Life* and its epistemology in the postwar world. The layouts of *Look*'s photo-essays were very similar to those of its progenitor (albeit with a bit more linearity) and, like Luce's publication, advertisements were inescapable within its pages. But one primary difference stands out: a decidedly liberal, pro–New Deal stance in *Look* from its very inception, which translated into more unqualified support of the civil rights movement in the years to follow. "Prizefights, Pugs, and Profits," its concise articulation of the Popular Front boxing narrative outlined in chapter 2, illustrates the nearness of the magazine to that social movement in sensibility. While *Look*'s circulation figures trailed far behind those of *Life* in the 1930s and 1940s, they began a steady rise in 1948 and by 1960 were beginning to match those of *Life* (Leonard 16). The existence of *Look* and its later success raises the question as to whether there was anything innately "reactionary" about the elements brought together in *Life*. After the war *Life* also moved closer to the anti-racism of the Popular Front, particularly in regard to African Americans. It published the "Joe Louis Story" in a two-part series in November 1948, in which it granted the prizefighter a space to describe his struggles against Jim Crow. Gordon Parks, hired that same year, would also struggle to present a complex portrait of black life in America from an African American position within the magazine; over the years he would experience a cycle of narrative control and narrative perversion that in many ways echoed that of Margaret Bourke-White. Significantly, the photo-essays that most reflected his politics followed a more linear narrative akin to realism, marking the survival of "the Bourke-White kind of essay" into the postwar years of *Life*.[20] Like mass-mediated, Popular Front realism in general, the new visual form pioneered in the U.S. by Luce, Bourke-White, and others became a terrain upon which multiple ideologies vied to establish their own ways of seeing. Also like other Popular Front realisms, the picture magazine retained the signature of its oppositional origins. The American Century had indeed begun, but its shape and implications were something ultimately beyond Henry Luce's control.

A detailed examination of the overall postwar fate of Popular Front mass-mediated realism is admittedly beyond the scope of this project. In this book, I have suggested that the realist forms advocated by the movement and reformatted for mass culture are still ubiquitous, though their political legacy has been uneven. The relevance of this body of work can be more definitively articulated here by putting aside, for a moment, the sociopolitical and aesthetic landscape of the second half of the twentieth century and turning instead to the cultural archeology of Walter Benjamin. In his *Arcades Project*, Walter Benjamin viewed consumer culture as constituting a dream world, and he held that the goal of any emancipatory project was to free mass-culture artifacts from the spell of capitalism, rescuing their power of enchantment for the purposes of social awakening. One way to do this was to critically examine them when they became *ruins*—that is to say, when their novelty in the marketplace had faded, revealing the unfulfilled promises they embodied. Despite their oppositional politics, the novels of Erskine Caldwell, Carlos Bulosan, Richard Wright, and Nelson Algren; the Hollywood adaptations of the work of Lillian Hellman and Clifford Odets; the visual innovations of Margaret Bourke-White in photo-journalism; and the creative work of so many others in the Popular Front nonetheless were commodities. But as commodities circulating in U.S. mass culture, they helped their audiences awaken, luring them into a dream that began to question some of the oppressive structures in their everyday lives. Following Benjamin once again, perhaps the most ascertainable legacy of this Popular Front cultural work, and the core of its didactic value today, lies in its legibility as ruins, and in our ability to unearth the potential that its fusion of realism, mass-culture modes, and progressive politics reveals.

Notes

INTRODUCTION
The People's Form Finds Its Audience
Popular Front Realism and the Culture Industries

1. *The Grapes of Wrath* (1940), *Mr. Smith Goes to Washington* (1939), and *Meet John Doe* (1941) all made the list of top money-making films of their years. *Sullivan's Travels* did not (Steinberg 16–18).
2. For comprehensive log lists of mid-century drama programming, see Martin Grams, Jr. *Radio Drama: American Programs, 1932–1962*. Jefferson, NC: McFarland, 2000.
3. In addition to the seminal study *The Cultural Front*, see also *Making a New Deal* by Lizbeth Cohen for the relationship between popular culture, ethnic identity, and the left in 1930s Chicago. For excellent, book-length studies of the relationship between African American cultural production and communist-inspired movements, see the *New Red Negro* by James Smethurst, *Hammer and Hoe* by Robin D. G. Kelley, and *Popular Fronts* by Bill Mullen. Chapter 1 of *Visions of Belonging* by Judith Smith also examines the impact of the Popular Front on representations of the family in 1940s popular culture.
4. I do not suggest here that recent scholars on mid-century left cultural production have elided a detailed discussion of realism because of New Critical leanings. Rather, I refer to the more general silence on the subject in literary studies outside this subfield. For an excellent account of the discomfort of scholars with realism and the curious silence on the topic within academic publishing, see Scott McLemee, "Keeping it Real," *Chronicle of Higher Education* 47 (2004), A11.
5. *The Grapes of Wrath* is also visually parodied by *Sullivan's Travels*. Not only do the latter's depictions of hobo jungles draw on John Ford's visually striking camp scenes, but the cover art for Steinbeck's novel is parodied in the opening frames of Sturges's film. The title frame presents the title of the film—*Sullivan's Travels*—on the cover of a novel. This novel shows two weary travelers—Sullivan and "The Girl"—dressed in raggedy clothes and looking down at their feet, a hilly landscape unfolding behind them. This is a clear evocation of the cover art for *The Grapes of Wrath* in its first Viking printing in 1939, which shows the backs of three Okies—one male and

two female—looking out into a valley ringed by mountains, also clad in plebeian clothes.
6. A stamp collection issued by the U.S. Postal Service in 1998, entitled "1930s: Celebrate the Century," obliquely references the Popular Front only twice, each time evoking the narrative of the Depression popularized by *The Grapes of Wrath*. The first evocation is a stamp depicting Dorothea Lange's famous photograph "Migrant Mother"; the second is the Dust Bowl, which forms the visual backdrop to the whole collection.
7. It is important to note that neither Denning nor Lye dismisses the political impact of *The Grapes of Wrath* entirely. Despite Denning's rejection of it as a master narrative of the Popular Front, he nonetheless views the campaign that it led as a "cultural success" (268). And though she questions the obvious racial implications of Steinbeck's notion of the people, Lye also argues that Steinbeck placed his Okies within a prior discourse of Asian unassimilability, and in doing so helped undermine the opposition between American and alien (144). This is a double-edged sword for Lye, as it helped pave the way for the model minority myth.
8. Takaki develops this argument in *Iron Cages*, chapters 1–3, and Jacobson does so throughout *Whiteness of a Different Color*.
9. FSA photographers such as Margaret Bourke-White, Walker Evans, Dorothea Lange, and Russell Lee turned away from the abstract modernism of Edward Steichen and Alfred Stieglitz, incorporating elements of this modernism as they "returned" to poverty, the subject of turn-of-the-century realist photographers such as Jacob Riis and Lewis Hine.
10. For a more detailed discussion of the indexical quality of realist representation in still photography, see Maren Stange, *Symbols of Ideal Life* (66).
11. See "The Genetic Basis of Democracy" (1939) in *Democracy Reborn* for Wallace's prewar homage to Boas.
12. In 1933 there were thirty-one strikes in California, involving a total of forty-eight thousand workers. By comparison, there were thirty strikes involving only eight thousand workers in the rest of the entire U.S. that year. Considering the fact that the vast majority of the California strikers were of Mexican or Filipino descent, that means that people of color formed the majority of striking workers in 1933 (Mitchell 134). For the sites of African American resistance in the 1930s and 1940s, see Savage, *Broadcasting Freedom* 3. For details on El Congreso and Mexican American CIO struggles in the Southwest, see Mario T. García, *Mexican Americans: Leadership, Ideology, and Identity, 1930–1960*. New Haven: Yale University Press, 1989. 145–98.
13. For the most explicit rejections of the core/periphery model, see Denning, *The Cultural Front* (4–21), Kelley, *Hammer and Hoe*, particularly chapters 6 and 7, and Foley, *Radical Representations*, chapter 2.
14. Singh was not the first to note the centrality of race and ethnicity in the politics of the 1930s and 1940s. A number of major texts dealing with the culture of this period have made compelling links between racial, class, and ethnic affiliation. A persuasive strand of scholarship, including Lizbeth Cohen's *Making a New Deal*, Robin D. G. Kelley's *Hammer and Hoe*, Barbara Foley's *Radical Representations*, James Smethurst's *New Red Negro*, and Jules Chametzky's earlier, pioneering work on Edward Dahlberg, suggests that the turbulent decades of Depression and war were about much more than

class unity—instead, these works show that cultural producers and ordinary people came to articulate race, ethnicity, and class in compatible terms. As he reflects on contemporary labor in *Yo Mama's Disfunktional*, Kelley reminds us that class politics and workers' movements have always been about complex identity formation, "from minstrelsy on up."

15. Imperialism, Lenin argued, was the highest stage in the development of capitalism, one that divided the globe between oppressor nations and oppressed nations. Within that context, the "right of nations to self-determination" was a properly anti-imperial (and hence anti-capitalist) stance.

16. Wallace had similarly noted that the revolutionary, democratic tradition in the U.S. was part of a shared international "people's revolution," which included France, Latin America, Germany, and even the Soviet Union (192).

17. The realist tendency within the literature of the 1930s has been discussed most extensively by Barbara Foley in *Radical Representations*, particularly chapter 7.

18. Citing Arthur John, Nancy Glazener notes that *McClure's* and *Century* reached circulations of 300,000 in 1893 and in 1894, respectively (338). This figure represents one half of one percent of the U.S. population at that time.

19. On the tension between populism and connoisseurship in *The Atlantic Monthly*, see Glazener 47.

20. A few examples of the poststructuralist critique of realism include Roland Barthes, *S/Z*, translated by Richard Miller (New York: Hill and Wang, 1974); Catherine Belsey, *Critical Practice* (New York: Methuen, 1980); and the criticism of the genre in *Screen* in the 1970s, summarized quite well by Dick Hebdige and Geoff Hurd in "Reading and Realism" *Screen Education* 28 (August 1978): 68–78. I have not found this body of criticism to be particularly helpful, as it tends to reduce realism to one feature—its lack of self-referentiality—and ignores many of its other historically specific elements. I would add two more assertions to counter the claim that all realist texts work to obscure their own status as representation and to mask the position of the author behind an elaborately constructed totality. First, this particular critique is rather ahistorical. In the late nineteenth century itself, the texts of nineteenth-century realism were very much questioned by critics and cultural commentators for the validity of their representations—in fact, they were held by some Victorian readers as highly offensive, the very antithesis of culture. It is safe to say that the very newness of realism as an aesthetic mode triggered a kind of defamiliarization for many readers at the time. (Jumping ahead to the early years of the twentieth century, it is telling that, in his essay "Art as Technique," the Russian formalist Viktor Shklovsky uses the realist Tolstoy as an example of the estrangement through form so valued by modernists.) Second, this critique focuses too narrowly on the individual text itself and gives too little agency to the reader. In my own observations of student responses to realist works in the classroom, I find that student readers inevitably view the individual work as only one of thousands of texts they have encountered, and their readings are mobilized both by their encounters with these other texts and by the interpretative frames provided by the sum total of institutions these texts produce/are produced by. Moreover, contact with a realist text narrated from a subject or historical position quite different from their own sometimes triggers a questioning of the reality they know. I have witnessed how some students' unfamiliarity with realist perspectives such

as those of Smedley, Conroy, Bulosan, or Wright can trigger interesting reflections on their own subjectivities.
21. *Appeal to Reason*, 11 January 1896, 2, and 2 January 1909, 3.
22. See "Concept of 'National Popular'" in *The Antonio Gramsci Reader: Selected Writings 1916–1935*. Ed. David Forgacs. New York: NYU Press, 2000. 364–70.
23. To cite but one critic of Twain's racial politics, Ronald Takaki has provided a compelling argument that Twain's *Connecticut Yankee* was a critique of the emergent and imperial "demonic iron cage" of white selfhood (chapter 7). For a more detailed look at the ways in which the key nineteenth-century realists avoided a concrete affiliation to a particular social class, see Borus's chapter "The Lure of Classlessness: The Antipolitics of Realism" in *Writing Realism*.
24. For an excellent account of the relationship between African American folk culture, African American poets, and the left in the 1930s and 1940s, see James Smethurst, *The New Red Negro*, particularly chapters 1, 2, and 4.
25. See Rozgonyi, *Preston Sturges's Vision of America: Critical Analyses of Fourteen Films* (Jefferson, NC: McFarland, 1995); Diane Jacobs, *Christmas in July: The Life and Art of Preston Sturges* (Berkeley: University of California Press, 1992); Brenda Wineapple, "Finding an Audience: *Sullivan's Travels*." *Journal of Popular Film and Television* 11.4 (1984): 152–57; and Kathleen Moran and Michael Rogin, "What's the Matter with Capra?: *Sullivan's Travels* and the Popular Front." *Representations* 71 (2000): 106–34.
26. I am indebted to Richard Ohmann and James Smethurst, whose works *Selling Culture* (11–16) and *The New Red Negro* (13) helped me formulate these definitions.

CHAPTER 1
Taking Down the Great White Hope
The Popular Front Boxing Narrative

1. The real Primo Carnera (1906–1976), nicknamed "The Ambling Alp," continued to achieve success in the ring until 1944, though his mafia-linked managers were widely reputed to have left him nearly penniless. Rumors of fixed fights dogged him his entire career; he sued Columbia Pictures for such allegations when it released *The Harder They Fall* in 1956, loosely based on his life.
2. In a lecture titled "Hyphen-Nation: The Politics of Diversity in a 'Nation of Immigrants,'" Matthew Frye Jacobson argued that key texts of the ethnic revival of the 1960s and 1970s posited an "Ellis Island whiteness" which displaced an earlier whiteness based on the iconography of Plymouth Rock, but remained every bit as exclusionary as the earlier racial formation.
3. See Jacobson, *Whiteness of a Different Color* and Roediger, *Working Toward Whiteness*.
4. Boxing had long been more amenable to urban naturalist narratives than any other sport, and some of the class elements of what I call the Popular Front boxing narrative were in place in pugilistic stories before the 1930s (Oriard 59, 97–103; Messenger 255). The figures of the ruthless promoter and the exploited working-class protagonist can be seen in Jack London's story "The Mexican" (1911), the novel *The Set-Up* (1928) by Joseph Mancure March, and even "The Champion" (1916) by Ring Lardner. A critical

treatment of American racial formations, however, was commonly absent from these earlier stories.
5. For a slice of this coverage, see the *Chicago Defender*, "Louis Plays Santa Claus to Detroiters," 1 January 1938: 1; "Joe Louis Off For His Camp in Stevensville," 8 January 1938: 10; and "The Champion Takes Time Out," 15 January 1938: 24. What is striking about these examples is that they are not promotional articles in advance of a big event; they appear almost a half a year before his next title bout, and a half a year after his last.
6. I am indebted here to Kegan Doyle's excellent article "Joe Louis in Black and White," which calls attention to a range of texts in which Wright exhibited a fascination for boxing, including *Native Son*.
7. The *Defender* promoted *The Spirit of Youth* in "Joe Louis Off For His Camp at Stevensville," 8 January 1938, 10; and "In Brown Bomber Film," 18 December 1937, 9.
8. For a few examples, see the *Chicago Defender*, 25 June 1938, 1; 13 January 1942, 21; and 17 January 1942, 21.
9. See "A Popular Victory," "Will to Crush Fascism Echoes in Harlem's Cheers for Louis Victory," and "People of Pittsburgh Hail Defeat of Nazi," all from the *Daily Worker* on 24 June 1938, 6.
10. See Ross Pudaloff, "Celebrity as Identity: Richard Wright, *Native Son*, and Mass Culture."
11. This peak year was the 1941–42 season, when the boxing films *City for Conquest* and *The Champ* were broadcast on the program. In addition, *Kid Galahad* was aired on Lux Radio Theater in December 1938, and *The Prizefighter and the Lady*, featuring the voice of John Garfield, was broadcast much later on *MGM Theater of the Air* in 1949. For the logs of these dramatic programs, see Grams, *Radio Drama*, 297, 301, 325. For the ratings of Lux Radio Theater in relation to other programs, see the compiled ratings data in Summers, *A Thirty-Year History of Programs Carried on National Radio Networks*, 69, 85, 93, 101, 109.
12. This reading of the genre is based on viewing most of the available films on boxing from 1930 through 1948. These include *The Champ* (1931), *Palooka* (1934), *Spirit of Youth* (1936), *Kid Galahad* (1937), *They Made Me a Criminal* (1939), *Golden Boy* (1939), *Keep Punching* (1939), *City for Conquest* (1940), *Gentleman Jim* (1942), *Body and Soul* (1947), and, though outside of the period of study, *The Harder They Fall* (1956). It is also based on plot synopses of the remaining boxing dramas, many of which are out of print, in *The American Film Institute Catalog of Motion Pictures Produced in the United States: Feature Films, 1931–1940*, Ed. Patricia King Hanson (Berkeley: University of California Press, 1993), and the subsequent volume on feature films from 1941–1950 (1999). These dramas include *Iron Man* (1931), *Winner Take All* (1932), *The Prizefighter and the Lady* (1933), *King for a Night* (1933), *The Life of Jimmy Dolan* (1933), *Ex-Champ* (1939), *Invitation to Happiness* (1939), *Knockout* (1941), *The Great John L* (1945), *Leather Gloves* (1948), and *The Big Punch* (1948). The vast majority of boxing films were dramas, though there were a few comedies about prizefighters, which include *Palooka* (1934), *Cain and Mabel* (1936), *Kid Nightingale* (1939), *Mr. Hex* (1946), and *The Kid from Brooklyn* (1946). I do not include this subgenre within my analysis.

13. Kimmel writes that, as a result of rapid mechanization in the 1920s and unemployment in the 1930s, the possession of a job could no longer be counted as a reliable marker of masculinity (192–94).
14. The nature of this transcendent arena, key to deciphering the overall meaning of the work, is once again a point of contention in the criticism. There is a tendency in the criticism of *Golden Boy* over the last twenty years to sideline Odets's overall politics when defining the meaning of his boxing metaphor in favor of personal, spiritual, or strictly ethnic concerns. Examples include Gabriel Miller, *Clifford Odets*, as well as John Frick, "'Odets, Where Is Thy Sting?' Reassessing the 'Playwright of the Proletariat.'" *Realism and the American Dramatic Tradition*. Ed. William Demastes. Tuscaloosa: University of Alabama Press, 1996, 123–38; and Michael Woolf, "Clifford Odets." *American Drama*. Ed. Clive Bloom. New York: St. Martin's Press, 1995: 46–67. To the contrary, I find that a consideration of his explicit politics is critical to an exploration of the spiritual, ethnic, and personal concerns in the play.
15. Groman has shown that Odets had an obsessive love for music, and even once stated that he regretted not becoming a musician. In the playwright's view, the sound of classical music preserved a sense of the transcendent and the beautiful in its listeners (Odets certainly would have agreed with Adorno on the didactic value of high art). The fact that Odets did not choose a career in music and instead chose a career as a political playwright, however, suggests that he desired something more than the creation of abstract beauty ascribed to high art—a need inscribed here in the doubtful words of his character.
16. The police detective appears in the novel in the figure of "One Eye" Tenczara. During an extended scene (135–52) he grills various downtrodden suspects at the police station for the amusement of viewers from the public, who are seated "as if for a double-feature" (137). Like other hardboiled detectives of the genre, Tenczara uses his skills in surveillance and his sharp wit to demolish those who cross his path. In this case, however, these aptitudes are directed at his victims in the lineup, who embody the underclass of Chicago. The spectacle of his surveillance at the police station, framed by the placard I HAVE ONLY MYSELF TO BLAME hanging in the interrogation room, shows his vision to be myopic, as it loses sight of the structural causes of urban poverty.
17. I have not referenced the criticism on *Never Come Morning* because there are not enough critical studies of it to constitute a dialogue. I have found only two contemporary essays on the novel: Ian Peddle's "Poles Apart?" (2001) and a chapter in Carla Cappetti's *Writing Chicago* (1993). The former discusses the progressive ways in which Algren combines race, ethnicity, and class in his work, but does so in order to erroneously exhibit him as a dissident voice among the mid-century left. Peddle also does not explore the role of probationary whiteness nor mass culture in Algren's figuring of race and class. The latter piece explores the ways in which the literary style of Algren, like those of Wright and Farrell, owes much to the Chicago school of sociology. As such, Cappetti underscores Algren's connection to American realism.
18. The first instance is during his imaginary bout with a Jewish fighter. When Bruno knocks out his fantasy Jewish opponent, Algren writes: "The lights of the park came up like a single light" (94). The second is when Bruno defeats Tucker: "[Tucker] hung there as though he'd been decapitated, till the lights came up like morning" (280).

19. Symbols of labor and reformist politics appear in the novel, but in conspicuously marginal ways. "Yesterday's relief stamps"—signs of the New Deal—are seen by Steffi as one more bit of trash in the gutter (212). Elsewhere, we find that Bruno lives by stealing his mother's relief checks, the very checks that organizations such as the Communist Party worked hard to ensure a steady flow of. And a union pin is just one of a random assortment of buttons on the jacket of the deranged character Snipes (178).
20. For one account of the relationship between late-1940s cinematic content and sociopolitical history, see Bodnar 89–92, 122.
21. While the first *Rocky* film, critically recognized as the best and most subtle of the series, is not a simple Horatio Alger tale, it can easily be seen as a muted expression of working-class white ethnic resentment. And while *Million Dollar Baby* promised an opening-up of the limited gender politics of the Popular Front boxing narrative by focusing on a female boxer, it undercut any potentially subversive thrust by containing that female protagonist's struggle within a father-daughter relationship (not to mention the classically problematic move of pitting her against a dark-skinned villain in the ring). *Cinderella Man*, though in many ways a homage to the 1930s cult of boxing, becomes a blatant Great White Hope story that would be regressive even by Depression-era standards. In one scene, Catholic fans of Jim Braddock (Cinderella Man) listen to the radio and pray for his victory over the dark-skinned, Jewish Max Baer—from within a church!

CHAPTER 2
Radio Soaps, Broadway Lights
Lillian Hellman, Shirley Graham, and the Interpellation of Female Audiences

1. One could object that Nathan clearly never saw *Pins and Needles* (1937–41), the Popular Front musical revue about young female garment workers that had a record run on Broadway for its genre. The case of *Pins and Needles* demonstrates there was indeed an audience for socially critical plays about women's labor, but I would also argue that it illustrates a lost opportunity for the left. Its content was quite unusual and not repeated in a significant production on Broadway in the 1930s and 1940s. Its focus on the problems of working-class women—or on women at all—was an exception, not the rule, in the long list of major Popular Front dramatic productions of the 1930s and 1940s.
2. Episode aired on 21 September 1939, on station WJSV in Washington, D.C.
3. Once again, Erskine Caldwell scored the record in this category with Jack Kirkland's adaptation of his *Tobacco Road*, which ran for 3,182 performances, a Broadway record for all categories of plays that held until the comedy *Life with Father*, which topped it only slightly with 3,224 performances (Atkinson 286; Goldstein 135). The 1935 play *Dead End* by Sidney Kingsley, another leftist playwright, was roughly equal to Hellman's *The Children's Hour* in popular success on Broadway, with 687 performances (Goldstein 135, 375).
4. If one regards Pearl S. Buck as a "writer on the left," then this claim needs qualification, as Buck's novels *The Good Earth* and *Dragon Seed*, read by millions and also adapted

to film, easily matched the circulation of Hellman's work. However, Buck was much more tentatively "on the left" than Hellman during the 1930s and 1940s; unlike Hellman, she generally rejected communism outside of a brief period during World War II, when she was retroactively embraced in CPUSA publications (see chapter 5).

5. Dashiell Hammett, a Marxist, was one of the major figures who shaped the form of the detective story in twentieth-century American fiction, first through his work in the pulp magazines of the 1920s and then on the big screen in the 1930s with the *Thin Man* series. The gangster films of the 1930s also revealed a decidedly left influence. Generally featuring the story of a street tough who rises from poverty only to be brought down in a hail of police bullets in the end, these films can be and have been read as a commentary on the failure of acquisitive individualism and working-class dreams of social mobility. Directly shaping the genre were the director Richard Rosson (*Scarface*, 1932), the screenwriters Francis Edward Faragoh (*Little Caesar*) and John Bright (*Public Enemy, Blonde Crazy, Three on a Match*), and the actor Edward G. Robinson (*Little Caesar*), all figures with definite and in some cases close connections to the left (Buhle 13–25).

6. Razlogova herself dates the "top-down" nature of this consolidation much later—in the 1940s, when broadcasters stopped revising the nuts and bolts of their programs in response to the wishes of listeners expressed in fan mail (140).

7. See Tania Modelski, *Loving with a Vengeance: Mass-Produced Fantasies for Women* (Hamden, CT: Archon Books, 1982); and Kathryn Weibel, *Mirror, Mirror: Images of Women Reflected in Popular Culture* (Garden City, NY: Anchor Books, 1977). For a summary of early feminist criticism of soaps, see Muriel G. Cantor and Suzanne Pingree, *The Soap Opera* (Beverly Hills: Sage Publications, 1983).

8. See Elaine Tyler May, "Rosie the Riveter Gets Married." *The War in American Culture: Society and Consciousness During WWII*. Eds. Lewis Erenberg and Susan Hirsch (Chicago: University of Chicago Press, 1996); and Karen Anderson, *Wartime Women: Sex Roles, Family Relations, and the Status of Women During World War II* (Westport, CT: Greenwood Press, 1981).

9. A study of the uncanny similarities between the strong, rural mothers Ma Perkins and Ma Joad has yet to be undertaken.

10. For example, *Our Gal Sunday* centered around an orphan named Sunday from a mining town in Colorado who married an English lord, and each episode began with the question: "Can this girl from a mining town in the West find happiness as the wife of a wealthy and titled Englishman?" While the villainesses of the show were rich and oftentimes snobbish suitors of Lord Henry Brinthrope, Brinthrope was depicted as a basically decent man, and his marriage to Sunday was an essentially good one that withstood constant challenges.

11. In 1983, Cantor and Pingree found that professionals were overrepresented in soap operas in relation to the real American population, and that the middle and upper classes received much more representation in daytime serials than in prime-time television (87–88, 90).

12. For an excellent study on radio and the Popular Front, see Judith E. Smith, "Radio's Cultural Front, 1938–1948." *Radio Reader: Essays in the Cultural History of Radio*. Ed. Michele Hilmes and Jason Loviglio (New York: Routledge, 2002). An adaptation of Guy Endore's *Babouk* was broadcast on *The Columbia Workshop* on 27 June 1937.

13. Though writers and actors received their paychecks from the ad agencies, the sponsor generally reserved the right to approve or disapprove scripts, or to withdraw its sponsorship on a few weeks' notice (MacDonald 33).
14. Irna Phillips, for example, stated at an NBC press conference in 1945 that her attempts to raise the issue of race had been censored by network executives (Hilmes 160).
15. On the American influence on American realism in theater, as well as the aesthetic nuts and bolts of the move from melodrama to realism on stage, see Brenda Murphy, *American Realism and American Drama, 1880–1940*.
16. While Michael Denning suggests that the new audience for theater in New York was pan-class and largely composed of activists, Richard Pells and Malcolm Goldstein both imply an expanded yet still mostly middle-class audience for left-wing (particularly Popular Front) theater (Denning, *Cultural Front* 286; Pells 254, 258; Goldstein 75, 218–19).
17. For the Broadway-Hollywood relationship, see Goldstein 366–67. Hollywood had a tendency to dilute the realism of the plays it selected, reformatting it as the realism-melodrama hybrid often associated with classic Hollywood cinema.
18. Realism was a common aesthetic mode in the radio plays by contemporary authors on the popular "prestige" program *The Columbia Workshop*. In addition to Elizabethan drama, sentimental and Victorian fiction, and some works of modernism, other nighttime "cultural" programs from the mid-1930s to 1950 also broadcast a broad range of realist classics and new realist work. Earlier realist work by Theodore Dreiser, Mark Twain, Leo Tolstoy, Heinrich Ibsen, Henry James, Stephen Crane, Edith Wharton, Ambrose Bierce, and Oscar Wilde, as well as newer work by Maxwell Anderson, Donald Ogden Stewart, Sinclair Lewis, Sidney Kingsley, John Steinbeck, Arthur Miller, and Lillian Hellman, could be heard on such national programs as *The Lux Radio Theatre* (one of the most popular shows on the air), *MGM Theater of the Air*, *NBC University Theater of the Air*, *The Columbia Workshop*, *Favorite Story*, *The Ford Theater*, and *Great Plays*. A disproportionate number of these realist classics were broadcast in the mid- to late 1940s, suggesting that a popular interest in realist literature had been cultivated over the course of the 1930s and 1940s (or, at least, that realism was more officially sanctioned after the war). Interestingly, Orson Welles's famous *Mercury Theater on the Air* aired no realist classics, though his *The Campbell Playhouse* dramatized a few. For log lists of the aforementioned programs, see Martin Grams, Jr. *Radio Drama: American Programs, 1932–1962* (Jefferson, NC: McFarland, 2000).
19. See Richard A. Blum, *American Film Acting: The Stanislavski Heritage* (Ann Arbor, MI: UMI Research Press, 1984).
20. For women as mass culture, see Andreas Huyssen, "Mass Culture as Woman: Modernism's Other." *After the Great Divide: Modernism, Mass Culture, Postmodernism* (Bloomington: Indiana University Press, 1986), 44–64. For examples of women's use of realism in literature, a short list would include Kate Chopin, Sarah Orne Jewett, Pauline Hopkins, Rose Terry Cook, Edith Wharton, Anzia Yezierska, Agnes Smedley, Ann Petry, and Josephine Herbst; in drama, the works of Rachel Crothers, Alice Childress, and Lorraine Hansberry come to mind, in addition to the women covered in this chapter.

21. *The Life of Mary Southern*, episode 22 (1934). The anecdote from *Just Plain Bill* comes from MacDonald 242.
22. The critical preference for realism over melodrama began around the turn of the century (Hallam 18–19).
23. Akins was one of only five women to be awarded the Pulitzer Prize for drama between 1918 and 1980. Four of these five women were recognized between 1918 and 1945, which suggests that post-realist critical criteria have also been unkind to women (perhaps even more so).
24. The following scholars have seen her work as either solidly realist or more realist than melodramatic: Ritchie Watson Jr., "Lillian Hellman's *The Little Foxes* and the New South Creed: An Ironic View of Southern History." *Southern Literary Journal* 28.2 (1996): 59–68; Thomas Carl Austenfeld, *American Women Writers and the Nazis: Ethics and Politics in Boyle, Porter, Stafford, and Hellman* (Charlottesville: University of Virginia Press, 2001); David Kennedy Sauer, "*Oleanna* and *The Children's Hour*: Misreading Sexuality on the Post/Modern Realistic Stage." *Modern Drama* 43 (Fall 2000): 421–41; Judith Barlow, "Into the Foxhole: Feminism, Realism, and Lillian Hellman." *Realism and the American Dramatic Tradition*. Ed. William DeMastes (Tuscaloosa: University of Alabama Press, 1996), 156–71; Theresa Mooney, "These Four: Hellman's Roots Are Showing." *Southern Women Playwrights: New Essays in Literary History and Criticism*. Ed. Robert McDonald and Linda Rohrer Paige (Tuscaloosa: University of Alabama Press, 2002), 27–41; and Jordan and Winifred Frazer. *American Drama Between the Wars: A Critical History* (Boston: Twayne, 1991). The exception here is Brenda Murphy in *American Realism and American Drama* (1987), who sees Hellman as more melodramatic than realist.
25. For example, one mainstream critic wrote in the *Nation* that Hellman's drama manages "to avoid the flat didacticism and the thinness of characterization usually so painfully evident in thesis plays" (Krutch 453). And in his review of *Watch on the Rhine* in the *New Masses*, Alvah Bessie praised "the sincerity of purpose of a dramatist who possesses potentialities far beyond the grasp of any other writer on the contemporary theater scene," even as he critiqued the politics of the play, namely, its vague depiction of European antifascism (Bessie 26–27).
26. See Jenny Spencer, "Sex, Lies, and Revisions: Historicizing Hellman's *The Children's Hour*." *Modern Drama* 47.1 (2004): 44–65; and Brett Elizabeth Westbrook, "The Lesbian Vanishes." *Bright Lights Film Journal* 28 (2000): no pagination. Also see Mary Titus, "Murdering the Lesbian: Lillian Hellman's *The Children's Hour*." *Tulsa Studies in Women's Literature* 10.2 (1991): 215–32.
27. "Other Current Shows." Review of *The Children's Hour*. *New Masses* 25 December 1934: 29.
28. *Lux Radio Theatre*, Episode 153. Aired 6 December 1937.
29. Throughout this section, I cite the *Modern Library* 1960 reprint of *Six Plays by Lillian Hellman* (1942). This collection preserves the original 1934 language of *The Children's Hour*, a play Hellman revised in the 1950s.
30. Westbrook, "The Lesbian Vanishes." On Hellman's view of homosexuality, see Spencer, "Sex, Lies, and Revisions," 46.
31. The A.N.T. constitution railed against the idea of theater "as a playground for dilettantes and escapists who are unable to withstand the hard realities of life." That

they carried through on this promise was revealed in the commentary of one critic who noted that the company "remains firmly on the ground, using themes about everyday people" (qtd. in Walker 253; Hatch 350).
32. Gerald Horne cites this incident as instilling in Graham a lesson about the perils of serious drama as opposed to the acclaim generated by light musicals (77). Given the structure of *The Big White Fog* and the overall theatrical milieu of the 1930s, I interpret her fears as more specific to the aesthetics of realism. Graham discontinued her direction of Ward's play after its test run, but it was later produced by the Chicago FTP at the Great Northern Theater under a different director, where it received a good audience and critical praise. *The Big White Fog* was revived several more times in New York soon after, once in Harlem at the Lincoln Theater with a cast that included Canada Lee.
33. See "Richard Wright's Long Black Shadow" in Bill Mullen's *Popular Fronts*.
34. Shirley Graham Du Bois Papers, Schlesinger Library, Radcliffe Institute, Harvard University, Box 25, folder 13, and Box 42, folder 7. Cambridge, MA. W. E. B. Du Bois Papers, Reel 50, p. 193, Reel 51, p. 580, and Reel 52, p. 1012. Amherst, MA. On the southern productions of *Ravens*, see Horne 300.
35. Though the character of Toussant is absent in *Elijah's Ravens*, Graham illustrates the female labor that enables male intellectualism in the very first scene of this play. While Rev. Cobb is reading from the Bible and taking notes, Mrs. Cobb and her daughter Mirah express annoyance that he is too deep in thought to move as they clean the rug under his feet (Shirley Graham Du Bois Papers, Box 42, folder 1).
36. See the *Cleveland News*, 22 February 1940, and the *Cleveland Plain Dealer*, 22 February 1940. Du Bois also informed her that a production of *Elijah's Ravens* he attended drew large crowds and was the talk of the campus (Letter to Graham, W. E. B. Du Bois Papers, Reel 52, p. 1016).
37. The script of *Track Thirteen* was published in *Yale Radio Plays: The Listeners Theatre*, ed. Constance Welch and Walter Prichard (Boston: Expression Company, 1939).
38. In the 1950s, four black-cast family dramas were aired under the umbrella of "Negro Radio Stories": *The Romance of Julia Davis*, *Ada Grant's Neighbors*, *My Man*, and *Rebecah Turner's Front Porch Stories*.

CHAPTER 3
Realism with a Little Sex in It
Erskine Caldwell's Challenge to *Gone with the Wind*

1. The figure of 8.6 million refers to the book's sales by 1975, as quoted in Alice Hackett and James Burke, *80 Years of Best Sellers, 1895–1975* (New York: R. R. Bowker, 1977), 10, 121–23.
2. These figures come from Alice Payne Hackett, *70 Years of Best Sellers, 1895–1965* (New York: R. R. Bowker, 1967), 12; Hackett and Burke 10; Edwin Arnold, ed. *Conversations with Erskine Caldwell* (Jackson: University Press of Mississippi, 1998), 81. According to Hackett and Burke, in 1975 *GWTW* was the ninth best-selling work of fiction since 1895, and *God's Little Acre* a close tenth (8.6 million and 8.2 million sold, respectively).

3. As a sales figure, Link's quote of 10 million is a hopeful exaggeration. By Hackett's count, *GWTW* had sold 6.9 million copies by 1965.
4. Laura Hapke's *Daughters of the Depression* is the only book-length study of writers on the left in the 1930s and 1940s I have found that gives Caldwell more than a passing mention.
5. I refer here to Murphy, *The Proletarian Moment* (1991); Denning, *The Cultural Front* (1997); Foley, *Radical Representations* (1993); and Wald, *Exiles from a Future Time* (2002). In his reading of Guy Endore, Wald has shown that even the figures of the classically constructed Stalinist core bear little resemblance to their Cold War portraits.
6. While scholarly work on African American stereotypes in the film *GWTW* abounds, much of the criticism that takes into account both the novel and the film has been guided by a second-wave feminism that takes Scarlett's agency as its central consideration. The political significance of the narrative, according to many critics, is the strength of its protagonist vis-à-vis the male characters, as well as the narrator's implicit and explicit rebukes of sentimental ideals of womanhood. Examples of this tendency include Laura Hapke, *Daughters of the Depression*; Charles Rowan Beye, "Gone with the Wind, and Good Riddance." *Southwest Review* 78 (1993): 366–80; Helen Taylor, *Scarlett's Women: Gone with the Wind and its Female Fans* (New Brunswick, NJ: Rutgers University Press, 1989); Morton, "My Dear, I Don't Give a Damn"; and Dieter Mendl, "A Reappraisal of Margaret Mitchell's *Gone with the Wind*." *Mississippi Quarterly* 19 (1981): 47–57. Other critics of *GWTW* focus on its aesthetic merits, its contribution to southern intellectual history, or its general message of survival. Examples here include Hayden Maginnis, "The Trouble with Scarlett." *Queen's Quarterly* 102 (1995): 641–53; Darden Asbury Pyron, "*Gone with the Wind* and the Southern Cultural Awakening." *Virginia Quarterly Review* 62 (1986): 565–87; and Pauly, "*Gone with the Wind* and *Grapes of Wrath*." Whether or not the novel and film are properly nostalgic—in other words, whether or not it subverts or maintains the plantation romance—has already been debated within this corpus, but the debate primarily has revolved around the implications of the "backward glance" (or lack thereof) for the narrative's gender politics. Breaking with this tendency of the criticism, Tara McPherson (2002) offers a refreshing third-wave feminist critique of the novel. She writes that "while at one level *GWTW* debates whether Scarlett should side with modernist Atlanta or the agrarian past, this struggle is not just about gender; her character's development also hinges upon a very specific and overt relationship to blackness." Tara McPherson, "Seeing the Black and White: Gender and Racial Visibility from *Gone with the Wind* to *Scarlett*." *Hop on Pop: The Politics and Pleasures of Popular Culture*. Ed. Henry Jenkins, Tara McPherson, and Jane Shattuc (Durham, NC: Duke University Press, 2002), 521. McPherson goes on to chart the ways in which the protagonist's whiteness is defined vis-à-vis the blackness of Mitchell's highly racialized portrayal of Mammy. One could add that Scarlett's relationship to modernity and to notions of blood and bloodlines (commonly associated with the more aristocratic, rural past) has everything to do with class as well.
7. Mitchell provides us with a rare moment of transparency between character and author in a "thank you" letter to one of her favorable reviewers: "[Prissy] aggravated me unendurably while I was writing her and, when Scarlett slapped her, it was really Margaret Mitchell yielding to an overwhelming urge" (Harwell 85).

8. James Murphy provides an excellent outline of RAPP theory and its dissemination in chapter 1 of *The Proletarian Moment*. George Lukács's *The Historical Novel* (Lincoln: University of Nebraska Press, 1983) is perhaps the most famous distillation of this theory, and not coincidentally, as Lukács was a RAPP theoretician.
9. See Granville Hicks's *The Great Tradition: An Interpretation of American Literature since the Civil War*, published in 1933 and again in 1935 (reprt. New York: Macmillan, 1969). That book's call for "people that live and breathe" (105) and for a dialectically informed, psychological depth (185, 205) clearly betray the influence of RAPP. Other (admittedly random) examples include Philip Rahv's review of *The Shadow Before*, Lukács "Propaganda or Partisanship," both in the April/May 1934 issue of *Partisan Review*, and, of course, the critiques of Caldwell above.
10. I do not suggest that comic repetition is found only in mass culture. It could rightfully be noted that this device—whether in the form of phrases that mark a particular character or of a character represented in a deliberately formulaic way—had been present in literary works for quite some time before the publication of *GLA* in 1933 (Charles Dickens and Herman Melville, for example). One could say the same for humor or eroticism. However, in the early-twentieth-century cultural milieu within which Caldwell produced his work, comic repetition was rather unusual in "serious" fiction and especially unusual in realism. As comic repetition could be much more commonly found in mass or popular culture than in the world of "serious" fiction in the 1920s, 1930s, and 1940s (not to mention proletarian literature), I have thus described it here as something belonging more to mass culture.
11. Works consulted on the southern grotesque include Alan Spiegel, "A Theory of the Grotesque in Southern Fiction." *Georgia Review* 26 (1972): 426–37; Flannery O'Connor, "Some Aspects of the Grotesque in Southern Fiction." *Mystery and Manners*. Ed. Sally and Robert Fitzgerald (New York: Farrar, Strauss, and Giroux, 1969), 36–50; Lewis Larson, "The Grotesque in Recent Southern Fiction." *Patterns of Commitment in American Literature*. Ed. Marston LaFrance (Toronto: University of Toronto Press, 1967), 165–79; and Sarah Gleeson-White, "Revisiting the Southern Grotesque: Mikhail Bakhtin and the Case of Carson McCullers." *Southern Literary Journal* 33 (2001). Burke discusses Caldwell's use of the grotesque in "Caldwell: Maker of Grotesques," in *The Philosophy of Literary Form: Studies in Symbolic Action* (Baton Rouge: Louisiana State University Press, 1941), 350–60. Gleeson-White discusses the southern grotesque as a subversive mode, and heavily draws from Mikhail Bakhtin's famous *Rabelais and His World* in constructing her argument. Both O'Connor and Lawson see the nonrealistic grotesque mode as a common choice for southern writers because, for people raised in a thoroughly religious world, reality is partially beyond the senses; hence one must go beyond what is empirically observable to the senses in representing that reality.
12. For an excellent account of Caldwell's marital relationships, see Klevar, *Erskine Caldwell*.
13. This is not meant to suggest that Caldwell was the only writer among the mid-century left to consent to pulp-fiction paperback art; Nelson Algren and James T. Farrell did as well.
14. The shift in the estimation of Caldwell as an artist is perhaps best illustrated by director John Ford. Released in 1941, Ford's rather serious adaptation of *Tobacco Road*

tried to bring out the novel's literary qualities. But in *Mr. Roberts*, a picture Ford co-directed in 1955, his assessment of the writer's artistic merits had apparently changed completely. Here the Erskine Caldwell reader is depicted as a complete buffoon in the form of Ensign Frank Pulver (Jack Lemmon). Lieutenant Roberts (Henry Fonda) chides Pulver for his philistinism, exclaiming to a fellow officer, "He's been reading *God's Little Acre* for over a year now! He's underlined every erotic passage and added exclamation points. And after a certain pornographic climax he's inserted the words 'well-written.'" By the 1960s, Caldwell's novels were marketed more aggressively as smut. The front cover of the 1965 McFadden-Bartlett edition of *Men and Women* pitched the book as "A startlingly frank look at love . . . the women who made it an art and the men who enjoyed their talents." But even then the book was partially advertised as realism: also on the front cover, a blurb from *Time* states that Caldwell creates "an impression of absolute reality."

15. Officially sanctioned literary theory in the Soviet Union during the 1930s was beginning to endorse a blend of realist and popular culture modes, though it did not necessarily discuss its preferences in those terms. Theories of socialist realism culled from Soviet theory, which can be found explicitly echoed in the *New Masses* (but not directly in criticisms of Caldwell), put the idea of positive characters front and center. Emerging as a literary model after RAPP's "living man" lost favor in the Soviet Union, socialist realism was not intended to highlight flawed, contradictory figures but rather heroic individuals with exalted traits. In *The Soviet Novel: History as Ritual* (Chicago: University of Chicago Press, 1981), Katerina Clark points out that this penchant for larger-than-life characters led to the creation of a wave of pulpy Soviet adventure novels in the late 1930s and 1940s (and into the postwar years as well). Socialist realism was explicitly to be a blend of realism and romanticism, and thus marked a trend within Soviet literary theory more amenable to pop-culture modes. But while the U.S. Popular Front embraced popular culture in many ways, this strand of literary theory did not cross the ocean in large measure.

16. A little-known fact and one of the great oddities of 1930s culture: the screenplay for the film *GWTW* was scripted by Sidney Howard, a Popular Fronter! Howard was a left-liberal playwright known for his realist work on Broadway, and for writing screen adaptations of the work of Sinclair Lewis. He also served on the advisory board of the communist Film and Photo League. This story illustrates the political and aesthetic contradictions of some writers in the 1930s scene.

17. I have based this synopsis of Brechtian theory from Brecht's essays in *Über Realismus*, ed. Werner Hecht (Leipzig: Reclam, 1968), and in *Brecht on Theater*, ed. John Willett (New York: Hill and Wang, 1974).

CHAPTER 4
Asian Yeomen and Ugly Americans
Carlos Bulosan, H. T. Tsiang, and the U.S. Literary Market

1. The Japanese and Japanese Americans were a constitutive part of the left, the labor movement, and the Communist Party on the West Coast and Hawaii up to and during

the 1930s. In fact, Japanese exile Sen Katayama was one of the founding members of the CPUSA in 1919. The party's Japanese-language newspaper in the U.S., *Rodo Shimbun*, peaked at a small but healthy circulation of 2,700 in the mid-1930s (Yoneda 98). Japanese radicals were also active in the struggle to unionize Alaskan cannery workers, leading to the formation of the Alaska Cannery Workers Union (ACWU) in 1936, and had essentially begun the labor movement in Hawaii at the turn of the century (85–86; Lee, "Hidden World" 282). Despite this activity, the CPUSA suspended Japanese and Japanese American party members and their spouses right after Pearl Harbor, its leadership supporting Executive Order 9066, which authorized the internment.
2. The biographical material in this paragraph has been drawn from Floyd Cheung, introduction to *And China Has Hands*, and Alan Wald, "Introduction to H. T. Tsiang." *Into the Fire: Asian American Prose*. Ed. Sylvia Watanabe and Carol Bruhac (New York: Greenfield Review Press, 1996).
3. To these ends, the Chinese Exclusion Act was repealed by Congress in 1943, and bars to the naturalization of Filipinos and Asian Indians were lifted in 1946; meanwhile, an image of the U.S. as a tolerant land in which many races and cultures lived harmoniously was exported abroad. Lye has noted how even the discourse surrounding Japanese internment was paradoxically inclusive, since the removal of Japanese Americans from ethnic enclaves was promoted, in a typically New Deal fashion, as being the first step toward their eventual assimilation.
4. Palumbo-Liu dates the transition to the late 1930s, by which time U.S. trade with China had doubled over the previous decade, and when the Sino-Japanese War made a large number of Americans deeply aware of Asia (66, 72). Lee locates the decisive shift a little later to the attack on Pearl Harbor, after which the U.S. needed to win the support of colonized people across the Pacific Rim in order effectively to fight the Japanese. Klein, finally, sees 1945 as the pivotal date. Immediately after the war, she argues, Popular Front and right-wing internationalisms were incorporated into a sentimental narrative of U.S./Asian integration necessary to wage the Cold War.
5. Denning's label for this narrative is not intended to cover all variants of pre-industrial nostalgia extant in the 1930s, but is rather a term he applies mainly (but not exclusively) to the work of radical modernists during the Depression. The emphasis of the Lincoln Republic narrative, as he describes it, is not necessarily an "agrarian" one, but rather is on the betrayal of the republican dream inherent in the North's victory in the Civil War (thus the place of the pre-industrial yeoman is not theorized in his work at all). For this reason, I have not used Denning's term as an overall label for "the usable past" constructed by the mid-century left.
6. For the praise of her work by the left in the Popular Front period, see "Pearl Buck's 'Dragon Seed' Is Epic Story of Embattled China," *Daily Worker*, 6 April 1942 (7); "The Good Earth's Warriors," *New Masses*, 10 February 1942 (21).
7. In three popular American wartime representations of the guerrilla struggles in the Philippines—the films *Bataan* (1943) and *Back to Bataan* (1945), and the purportedly nonfiction adventure story by Ira Wolfert, *American Guerilla in the Philippines* (1945)—American agency is privileged while Filipino self-determination is seriously downplayed. The Huk resistance movement is not mentioned at all, a silence which

Huk leader Luis Taruc's *Born of the People* (1953) and Benedict Kerkvliet's later study *The Huk Rebellion* (1977) attempt to correct (both cite American guerilla resistance as minimal and largely ineffectual). In the three American texts, however, Filipinos are presented as all courage and no strategy, and thus in need of American direction. In *Back to Bataan*, for instance, Filipino officer Andrew Bonifacio states: "Don't talk to me about the Filipinos. You mention the word 'freedom' around them [and] they don't stop to think. They walk empty-handed into blazing machine gun fire." And while the child Maximo embodied the spirit of democracy by bravely sacrificed himself for his unit, he could not spell "liberty" correctly, a source of amusement in the film.

8. While reviewed extensively in the mainstream press, *America* was not reviewed in the major periodicals of the American left at all (apart from its listing as "Recommended Reading" by *P.M.*). *Laughter* received only one review in these periodicals, in *New Masses* on 13 June 1944, p. 28. Literary works by African Americans were reviewed regularly in U.S. communist presses, however. In the period *America* was reviewed by liberal and conservative newspapers and magazines, for example, the *New Masses* (21 May 1946, 25) and the *Daily Worker* (20 March 1946, 11) covered Ann Petry's *The Street,* and the *Daily Worker* wrote on Fannie Cook's *Mrs. Palmer's Honey* (28 March 1946, 13).

9. In regard to *Flower Drum Song*, I refer to the popular musical adaptation in the following discussion, not Lee's novel, which was more nuanced and critical of American racial formation.

10. Palumbo-Liu has noted that Wan-Lee's time as a laundryman represents a naive stage in his development, as his character is marked by both a "nostalgic identification with China" and a "sojourner mentality" grounded in a belief in private enterprise (51, 54). Wan-Lee believes his laundry will allow him to accumulate a fortune that will enable his return to China, and the inside of his laundry has been decorated as a "temple" to commemorate his country of origin. His shift to the space of the cafeteria marks the culmination of Wan-Lee's development: his political awakening in that space, one that arises from his experience of exploitation there, involves the connection of a new form of nationalism to a multiracial class consciousness.

11. Though Tsiang appeared in a wide number of films and television programs from the 1930s to the 1960s (including *Oceans Eleven* and *Gunsmoke*), he was always given minor parts. His wartime appearances in anti-Japanese films such as *Betrayal From the East* (1945), in which he played a Japanese spy, even served to justify the internment. While such roles furthered his desire to drive the Japanese from China, they also illustrate the impossibility of a pan–Asian American, Popular Front solidarity in U.S. popular culture at this time. There were moments of such solidarity outside of Hollywood, however. Japanese American organizer Karl Yoneda recalled how many Chinese and Korean trade unionists expressed solidarity with Japanese anti-fascists during the war by refusing to wear buttons reading "Chinese American" and "I'm a Korean" (117–18).

12. Wan-Lee's encounters with such brazenly villainous Chinese nationalists in the U.S. might seem highly unrealistic, historically speaking; but they can also be seen as the author's way of figuring the very real efforts of the nationalist Chinese government to extradite him. Further, Tsiang's observation of the racial purity inherent in early-

twentieth-century Chinese nationalism has been noted by scholars. See Prasenjit Duara, "Nationalists among Transnationals: Overseas Chinese and the Idea of China,1900–1911." *Ungrounded Empires: The Cultural Politics of Modern Chinese Transnationalism.* Ed. Aihwa Ong and Donald Nonini (London: Routledge, 1997): 39–60.

13. While the plots and certain details from individual stories in the two collections bear an uncanny similarity (for instance, between "My Old Man's Political Appointment" in *Georgia Boy* on one hand and both "My Father's Political Appointment" and "Uncle Manuel's Homecoming" in *Laughter* on the other), this is not a matter of plagiarism, as both collections have distinct tones, dialects, and cultural references. The question of who influenced whom is not easy to answer with 100 percent certainty, as there has been no detailed biography of Bulosan to date, but it appears that the influence was from Caldwell to Bulosan, not vice versa. *Georgia Boy* was published in April 1943 and most of its constituent stories appeared from 1940–42 in *New Republic, Collier's,* and *Coronet.* Many were conceived in May 1941 in the seclusion of a Moscow hotel room (Klevar 237, 445, Miller 304). A template story for the collection, "The Night My Old Man Came Home," appeared in *The New Yorker* as early as 1937 (Miller 302). Meanwhile, *Laughter* was published in 1944, and its constituent stories appeared in *The New Yorker* in December 1942, September 1943, and October 1943, and in *Harper's Bazaar* in March 1944. "Court" was originally written in 1939, however, and has a very different tone and structure from the other stories in *Laughter* and *Georgia Boy.*
14. See L. M. Grow, "*The Laughter of My Father*: A Survival Kit," and Joel Slotkin, "Igorots and Indians: Racial Hierarchies and Conceptions of the Savage in Carlos Bulosan's Fiction of the Philippines."
15. Both Ronald Takaki in *Iron Cages* and David Roediger in *Wages of Whiteness* discuss in great detail the ways in which whiteness has been linked to a racial aptitude for modern discipline. The absence of this aptitude, they have both shown, has served as the basis for racialization.
16. To Lye, the attribution of an "unusual capacity for economic modernity" to East Asians has made them sources of anxiety (the mechanical, massified coolie from before World War II) as well as symbols of emulation (the enterprising model minority of the postwar period). This racial form, moreover, stands in contrast to primitivist types of Orientalism and to representations of other U.S. minority groups as pre-industrial others. While I ultimately agree with Lye's argument, a consideration of pre–World War II, American renderings of Filipinos complicates her application of this notion to all East Asian groups.
17. Roy Rosenzweig's study of saloon culture in *Eight Hours for What We Will: Workers and Leisure in an Industrial City, 1870–1920* (Cambridge, UK: Cambridge University Press, 1983), is an excellent case study of how masculinity and capitalist discipline have sometimes been opposed within American culture.
18. Also, Erskine Caldwell's *Georgia Boy* (1943) illustrates how very similar narratives of manhood were in circulation in American culture at that time (and in wide circulation, given that *Georgia* sold 3.5 million copies). Its stories also revolve around a father-son bond, remembered by the son who has now reached adulthood; and this bond is also strengthened as the son is enlisted as a co-conspirator with a sinful father

against a more practical and upright mother. When compared side to side, *Laughter* appears an attempt to show Filipinos as just like libidinous American men at heart, except for minor cultural differences (a preference for wine rather than whisky, the use of *carabaos* instead of horses, and so on).

19. For the debate on whether Bulosan's nationalism is ironic or genuine, see Marilyn Alquizola, "Subversion or Affirmation: The Text and Subtext of *America Is in the Heart.*" *Asian Americans: Comparative and Global Perspectives*. Ed. Shirley Hume et al. (Pullman: Washington State University Press, 1991): 199–209; and Susan Evangelista, *Carlos Bulosan and His Poetry: A Biography and an Anthology* (Seattle: University of Washington Press, 1985).

20. From 1898 to 1934, Filipinos were neither aliens nor citizens but U.S. nationals, a colonial status that enabled them to migrate to the U.S. and work but not to obtain citizenship. The Tydings-McDuffie Act of 1934 reclassified them as aliens ineligible for citizenship, and this was not reversed until 1946. In general, legal and extralegal backlashes against Filipinos in the U.S. intensified during the Depression. I write that *America* is more of an appeal for citizenship in the cultural and not the legal sense, not only because Filipinos became eligible for citizenship in the year of its publication, but also because it is unknown whether Bulosan ever applied for naturalized citizenship (though it is known that he never became a citizen).

21. Josephine Herbst similarly wrote, for example, that "Americanism ... has been a dream rather than a reality" and that "America to me is a country that has never fulfilled itself." "What is Americanism?" *Partisan Review and Anvil* (April 1936): 5–6.

22. While the left nationalisms of second-generation European American authors are varied, they also tend to cast their lot with an American tradition (whether for strategic or for heartfelt reasons) over that of their parents' homelands. The writings of these second-generation Americans are set almost entirely in the U.S.; they rarely involve sustained engagements with the cultural and political situations in their ancestral countries, and even where they do they ultimately renounce the country of origin in favor of either the U.S. or a U.S./U.S.S.R. dyad. In Jerre Mangione's *Mount Allegro*, for example, we find a lengthy description of the Italian American narrator's nostalgic journey "home" to the Sicily of his parents. But even here, the fascist erosion of both Sicilian culture and the regional economy described by Mangione reaffirms for its reader a sense of the U.S. as an antifascist land of liberty, and hence a primary node of identification. Similarly, Mike Gold famously begins *Jews Without Money* by linking his narrative to the persecution of the Jews in Europe, thereby indicating an investment in the politics of his parents' homelands, yet nothing in the narrative leads one to believe that he harbors any deep nostalgia for Europe. In a 1944 editorial in the *Daily Worker*, he even sentimentally describes the Statue of Liberty as unchanging "beacon" of hope that unites generations ("Miss Liberty" 7).

23. As Ronald Takaki and David Roediger have argued in *Iron Cages* and *Wages of Whiteness* (respectively), republican discourse constructed a highly disciplined and even "bourgeois" subject that was part and parcel to the modern, even though the discourse was in operation long before capitalism became full-blown in the U.S. And as the virtuous yeoman of agrarian discourse stems from this republicanism as well, one could also argue that agrarianism was, paradoxically, a "modern" discourse in some ways as well.

24. One critic has also noted a range of stylistic similarities between *America* and the realist autobiography *Black Boy* by Richard Wright: see Helen Jaskoski, "Carlos Bulosan's Literary Debt to Richard Wright." *Literary Influence and African American Writers: Collected Essays*. Ed. Tracy Mishkin (New York: Garland, 1996), 231–43. While the development of the narrator's consciousness is not linear as in the classic bildungsroman, I find *America* to be a realist text because of the rough chronology of its narration, the clarity and accessibility of its prose, and its thematization of environmental factors on the narrator's development. In the brutality of its environment, it also borrows from naturalism. Realism, furthermore, need not be written in the third person.
25. *America* begins with an embittered homecoming, the narrator's brother returning to poverty after wartime service to the U.S. in World War I. The book ends after another round of Filipino military volunteerism has begun, this time in World War II.

CHAPTER 5
The Popular Front in the American Century
Life Magazine, Margaret Bourke-White, and Partisan Objectivity

1. For a few examples, see "Some Like It Here" and "You and the Next Administration," *Collier's*, 12 August 1939; "The Court is Now His," by Wendell Willkie, *Saturday Evening Post*, 9 March 1940; review of film "The Grapes of Wrath," *Time*, 29 January 1940; "Let Me Call You Comrade," *Collier's*, 10 February 1940; and "How About Taxing the TVA?" *Collier's*, 27 January 1940.
2. In an article clearly supportive of Roosevelt's Republican challenger Wendell Willkie, *Life* joyfully reported figures from *Editor and Publisher* showing that far more papers backed Republican presidential candidates than F.D.R. in 1936 and 1940 (30 September 1940, 84). However, there were left and liberal reporters on the staff of papers with conservative editorial boards, struggling to and sometimes succeeding in airing their views. That deep divisions between publishers and staff existed in newspapers is evidenced by the organization of the American Newspaper Guild in 1933, which met with vehement opposition from newspaper publishers. See Charles Dale, "An Integral Part of Journalism: the Newspaper Guild." *With Just Cause: Unionization of the American Journalist*. Ed. Walter Brasch (Lanham, MD: University Press of America, 1991), 3.
3. The three main book-length studies of *Life* today are Loudon Wainwright, *The Great American Magazine: An Inside History of Life* (1986), Wendy Kozol, *Life's America: Family and Nation in Postwar Photojournalism* (1994), and the more recent collection of essays *Looking at Life Magazine*, ed. Erica Doss (2001). James Baughman's *Henry Luce and the Rise of the American News Media* (1987) also provides essential, behind-the-scenes information about the operations of the Luce empire, without which this study would be nearly impossible. See also Aden Hayes, "The Spanish Civil War in Life Magazine." *The Spanish Civil War and the Visual Arts*. Ed. Kathleen Vernon (Ithaca, NY: Center for International Studies, 1990), and Robert Herzstein, *Henry Luce, a Political Portrait* (1994).

4. In addition to Michael Denning's *The Cultural Front*, examples include James Cronin, *The World the Cold War Made: Order, Chaos, and the Return of History* (New York: Routledge, 1996); Nikhil Pal Singh, "Culture/Wars: Recoding Empire in an Age of Democracy." *American Quarterly* 50 (1998): 471–522; and Christina Klein, *Cold War Orientalism: Asia in the Middlebrow Imagination, 1945–1961* (Berkeley: University of California Press, 2003).

5. American writers on the left at mid-century inherited a strand of thought from the earlier Soviet Proletkult movement, which peaked in influence between 1917 and 1920. The Proletkult called on proletarian writers to tell their own stories, to reveal authentic, revolutionary working-class life through their subjective experiences. Mike Gold continued this trend in 1930, when he admonished proletarians to "write with the courage of our own experience" ("Proletarian Realism" 207). The Proletkult was formally dissolved in 1932, but the subjective tendency never quite died in the U.S., taking on a life of its own in a number of proletarian autobiographies narrated in a first-person, realist mode, including Agnes Smedley's *Daughter of Earth* (1929), Jack Conroy's *The Disinherited* (1933), Richard Wright's *Black Boy* (1945), Carlos Bulosan's *America is in the Heart* (1946), as well as others written in a modernist vein, including those by Tillie Olsen, Meridel LeSueur, and by Mike Gold himself.

6. For examples of self-referentiality in *P.M.*, see "How Hitler Deceives His People—A Picture Analysis," *P.M.*, 22 September 1940, 35–38; and "Camera Reveals How Campaigning Has Altered Willkie's Personality," *P.M.*, 22 October 1940, 47–49.

7. See "Speaking of Pictures . . . LIFE Looks Back 5 Years to See How its 1st Big Story Has Changed." 1 December 1941: 10–11. It should also be noted that Henry Luce even condemned Roosevelt's leadership right after Pearl Harbor in his editorial "Day of Wrath" (22 December 1941: 10–11). *Life* also embraced F.D.R.'s Republican opponents in the 1940 and 1944 presidential elections.

8. To illustrate, in elections, the *Digest* simply reports basic or flattering information about each contender as if the candidates themselves wrote them, and such courtesy is even extended to the Socialist candidate (7 July 1900, p. 8). But in covering subjects not marked by the authors as "contested," such as British imperialism in China, it takes a clear position by assuming the righteousness of the British presence (21 July 1900, p. 81). Further, news articles in the *Digest* are composed largely of a series of quotes strung together from newspapers around the world, which, when added together, generally form a rough consensus on what "actually happened." The individual quotes appear subjective and local, but when added together by the invisible editorial hand of the *Digest*, they appear as fact. In other words, while the quotes are traceable to a definite authorial source, the *Digest* itself appears as unauthored discourse in its purest form. Its practices, incidentally, stay consistent from the turn of the century up until the late 1920s.

9. Some examples of the "found object" quality of *Life* captions include "The people of Mexico sell to the people of the United States things like these," 14 March 1938, 41; "These are Modern Tintypers," 20 September 1937, 17; "Here are pictures . . ." 11 April 1938, 5; "This is a picture of a courtroom scene," 6 September 1937, 19.

10. For an example, see "Lily Pons Sings Before Record-Breaking Crowd of 175,000 in Chicago." 13 September 1937: 28–29. The writer tells us that the singer "hates bread

[and] fills up on potatoes. She once owned a pet jaguar. Her favorite number is 13 and her car license is LP 13."

11. See the editorial by Luce entitled "Negro Rights," 24 April 1944, 32. See also "Robeson in Moscow," 11 January 1937, 49; "Slave-Born Negro Scientist is Honored in Alabama," 22 March 1937, 37–38.
12. See "Out of the Deep South: A Lynching, Oil and Feathers, The Ku Klux Klan and Mr. Justice Black," 23 August 1937, 30–33; "Scottsboro Boys Once More on Trial," 19 July 1937, 29–31.
13. My claims here are drawn from a number of secondary sources as well as my comprehensive research on *Life* from 1937 to 1945. For *Life* and the Chinese, see Herzstein, *Henry R. Luce, Time, and the American Crusade in Asia* (2005), and Kelly Ann Long, "Friend or Foe: *Life*'s Wartime Images of the Chinese" in *Looking at Life Magazine* (2001). For representational patterns vis-à-vis the Japanese and the U.S.S.R., see Herzstein, *American Crusade* (38, 42, 44). For the struggle over anti-Semitic representation within Time Inc., see Herzstein, *Henry Luce: A Political Portrait of the Man Who Created the American Century* (1994), chapter 8. For an example of British support and Arab vilification, see "Emir Abdullah: the Smart Little Arab Ruler of Trans-Jordan is No. 1 British Pawn in the Middle East," 1 December 1941, 67–70.
14. I found no definite increase or decrease in this pattern between 1936 and 1941. The 5 April 1937 issue featured thirty-seven pages of ads out of a total of eighty-six pages (43 percent ads); 22 May 1939 contained thirty-nine pages of advertisements out of ninety (43 percent), and in the 23 June 1941 issue, forty out of ninety-four pages consisted of ads (42 percent).
15. Examples of the poststructuralist critique of realism include Roland Barthes, *S/Z*, trans. Richard Miller (New York: Hill and Wang, 1974), and Catherine Belsey, *Critical Practice* (New York: Methuen, 1980).
16. Christopher Wilson, "The Rhetoric of Consumption: Mass Market Magazines and the Demise of the Genteel Reader, 1880–1920." *The Culture of Consumption: Critical Essays in American History, 1880–1980*. Ed. T. J. Jackson Lears and Richard Fox Wightman (New York: Pantheon, 1983). Richard Ohmann provides the most comprehensive look to date at the magazine revolution in his *Selling Culture: Magazines, Markets, and Class at the Turn of the Century* (London: Verso, 1996).
17. This is not to say that Bourke-White turned her back on modernism entirely. For instance, in some of her work for *Life*'s first photo-essay on the Fort Peck Dam in 1936, she defamiliarized and glorified the construction project with images that broke it down into its elemental lines and shapes, reminiscent of modernist design. And this chapter will reference a few more examples of her continuing modernism for *Life*. But the vast majority of her 1930s photographs bear more in common with American realism than they do the various strands of mid-century modernism.
18. Within a culture that does not offer any viable political choices, Caldwell writes: "religion fits his needs and fulfills his desires. Usually he is a man, who, under other circumstances, might have found religion a comforting thought, but not a panacea" (39). You or I would be dancing before the altar, too, he suggests, were it not for our relatively privileged lives.
19. "The Camera Overseas: Brazil Presents the Bogey of Fascism to the Americas," 22 November 1937, 98–99.

20. See "Harlem Gang Leader." 1 November 1948, 44. Particularly in his early career (which began in the F.S.A.), Gordon Parks can also be considered a realist. He told *Ebony* that his job was to report "the ugly and the beautiful," and "to report accurately the truth as he sees it" (qtd. in Doss 227). He shared the general epistemological tenets of partisan objectivity by stating a desire to both fight for racial justice and be "objective."

Works Cited

Alexander, William. *Film on the Left: American Documentary Film from 1931 to 1942.* Princeton, NJ: Princeton University Press, 1981.
Algren, Nelson. *Never Come Morning.* 1942. New York: Seven Stories Press, 1987.
Allen, Robert. *Speaking of Soap Operas.* Chapel Hill: University of North Carolina Press, 1985.
Allmendinger, Blake. "Little House on the Rice Paddy." *American Literary History* 10.2 (1998): 360–77.
"Another All-Negro Serial in Web Bid." *Variety.* 7 March 1945: 31.
Arnold, Edwin, ed. *Conversations with Erskine Caldwell.* Jackson: University Press of Mississippi, 1988.
Atkinson, Brooks. *Broadway.* New York: Macmillan, 1970.
Back to Bataan. Directed by Edward Dmytryk. Screenplay by Ben Barzman and Richard Landau. RKO Pictures, 1945.
Baker, Kenneth. "Radio Listening and Socio-Economic Status." *The Psychological Record* 1 (1937): 95–144.
Barlow, Judith. "Into the Foxhole: Feminism, Realism, and Lillian Hellman." *Realism and the American Dramatic Tradition.* Ed. William De Mastes. Tuscaloosa: University of Alabama Press. 1996. 156–71.
Baughman, James. *Henry Luce and the Rise of the American News Media.* Boston: Twayne Publishers, 1987.
———. "Who Read *Life*? The Circulation of America's Favorite Magazine." *Looking at Life Magazine.* Ed. Erica Doss. Washington: Smithsonian Institute Press, 2001. 41–51.
Bell, Michael Davitt. *The Problem of American Realism: Studies in the Cultural History of a Literary Idea.* Chicago: University of Chicago Press, 1996.
Bessie, Alvah. Review of *Watch on the Rhine. The New Masses.* 15 April 1941: 26–28.
Black, Allida. *Casting Her Own Shadow: Eleanor Roosevelt and the Shaping of Postwar Liberalism.* New York: Columbia University Press, 1996.
Bodnar, John. *Blue Collar Hollywood: Liberalism, Democracy, and Working People in American Film.* Baltimore: Johns Hopkins University Press, 2003.
Body and Soul. Directed by Robert Rossen. Screenplay by Abraham Polonsky. Enterprise Studios, 1947.

Bogle, Donald. *Toms, Coons, Mulattoes, Mammies, and Bucks: An Interpretive History of Blacks in American Films*. 1973. New York: Continuum, 1996.
Booth, Michael. Introduction. *Hiss the Villain: Six English and American Melodramas*. New York: B. Blom, 1964.
Borus, Daniel. *Writing Realism: Howells, James, and Norris in the Mass Market*. Chapel Hill: University of North Carolina Press, 1989.
Bourke-White, Margaret. *Portrait of Myself*. New York: Simon and Schuster, 1963.
Bourke-White, Margaret, and Erskine Caldwell. *You Have Seen Their Faces*. 1937. Athens: University of Georgia Press, 1995.
Browder, Earl. *What is Communism?* New York: Vanguard Press, 1936.
Brown, Bill. "Monstrosity." *The Material Unconscious: American Amusement, Stephen Crane, and the Economics of Play*. Cambridge, MA: Harvard University Press, 1996. 199–245.
Bryer, Jackson, ed. *Conversations with Lillian Hellman*. Jackson: University Press of Mississippi, 1986.
Buckman, Gertrude. "A Slum on the Way to the End of the Night." Review of *Never Come Morning*. *Partisan Review* 9 (September-October 1942): 426–27.
Buhle, Paul, and Dave Wagner. *Radical Hollywood: The Untold Story Behind America's Favorite Movies*. New York: New Press, 2002.
Bulosan, Carlos. *America Is in the Heart: A Personal History*. 1946. Seattle: University of Washington Press, 2000.
———. "Freedom from Want." *Saturday Evening Post*. 6 March 1943: 12–13.
———. *The Laughter of My Father*. 1944. New York: Bantam Books, 1946.
———. "The Growth of Philippine Culture." *On Becoming Filipino*. Ed. E. San Juan Jr. Philadelphia: Temple University Press, 1995. 115–23.
———. "I am Not a Laughing Man." *On Becoming Filipino*. Ed. E. San Juan Jr. Philadelphia: Temple University Press, 1995. 138–42.
———. "Letters (1937–1955)." *On Becoming Filipino*. Ed. E. San Juan Jr. Philadelphia: Temple University Press, 1995. 173–214.
———. "My Education." *On Becoming Filipino*. Ed. E. San Juan Jr. Philadelphia: Temple University Press, 1995. 124–30.
Burch, Noël. "Porter, or Ambivalence." *Screen* 19 (Winter 1978–79): 91–105.
Burke, Kenneth. "Caldwell: Maker of Grotesques." 1935. *The Critical Response to Erskine Caldwell*. Robert McDonald, ed. Westport, CT: Greenwood Press, 1997, 48–54.
———. "Revolutionary Symbolism in America." *American Writers' Congress*. Ed. Henry Hart. New York: International Publishers, 1935. 87–93.
Caldwell, Erskine. *God's Little Acre*. 1933. New York: Penguin Books, 1946.
———. *Journeyman*. 1935. New York: Penguin Books, 1947.
———. *Tobacco Road*. 1932. *Three by Caldwell: Tobacco Road, Georgia Boy, Sure Hand of God*. Boston: Little, Brown, and Co., 1960.
———. *Tragic Ground*. 1944. New York: Penguin Books, 1948.
———. *Trouble in July*. 1940. Savannah, GA: Beehive Press, 1977.
Cantor, Muriel, and Suzanne Pingree. *The Soap Opera*. Beverly Hills, CA: Sage Publications, 1983.
Cappetti, Carla. *Writing Chicago: Modernism, Ethnography, and the Novel*. New York: Columbia University Press, 1993.

Cawelti, John. *Adventure, Mystery, and Romance: Formula Stories as Art and Popular Culture*. Chicago: University of Chicago Press, 1976.
Chametzky, Jules. "Edward Dahlberg: Early and Late." *Proletarian Writers of the Thirties*. Carbondale: Southern Illinois University Press, 1968. 64–73.
City for Conquest. Directed by Anatole Litwak. Screenplay by John Wexley. Warner Bros., 1940.
The Champ. Directed by King Vidor. Screenplay by Leonard Praskins. MGM, 1931.
Chandler, Raymond. "The Simple Art of Murder." *The Simple Art of Murder*. New York: W. W. Norton, 1968. 519–33.
Cheung, Floyd. Introduction. *And China Has Hands*. By H. T. Tsiang. Forest Hills, NY: Iron Weed Press, 2003. 7–15.
Cohen, Lizbeth. *Making a New Deal: Industrial Workers in Chicago, 1919–1939*. Cambridge, UK: Cambridge University Press, 1990.
Conroy, Jack. "Passion and Pellagra." 1932. *The Critical Response to Erskine Caldwell*. Robert McDonald, ed. Westport CT: Greenwood Press, 1997. 27–28.
Cox, Jim. *The Historical Dictionary of American Radio Soap Operas*. Lanham, MD: Scarecrow Press, 2005.
Cowley, Malcolm. "Chicago Poem." Review of *Never Come Morning*. *New Republic* 4 May 1942: 613–14.
Crowther, Bosley. "Comic Tour in 'Sullivan's Travels' on the Paramount's Screen." *New York Times*. 29 January 1942: 25.
Dawahare, Anthony. *Nationalism, Marxism, and African American Literature between the Wars: A New Pandora's Box*. Jackson: University Press of Mississippi, 2003.
Day, Daniel. "Local Fans Drop Cares, Unleash Mighty Flood of Happiness as Brown Bomber Trounces Schmeling." *Chicago Defender*. 25 June 1938: 1–2.
Denning, Michael. *The Cultural Front: The Laboring of American Culture in the Twentieth Century*. London: Verso, 1997.
———. *Culture in the Age of Three Worlds*. London: Verso, 2004.
Dexter, Charles. "Group Back on Broadway with Odets' Latest Play." *Daily Worker*. 12 November 1937: 7.
Donohue, H. E. F. *Conversations with Nelson Algren*. New York: Hill and Wang, 1964.
Doss, Erica. "Visualizing Black America: Gordon Parks at *Life*: 1948–1971." *Looking at Life Magazine*. Ed. Erica Doss. Washington: Smithsonian Institute Press, 2001. 221–41.
Doyle, Kegan. "Joe Louis in Black and White." *Aethlon: The Journal of Sport and Literature* 18.1-2 (2000): 113–33.
Drabeck, Bernard, and Helen Ellis, ed. *Archibald MacLeish: Reflections*. Amherst: University of Massachusetts Press, 1986.
Du Bois, W. E. B. *The Souls of Black Folk*. 1903. *Three Negro Classics*. New York: Avon Books, 1965. 206–389.
———. Letter to Shirley Graham. 7 July 1941. W. E. B. Du Bois Papers, Reel 52, page 1016. Amherst, MA.
Early, Gerald. *The Culture of Bruising: Essays on Prizefighting, Literature, and Modern American Culture*. Hopewell, NJ: Ecco Press, 1994.
Farnsworth, Robert. *From Vagabond to Journalist: Edgar Snow in Asia, 1928–1941*. Columbia: University of Missouri Press, 1996.

Farrell, James T. Foreword. *James T. Farrell: Short Stories*. New York: Penguin, 1946.
Fiske, John. "Television: Polysemy and Popularity." *Critical Studies in Mass Communications* 3 (1986): 391–408.
Fletcher, Winona. "From Genteel Poet to Revolutionary Playwright: Georgia Douglas Johnson." *Theatre Annual* 40 (1985): 41–64.
Foley, Barbara. *Radical Representations: Politics and Form in U.S. Proletarian Fiction, 1929–1941*. Durham: Duke University Press, 1993.
Freeman, Joseph. *An American Testament*. New York: Ferrar and Rinehart, 1936.
Frick, John. "'Odets, Where Is Thy Sting?' Reassessing the 'Playwright of the Proletariat.'" *Realism and the American Dramatic Tradition*. Ed. William Demastes. Tuscaloosa: University of Alabama Press, 1996. 123–38.
Gary, Brett. "The Pitiless Spotlight of Publicity: *Life* and the World War II–Era Exposure of American Extremists." *Looking at Life Magazine*. Ed. Erica Doss. Washington: Smithsonian Institute Press, 2001. 77–101.
Gissen, Max. "The Darker Brothers." Review of *America Is in the Heart* by Carlos Bulosan and *My Africa* by Mbonu Ojike. *New Republic* 25 March 1946: 420–22.
Gold, Mike. *Jews without Money*. 1930. New York: Carroll and Graf Publishers, 1998.
———. "Miss Liberty's Beacon Still Shines." *Daily Worker*. 6 October 1944: 7.
———. "Proletarian Realism." 1930. *Mike Gold: A Literary Anthology*. New York: International Publishers, 1972. 203–8.
Goldberg, Vicki. *Margaret Bourke-White: A Biography*. New York: Harper and Row, 1986.
Golden Boy. Directed by Rouben Mamoulian. Screenplay by Lewis Meltzer, Daniel Taradash, Sarah Mason, and Victor Heerman. Columbia Pictures, 1939.
Goldstein, Malcolm. *The Political Stage: American Drama and Theater of the Great Depression*. New York: Oxford University Press, 1974.
Gompers, Samuel, and Herman Gutstadt. "Meat vs. Rice: American Manhood against Asiatic Coolieism, Which Shall Survive?" San Francisco: American Federation of Labor, 1908.
Gorn, Elliot. *The Manly Art: Bare-Knuckle Prize Fighting in America*. Ithaca, NY: Cornell University Press, 1986.
Gorn, Elliot, and Warren Goldstein. *A Brief History of American Sports*. Urbana: University of Illinois Press, 1993.
Graham, Shirley. *I Gotta Home*. *Black Female Playwrights: An Anthology of Plays Before 1950*. Ed. Kathy Perkins. Bloomington: Indiana University Press, 1989. 225–79.
———. "The Bannekers." Ts. 41.6. Shirley Graham Du Bois Papers: Schlesinger Library, Radcliffe Institute, Harvard University.
———. "The Bannekers: A Prospectus for a Radio Story." Ts. 41.7. Shirley Graham Du Bois Papers. Schlesinger Library, Radcliffe Institute, Harvard University.
———. Letter to W. E. B. Du Bois. 30 December 1939. Reel 50, page 193. W. E. B. Du Bois Papers, W. E. B. Du Bois Library, University of Massachusetts Amherst.
———. Letter to W. E. B. Du Bois. 6 March 1940. Reel 51, page 580. W. E. B. Du Bois Papers, W. E. B. Du Bois Library, University of Massachusetts Amherst.
———. Letter to W. E. B. Du Bois. 25 April 1940. Reel 51, page 582. W. E. B. Du Bois Papers, W. E. B. Du Bois Library, University of Massachusetts Amherst.
———. Letter to W. E. B. Du Bois. 15 May 1941. Reel 52, page 1014. W. E. B. Du Bois Papers, W. E. B. Du Bois Library, University of Massachusetts Amherst.

———. Letter to W. E. B. Du Bois. 19 March 1942. Reel 53, page 1044. W. E. B. Du Bois Papers, W. E. B. Du Bois Library, University of Massachusetts Amherst.

———. Letter to W. E. B. Du Bois. 19 June 1943. Reel 55, page 322. W. E. B. Du Bois Papers, W. E. B. Du Bois Library, University of Massachusetts Amherst.

Grams, Martin Jr. *Radio Drama: American Programs, 1932–1962.* Jefferson, NC: McFarland, 2000.

Gramsci, Antonio. "Concept of National Popular." *The Antonio Gramsci Reader: Selected Writings, 1916–1935.* Ed. David Forgacs. New York: NYU Press, 2000. 364–70.

Gregory, James. *American Exodus: The Dust Bowl Migration and Okie Culture in California.* New York: Oxford University Press, 1989.

Grow, L. M. "*The Laughter of My Father*: A Survival Kit." *MELUS* 20 (1995): 35–46.

Hackett, Alice. *70 Years of Best Sellers, 1895–1965.* New York: R.R. Bowker, 1967.

Hackett, Alice, and James Henry Burke. *80 Years of Best Sellers, 1895–1975.* New York: R.R. Bowker, 1977.

Hallam, Julia, with Margaret Marshment. *Realism and Popular Cinema.* Manchester, UK: Manchester University Press, 2000.

Hapke, Laura. *Daughters of the Depression: Women, Work, and Fiction in the American 1930s.* Athens: University of Georgia Press, 1995.

Harwell, Richard, ed. *Margaret Mitchell's "Gone with the Wind" Letters, 1936–1949.* London: Macmillan, 1976.

Hatch, James. "Creeping toward Integration." *A History of African American Theatre.* Ed. Errol Hill and James Hatch. Cambridge, UK: Cambridge University Press, 2003. 335–74.

———. "The Great Depression and Federal Theatre." *A History of African American Theatre.* Ed. Errol Hill and James Hatch. Cambridge, UK: Cambridge University Press, 307–34.

Hau, Caroline, and Benedict Anderson. Introduction. *All the Conspirators.* Seattle: University of Washington Press, 1998. vii–xxiv.

Hellman, Lillian. *The Children's Hour. Six Plays by Lillian Hellman.* 1942. New York: Modern Library, 1960. 5–86.

———. Introduction. *Six Plays by Lillian Hellman.* 1942. New York: Modern Library, 1960. vii–xiv.

———. *The Little Foxes. Six Plays by Lillian Hellman.* 1942. New York: Modern Library, 1960. 167–248.

Herr, Christopher. *Clifford Odets and American Political Theatre.* Westport, CT: Praeger, 2003.

Herzstein, Robert. *Henry R. Luce: A Political Portrait of the Man Who Created the American Century.* New York: Macmillan, 1994.

———. *Henry R. Luce, Time, and the American Crusade in Asia.* Cambridge, UK: Cambridge University Press, 2005.

Himes, Chester. *If He Hollers Let Him Go.* 1945. New York: Thunder's Mouth Press, 2002.

Hoopes, Roy. *Ralph Ingersoll: A Biography.* Atheneum, New York, 1985.

Horne, Gerald. *Race Woman: The Lives of Shirley Graham Du Bois.* New York: New York University Press, 2000.

Howells, William Dean. "Criticism and Fiction." *Criticism and Fiction, and Other Essays.* New York: New York University Press, 1959.

Hughes, Langston. "Some Practical Observations: A Colloquy." *Phylon* 11 (1950). *Collected Works of Langston Hughes. Vol. 9: Essays on Art, Race, Politics and World Affairs*. Ed. Christopher De Santis. Columbia: University of Missouri Press, 2002. 307–11.

Isaacs, Harold. *Images of Asia: American Views of China and India*. New York: Capricorn, 1962.

Ivy, James. Review of *Trouble in July*. *The Crisis* 47:4 (1940): 122, 124.

Jacobson, Matthew Frye. *Whiteness of a Different Color: European Immigrants and the Alchemy of Race*. Cambridge, MA: Harvard University Press, 1998.

———. "Hyphen Nation: The Politics of Diversity in a 'Nation of Immigrants.'" Eighth Annual Sidney Kaplan Lecture. Amherst, MA. 6 May 2003.

Kaplan, Amy. *The Social Construction of American Realism*. Chicago: University of Chicago Press, 1988.

Kazin, Alfred. *On Native Grounds: An Interpretation of Modern American Prose Literature*. New York: Reynal and Hitchcock, 1942.

Kelley, Robin D. G. *Hammer and Hoe: Alabama Communists during the Great Depression*. Chapel Hill: University of North Carolina Press, 1990.

Kerkvliet, Benedict. *The Huk Rebellion: A Study of Peasant Revolt in the Philippines*. Berkeley: University of California Press, 1977.

Kid Galahad. Directed by Michael Curtiz. Screenplay by Seton Miller. Warner Bros., 1937.

Kim, Elaine. *Asian American Literature: An Introduction to the Writings and Their Social Context*. Philadelphia: Temple University Press, 1982.

Kimmel, Michael. *Manhood in America: A Cultural History*. New York: Free Press, 1996.

Klein, Christina. *Cold War Orientalism: Asia in the Middlebrow Imagination, 1945–1961*. Berkeley: University of California Press, 2003.

Klevar, Harry. *Erskine Caldwell: A Biography*. Knoxville: University of Tennessee Press, 1993.

Kozol, Wendy. *Life's America: Family and Nation in Postwar Photojournalism*. Philadelphia: Temple University Press, 1994.

Krutch, Joseph Wood. "No Such Animal." Review of *Watch on the Rhine*. *The Nation*. 12 April 1941: 453.

Laclau, Ernesto, and Chantal Mouffe. *Hegemony and Socialist Strategy: Toward a Radical Democratic Politics*. 1985. London: Verso, 1994.

Lee, Robert G. "The Hidden World of Asian Immigrant Radicalism." *The Immigrant Left in the United States*. Ed. Paul Buhle and Dan Georgakas. Albany: State University Press of New York, 1996. 256–88.

———. *Orientals: Asian Americans in Popular Culture*. Philadelphia: Temple University Press, 1999.

Lefebvre, Georges. *The Coming of the French Revolution*. Trans. by R. R. Palmer. Princeton, NJ: Princeton University Press, 1971.

Leonard, George. *Walking on the Edge of the World*. Boston: Houghton Mifflin, 1988.

Littledale, Clara Savage. "The Way Father Stretched His Mouth." Review of *The Laughter of My Father* by Carlos Bulosan. *Saturday Review of Literature*. 3 June 1944: 22.

Lomax, Alan. *Selected Writings, 1934–1997*. Ed. Ronald Cohen. New York: Routledge, 2003.

Lovell, Terry. *Pictures of Reality: Aesthetics, Politics, Pleasure*. London: British Film Institute, 1980.

Luce, Henry. "Address to the Commissars." *The Ideas of Henry Luce*. Ed. John Jessup. New York: Atheneum, 1969. 35–43.
———. "The American Century." *Life*. 17 February 1941: 61–65.
———. "Causes, Causes!" *The Ideas of Henry Luce*. Ed. John Jessup. New York: Atheneum, 1969. 54–57.
———. "A Prospectus for a New Magazine." *Printer's Ink*. 20 August 1936: 33–40.
Lukács, Georg. *The Historical Novel*. Trans. Hannah and Stanley Mitchell. Lincoln: University of Nebraska Press, 1983.
Lunacharsky, Anatoly. "Der sozialistische Realismus." 1933. *Vom Proletkult zum sozialistische Realismus: Aufsätze zur Kunst der Zeit*. East Berlin: Dietz Verlag, 1981. 326-350.
Lye, Colleen. *America's Asia: Racial Form and American Literature, 1893–1945*. Princeton: Princeton University Press, 2005.
Lynch, William. "Loyalty in Spite of All." Review of *America Is in the Heart* by Carlos Bulosan. *Saturday Review of Literature* 9 March 1946: 7–8.
MacDonald, J. Fred. *Don't Touch That Dial! Radio Programming in American Life, 1920–1960*. Chicago: Nelson Hall, 1979.
Macleod, Norm. "A Hardboiled Idealist." 1931. *The Critical Response to Erskine Caldwell*. Robert McDonald, ed. Westport, CT: Greenwood Press, 1997. 21.
Marchand, Roland. *Advertising the American Dream: Making Way for Modernity, 1920–1940*. Berkeley: University of California Press, 1985.
McElvaine, Robert. *The Great Depression: America, 1929–1941*. 1984. New York: Times Books, 1993.
Messenger, Christian. *Sport and the Spirit of Play in American Fiction: Hawthorne to Faulkner*. New York: Columbia University Press, 1981.
Miller, Dan. *Erskine Caldwell: The Journey From Tobacco Road*. New York: Alfred Knopf, 1995.
Miller, Gabriel. *Clifford Odets*. New York: Continuum, 1989.
Miller, Jordan, and Winifred Frazer. *American Drama between the Wars: A Critical History*. Boston: Twayne Publishers, 1991.
Mitchell, Don. *Lie of the Land: Migrant Workers and the California Landscape*. Minneapolis: University of Minnesota Press, 1996.
Mitchell, Margaret. *Gone with the Wind*. 1936. Garden City, NY: Garden City Books, 1954.
Monaghan, John. Review of *America is in the Heart* by Carlos Bulosan. *The Commonweal* 24 May 1946: 149.
Morison, James. "Pearl Buck's 'Dragon Seed' Is Epic Story of Embattled China." *Daily Worker*. 6 April 1942: 7.
Morton, Marian. "'My Dear, I Don't Give a Damn': Scarlett O'Hara and the Great Depression." *Frontiers: A Journal of Women's Studies* 5 (1980): 52–56.
Mullen, Bill. *Popular Fronts: Chicago and African-American Cultural Politics, 1935–1946*. Urbana: University of Illinois Press, 1999.
Murphy, Brenda. *American Realism and American Drama, 1880–1940*. Cambridge, UK: Cambridge University Press, 1987.
Murphy, James. *The Proletarian Moment: The Controversy over Leftism in Literature*. Urbana: University of Illinois Press, 1991.

Nathan, George Jean. "Dour Octopus." Review of *The Little Foxes*. *Newsweek*. 27 February 1939: 26.

———. *The Entertainment of a Nation, or Three-Sheets in the Wind*. New York: Alfred Knopf, 1942.

Nettels, Elsa. *Language, Race, and Social Class in Howells's America*. Lexington: University Press of Kentucky, 1988.

Nguyen, Viet Thanh. *Race and Resistance: Literature and Politics in Asian America*. Oxford, UK: Oxford University Press, 2002.

Odets, Clifford. *Golden Boy*. 1937. *Waiting for Lefty and Other Plays*. New York: Grove Press, 1993.

Oriard, Michael. *Dreaming of Heroes: American Sports Fiction, 1868–1980*. Chicago: Nelson Hall, 1982.

Ohmann, Richard. *Selling Culture: Magazines, Markets, and Class at the Turn of the Century*. London: Verso, 1996.

Palumbo-Liu, David. *Asian/American: Historical Crossings of a Racial Frontier*. Stanford, CA: Stanford University Press, 1999.

Pauly, Thomas. "*Gone with the Wind* and *The Grapes of Wrath* as Hollywood Histories of the Depression." *Movies as Artifacts*. Ed. Michael Marsden et al. Chicago: Nelson Hall, 1982. 164–76.

Pearson, R. E. *Eloquent Gestures: The Transformation of Performance Style in the Griffith Biograph Films*. Berkeley: University of California Press, 265.

Peddle, Ian. "Poles Apart? Ethnicity, Race, Class, and Nelson Algren." *Modern Fiction Studies* 47 (2001): 118–44.

Peiss, Kathy. *Cheap Amusements: Working Women and Leisure in Turn-of-the-Century New York*. Philadelphia: Temple University Press, 1986.

Perkins, Kathy. Introduction. *Black Female Playwrights: An Anthology of Plays before 1950*. Ed. Kathy Perkins. Bloomington: Indiana University Press, 1989. 1–17.

"Prizefights, Pugs, and Profits." *Look*. 31 January 1939: 6–13.

Pudaloff, Ross. "Celebrity as Identity: Richard Wright, *Native Son*, and Mass Culture." *Studies in American Fiction* 11.1 (1983): 3–18.

Pullen, Glenn. "'Coal Dust' is Violent and Vivid Drama." *Cleveland Plain Dealer*. 27 April 1939.

Pyron, Darden Ashbury. *Southern Daughter: The Life of Margaret Mitchell*. Oxford, UK: Oxford University Press, 1991.

Rabinowitz, Paula. *Labor and Desire: Women's Revolutionary Fiction in Depression America*. Chapel Hill: University of North Carolina Press, 1991.

Rabinowitz, Paula. *They Must Be Represented: The Politics of Documentary*. New York: Verso, 1994.

Razlogova, Elena. "True Crime Radio and Listener Disenchantment with Network Broadcasting, 1935–1946." *American Quarterly* 58.4 (2006): 137–58.

Reid, James. "Reid Cites Qualities of Louis Which Have Inspired Race Youth." *Chicago Defender*. 25 June 1938: 22.

Review of *The Laughter of My Father* by Carlos Bulosan. *Booklist* 1 May 1944: 300.

Review of *The Laughter of My Father* by Carlos Bulosan. *The New Yorker*. 22 April, 1944: 89.

Roediger, David. *Wages of Whiteness: Race and the Making of the American Working Class*. Rev. ed. London: Verso, 1999.

———. *Working toward Whiteness: How America's Immigrants Became White: The Strange Journey from Ellis Island to the Suburbs.* New York: Basic Books, 2005.
Rodney, Lester. "Brilliant Saga of Our Negro Athletes." *Daily Worker.* 23 June 1938: 8.
Rogin, Michael. *Blackface, White Noise: Jewish Immigrants in the Hollywood Melting Pot.* Berkeley: University of California Press, 1996.
Rolfe, Edwin. Review of *God's Little Acre.* 1933. *The Critical Response to Erskine Caldwell.* Robert McDonald, ed. Westport CT: Greenwood Press, 1997. 31–33.
Rollyson, Carl. *Lillian Hellman: Her Legend and Her Legacy.* New York: St. Martin's Press, 1988.
San Juan Jr., E. Introduction. *The Cry and the Dedication.* By Carlos Bulosan. Philadelphia: Temple University Press, 1995. ix–xxxvi.
———. Introduction. *On Becoming Filipino.* By Carlos Bulosan. Ed. E. San Juan Jr. Philadelphia: Temple University Press, 1995. 1–44.
Savage, Barbara Diane. *Broadcasting Freedom: Radio, War, and the Politics of Race.* Chapel Hill: University of North Carolina Press, 1999.
Schick, Frank. *The Paperbound Book in America.* New York: R.R. Bowker, 1958.
Schudson, Michael. *Discovering the News: A Social History of American Newspapers.* New York: Basic Books, 1978.
Schuyler, George. "*Not* Gone With the Wind." *The Crisis* 44:7 (1937): 2–3.
Shadegg, Stephen. *Claire Booth Luce: A Biography.* New York: Simon and Schuster, 1970.
Shaffer, Robert. "Pearl S. Buck's Critique of the Cold War." *Journal of Women's History* 11.3 (1999): 151–75.
Shukotoff, Arnold. "Journey Down Tobacco Road." *New Masses.* 22 June 1938: 24.
Shuman, Amy. "Dismantling Local Culture." *Western Folklore* 52 (1993): 345–61.
Shuman, R. Baird. *Clifford Odets.* New York: Twayne, 1962.
Sillen, Samuel. "The Good Earth's Warriors." *New Masses.* 10 February 1942: 27–28.
Singh, Nikhil Pal. "Culture/Wars: Recoding Empire in an Age of Democracy." *American Quarterly* 50 (1998): 471–522.
Slotkin, Joel. "Igorots and Indians: Racial Hierarchies and Conceptions of the Savage in Carlos Bulosan's Fiction of the Philippines." *American Literature* 72 (2000): 843–66.
Smethurst, James. *The New Red Negro: The Literary Left and African-American Poetry.* New York: Oxford University Press, 1999.
Smith, Judith. "Radio's 'Cultural Front,' 1938–1948." *Radio Reader: Essays in the Cultural History of Radio.* Ed. Michele Himes and Jason Loviglio. New York: Routledge, 2002. 209–30.
———. *Visions of Belonging: Family Stories, Popular Culture, and Postwar Democracy, 1940–1960.* New York: Columbia University Press, 2004.
Smulyan, Susan. *Selling Radio: The Commercialization of American Broadcasting, 1920–1934.* Washington: Smithsonian Institution Press, 1994.
Snow, Edgar. *People on Our Side.* 1944. Cleveland: World Publishing, 1945.
———. *Red Star over China.* 1938. New York: Modern Library, 1944.
Spencer, Jenny. "Sex, Lies, and Revisions: Historicizing Hellman's *The Children's Hour.*" *Modern Drama* 47.1 (2004): 44–65.
Stange, Maren. *Symbols of Ideal Life: Social Documentary Photography in America.* Cambridge, UK: Cambridge University Press, 1989.

Stein, Sally. "The Graphic Ordering of Desire: Modernization of a Middle-Class Women's Magazine, 1919–39." *The Contest of Meaning.* Ed. Richard Bolton. Cambridge, MA: MIT Press, 1992. 145–61.

Steinberg, Cobbett. *Reel Facts: The Movie Book of Records.* Updated ed. New York: Vintage, 1982.

Steinbeck, John. *The Grapes of Wrath.* 1939. New York: Penguin, 2002.

Stewart, Donald Ogden, ed. *Fighting Words.* New York: Harcourt Brace, 1940.

Sugrue, Thomas. "Laughter in the Philippines." Review of *The Laughter of My Father* by Carlos Bulosan. *New York Times Book Review.* 23 April 1944: 7.

Sullivan's Travels. Directed and screenplay by Preston Sturges. Paramount Studios, 1942.

Summers, Harrison. *A Thirty-Year History of Programs Carried on National Radio Networks in the United States, 1926–1956.* 1958. New York: Arno, 1971.

Susman, Warren. *Culture as History: The Transformation of American Society in the Twentieth Century.* 1973. Washington: Smithsonian Institution Press, 2003.

Swindell, Larry. *Body and Soul: The Story of John Garfield.* New York: William Morrow, 1975.

Takaki, Ronald. *Iron Cages: Race and Culture in Nineteenth-Century America.* 1979. New York: Oxford University Press, 1990.

"The Telephone Company." *Life.* 17 July 1939: 56–63.

They Made Me a Criminal. Directed by Busby Berkeley. Screenplay by Sig Herzig. Warner Bros., 1939.

Tracy, Susan. *In the Master's Eye: Representations of Women, Blacks, and Poor Whites in Antebellum Southern Fiction.* Amherst: University of Massachusetts Press, 1995.

Tsiang, H. T. *And China Has Hands.* 1937. Forest Hills, NY: Iron Weed, 2003.

Volosinov, V. N. *Marxism and the Philosophy of Language.* 1929. Cambridge, MA: Harvard University Press, 1986.

"Under New Management." *Time.* 24 April 1939: 63.

Wainwright, Loudon. *The Great American Magazine: An Inside History of Life.* New York: Alfred Knopf, 1986.

Wald, Alan. *Exiles from a Future Time: Forging the Mid-Twentieth-Century Literary Left.* Chapel Hill: University of North Carolina Press, 2002.

Walker, Ethel Pitts. "The American Negro Theatre." *The Theatre of Black Americans: A Collection of Essays.* Ed. Errol Hill. New York: Applause, 1987.

Wallace, Henry. *Democracy Reborn.* Ed. Russell Lord. New York: Reynal and Hitchcock, 1944.

Wang, Xing, ed. *China Remembers Edgar Snow.* Beijing: Beijing Review, 1982.

"We Shoot Down the First Japs." *Life.* 22 December 1941: 29–35.

Weales, Gerald. *Odets the Playwright.* London: Methuen, 1985.

Williams, Linda. "Melodrama Revised." *Refiguring American Film Genres: History and Theory.* Ed. Nick Browne. Berkeley: University of California Press, 1998. 42–88.

Williams, Raymond. "A Lecture on Realism." *Screen* 18 (1977): 61–74.

Wilson, Christopher. "The Rhetoric of Consumption: Mass Market Magazines and the Demise of the Genteel Reader, 1880–1920." *The Culture of Consumption: Critical Essays in American History, 1880–1980.* Ed. Richard Wightman Fox and T. J. Jackson Lears. New York: Pantheon, 1983. 39–64.

Winfield, Betty Houchin. *F.D.R. and the News Media*. Urbana: University of Illinois Press, 1990.

Woolf, Michael. "Clifford Odets." *American Drama*. Ed. Clive Bloom. New York: St. Martin's, 1995. 46–67.

Wright, Richard. "And Oh—Where Were Hitler's Pagan Gods." *Daily Worker*. 24 June 1938: 1, 8.

———. "High Tide in Harlem." *New Masses*. 5 July 1938: 18–20.

———. "Joe Louis Uncovers Dynamite." 1935. *Richard Wright Reader*. Ed. Ellen Wright and Michel Fabre. New York: Harper and Row, 1978. 31–35.

———. "King Joe, Part I." Recorded 1941. Performed by Paul Robeson and Count Basie and his Band. *Joe Louis, an American Hero*. Rounder Records, 2001.

———. "Lynching Bee." 1940. *The Critical Response to Erskine Caldwell*. Robert McDonald, ed. Westport, CT: Greenwood Press, 1997. 114–15.

———. *Native Son*. 1940. New York: Perennial, 2001.

Yoneda, Karl. *Ganbatte: Sixty-Year Struggle of a Kibei Worker*. Los Angeles: Resource Development and Publications, Asian American Studies Center, University of California, 1983.

Index

Achenhurst, Anne, 49
Actor's Repertory Company, 51
Actor's Studio, 53
Agee, James, and Walker Evans, *Let Us Now Praise Famous Men*, xix
agrarianism, xix, 80, 95, 113–14, 115–17, 119, 136–37, 140–44, 205, 208
Aiken, George, *Uncle Tom's Cabin* (play), 100
Akins, Zoë, 56, 58, 200
Algren, Nelson, xxiv, xxx, xxxix, 3, 93, 110, 189; *Never Come Morning*, 26–31, 34, 35, 196–97
Allison, Hughes, 67
American Negro Theater (ANT), 51, 68, 69, 200–1
American Newspaper Guild, 209
Anderson, Marian, 37, 38
Anderson, Maxwell, xiv, 48, 52
Appeal to Reason, xxxvii
Armstrong, Henry, 5, 14, 15, 34
Arnheim, Rudolph, 47
Atlantic Monthly, xxxii, xxxiii, xxxiv

Back to Bataan (film), xl, 122, 205–6
Baker, Kenneth, 47
Barlow, Judith, 65
Barney Google (comic), 185
Barzman, Ben, 122
Bataan (film), xx, 205–6
Belafonte, Harry, 68
Bell, Michael Davitt, xxxiv–xxxv

Benjamin, Walter, 189
Bessie, Alvah, 200
Betrayal From the East (film), 206
Bierce, Ambrose, xiv, 177
Birth of a Nation (film), 90
Boas, Franz, xxv
Body and Soul (film), xxviii, xxxviii, 31–34, 35
Bogle, Thomas, 66
Boleslavski, Richard, 53
Bourke-White, Margaret, xxiii, xxx, xli, 83, 178, 189; explicit politics, 180; work for *Life* (magazine), 153, 158, 180–87, 211; *You Have Seen Their Faces* (co-authored by Erskine Caldwell), 92–93, 109, 181–86
boxing narratives, xiv, xxiii–xxiv, xxxix, 194–95; by African American writers, 5–6, 8–16; in film, 10, 17–21, 25–26, 31–34; about Joe Louis, 9–17; as melodrama, 20–21, 34, 35; postwar variants, 36; on radio, 195; as realism, 19–20; by white Popular Front writers, 4–5, 8, 19, 21–31; women in, 35–36
Brecht, Bertolt, 108–9
Brenda Curtis (radio show), 39–40, 76
Browder, Earl, xxvii, xxix
Buck, Pearl, xl, 111, 113, 169, 170; *Dragon Seed*, xiv, 116, 118; explicit politics of, 118, 197–98; *The Good Earth*, xiv, 80, 116–19, 134; as realist, 118–19; reception of, 118–19, 139–40

Bulosan, Carlos, xl, 111, 189; *All the Conspirators*, 147; *America Is in the Heart*, xxi, xxii, 112–14, 129, 137–47, 208–9; and Erskine Caldwell, 132, 144, 207–8; and the Cold War, 114–15, 144–47; *Cry and the Dedication*, 139, 147; "Freedom From Want," xxi–xxiii, xxiv, xxv, 147; *Laughter of My Father*, 110, 112–14, 129–37, 138, 142, 207; marketing of his work, 131–33; and masculinity, 135–36; and Margaret Mitchell, 144; and Popular Front, 111–14, 138, 144, 147; and realism, xxii–xxiii, xxx, 113–14, 131–32, 140, 209; reception of, 112–14, 129–30, 139–40, 142–43, 145, 148, 206; and U.S. agrarianism, 113–14, 136–37, 140–44; use of Philippine folklore, 133
Burke, Kenneth, xxvii, 91, 97, 98, 99, 100

Cahan, Abraham, xxxvi
Caldwell, Erskine, xiv, xxiii, xl, 189; aesthetics of, 84, 98–102, 108–10; audiences for, 82, 83, 104–5, 201, 204; and Margaret Bourke-White, collaboration with, 181–85, 211; and Carlos Bulosan, 132, 144, 207–8; explicit politics, 83; and gender, 102–4; *Georgia Boy*, 85, 91, 94, 132, 207–8; *God's Little Acre*, xl, 81–82, 85, 91–94, 98–104, 113, 115; *Journeyman*, 85, 91, 94–96, 103; and left-wing critics, 84–85, 91–92, 97–99; plot formulas of, 91, 94; and pluralism, 82, 96–97; *Tobacco Road*, xxiv, 85, 91–93, 95, 98–100, 103–4, 115; *Tobacco Road* (play), 197; *Tragic Ground*, 85, 91–93, 95, 99–101, 105–6; *Trouble in July*, 85, 91, 94–96; and Richard Wright, 83, 96, 97
Calloway, Cab, 5
Cantwell, Robert, 93
Cappetti, Carla, 196
Capra, Frank, xiii, xiv, xviii, xix, xx
Carnera, Primo, 3–4, 194
Cawelti, John, 20
Champ, The (film), 18, 19, 30
Chandler, Raymond, 54
Chesnutt, Charles, xxxvi, 131–32
Cheung, Floyd, 112, 123
Chiang Kai-shek, 121, 169

Chicago Defender, 5, 10, 12, 86
Childress, Alice, 58, 68, 69, 78
Chinese communism: appeal to U.S. leftists, 70, 119–21; representations of, 119–21, 128, 168
Chinese nationalists, representations of, 119, 121, 127–28, 168–70
Cinderella Man (film), 36, 197
City for Conquest (film), 18, 19
civil rights movement, xxvi, 148
Clark, Katerina, 204
Clurman, Harold, 32, 53
Collier's, 156
Colón, Jesús, xlii
Columbia Workshop (radio show), xiv, 199
Commonweal, 140, 142
Communist International (Comintern), xxvii, xxviii, xxix, xlii
Communist Party of the United States (CPUSA), xxvii, xxix, 41, 86, 111, 205
Congreso del Pueblo de Habla Española, El, xxvi
Conroy, Jack, xxx, 83, 91, 93, 98, 210
Crane, Stephen, xiv, xxxi, 177
Crisis, 5
Crothers, Rachael, 49
culture industries, lack of access for people of color, xxiv, xl–xli, 13, 38, 48, 52–53, 67–68, 110, 114, 127, 147–48

Daily Worker, 11, 13, 22, 85, 112, 118, 123
Daughters of the American Revolution (DAR), 37
DeMille, Cecil B., 125
Debs, Eugene, xxxvi
Denning, Michael, xvii, xxvi, xxvii, 52–53, 85, 116, 136, 144, 192, 205
detective stories, xiv, xlii, 16, 27, 43, 196, 198
Dickens, Charles, 203
Disney films, xiii
Dmytryk, Edward, xl, 122, 140
Dos Passos, John, 83, 84, 93, 115
Doyle, Kegan, 10–11, 14, 15, 195
Dreiser, Theodore, xiv, xxxi, xxxvi, 177
Du Bois, W. E. B., 70, 94, 182
Dust Bowl, xix–xx, 192

Early, Gerald, 19
Ellison, Ralph, xxvi, 6
Endore, Guy, 48, 198
Engels, Friedrich, xxxvi
ethnic revival, 4, 194
Evans, Walker, xix, xxx, 178, 192
Executive Order 8802, xxvi

Fair Employment Practices Commission, xxvi
Farm Security Administration (FSA), xix, xxiii, xxx, 115, 142
Farrell, James T., xv, xxx, 93, 203
Favorite Story, xiv, 199
Federal Theater Project, xiv, xli, 40, 42, 50, 51–52, 53, 68, 69
Film and Photo League, 83, 85, 180, 204
Fiske, John, 146
Flanigan, Hallie, 42, 51
Flaubert, Gustav, xiv
Foley, Barbara, xvii, 85, 104–5, 192
Ford, John, xiv, xix, 191, 203–4
Fortune (magazine), 149, 179
"Four Freedoms," xxi, 121, 128, 147
Frazer, Winifred, 50
Freeman, Joseph, xxxii, 180

gangster films, xiv, xlii, 43, 198
Garfield, John, xiii, xxxviii, xxxix, 19, 31–32, 110, 195
Glazener, Nancy, xxxiii, 193
God's Little Acre (film), 82
Gold, Michael, xxxii, xxxiv–xxxv, 83, 85, 208, 210; *Jews Without Money*, 208
Golden Boy (film), 19, 25–26, 35
Goldstein, Warren, 7
Gompers, Samuel, xxxvi
Gone with the Wind (film), 81, 86, 204
Gorelik, Mordecai, 22, 51
Gorki, Maxim, 140
Gorn, Elliot, 7
Graham Du Bois, Shirley, xxiv, xxxix, xl, 41, 42, 68–69, 110, 148; aesthetics of, 69–71, 72–73, 128; *The Bannekers* (radio pilot), 69, 70, 76–78; biographies by, 76; *Elijah's Ravens* (play), 71, 72, 73, 75, 201; explicit politics, 70, 78; *I Gotta Home* (play), 69, 70, 71–75; *It's Morning* (play), 69, 70; production of her work, 68–69, 70, 71, 75, 76, 78; and radio script writing, 76–77; reception of, 70, 75; *The Swing Mikado* (musical), 41, 42, 68, 71, 78; *Track Thirteen* (radio play), 76; and Richard Wright, 69, 71
Gramsci, Antonio, xxxvii
Grapes of Wrath (film), xiv, xix, xxiii, 191
Great Train Robbery, xxxi
Griffith, D. W., 53, 126
grotesque, as southern literary device, 101–2, 203
Group Theatre, 21, 32, 51, 52, 53
Guiding Light (radio show), 47, 49, 71, 73

Hale, Hope, 43, 55
Hall, Stuart, xlii
Hammerstein, Oscar, II, 67, 146
Hammett, Dashiell, 4, 54, 198
Hansberry, Lorraine, 58, 68, 69, 78
Hapke, Laura, 99, 102
Harder They Fall, The, 36, 194
Harris, Joel Chandler, 132
Harte, Bret, 132
Hellman, Lillian, xiv, xxiii, xxxix, 41–42, 110, 189; aesthetics of, 58–59, 64, 100; *Children's Hour*, 41–42, 59–63; *Little Foxes* (play), 41–42, 63–66, 98; politics of, 56–57, 62; reception of, 37–38, 41–42, 56, 58, 197, 200; *Watch on the Rhine* (play), 66, 67, 200
Herbst, Josephine, 83, 208
Herder, Johann Gottfried von, 133
Herndon, Angelo, xxvi
Herzstein, Robert, 165
Hicks, Granville, xxxvii, 203
High Time (newsletter), 179
Hill, Abram, 52, 67, 69
Hilmes, Michelle, 46
Himes, Chester, *If He Hollers Let Him Go*, 6, 15–17
Hine, Lewis, xv, 178, 192
Hitler-Stalin Pact, xxvii–xxviii
Hollywood Theatre Alliance, 52

228   Index

Hopkins, Pauline, xxxvi
Horne, Gerald, 70, 201
House Committee on Un-American Activities (HUAC), 32, 180
"House I Live In, The" (film), xx
Howard, Sidney, 50, 52, 204
Howells, William Dean, xv, xxii, xxxi, xxxii, xxxiv–xxxv, xxxvi–xxxvii, 72, 98, 132
Hughes, Langston, xlii, 13, 51, 67, 68
Huk guerillas, 119, 205–6
Hummert, Frank, 49

Ibsen, Heinrich, xiv
Ingersoll, Ralph, 179–80
International Literature of the World Revolution, 97
Isaacs, Harold, 116

Jacobson, Matthew Frye, xx, 4–5, 194
James, Henry, xiv, 98
Joe Louis Story, The (film), 36
Johnson, Georgia Douglas, 43, 52, 69
Johnson, Jack, 7, 10
Just Plain Bill (radio show), 55

Kaplan, Amy, xv, xxxi
Karamu Theater, 52, 71
Katayama, Sen, 205
Kazan, Elia, 53
Kazin, Alfred, xvi, xvii
Kelley, Robin D. G., 86, 192–93
Keep Punching, 5
Kid Galahad (film), 18, 19, 35
Kim, Elaine, 114
Kingsley, Sidney, xiv, 52; *Dead End* (play), 197
Klein, Christina, 111, 114, 124, 125, 144–45, 167, 205
Klevar, Harry, 108
Kozol, Wendy, 157, 162
Ku Klux Klan, 89

Ladies' Home Journal, 156
Lange, Dorothea, xxiii, xxx, 178; "Migrant Mother," xxiii, 192

Lee, C. Y., 123, 206
Lee, Canada, 32, 67
Lee, Robert G., 111, 114, 205
Lee, Russell, xxx, 178, 192
Lenin, Vladimir Illich, 193
Lewis, Sinclair, xiii, xiv, 53
Life (magazine), xli, 150; aesthetics of, 153–56, 157–63, 171–77, 187; Asia, representations of, 168–71; circulation, 150, 152, 187; and consumerism, 150–51, 156, 160–61, 164–65, 171–76, 185–86, 211; crowds, representation of, 154–56, 158, 164–66; explicit politics, 152–61, 179, 209; and New Deal, 158–59; and objectivity, 157, 161–62; photography, use of, 162–63, 172, 174–75, 180–81, 185; and pluralism, 151, 164–71; and Popular Front, 151–53, 157–59, 176–89; precursors, 149–50, 156, 177–78; and race, 158, 166–71, 183, 185, 188
Life of Mary Southern (radio show), 55
Link, Dr. Henry, 82
Linkskurve (journal), 97
Literary Digest, 149, 161, 210
Living Newspaper project, 52
Llewellyn, Richard, 80
London, Jack, xxxvi, 177
Long, Earl, 154–56
Look (magazine), 3, 113, 188
Lorentz, Pare, xix, 95, 115
Louis, Joe, xxxix, 5, 8–13, 14, 15, 16–17, 34, 188, 195
Lovell, Terry, 162–63
Lowe, Pardee, 124
Luce, Clair Booth, xiv, 56, 58
Luce, Henry: "The American Century," xxiv, xli, 149, 150–51, 153, 176; career, 149–50; and China, 168–69; explicit politics, 151, 159, 165, 166, 179, 187, 210; hiring of leftists, 179; journalistic mission, 151, 157, 161; "partisan objectivity," concept of, 156, 157–63; "Prospectus" for *Life*, 163, 179. See also *Life* (magazine)
Lukács, Georg, 11, 97, 106–8, 203
Lumiere, August and Louis, xxx

Lunacharsky, Anatoly, 106
Lux Radio Theatre, xiv, 17, 60, 195, 199
Lye, Colleen, 114, 116, 117, 120, 121, 133, 192, 207

Ma Perkins (radio show), 47
MacLeish, Archibald, 179, 180
MacLeod, Norm, 91
magazines: in nineteenth and turn of century, xxxiii, 152, 177–78, 193; in twentieth century, 152, 156. See also *Life* (magazine)
Mangione, Jerre, xlii, 208
Mao Tse-Tung, 119, 120–21
March of Time (newsreels), 149, 156
Marx, Karl, xxxvi, xxxvii
mass culture, definition of, xli
McClendon, Rose, 68
McPherson, Tara, 202
"Meat vs. Rice," 125
Meet John Doe (film), xiv, xix, xx, 191
Mehring, Franz, 97
melodrama, xiv, xxxi, xxxii, 19–21, 34, 49–50, 54–56, 63, 156
Mercury Theater, 51, 52
Mercury Theater of the Air (radio show), 199
Miller, Arthur, xiv, 48
Miller, Jordan, 50
Miller, May, 43, 52, 69
Million Dollar Baby (film), 17, 197
Minnie, Memphis, 5
Mitchell, Don, 144
Mitchell, Margaret, xl; audiences for, 81–82, 201; explicit politics, 82, 86–87; *Gone with the Wind* (novel), 80, 81–82, 85–90, 107–8, 113, 202; and literary critics, 87, 202; and plantation romance, 90, 107; as realist, 81, 107–8, 110
"model minority" discourse, 114–15
Modern Romances, 43
modernism, xviii, xxix–xxx, 52, 178, 192, 211
Mori, Toshio, 111
Mr. Roberts (film), 204
Mr. Smith Goes to Washington (film), xiv, 191
Mullen, Bill, 13, 71
Mulvey, Laura, 103

Murphy, James, xvii, 85
Mydans, Carl, 181

Nathan, George Jean, 38–39, 56
National Negro Congress, xxvi, 86
Native Ground (play), xix
naturalism, xvi, 20, 31, 91–92, 106
NBC Theatre of the Air, xiv
Negro People's Theater (Chicago), 52, 68
Negro People's Theatre (New York), 51, 68
Negro Story, 6
New Masses, xxxiii, xxxvii, 11, 13, 85, 97, 98, 112, 113, 118, 123, 204
New Republic, 139, 142
New Theater League, 51
New York Times, 113, 129
New Yorker, 131
Nguyen, Viet Thanh, 135, 139
Norris, Frank, xxxvi, 177

Odets, Clifford, xxiv, xxxix, 3, 21, 110, 189; *Golden Boy* (play), 21–25, 34, 63, 196
Okada, John, 111
Okubo, Mine, 111
Ortega y Gasset, José, 164
Our Gal Sunday (radio show), 198

Page, Myra, xxx, 93
Palumbo-Liu, David, 205, 206
paperback books, xv, xxx, 105–6, 113, 130–31, 203
Parker, Dorothy, 48
Parks, Gordon, 167, 188, 212
Partisan Review, xvii, 30, 97, 123
Petry, Ann, xiv, xxx, 13, 40, 78
Philippines, 112, 129; colonial relationship to U.S., 130; representation by Bulosan, 129–47; and U.S. immigration policy, 208; white representations of, 121–22, 133–34, 139–40, 168, 170–71, 205–6
Phillips, Irna, 45, 49, 55, 199
Pins and Needles (musical), 42, 61, 62–63, 197
Plekhanov, Georgi, 97
pluralism, xvi–xvii; "The People's Century" as variant of, xxi–xxvi, xxxvii–xxxviii,

pluralism (*cont.*)
    xli, 82, 116, 147, 149, 151; "We're the People" as variant of, xviii–xxi, xxii–xxiv, 95, 113–14, 116, 151. *See also* realism: and pluralism
P.M. (magazine), 83, 157, 179, 181, 187
Poitier, Sidney, 68
Polonsky, Abraham, 19
popular culture, definition of, xli
Popular Front: and Cold War, 144–47, 153, 187–89; and CPUSA, xxvii; definition of, xiii, xxvi–xxvii; in historical memory, xxxvii–xxxviii; and nationalism, xxviii–xxix; periodization of, xxvii–xxviii; and pluralism, xvi–xxvii; political subjectivity within, xxviii; and popular culture, xvii, xxiii–xxiv. *See also* realism: and the Popular Front
Proletkult movement, 210
Pulitzer press, 177
Pyron, Darden Ashbury, 86

Rabinowitz, Paula, xxxv, 183
radio: African American access, 48; corporate structure of, 44–45, 46–49, 199; and female audiences, 39–40, 44; and Popular Front, 44, 47–48; and realism, xiv–xv, 199; serial program genres, 44–45, 48; and working class audiences, 44. *See also* soap opera
Randolph, A. Philip, xxvi
realism: in advertising, xxx; in bestselling novels, xiv–xv, xxx; class politics of, xxxiii–xxxv, xxxvi–xxxvii; definition of, xvi; as epistemology, xxxiii–xxxvi, 162–63; and film, xiv, xxx–xxxi; gender politics of, xxxv, 42–43, 54–56, 199; in Hollywood cinema, 19–20, 199; and journalism, 162–63, 177–78; and literary studies, xiv, xviii, xxix–xxx; local color subgenre, xl, 80, 131–32; in magazines, xxxii–xxxiii, 177–78; Marxist theories of, xxxvi, 12, 97–98, 106–9; and mass culture, xiii–xvii, xxx–xxxiii; and melodrama, xiv, xxxi, xxxii, 19–21,

54–56; in nineteenth century, xv–xvi, xxxi–xxxvii, 131–32; and photography, xxiii, xxx, 162–63, 178; and pluralism, xvi–xvii, xxii–xxiv, xxxiii–xxxvii; and Popular Front, xii–xviii, xxiii–xxiv, xxxii–xxxv; poststructuralist critique of, xxxiv, 175–76, 193–94; racial politics of, xxxv–xxxvi; and radio, xiv–xv, 199; socialist realism, 204; and *Sullivan's Travels*, xii; and theater, xiv, xxx, xxxi, 19, 49–50, 52–53; in twentieth century, xiii–xiv, xxx–xxxvi, xlii; in USSR, xxx, 97, 204
Reid, James, 10
republicanism, xix–xx, xxiii, xxv, 117, 119–21, 140, 205, 208
Revolutionary Association of Proletarian Writers (RAPP), 97–98, 108, 203
Rice, Elmer, xiv, 50, 52
Riis, Jacob, xv, xxx, 178, 192
Robeson, Paul, xxxviii, 6, 48, 67, 166
Rockwell, Norman, xxiii
Rocky (film), 17, 36, 197
Rodney, Lester, 11
Roediger, David, xx, 4–5, 94, 208
Rohmer, Sax, 111, 116, 126
Rolfe, Edwin, 91, 98
Roosevelt, Eleanor, 37–38
Roosevelt, Franklin Delano, xxi, xxiv, xxvi, 152–53, 158–59, 210
Rose McClendon Players, 51, 68
Ross, Barney, 33, 34
Rossen, Robert, 4, 19
Roxborough, John, 10

San Juan, E., Jr., 148
Saturday Evening Post, xxiii, 13, 113, 116, 119, 156
Saturday Review of Literature, 131, 139, 145
Savage, Barbara, 48, 76
Schudson, Michael, 161, 177
Schuyler, George, 86
sensational journalism, 177
sentimental fiction, xxxv
Simpsons, The (TV show), 100

Sin Far, Sui, xxxvi
Sinclair, Upton, xiii, xxiv, xxxvi, 84
Shaw, George Bernard, 50
Shaw, Irwin, 48
Sheldon, Edward, xv, 49
Shlovsky, Viktor, 193
Sinatra, Frank, xx
Sklaroff, Lauren, 9–10
Smedley, Agnes, xxx, 120; *Daughter of Earth*, xxxv, 210
Smethurst, James, xvii, 192, 194
Smith, Judith, 40, 48
Smith, Lillian, 13
Snow, Edgar, xl, 113, 116, 119, 169, 170; *Battle for Asia*, 121; *People on Our Side*, 121–22; *Red Star Over China*, 119–21
soap operas, 45, 201; politics of, xxxix, 39–40, 45–47, 78, 198; and realism, xv, 55
Soong Mei-ling ("Madame Chiang"), 169, 170
Spencer, Jenny, 59
Spirit of Youth (film), 5, 10, 35
Stanislavski, Constantin, 53
Stanwyck, Barbara, 60
Steichen, Edward, 178, 192
Stein, Sally, 172–74
Steinbeck, John, xiii, xviii, xxx, 95, 113, 141, 142; *Grapes of Wrath* (novel), xiv, xix–xx, xxi–xxiii, xxv, 80, 96, 114, 115, 143, 191–92; *In Dubious Battle*, xx
Stewart, Donald Ogden, xiv
Stowe, Harriet Beecher, 132
Strasberg, Lee, 53
Stryker, Roy, xix
Sturges, Preston, xi–xiv, xxxviii
Sullivan, John L., 7
Sullivan's Travels (film), xi–xiv, xxiv, xxvii, xxxvii–xxxviii, 106, 191
Susman, Warren, xiii

Takaki, Ronald, xx, 194, 207, 208
Taruc, Luis, 206
Theater Guild, 50, 75
Theater Union, 50, 51
Theatre Arts Committee, 51

These Three (film), 59, 61, 79; radio adaptation, 60
They Made Me a Criminal (film), 18, 19, 30
Third Period, xxvii, xxviii, xxix, xlii
Time (magazine), 149, 161
Tobacco Road (film), 203–4
Tolstoy, Leo, xiv, 140
Tracy, Susan, 90
tragedy, xii
transnational, definition of, xli
Trilling, Lionel, xvii
True Story, 55
Tsiang, H. T., xl, 147–48; *And China Has Hands*, xxiv, 110–14, 122–29, 206–7; *China Red*, 123; explicit politics, 112; film career, 127, 147, 206; *Hanging on Union Square*, 123; and Popular Front, 111–12, 122, 124; reception of, 112–14, 123–24
Twain, Mark, xiv, xv, xxx, xxxvi, 132, 194

Vidor, King, 4, 18, 43
Volosinov, V. N., 9

Wald, Alan, xvii, 85
Wallace, Henry, xxiv–xxvi, 149, 193
Ward, Theodore, 52, 69, 71
Welles, Orson, 199
Westbrook, Brett Elizabeth, 59, 62
Weston, Edward, 178
Wharton, Edith, xiv, xxxi, xxxii
White, Walter, 83
Why We Fight (film), xx
Williams, Linda, 20
Williams, Raymond, xxxiii, 156
Willkie, Wendell, 165–66, 209
Wilson, Christopher, 178
Wolfert, Ira, 205–6
"Woman's Film," 43
Wong, Jade Snow, 123–24
Wright, Richard, xxiv, xxx, xxxix, 52, 69, 189; and Nelson Algren, 31; "And Oh—Where Were Hitler's Pagan Gods," 12; *Black Boy*, xiv, 110, 114, 209, 210; and boxing, 11–13; "Bright and Morning

Wright, Richard (*cont.*)
  Star," 74; and Carlos Bulosan, 209; and Erskine Caldwell, 83, 96, 97; "High Tide in Harlem," 12–13; "Joe Louis Uncovers Dynamite," 11–12; *Native Son* (novel), xiv, 3, 13–15, 71, 73, 96, 110; *Native Son* (play), 67; reception of, 13–14
Wyler, William, 64

Xiao Qian, 121

Yamamoto, Hisaye, 111
"Yellow Peril" discourse, 111, 114–15, 116, 120, 125–26
Yellow Power movements, 116–17, 148
yeoman farmer, xix, xl, 95, 96–97, 113–14, 117, 118–21, 140–43, 169, 208
Yoneda, Karl, 206

Zola, Émile, xiv

www.ingramcontent.com/pod-product-compliance
Lightning Source LLC
Chambersburg PA
CBHW030338240426
43661CB00052B/1678